PERSPECTIVES ON WRITING
Series Editor, Susan H. McLeod

PERSPECTIVES ON WRITING
Series Editor, Susan H. McLeod

The Perspectives on Writing series addresses writing studies in a broad sense. Consistent with the wide ranging approaches characteristic of teaching and scholarship in writing across the curriculum, the series presents works that take divergent perspectives on working as a writer, teaching writing, administering writing programs, and studying writing in its various forms.

The WAC Clearinghouse and Parlor Press are collaborating so that these books will be widely available through free digital distribution and low-cost print editions. The publishers and the Series editor are teachers and researchers of writing, committed to the principle that knowledge should freely circulate. We see the opportunities that new technologies have for further democratizing knowledge. And we see that to share the power of writing is to share the means for all to articulate their needs, interest, and learning into the great experiment of literacy.

OTHER BOOKS IN THE SERIES

Charles Bazerman and David R. Russell (Eds.), *Writing Selves/Writing Societies* (2003)

Gerald P. Delahunty and James Garvey, *The English Language: From Sound to Sense* (2009)

Charles Bazerman, Adair Bonini, and Débora Figueiredo (Eds.), *Genre in a Changing World* (2009)

David Franke, Alex Reid, and Anthony Di Renzo (Eds.), *Design Discourse: Composing and Revising Programs in Professional and Technical Writing* (2010)

Martine Courant Rife, Shaun Slattery, and Dànielle Nicole DeVoss (Eds.), *Copy(write) : Intellectual Property in the Writing Classroom* (2011)

WRITING IN KNOWLEDGE SOCIETIES

Edited by

Doreen Starke-Meyerring
Anthony Paré
Natasha Artemeva
Miriam Horne
Larissa Yousoubova

The WAC Clearinghouse
wac.colostate.edu
Fort Collins, Colorado

Parlor Press
www.parlorpress.com
Anderson, South Carolina

The WAC Clearinghouse, Fort Collins, Colorado 80523-1052
Parlor Press, 3015 Brackenberry Drive, Anderson, South Carolina 29621

© 2011 by Doreen Starke-Meyerring, Anthony Paré, Natasha Artemeva, Miriam Horne, and Larissa Yousoubova. This work is licensed under a Creative Commons Attribution-Noncommercial-No Derivative Works 3.0 United States License.

Printed in the United States of America

Library of Congress Cataloging-in-Publication Data

Writing in knowledge societies / edited by Doreen Starke-Meyerring ... [et al.].
  p. cm. -- (Perspectives on writing)
 Includes bibliographical references.
  ISBN 978-1-60235-268-1 (pbk. : acid-free paper) -- ISBN 978-1-60235-269-8 (hardcover : acid-free paper) -- ISBN 978-1-60235-270-4 (adobe ebook) -- ISBN 978-1-60235-271-1 (epub)
 1. Authorship--History. 2. Academic writing. 3. Scholarly electronic publishing. I. Starke-Meyerring, Doreen, 1966-
 PN149.W76 2011
 808.02--dc23
                           2011042910

Copyeditor: Amanda Purnell
Designers: Mike Palmquist and Adam Mackie
Series Editor: Susan H. McLeod

This book is printed on acid-free paper.

The WAC Clearinghouse supports teachers of writing across the disciplines. Hosted by Colorado State University, it brings together scholarly journals and book series as well as resources for teachers who use writing in their courses. This book is available in digital format for free download at http://wac.colostate.edu.

Parlor Press, LLC is an independent publisher of scholarly and trade titles in print and multimedia formats. This book is available in paperback, cloth, and Adobe eBook formats from Parlor Press at http://www.parlorpress.com. For submission information or to find out about Parlor Press publications, write to Parlor Press, 3015 Brackenberry Drive, Anderson, South Carolina 29621, or e-mail editor@parlorpress.com.

Acknowledgment

We wish to acknowledge the research funding provided by the Social Sciences and Humanities Council of Canada in support of two CASDW (Canadian Association for the Study of Discourse and Writing) conferences, *Writing in the Knowledge Society* (Toronto, Canada, May 28-30, 2006) and *Writing in Changing Communities—Communities Writing Change* (Saskatoon, Canada, May 27-29, 2007), from which the chapters in this book emerged.

CONTENTS

Writing in Knowledge Societies 1

1 The Roles of Writing In Knowledge Societies: Questions, Exigencies, and Implications for the Study and Teaching of Writing 3
   Doreen Starke-Meyerring and Anthony Paré

Conceptual, Methodological, and Historical Perspectives on Studying Writing as an Epistemic Practice 29

2 Investigating Texts in their Social Contexts: The Promise and Peril of Rhetorical Genre Studies .... .31
   Catherine F. Schryer

3 "Curious Gentlemen": The Hudson's Bay Company and the Royal Society, Business and Science in the Eighteenth Century .... .53
   Janet Giltrow

4 Electrons Are Cheap; Society Is Dear .... .75
   Charles Bazerman

Writing as Knowledge Work in Public and Professional Settings 85

5 Risk Knowledge and Risk Communication: The Rhetorical Challenge of Public Dialogue .... .87
   Philippa Spoel and Chantal Barriault

6 The Evolution of an Environmentalist Group Toward Public Participation: Civic Knowledge Construction and Transgressive Identities .... .113
   Diana Wegner

7 Making Legal Knowledge in Global Digital Environments: The Judicial Opinion as Remix .... .139
   Martine Courant Rife

8   Understanding and Supporting Knowledge Work in Schools,
    Workplaces, and Public Life.................................. *161*
    William Hart-Davidson and Jeffrey T. Grabill

**The Role of Writing in the Production of Knowledge in Research
Environments**.. **177**

9   Rhetoric, Knowledge, and "The Brute Facts of Nature" in
    Science Research... *179*
    Heather Graves

10 Disciplines and Discourses: Social Interactions in the
    Construction of Knowledge.................................. *193*
    Ken Hyland

11 Knowledge and Identity Work in the Supervision of Doctoral
    Student Writing: Shaping Rhetorical Subjects *215*
    Anthony Paré, Doreen Starke-Meyerring, and Lynn McAlpine

12 Writing into the Knowledge Society: A Case Study of
    Vulnerability in Inkshedding............................... *237*
    Miriam Horne

The Teaching of Writing as an Epistemic Practice in Higher Education ... 257

13 Writing and Knowledge Making: Insights from an Historical Perspective... *259*
    Paul M. Rogers and Olivia Walling

14 Reinventing WAC (again): The First-Year Seminar and Academic Literacy *275*
    Doug Brent

15 A Code of Ethics as a Collaborative Learning Tool: Comparing a
    Face-to-Face Engineering Team and Multidisciplinary Online Teams.. *299*
    Anne Parker and Amanda Goldrick-Jones

16 "An Engrained Part of My Career": The Formation of a
    Knowledge Worker in the Dual Space of Engineering
    Knowledge and Rhetorical Process........................... *321*
    Natasha Artemeva

17 International Students and Identity: Resisting Dominant
    Ways of Writing and Knowing in Academe *351*
    Heekyeong Lee and Mary H. Maguire

**Articulating and Implementing Rhetoric and Writing as a
Knowledge-Making Practice in Higher Education** 371

18 Representing Writing: A Rhetoric for Change *373*
    Roger Graves

19 Building Academic Community through a Town Hall Forum:
    Rhetorical Theories in Action. *389*
    Tania Smith

20 Talking the Talk and Walking the Walk: Establishing
    the Academic Role of Writing Centres *415*
    Margaret Procter

Author and Editor Institutional Affiliations *441*

WRITING IN KNOWLEDGE SOCIETIES

1 THE ROLES OF WRITING IN KNOWLEDGE SOCIETIES: QUESTIONS, EXIGENCIES, AND IMPLICATIONS FOR THE STUDY AND TEACHING OF WRITING

Doreen Starke-Meyerring and Anthony Paré

For as long as human beings have used it to organize and conduct their activities, writing has played an integral role in the creation, sharing, and contestation of knowledge. Tracing the intertwined history of writing and secular knowledge of civilizations in Europe, the Middle East, the Mediterranean, China, India, and Mesoamerica, and Europe, Bazerman and Rogers (2008a, b), for example, map out the complex ways in which writing has been instrumental to the formation of knowledge institutions, disciplines, and communities. In the last few decades, however, the question about the role of writing in the production of knowledge has gained new salience with the rise of what has commonly been termed the knowledge society, where civic life as well as much economic activity depend on the production and sharing of knowledge. Indeed, according to some estimates, knowledge accounts for about three fourths of the value produced in the knowledge economy (Neef, 1998, ctd. in Brandt, 2005), rendering it "more valuable than land, equipment, or even money" (Brandt, p. 167). And because much of this knowledge is created, shared, inscribed, contested, and used largely through various textual forms, writing has moved centre stage in all sectors of society.

As Brandt (2005) observes in her study of writing in contemporary knowledge-intensive organizations, with its integral role in the production of knowledge, writing fuels the knowledge economy, with written products becoming "the chief vehicles for economic transactions and the chief ground for making profits or achieving advantage" (p. 180), so that "such high-stakes factors as corporate reputation, client base, licensing, competitive advantage, growth, and profit rely on what and how people write" (p. 174). In short, writing has become an important means of production and as such forms a vital component of the epistemological infrastructure of knowledge-intensive organizations and societies. In Brandt's (2005) words, writing has become "hot property" (p. 167). In addition, as a growing body of research in writing studies indicates, writing is vital to citizen participation in the shaping of public knowledge, in policy deliberation, and in public decision making (e.g., Flower, 2008; Grabill, 2007; Long, 2008). Not coincidentally, as Bazerman (2008) observes, there is "clearly a global renaissance in writing studies at all levels on every continent" (p. 2), reflected in a fast increasing number of writing studies conferences, as well as handbooks of research in rhetoric and writing studies (e.g., Bazerman, 2008; Beard, Myhill, Riley, & Nystrand, 2009; Lunsford, Wilson, & Eberly, 2009; MacArthur, Graham, & Fitzgerald, 2005). As this book demonstrates, this renaissance in writing studies and the growing salience of knowledge in all sectors of society are intimately related.

For writing studies as a discipline that traces its intellectual roots to ancient studies of the rhetoric of civic discourse and thus to 2,500 years of inquiry into human thought and knowledge, the renewed attention to writing as a knowledge-making practice raises a number of urgent questions: What roles does writing play in knowledge-intensive societies? What specific exigencies arise for writing in knowledge-intensive settings? How do rhetoric and writing work to produce, share, question, or advance knowledge in civic, workplace, and institutional spaces whose main purpose either is or depends on the production of knowledge? That is, in what ways is writing epistemic? In turn, these questions have implications for the institutional, organizational, and community environments in which writing happens: How do institutional and organizational contexts constrain, enable, or otherwise shape writing as a knowledge-making practice? Conversely, how does writing as a knowledge-making practice shape institutions and organizations? How do people come to participate in collective knowledge-making endeavors?

This book addresses these questions with the aim to examine, illustrate, and articulate the vital roles rhetoric and writing play as knowledge-making practices in diverse knowledge-intensive settings. The contributions to this book examine the multiple and often decidedly subtle, but no less consequential ways in which writing is epistemic, and they articulate the central role of writing in creating, shaping, sharing, or contesting knowledge in a range of human activities in workplaces and civic settings as well as in higher education. The chapters illustrate and conceptualize the ways in which rhetoric and writing work to organize, (re-)produce, undermine, dominate, marginalize, or contest knowledge-making practices in diverse settings, showing the many ways in which rhetoric and writing operate in knowledge-intensive organizations and societies.

To be sure, there has been much important discussion and critique of the construct termed knowledge society, including ways in which the construct has been used to legitimize policy decisions to favor particular economic interests, especially in the commercialization of knowledge over broader public interests (e.g., Delanty, 2003; Peters, 2007; Välimaa & Hoffman, 2008). Our purpose here is not to essentialize or legitimize a particular kind of social formation as "the knowledge society"—quite the contrary: Our purpose is to provide rich accounts of the diversity of knowledge-making practices and the roles rhetoric and writing play in organizing and (re)producing them. We invoke the term here largely to reflect the widespread sense of the growing importance and centrality of knowledge to all human activity. At the same time, we hope to facilitate and inspire continued critical inquiry into notions of the knowledge society as a monolithic or unproblematic formation by providing detailed accounts of the diverse and locally situated practices of rhetoric and writing in the production and sharing of knowledge as well as by addressing such questions as what exigencies give rise to writing; who is invited to participate under what conditions in the discursive practices designed to arrive at truths, decisions, judgments, actions; or how discursive practices are regulated, in whose interests, and with what consequences for diverse participants.

These are consequential questions that not only reflect the centrality of rhetoric and writing to human activity, but also signal the growing need to articulate, reconsider, and reposition writing studies as a discipline in increasingly knowledge- and therefore writing-intensive societies. These questions therefore inspire a second important purpose of the book: to advance writing studies as a discipline dedicated to the study of human thought and knowledge.

Given this dual purpose, the book is organized into five sections. Following this introductory chapter, which functions to situate the contributions in a rich tradition of inquiry into the epistemic nature of rhetoric and writing, section one of the book offers conceptual, methodological, and historical perspectives on the study of writing as an epistemic practice that inform and cut across many of the chapters in the book. Section two examines writing as knowledge work in civic and professional settings, while section three explores the role of writing in the production of knowledge in research environments. Sections four and five address the pedagogical and disciplinary implications for rhetoric and writing studies, with section four taking up questions surrounding the teaching of writing as an epistemic practice in higher education, and section five addressing the articulation and implementation of writing as a knowledge-making practice in higher education.

In pursuing these aims, the chapters in this book draw on rich traditions of scholarly inquiry into the epistemic nature of rhetoric and writing, extending from the important roots of this inquiry in classical rhetorical studies of civic discourse. These roots have resurfaced most poignantly perhaps in the debate about the epistemic nature of rhetoric initiated by Scott (1967, 1976, 1993) in the context of the larger rhetorical turn in academic inquiry across disciplines (Simons, 1989, 1990), and they have continued to pervade the intensive research efforts that have shaped rhetoric and writing studies as a discipline over the last 50-60 years. Before we introduce each of the sections in this book, therefore, we begin this chapter by briefly revisiting some of these traditions. Although an exhaustive review of that long line of inquiry is beyond the scope of any single chapter, our purpose here is to situate the contributions to this book in these rich traditions to provide some of the historical and theoretical context for the ways in which the chapters in this book work to tease out the complex, diverse, and locally situated ways in which rhetoric and writing work to produce and share knowledge in knowledge-intensive societies.

TRADITIONS OF INQUIRY INTO RHETORIC AND WRITING AS KNOWLEDGE-MAKING PRACTICES

The history of rhetoric and writing studies traces a persistent and restless curiosity in the relationship between writing and knowledge, a curiosity that—like the field itself—has important roots in classical studies of rhetoric. Indeed, long before the current renaissance of inquiry into rhetoric and writing, the link between rhetoric and knowledge was a vital concern in rhetorical study in classical Greece and Rome, where rhetoric emerged as a theory informing the education of citizens for participation in the civic life of the polis—its political, legal, and other institutions. Participation in these institutions naturally raised questions of deliberation, knowledge, argument, and persuasion—ways in which participants would generate the knowledge needed to arrive at truths and decisions.

Articulated early by Plato, at the heart of this concern with rhetoric as a theory of civic discourse was the question of rhetoric's role in the production of knowledge: Do truths exist independently of human beings as fixed certainties waiting to be discovered, with rhetoric's role as a supplementary art of presenting those truths persuasively and effectively, or does rhetoric have a constitutive role, a productive force? That is, does rhetoric work to constitute, shape, enable, constrain, challenge, and contest knowledge? Is knowledge rhetorical—the product of human sociality—always contested, contingent, socioculturally situated, resulting from advancing, defending, contesting knowledge claims based on arguments and evidence whose acceptability depends on the practices, values, and standards of the communities, institutions, and organizations whose work they do?

As Nelson and Megill (1986) observed, the way this question is debated is itself highly socio-historically situated: In much debate over the centuries, the rhetorical nature of knowledge production tends to be questioned or denied at points and locations in human history when societal conflict, turmoil, and decline feed a quest for certainty—for certain truths to re-establish a dominant social order. Such processes of reasserting certainties in the interests of ensuring a dominant social order naturally depend on the denial of the rhetorical nature of knowledge production, that is, on the denial of its contestation, contingency, and situatedness. Thus, Nelson and Megill situated Plato's ambivalence toward rhetoric at a time of turmoil in the Greek polis, and they situated the later enlightenment quest for certainty through reason, demonstration, and empiricism, or as Nelson and Megill put it, "the enlightenment dream of a single, certain, natural, and rational order authoritative for everyone" (p. 28) at a time of instability and unrest in Europe.

Despite these socio-historically situated ups and downs in the debate about rhetoric's role in the production of knowledge, rhetoric's epistemic role has been examined tenaciously over the centuries. Most notably in early rhetorical theory, Aristotle, in his *On Rhetoric: A Theory of Civic Discourse,* defined rhetoric as "an ability, in each [particular] case, to see the available means of persuasion" (Aristotle, 2007, [1355b]). As Kennedy remarks in his 2007 translation of Aristotle's *Rhetoric,* the word to "see" in the original Greek is theōrēsai, meaning "to be an observer of and to grasp the meaning or utility of" (p. 37), a word that is related to the noun theōria, the ethymological root of theory. As such, rhetoric was understood early on as involving the study and understanding of discursive practices in particular social situations. For our purpose of tracing the link between rhetoric and knowledge, two points about this early understanding of rhetoric are important. First, rhetoric, according to Aristotle, is generative—a point that was developed in great detail by Enos and Lauer (1992) in their examination of the use of the term "heuristic" (heurein, heuresis, meaning to find out, discover, invent) in Aristotle's *Rhetoric.* As Enos and Lauer showed, Aristotle saw rhetoric as about finding [heurein] or generating what he called entechnic or artistic proofs, that is—roughly—the necessary arguments, evidence, credibility, and emotional appeals for the construction of probable truths, judgments, and decisions in a particular situation with a particular audience. In Enos and Lauer's words, "Aristotle used the term heuristic to capture the way meaning is co-created between rhetor and audience ... in constructing probable knowledge" (p. 79). Accordingly, Enos and Lauer emphasized, "for Aristotle, rhetoric was concerned with conceptualization through discourse" (p. 80).

This notion of rhetoric as generative or productive of conceptualization, understanding, and knowledge was further extended by Atwill (1993) in her careful re-reading of Aristotle's *Rhetoric* from a knowledge production perspective. As Atwill pointed out, Aristotle categorized rhetoric as one of the technēs, that is, one of the human modes of inquiry that are concerned with making or producing something (e.g., architecture, medicine, engineering, poetics). That is, for Aristotle, rhetoric was concerned with productive knowledge, which he understood, in some ways, as different from disciplines concerned with theoretical or interpretive knowledge, epistēme (e.g., philosophy, mathematics), and disciplines concerned with practical knowledge, that is with acting, (e.g., political science, ethics, etc.). Although Aristotle reserved the term "episteme" for what he identified as interpretive knowledge, Atwill showed that early on, rhetoric was seen as a kind of productive knowledge, that is, knowledge generated to produce certain outcomes, such as judgments in courts and elsewhere, truths and decisions in policy deliberation, or value statements in ceremonial events.

In addition to the focus on rhetoric as a generative and productive force in Aristotle's definition of rhetoric, his definition of rhetoric as requiring the study of discursive practices "in each [particular] case" holds another important insight that has continued to inform the current study of the link between writing and knowledge: Rhetoric and writing are highly social practices, which are locally and socio-culturally situated as they are developed by communities over time, and, as such, they are specific to the particular socio-cultural and economic locales in which they originate and whose work they accomplish. Concerned with the instruction of his students in the participation in Greek civic life, Aristotle, for example, developed early notions of genres as repeated practices shared by a body politic—practices that do the work, including the knowledge work, of the city state's institutions. For example, Aristotle described forensic rhetoric as the discourse of the courts focused on the production of court decisions, deliberative rhetoric as the discourse concerned with the production of policy decisions, and epideictic rhetoric as discourse focused on the production of values in public ceremony.

Although concerns about its epistemic nature have surfaced regularly in scholarly inquiry into rhetoric (although perhaps not always articulated in such terms), what brought the debate about the epistemic nature of rhetoric to the forefront of contemporary research and inquiry in rhetoric was a debate around rhetoric as epistemic initiated by Scott (1967, 1976, 1993) in the context of what has become known variably as the linguistic, interpretive, and rhetorical turn in the social and human sciences (Simons, 1989, 1990) or the rhetoric of inquiry (e.g., Lyne, 1985; Nelson & Megill, 1986). Captured by the 1984 Iowa Symposium on Rhetoric and the Human Sciences and the 1986 Temple University follow-up conference, the rhetorical turn united scholars who had come to understand "reason ... [as] inherently rhetorical" (p. 13). As Simons (1990) articulated the realization at the heart of this shift in academic knowledge production, "virtually all scholarly discourse is rhetorical in the sense that issues need to be named and framed, facts interpreted and conclusions justified ..." (p. 9). That insight into the rhetorical nature of knowledge was not limited to scholars in rhetoric and writing studies, but extended far beyond the boundaries of rhetoric, with scholars from a wide range of disciplines studying the discursive construction of knowledge in the social and human sciences, such as Foucault (1972) or Geertz (1973), Nelson, Megill, & McCloskey, (1985) and Brown (1987) as well as in the natural sciences, such as Kuhn (1972) and Feyerabend (1975).

In the context of this larger movement toward a revived rhetorical understanding of knowledge, Scott (1967), drawing on his analysis of rhetorical scholarship around the link between rhetoric and knowledge, famously declared, "in human affairs, then, rhetoric ... is a way of knowing; it is epistemic" (p. 17), arguing that "truth is not prior and immutable but is contingent.... it is in time, ... [and] rhetoric ... [is] not a matter of giving effectiveness to truth but of creating truth" (p. 13). In other words, rhetoric's function is not simply to dress up and effectively convey some prior truth, but its role is in the creation and contestation of understanding and knowledge itself. This articulation of the epistemic nature of rhetoric opened up a set of new implications and questions for studying the link between rhetoric/writing and knowledge and raised new ethical concerns. As Scott (1976) emphasized, for example, in a world of competing, contingent, and situated knowledge claims, enlightenment-like claims to universal, stable, and certain knowledge are untenable. Rather, according to Scott (1976), knowledge claims must be rhetorically established and negotiated, requiring a greater need for the appreciation of different ways of knowing as well as a responsibility to participate in the negotiation and repeated renewal of circumstances and norms under which knowledge is created. Accordingly, as Scott (1993) urged, "we must see truth as moments in human, creative processes, and we must see rhetoric as finding its being in those processes and those moments" (p. 133).

Indeed, inquiry into human processes and moments of knowledge creation, especially in research, including in the human, social, and natural sciences, has become an important area of scholarly inquiry in rhetoric and writing studies, giving rise to a broad spectrum of research into the rhetorical construction of knowledge across the disciplines, whether that was the rhetoric of the natural sciences (e.g., Bazerman, 1988; Ceccarelli, 2004; Graves, 2005; Gross, 1990; Harris, 1997; Segal, 2005) or the social sciences and humanities (e.g., Bazerman, 1988; Brown, 1987; McCloskey, 1994). Importantly, as this work in the rhetoric of the disciplines has shown, rhetoric and writing are not merely complementary to, but constitutive of disciplinary knowledge production at all stages of inquiry regardless of the particular discipline. Accordingly, that constitutive role takes on many forms. It surfaces in the construction of knowledge claims, for example, in the form of complex social interactions involved in arguing for one of many possible interpretations of data generated by experiments or other forms of inquiry (e.g., Hyland, 2004, 2009; Myers, 1989). As well, as Bazerman (1988) demonstrated early on in his detailed historical analysis of the evolution of the scientific article in the *Philosophical Transactions of the Royal Society*, the very standards for how experiments are to be conducted, for example, and for what constitutes acceptable accounts of scientific investigations and knowledge claims were negotiated over time through writing.

These conceptual concerns about the rhetorical nature of knowledge production have infused the study and teaching of writing from the earliest days of process theory in the mid-1960s to the chapters in this book. Writing studies scholars have long sought to understand how the activity of writing is related to the production of new conceptions and perspectives: what can and cannot be known; how do we come to know; how do we decide on acceptable or less acceptable ways of knowing; what or whose knowledge is acceptable or not?

When contemporary researchers and teachers of writing first shifted their gaze from the written product to the writer's process, the heuristic power of writing seemed obvious: knowledge is not merely expressed in writing, it is created by writing. The very act of composing encourages and extends the possibilities for thought.

That understanding prompted calls in the 1970s for writing to be employed across the curriculum as a means to engage individual students in the intellectual work that writing promotes, and it led to writing-to-learn theories and pedagogies (e.g., Emig, 1977) and the writing across the curriculum movement (e.g., Gray & Myers, 1978). However, that attention to the full curriculum, combined with research into workplace writing, soon made two things abundantly clear: first, writing is deployed quite distinctly in different disciplines and organizations, and, second, knowledge production through writing is not the result of individual contributions, but, rather, a collective and ongoing effort made possible, in large part, by writing itself. Moreover, as research through the 1980s revealed, the differences in writing from one group to another are in fact calculated and strategic adaptations in writing forms and practices that are designed to produce the sort of knowledge required by specific collectives. It is not just that biologists have a different vocabulary than economists or social workers or physicians, it is that each of these groups exploits the infinite malleability of language in order to generate and promote the knowledge and ways of knowing that advance their work.

Throughout the 1990s, equipped with this recognition of the socially and culturally situated nature of writing, writing studies researchers fanned out across various fields of human activity to document the ways in which texts and writing practices have been tailored to produce particular knowledges, the effects of that tailoring, the community-specific methods for introducing newcomers to textual practices, and the consequences for individuals and collectives of participation in those practices. Before considering these new explorations of the writing-knowledge link, it might help to review what we have learned from over four decades of writing studies research.

Rohman (1965), in the article usually credited with the first reference to writing as a "process," argued that writing preceded thinking and should not be confused with thought (p. 106). Nonetheless, process theories of composing that developed over the late 1960s and into the 1970s foregrounded the heuristic power of writing—that is, its ability to generate or "discover" ideas—and discounted the prevailing notion that writing expressed knowledge already formed in the mind. One of those theories—often referred to as "expressivism"—grew from pedagogical approaches that countered the earlier current-traditional focus on correctness and form. The chief proponents of this approach (e.g., Coles, 1978; Elbow, 1973, 1981; Macrorie, 1970; Murray, 1968 1980) situated the writer at the centre of the composing process and stressed the notion of "voice," generally conceived as the unique expression of an individual identity. Despite later critiques of the "authentic self" at the heart of expressivism (e.g., Faigley, 1992), the idea that the act of writing allows writers to make new meanings, to link previously separated concepts, and to know a topic in a different way has remained a central tenet of writing studies.

Writing and knowledge-making were also central in cognitive process theories of writing—theories that borrowed heavily from cognitive psychology for both research methodologies and theoretical antecedents. Cognitive theorists (e.g., Bereiter & Scardamalia, 1987; Flower & Hayes, 1981) offered a complex and dynamic picture of the individual's composing process—a picture that focussed mainly on the mental or intellectual steps that made text production possible. A central feature in cognitive models was what Flower and Hayes (1981) referred to as the "text produced so far," which served as a prompt for further idea generation.

As the writer produced ideas in language, those ideas in turn inspired new ideas. Later developments in research and theory led to a rejection of the cognitive model of composing—mainly on the grounds that it ignored context and posited a fixed, mechanistic view of human mental activity, but much of the empirical evidence from studies of this era is difficult to reject: the cyclical movement between mental representations in the mind and symbolic representations on the page is generative and clearly heuristic. Writers do not simply transcribe ideas; in their effort to make meaning, writers generate ideas, and they challenge, rethink, extend, and revise them. Writing leads to new and different knowledge.

The next breakthrough in our understanding of the relationship between writing and knowledge occurred when researchers began to recognize that individual mental and scribal activities are inseparable from—and, in fact, deeply shaped by—the social or cultural contexts within which writers work (e.g., Knoblauch, 1980; Selzer, 1983). In the same way in which the languages we acquire exist long before we are born, so do the discursive practices of the disciplinary, workplace, or civic settings long before people enter them. This expanded research focus in writing studies corresponded with the larger "discursive turn" in contemporary intellectual debate mentioned earlier: the contention that what we know about the world is the product of our signifying practices—our discourses—and that "reality" is a provisional truth constructed, temporarily maintained, and eventually changed by the dialectical action of rhetoric—that is, by the ongoing interactions between and among different perspectives and beliefs (e.g., Bazerman, 1981, 1988; Berlin, 1987, 2003; Faigley, 1992). This rhetorical dynamic, according to social (or social-epistemic) theories of the writing-knowledge relationship, is as true for aesthetics as for astrophysics. Within any field of human activity, the dominant beliefs, values, facts, and theories are held in place by a dialogue among members of the collective, and challenges to dominance are essential if new knowledge is to be made. Thus, collectives create communal discourse strategies designed to produce the rhetorical friction that makes new knowledge and new ways of knowing. As a result, we get parliaments, senates, law courts, medical rounds, newspaper editorials, public debates, scientific conferences, academic journals, and other forums for the exchange of views.

As noted above, a critical point in this conception of the writing-knowledge link is that these collective discourse strategies are culturally and socially situated—that is, they vary from location to location or from field to field in ways that are deliberately (though rarely self-consciously) designed to produce particular kinds of knowledge and, conversely, to prohibit or reduce the likelihood of other kinds of knowledge. So, for example, hearsay evidence is inadmissible in court; Robert's Rules govern what can be said, by whom, and when in governance forums; and scientific disciplines impose strict regulations on the nature and provision of evidence. The rich body of research on workplace writing that began in the early 1980s (e.g., Bazerman & Paradis, 1991; Knoblauch, 1980; Odell & Goswami, 1982, 1985; Selzer, 1983; Smart, 2007; Spilka, 1993; Winsor, 1996, 2003; Zachry & Thralls, 2007;), as well as research on rhetoric in the disciplines, offers detailed reports of the complex ways in which organizations, disciplines, corporations, and other collectives develop, regulate, protect, and adjust discourse strategies to meet their knowledge ends.

One of the contemporary strands of writing studies that has been particularly concerned with the writing-knowledge connection is rhetorical genre studies (e.g., Artemeva & Freedman, 2006; Bawarshi & Reiff, 2010; Bazerman, 1988; Bazerman, Bonini, & Figueiredo, 2009; Bazerman & Russell, 2003; Coe, Lingard, & Teslenko, 2002; Devitt, 2004; Freedman & Medway, 1994; Miller, 1984; Schryer, 1993), which assumes that these repeated discourse strategies—or genres—maintain stability in the production of discourse and (thus) knowledge by typifying or standardizing key components of the rhetorical situation: the moments at which discourse is called for or elicited (the exigence, or need); the appropriate textual format and content for the response to each exigence; the roles and relationships played out by community members in the performance or enactment of the genre; and the consequences or outcomes of the genre. A discourse strategy that becomes a genre has been successful at reproducing the ways of knowing and the knowledge valued by the collective. As Giltrow (2002) has argued, such genres are sometimes explicitly controlled through what she calls "meta-genres," which are themselves discourse strategies that are manifest in such texts as guidelines, policy statements, style guides, and other regulatory texts. Meta-genres provide writers with "a kind of pre-emptive feedback, ... ruling out some kinds of expression, endorsing others" (p. 190).

Most significantly perhaps, this tradition of research has come to understand rhetoric and writing as a social practice—as constitutive of human activity and thus of the work, civic, and personal lives of people, as well as the educational, social, political and economic institutions of communities and societies. In *Writing Selves/Writing Societies,* the first book in this WAC Clearinghouse & Parlor Press series on Perspectives on Writing, Bazerman and Russell (2003), for example, bring together writing studies researchers whose work shows how writing organizes human activity and produces outcomes that are valued by institutions, organizations, disciplines, communities—whether they are educational or government institutions, health care providers, national banks, or community think-tanks. Continuing this line of inquiry, the chapters in this book draw particular attention to the role of writing as an epistemic practice in the production of these outcomes as well as in the production of knowledge as a particular kind of outcome itself. As such, they draw extensively on theories of genre (either implicitly or explicitly) as a productive, constraining, constitutive, and regulatory force in human activity as demonstrated richly by the work gathered in *Genre in a Changing World* edited by Bazerman, Bonini, and Figueiredo (2009), the second book in the series.

Given these kinds of concerns at the centre of attention in genre studies, this strand of writing studies has also brought critical perspectives on discourse and knowledge production to the foreground. Although most genres are flexible—and necessarily so, if change is desired—the fact that it is possible to discern patterns in a collective's discourse strategies raises certain critical questions: What knowledge is afforded and constrained by a collective's discourse regulations? That is, what can and cannot be said and known? Who is allowed to or called on to speak, and who is not? How flexible are the conventions inscribed in genres, and who has licence to alter them? Does the knowledge afforded by a particular genre benefit some members of the collective over others? One collective over another?

Finally, recognizing that specialized discourse practices are rarely explicitly taught, writing studies researchers have a tradition of investigating the process whereby a collective's new members learn to participate in the community's knowledge-making activities (e.g., Berkenkotter, Huckin, & Ackerman, 1988; Casanave & Li, 2008; Dias, Freedman, Medway, & Paré, 1999; Dias & Paré, 2000; Freedman, 1987; McCarthy, 1987; Prior, 1998; Winsor, 1996). That work has demonstrated that discourse conventions are not merely etiquette; rather, they are deeply transformative for both individuals and collectives, influencing identity, epistemology, ideology, even ontology. In other words, participation in a community's knowledge-making practices does not just produce knowledge; it produces ways of knowing, ways of seeing, ways of believing, ways of being.

As the contributions to this book show, these multiple traditions of inquiry into the epistemic nature of rhetoric and writing are vital to helping us understand how knowledge is produced discursively; at the same time, the contributions to this book replenish these traditions by examining the new complexities, functions, and roles of rhetoric and writing in knowledge-intensive endeavors, as we illustrate in the following overview of the book.

CONCEPTUAL, METHODOLOGICAL, AND HISTORICAL PERSPECTIVES ON STUDYING WRITING AS AN EPISTEMIC PRACTICE

Grounded in these extensive traditions of inquiry, section 1 offers conceptual, methodological, and historical perspectives on the study of writing as an epistemic practice that inform or cut across many of the chapters in the book. In chapter 2, Catherine Schryer offers methodological considerations, arguing that

Rhetorical Genre Studies (RGS) offer an ideal approach to studying how writing produces knowledge because of how and where RGS locates itself theoretically and methodologically: first, it positions itself between texts and the worlds they construct, looking both ways, and seeks to understand how knowledge is produced through the operation of those texts in their worlds; second, it works at the borders of writing studies and the fields whose writing and knowledge-making practices it seeks to understand. Finally, Schryer argues that a variety of contemporary theories from linguistics, sociology, and psychology offer strong conceptual support to an RGS approach to the study of writing as knowledge work. In the next chapter, Janet Giltrow offers an extended example of the conceptual power of genre that Schryer (this volume) describes. By analyzing the rhetorical history of an 18th century trader for the Hudson's Bay Company, her study shows how genre knowledge and genre learning emerge through social interactions in the overlaps, or "interstices," as Schryer says, of "multiple scenes of activity," including—in Giltrow's study—science, travel, and trade. And as Giltrow notes, this versatility of genre—its local situatedness in multiple activities raises questions for the ways in which we understand the role of genre and genre knowledge in digital environments, especially for trends in the design of digital environments to focus on reproducing what are perceived to be standard features or conventions of genre. Extending Giltrow's considerations about writing and knowledge in digital environments, Charles Bazerman, in the next chapter, urges us to take a step back from immediate concerns over multimedia writing and persuasive screen design that have occupied the centre of attention in writing studies scholarship. Instead, he argues for a deeper look at how technologies affect human sociality—opportunities to connect in meaningful ways for deeper sharing of knowledge and deeper cooperation. Tracing the impact of digital technologies on various institutions of knowledge and cultural production, Bazerman warns that technologies tend to be first deployed by established social systems, which means that technologies tend to be designed to facilitate existing work that reproduces the economic interests of those systems and the social relations of power that maintain those interests. Much is at stake, Bazerman reminds us. In academic publishing, for example, the question is one of monopoly control by elites over often publicly funded knowledge versus the free flow of that knowledge "for the good of all."

WRITING AS KNOWLEDGE WORK IN PUBLIC AND PROFESSIONAL SETTINGS

Public access to knowledge, and, indeed, public participation in the production of knowledge that shapes consequential public decisions, is the subject of more detailed attention in section 2, which examines the vital roles writing plays in the construction and shaping of knowledge in public and professional settings. In public life, writing studies research, continuing a 2,500-year tradition of inquiry into civic discourse, has continually shown the central role of writing and rhetoric in organizing and (re)producing the activities of communities, including the ways in which citizens develop the understanding and knowledge necessary to deliberate and make decisions about public life, the ways in which they claim their roles as participants, or the ways in which those roles are regulated and constrained. As the chapters in this section confirm, writing is vital to citizen participation in the shaping of public knowledge, in policy deliberation, and in public decision making with new exigencies and challenges arising in the contexts of environmental crisis (Wegner and Spoel), digital network technologies (Hart-Davidson and Grabill; Rife), and globalization (Rife).

The role of writing in the construction of public knowledge as motivated by environmental crisis is the focus of attention in chapters 5 and 6. In chapter 5, Philippa Spoel and Chantal Barriault analyze the rhetorical model of public engagement in the construction of risk knowledge deployed by a study assessing the environmental risks of mining-related soil contamination in a Northern Ontario community. Although the study is promoted by the Canadian government as a model for community involvement in the assessment of risks, Spoel and Barriault's insightful analysis reveals that the mining-company-funded study uses a model of public engagement that amounts largely to a well orchestrated public relations campaign designed to produce the assuring illusion of public participation in the construction of risk knowledge, while effectively limiting public participation through an information transfer model. In this model, for example, the public advisory committee is separate and subordinate to the technical committee, web sites—as Bazerman in this volume would predict—serve as one-way channels of information flow restricting public debate and participation, and open-house forums and their agendas are controlled by those in charge of the study. Ultimately, here, risk communication works to reinforce a hierarchy between "expert" and public knowledge, to ensure the credibility of the company as "open" to public participation, and to manage the public response, leaving little room for shared knowledge and decision making. By offering alternative models for public participation in the construction of environmental risk knowledge, Spoel and Barriault illustrate how vital an understanding of the epistemic nature of rhetoric and writing is for citizens to ensure their participation in the construction of knowledge, such as here about the risks posed by soil contamination for the public food supply, risks that affect them in most immediate ways.

The struggle of citizens to ensure their participation in public knowledge and decision making processes is also at the heart of Diana Wegner's chapter, which analyzes the activist identity work an environmentalist group performs in order to ensure its participation in environmental decision making about development projects in a community in British Columbia. Specifically, Wegner examines the paradoxical situation of activist groups having to engage in and to some extent reproduce dominant discursive practices, in this case of the city government, while simultaneously engaging in the activist discursive practices that are vital to their transgressive identity. The chapter's detailed analysis of the discursive practices of the group provides nuanced testimony to the intricate relationships between discourse, identity, and knowledge, showing how identities are not only discursively produced and challenged, but also how discourses, e.g., that of the city government, inscribe a limited range of identities that allow for participation in public knowledge and decision making about the environment.

In chapter 7, Martine Courant Rife directs our attention to the role of writing in the production of legal knowledge for a judicial opinion that itself has wide-ranging implications for the degree to which the citizens of a country are able to share and draw on existing knowledge in their writing in order to build new knowledge. Drawing on the landmark Canadian Supreme Court case CCH Canadian Ltd. V. Law Society of Upper Canada (2004), Rife shows how writing works to shape knowledge used to inform the judicial opinion. Specifically, as Rife shows, Judge McLachlin's reliance on new forms of intertextuality and remixing of judicial opinions and laws in other international jurisdictions enables her to arrive at a judicial opinion that allows her to meet the needs of Canadian citizens for the sharing and fair dealing in knowledge and cultural production needed for innovation and new knowledge production, while setting a significant example for fair dealing in copyrighted work worldwide. Given its focus on copyright and fair dealing, however, the chapter shows not only how writing shapes legal knowledge, but also how legal writing, in this case, the judicial opinion, shapes the ability of millions of citizens to draw on existing knowledge in their writing to produce new knowledge.

In the last chapter in this section, Bill Hart-Davidson and Jeff Grabill offer this succinct summary of the book's and in particular this section's main thesis: "the activity of citizenship, as well as the activity of professionals working in organizational settings (including technical writers), is knowledge work that is either supported by writing or embodied as writing." To support that claim, they consider the knowledge/writing work done in a variety of different public and professional settings—settings shaped by or consisting of digital technologies—and raise critical issues about how writing researchers and teachers can support such work and facilitate the meaningful connections for knowledge work Bazerman calls for earlier in this volume. As they demonstrate, new technologies and new textual practices are changing the ways in which knowledge is produced, disseminated, and applied.

THE ROLE OF WRITING IN THE PRODUCTION OF KNOWLEDGE IN RESEARCH ENVIRONMENTS

Like public and professional environments, research environments "run on writing, in myriad, constantly-changing genres and media" (Bazerman & Russell, 2003). In academic contexts, disciplinary and interdisciplinary knowledge is created, shared, advanced, contested, revised, and recognized largely through writing. Not surprisingly, writing constitutes much of what researchers do, from the research funding proposals that make research possible in the first place to the peer-reviewed journal articles, book chapters, book reviews, conference presentations, books, peer-reviewer reports, and more that organize and produce the work of research and ensure its contribution to the larger collective ongoing knowledge-making endeavor. In the first chapter in this section, chapter 9, Heather Graves goes to the heart of the question around the rhetorical nature of scientific knowledge production, producing a detailed account of how rhetoric contributes to the construction of scientific facts. Drawing on examples from her studies of rhetoric in experimental and theoretical physics, Graves takes the question of rhetoric's role in scientific knowledge production a step beyond epistemological questions, arguing that rhetoric not only has an epistemic role, but indeed an ontological one. As her analysis of an experimental physics case shows, for example, the reshifting of an argument through the rhetorical figure of metonymy in ways that are acceptable to the physics community makes the difference between whether a claimed method for producing a particular silicon thin film is believed to exist or not.

The important role of social interaction in the construction of scientific knowledge illustrated in Heather Graves' chapter is the central focus of study in chapter 10. In this chapter, Ken Hyland draws on a corpus analysis of 240 published research papers from eight disciplines as well as on interviews with researchers from these disciplines to propose a taxonomy of strategies for social interaction in research papers. As Hyland's study shows, these strategies—ranging from writer's expressions of stance, such as hedges, boosters, attitude markers, and self-mention to expressions of reader engagement, such as reader mention, directives, or questions—have important epistemic functions as they help writers anticipate possible negative reactions or alternative interpretations of their knowledge claims and to build the social relations that make the negotiation and acceptance of knowledge claims possible. In Hyland's vivid words, researchers "don't just produce texts that plausibly represent an external reality. They are not just talking about garlic proteins, stress fractures or brains in vats. Instead, they use language to acknowledge, construct and negotiate social relations." Perhaps most importantly, Hyland's study reveals that these strategies for social interaction are culturally constructed, varying across disciplines, with each discipline developing its own norms for what strategies of interaction are appropriate and credible.

One of the most critical tasks faced by all research communities is the socialization of newcomers to carry on and renew the community's knowledge-making endeavors, a process that involves the formation of subject positions or identities capable of participating in the rhetorical practices that sustain these knowledge-making endeavors—a task studied in chapter 11 by Paré and colleagues in the context of dissertation supervision sessions and in chapter 12 by Horne in the context of new members to a research community learning to participate in the discursive knowledge-making practices called inkshedding at the community's conference. Drawing on their analysis of dissertation supervision sessions, Paré, Starke-Meyerring, and McAlpine illustrate how supervisors attempt to locate and align students with the various competing factions of these communities along with their often conflicting epistemological, ontological, and ideological commitments and practices. However, as their analysis shows, much of the identity work during supervision sessions happens without attention to the rhetorical nature of this process, providing few opportunities for students to reflect on what kinds of researchers they are becoming, with what kind of ideological, epistemological, or ontological alignments. Describing a somewhat similarly arhetorical process of new member induction into the knowledge-making practices of a conference, Horne draws on her longitudinal study of the Inkshed community to account for the human experience of learning how to participate in disciplinary conversations whose norms and expectations have become normalized over a long time, but are the source of vulnerability, insecurity, and anxiety among newcomers. As Horne argues persuasively, "the institutional context that does not acknowledge these insecurities is sure to constrain the potential knowledge of its collective, for the link between writing and knowledge is not only theoretical, but also human."

THE TEACHING OF WRITING AS AN EPISTEMIC PRACTICE IN HIGHER EDUCATION

The integral role of rhetoric and writing in the production of knowledge-making practices, outcomes, and identities is not only instrumental to the research function of universities, but also to the teaching of students as gradual participants in these knowledge-making practices. At the same time, the epistemic nature of rhetoric and writing—not only in research but also in civic and professional settings—also raises important questions for how writing might be taught in higher education. In chapter 13, Paul Rogers and Olivia Walling further expand our understanding of the deeply social nature of writing as knowledge work developed in the previous chapters by offering a historical and systemic perspective on writing as an epistemic practice. Drawing on a study of the complex interactions between scientists, government committees, and military officials in the development of French military weaponry in the late 18th century, Rogers and Walling illustrate the systemic role of writing in complex interacting activity systems. As they show, this role is facilitated by writing's ability to coordinate the relationships between people "doing different things" within and across communities, the constraints placed on writing by those communities, and the ambiguity of texts as representational systems, all of which render writing a technology that allows for and participates in the creation of complex systems of knowledge. Importantly, the authors show how their historical and systemic perspective allows them to draw conclusions for the teaching of writing, such as the need for specialized theoretical introductions to the study of discourse and writing as well as the need for embedding writing instruction in the systems of knowledge in which the students are to participate.

These recommendations generated by Rogers and Walling underlie many of the specific approaches to the teaching of writing in higher education developed in the remaining chapters in this section. Doug Brent, in chapter 14, for example, illustrates this systemic alignment of writing instruction in two important ways, first by joining many other writing studies scholars (e.g., McLeod, 2007; Russell, 2006; Walvoord, 1996) in integrating writing instruction, specifically Writing Across the Curriculum, into a system of larger reform movements in higher education designed to facilitate student roles as knowledge creators rather than only recipients, such as the Boyer report movement and in particular the First-Year-Experience or First-Year-Seminar movement. Brent's study shows how the integration of WAC into the first-year experience allowed students to develop a deeper understanding of the social nature of the knowledge work accomplished through writing, to explore existing work less to confirm their preconceived views and more to pursue genuine questions, and to tap more into the social system of knowledge production in the form of libraries, more frequent contact with faculty, and peer collaboration in knowledge production.

Similarly, Anne Parker and Amanda Goldrick-Jones in chapter 15 make the social nature of writing the central focus of their engineering communication courses and illustrate how students in traditional as well as online teams work to produce a shared understanding of ethical interaction or a "code of ethics" that makes knowledge production in engineering possible. In effect, the students that Parker and Goldrick-Jones studied created a form of meta-genre (Giltrow, 2002) that governed their discourse and knowledge work. As Parker and Goldrick-Jones argue, the assignment they designed provided students "with a glimpse, at least, of what it's like to be part of an ethical 'community of practice'; that is, a group of people who both perform a function and learn together – thus understanding to some extent what it means to participate in a knowledge society."

Drawing on her longitudinal study of novices developing genre knowledge in engineering in university as well as in the workplace, Natasha Artemeva in chapter 16 illustrates persuasively that this genre knowledge—not unlike the genre knowledge of the 18th century Hudson Bay trader described earlier by Janet Giltrow—is composed of complex components learned in multiple activity systems and that the development of this genre knowledge is an ingrained part of students' careers. Importantly, as Rogers and Walling in this section suggest and as Artemeva's meticulous tracing of genre learning through a university-workplace trajectory is able to show, students are best able to begin working with the theoretical knowledge about writing provided in their engineering communication classroom once they have been introduced to the larger systems of knowledge production in engineering over the course of several years of engineering education, making perhaps the third year of engineering programs a particularly opportune time for the integration of engineering communication courses into the curriculum.

In the final chapter in this section, Heekyeong Lee and Mary Maguire remind us that questions of identity play an important role in the writing-knowledge equation not only in public settings (as articulated in this volume by Diana Wegner) or in research environments (as articulated by Paré and colleagues as well as Horne), but also in the teaching of writing in higher education. And, as they show, ignoring these questions comes at a high cost to students. Here students from South Korea study in Canadian universities, where dominant discursive practices inscribe identities that may be at odds with those embraced by the students. The personal literacy narratives of two students presented in this chapter illustrate that students understand quite well who they are being asked to be in their writing, but not why, let alone what options they have to negotiate the identities inscribed in the academic discourse they encounter, leading to feelings of alienation and exclusion. Their stories are a compelling argument about the cost of leaving students to struggle with these identity questions, leading the authors to urge a critical approach to the teaching of writing and language in higher education that explores the links between questions of power, dominance, identity, and alignment in academic discourse and empowers students with diverse identities to "write with authority."

ARTICULATING AND IMPLEMENTING RHETORIC AND WRITING AS A KNOWLEDGE-MAKING PRACTICE IN HIGHER EDUCATION

As the contributions to this volume illustrate, the link between writing and knowledge is a deep and intricate one: indeed, writing is knowledge work—writing and knowledge form an "as" rather than an "and" relationship, rendering writing a vital means of production in knowledge-intensive societies, with high-stakes consequences not only for the direct economic concerns, such as corporate client base or profits, identified by Brandt (2005), but also for the extent to which citizens shape and participate in democratic processes of environmental risk assessment and decision making, the ways in which law shapes the extent to which citizens can engage in the sharing and creation of new knowledge, the ways in which scientific knowledge claims are created and contested or accepted, the kinds of researchers that emerge from doctoral education programs, the extent to which new researchers as well as students are able to participate in and contribute to collective knowledge-making endeavors in academe, public settings, as well as the workplace, and much more.

As societies—citizens, governments, businesses, professionals, and many others—increasingly sense these high-stakes roles of writing in the production and sharing of knowledge, they naturally turn to education and specifically higher education as the institution charged with original knowledge production and the education of knowledge workers and civic leaders. Unfortunately, although writing is a vital part of the epistemological infrastructure of knowledge-intensive societies, the study and teaching of writing are often still absent from university programs in many countries, receive little systematic research-based attention in university or national policy planning, or lack institutional conditions that would allow for the development of vital research capacity in writing studies. Not surprisingly, therefore—and in many ways typical of emerging disciplines, rhetoric and writing studies teachers, scholars, and program directors spend much of their time articulating the role of writing in knowledge production, the insights the discipline of writing studies has produced into how discourse and writing work and how writing is learned, and what roles rhetoric and writing play in the life of higher education institutions themselves. In short, they become change agents (McLeod, 2007; Russell, 2006).

The contributions to this final section, therefore, illustrate and examine some of that vital work involved in articulating and implementing writing as a knowledge-making practice in higher education, for example, in program and curricular development or in the creation of institutional space for critical, research-based attention to writing. In chapter 18, Roger Graves presents a self-study of a program administrator working to articulate the role of his writing studies program to various constituents to secure positions and funds that allow the program to grow, to involve students, and to create institutional and curricular space for the new program.

In the next chapter, Tania Smith offers a case study of ways in which scholarship in rhetoric and writing can inform the work of institutions beyond individual programs. Her case study shows how the genre of a town hall forum served as a boundary event to bridge the deepening divides among faculty, students, and administrators, resulting in new courses, a community service learning initiative, a peer-mentoring initiative, and a part-time senior administrative position to continue the work of bridging administrative and student communities and of involving students as co-producers of institutional knowledge for curricular decision making. Situating the event in higher education reform movements, such as those inspired by the Boyer Commission Report and the Wingspread Statement on Student Civic Engagement, Smith illustrates how scholarship in rhetoric and writing, with its long tradition of studying civic discourse, can inform democratic deliberation and decision making in institutions of higher education, making these institutions working examples of the kind of student participation in knowledge production and civic engagement envisioned by these reform movements.

Margaret Procter, in chapter 20, advances a longitudinal case study of her home institution, the University of Toronto, as what she calls "a kind of display cabinet for structural and theoretical issues likely to be shared by other writing centres in Canada." However, without doubt, the issues will be familiar to anyone working in writing studies anywhere. Chief among those issues, and a source of great frustration to many in university writing centres, is the challenge of convincing administrators and colleagues in other disciplines to base their decision making on research illustrating the central role writing plays in knowledge-making in all disciplines. Procter's case study provides heartening evidence that concerted efforts by writing centre staff can help establish the importance of writing instruction and can even secure long-term and well remunerated positions for writing teachers, but she acknowledges that she and her colleagues have not yet achieved recognition as knowledge-makers themselves, and so are not expected to engage in the research needed to advance the field.

Together, the contributions to this book paint a compelling and nuanced picture of the diverse roles writing plays in knowledge-intensives societies, the exigencies that arise for writing in knowledge-intensive societies, and the ways in which rhetoric and writing work to produce, share, question, marginalize, or advance knowledge in civic, workplace, and institutional spaces. Drawing on diverse theoretical traditions, the chapters also offer important insights into the ways in which we conceptualize the epistemic nature of writing and the implications these have for the study and teaching of writing. What unites the work presented in this book is the recognition that what knowledge is, what counts as knowledge, how we arrive at knowledge, who gets to participate in the production and sharing of knowledge are questions negotiated rhetorically by local communities, institutions, disciplines, or other groups engaged in the production of knowledge.

Most importantly, perhaps, what cuts across all chapters is the realization that in knowledge-intensive societies, we mark an historical moment in the development of writing studies as a discipline dedicated to the study of human thought and knowledge: It is an historical moment in which much depends on the ways in which the discipline finds its curricular and research space in institutions tasked with the production of knowledge. As the contributions to this book testify, we have arrived at a stage in human development where we can no longer afford to produce knowledge without a discipline that offers the research base and theory to allow for rigorous critiques of how our discursive knowledge-making practices enable and constrain what we can and cannot know.

REFERENCES

Aristotle. (2007). *On rhetoric: A theory of civic discourse* (G. A. Kennedy, Trans., 2nd ed.). New York: Oxford University.

Artemeva, N., & Freedman, A. (Eds.). (2006). *Rhetorical genre studies and beyond.* Winnipeg: Inkshed Publications.

Atwill, J. (1993). Instituting the art of rhetoric: Theory, practice, and productive knowledge in interpretations. In T. Poulakos (Ed.), *Rethinking the history of rhetoric* (pp. 91-117). Boulder, CO: Westview.

Bawarshi, A. S., & Reiff, M. J. (2010). *Genre: An introduction to history, theory, research, and pedagogy.* Reference Guides to Rhetoric and Composition. West Lafayette, IN, and Fort Collins, CO: Parlor Press & The WAC Clearinghouse. Available at http://wac.colostate.edu/books/.

Bazerman, C. (1981). What written knowledge does: Three examples of academic discourse. *Philosophy of the Social Sciences,* 11, 361-87.

Bazerman, C. (1988). *Shaping written knowledge.* Madison, WI: University of Wisconsin Press.

Bazerman, C. (2008). Introduction. In C. Bazerman, (Ed.), *Handbook of research on writing: History, society, school, individual, text* (pp. 1-4). New York: Erlbaum.

Bazerman, C. & Paradis, J. (Eds.). (1991). *Textual dynamics of the professions: Historical and contemporary studies of writing in professional communities.* Madison, WI: University of Wisconsin Press.

Bazerman, C., Bonini, A., & Figueiredo, D. (Eds.). (2009). *Genre in a changing world.* Perspectives on Writing. Fort Collins, CO, and West Lafayette, IN: The WAC Clearinghouse & Parlor Press Available at http://wac.colostate.edu/books/.

Bazerman, C., & Rogers, P. (2008a). Writing and secular knowledge apart from modern European institutions. In C. Bazerman (Ed.), *Handbook of research on writing: History, society, school, individual, text* (pp. 143-156). New York: Erlbaum.

Bazerman, C., & Rogers, P. (2008b). Writing and secular knowledge within modern European institutions. In C. Bazerman (Ed.), *Handbook of research on writing: History, society, school, individual, text* (pp. 157-175-4). New York: Erlbaum.

Bazerman, C., & Russell, D. (Eds.). (2003). *Writing selves/writing societies: Research from activity perspectives.* Fort Collins, Colorado: The WAC Clearinghouse and Mind, Culture, and Activity. Available at http://wac.colostate.edu/books/selves_societies/

Beard, R., Myhill, D., Riley, J., & Nystrand, M. (Eds.). (2009). *The Sage handbook of writing development.* London, UK: Sage.

Bereiter, C. & Scardamalia, M, (1987). *The psychology of written composition.* Hillsdale, NJ: Erlbaum.

Berkenkotter, C., Huckin, T., & Ackerman, J. (1988). Conventions, conversations, and the writer: Case study of a student in a rhetoric Ph.D. program. *Research in the Teaching of English,* 22, 9-43.

Berlin, J. A. (1987). *Rhetoric and reality: Writing instruction in American colleges, 1900-1985.* Carbondale, IL: Southern Illinois University Press.

Berlin, J. A. (2003). *Rhetorics, poetics, and cultures: Refiguring college English studies.* West Lafayette, IN: Parlor Press.

Brandt, D. (2005). Writing for a living. Literacy and the knowledge economy. *Written Communication,* 22, 166-197.

Brown, R. H. (1987). *Society as text.* Chicago: University of Chicago Press.

Casanave, C. P., & Li, X. (Eds.). (2008). *Learning the literacy practices of graduate school: Insiders' reflections on academic enculturation.* Ann Arbor: University of Michigan Press.

Ceccarelli, L. (2004). *Shaping science with rhetoric: The cases of Dobzhansky, Schrödinger, and Wilson.* Chicago: University of Chicago Press.

Coe, R., Lingard, L. & Teslenko, T. (Eds.). (2002). *The rhetoric and ideology of genre: Strategies for stability and change.* Cresskill, NJ: Hampton Press.
Coles, W. E. (1978). *The plural I: The teaching of writing.* New York: Holt.
Delanty, G. (2003). Ideologies of the knowledge society and the cultural contradictions of higher education. *Policy Futures in Education,* 1(1), 71-82.
Devitt, A. J. (2004). *Writing genres.* Carbondale, IL: Southern Illinois University Press.
Dias, P. & Paré, A. (Eds.). (2000). *Transitions: Writing in academic and workplace settings.* Cresskill, NJ: Hampton Press.
Elbow, P. (1973). *Writing without teachers.* New York: Oxford University Press.
Elbow, P. (1981). *Writing with power.* New York: Oxford University Press.
Emig, J. (1977). Writing as a mode of learning. *College Composition and Communication,* 28, 122-28.
Enos, R. L., & Lauer, J. (1992). The meaning of heuristic in Aristotle's Rhetoric and its implications for contemporary rhetorical theory. In S. P. Witte, N. Nakadate, & R. D. Cherry (Eds.), A rhetoric of doing: Essays on written discourse in honor of James L. Kinneavy (pp. 79-87). Carbondale: Southern Illinois University Press.
Faigley, L. (1992). *Fragments of rationality: Postmodernity and the subject of composition.* Pittsburgh, PA: University of Pittsburgh Press.
Feyerabend, P. K. (1975). *Against method: Outline of an anarchistic theory of knowledge.* London: New Left Books.
Flower, L. (2008). *Community literacy and the rhetoric of public engagement.* Carbondale: Southern Illinois University Press.
Flower, L. S. & Hayes, J. R. (1981). A cognitive process theory of writing. *College Composition and Communication,* 32, 365-87.
Foucault, M. (1972). *The archeology of knowledge & the discourse on language.* New York: Pantheon Books.
Freedman, A. (1987). Learning to write again: Discipline-specific writing at university. *Carleton Papers in Applied Language Studies,* 4, 95-115.
Freedman, A., & Medway, P. (Eds.) (1994). *Genre in the new rhetoric.* London: Taylor and Francis.
Geertz, C. (1973). *The interpretation of cultures: Selected essays.* New York: Basic.
Giltrow, J. (2002). Meta-genre. In R. Coe, L. Lingard & T. Teslenko (Eds.), *The rhetoric and ideology of genre: Strategies for stability and change* (pp. 187-205). Cresskill, NJ: Hampton Press.
Grabill, J. (2007). *Writing community change: Designing technologies for citizen action.* Cresskill, NJ: Hampton Press.
Graves, H. (2005). *Rhetoric in(to) science.* Cresskill, NJ: Hampton Press.
Gray, J., & Myers, M. (1978). The Bay Area writing project. *The Phi Delta Kappan,* 59(6), 410-413.

Gross, A. (1990). *The rhetoric of science.* Cambridge, MA: Harvard University Press.

Harris, R. (Ed.). (1997). *Landmark essays on rhetoric of science: Case studies.* Mahwah, NJ: Erlbaum.

Hyland, K. (2004). *Disciplinary discourses: Social interactions in academic writing.* Ann Arbor, MI: Michigan University Press.

Hyland, K. (2009). *Academic discourse: English in a global context.* London, UK: Continuum.

Kennedy, G. (2007). Translation notes. In *Aristotle, On Rhetoric: A theory of civic discourse.* New York: Oxford University.

Knoblauch, C. H. (1980). Intentionality in the writing process: A case study. *College Composition and Communication, 31*(2), 153-159.

Kuhn, T. S. (1972). *The structure of scientific revolutions (3rd ed.).* Chicago: University of Chicago Press.

Long, E. (2008). *Community literacy and the rhetoric of local publics.* Reference Guides to Rhetoric and Composition. West Lafayette, IN, and Fort Collins, CO: Parlor Press & The WAC Clearinghouse. Available at http://wac.colostate.edu/books/.

Lunsford, A. A., Wilson, K. H., & Eberly, R. A. (Eds.). (2009). *The Sage handbook of rhetorical studies.* Thousand Oaks, CA: Sage.

Lyne, J. (1985). Rhetorics of inquiry. *Quarterly Journal of Speech, 71*, 65-73.

MacArthur, C. A., Graham, S., & Fitzgerald, F. (Eds.). (2005). *The handbook of writing research.* New York: Guilford.

Macrorie, K. (1970). *Telling writing.* Rochelle Park, NJ: Hayden.

McCarthy, L. P. (1987). A stranger in strange lands: A college student writing across the curriculum. *Research in the Teaching of English, 21*, 233-265.

McCloskey, D. (1994). *Knowledge and persuasion in economics.* Cambridge, UK: Cambridge University Press.

McLeod, S. (2007). *Writing program administration.* Reference Guides to Rhetoric and Composition. West Lafayette, IN, and Fort Collins, CO: Parlor Press & The WAC Clearinghouse. Available at http://wac.colostate.edu/books/.

Miller, C. (1984). Genre as social action. *Quarterly Journal of Speech, 70*, 151-167.

Murray, D. (1968). *A writer teaches writing.* New York: Holt.

Murray, D. (1980). Writing as process: How writing finds its own meaning. In T. R. Donovan & B. McClelland (Eds.), *Eight approaches to teaching composition* (pp. 3-20). Urbana, IL: National Council of Teachers of English.

Myers, G. (1989). The pragmatics of politeness in scientific articles. *Applied Linguistics, 10*(1), 1-35.

Nelson, J., & Megill, A. (1986). Rhetoric of inquiry: Projects and prospects. *Quarterly Journal of Speech, 72*, 20-37.

Nelson, J., Megill, A., & McCloskey, D. (1985). *The rhetoric of the human sciences.* Madison: University of Wisconsin Press.

Odell, L., & Goswami, D. (1982). Writing in a non-academic setting. *Research in the Teaching of English, 16,* 201-223.

Odell, L., & Goswami, D. (Eds.). (1985). *Writing in nonacademic settings.* New York: Guilford Press.

Peters, M. (2007). *Knowledge economy, development and the future of higher education.* Rotterdam, The Netherlands: Sense Publishers.

Rohman, G. (1965). Pre-writing: The stage of discovery in the writing process. *College Composition and Communication, 16,*106-112.

Russell, D. (2006). WAC's beginnings: Developing a community of change agents. In S. H. McLeod & M. I. Soven (Eds.), *A history of Writing Across the Curriculum: Composing a community* (pp. 3-15). West Lafayette, IN: Parlor Press.

Schryer, C. F. (1993). Records as genre. *Written Communication, 10,* 200-234.

Scott, R. L. (1967). On viewing rhetoric as epistemic. *Central States Speech Journal, 18,* 9-16.

Scott, R. L. (1976). On viewing rhetoric as epistemic: Ten years later. *Central States Speech Journal, 27,* 258-266.

Scott, R. L. (1993). Rhetoric is epistemic: What difference does that make? In T. Enos & S. Brown (Eds.), *Defining the new rhetorics* (pp. 120-136). Englewood Cliffs, NJ: Prentice Hall.

Segal, J. (2005). *Health and the rhetoric of medicine.* Carbondale, Southern Illinois University Press.

Selzer, J. (1983). The composing processes of an engineer. *College Composition and Communication, 34*(2), 178-187.

Simons, H. W. (1989). *Rhetoric in the human sciences.* London: Sage.

Simons, H. W. (1990). *The rhetorical turn. Invention and persuasion in the conduct of inquiry.* Chicago: University of Chicago Press.

Smart, G. (2007). *Writing the economy: Activity, genre and technology in the world of banking.* London, UK: Equinox.

Spilka, R. (Ed.). (1993). *Writing in the workplace: New research perspectives.* Carbondale, IL: Southern Illinois University Press.

Välimaa, J., & Hoffman, D. (2008). Knowledge society discourse in higher education. *Higher Education, 56,* 265-285.

Walvoord, B. E. (1996). The future of WAC. *College English, 58,* 58-79.

Winsor, D. (1996). *Writing like an engineer: A rhetorical education.* Mahwah, NJ: Erlbaum.

Winsor, D. (2003). *Writing power: Communication in an engineering centre.* Albany, NY: SUNY Press.

Zachry, M., & Thralls, C. (Eds.). (2007). *Communicative practices in workplaces and the professions: Cultural perspectives on the regulation of discourse and organizations.* Amityville, NY: Baywood.

CONCEPTUAL, METHODOLOGICAL, AND HISTORICAL PERSPECTIVES ON STUDYING WRITING AS AN EPISTEMIC PRACTICE

2 INVESTIGATING TEXTS IN THEIR SOCIAL CONTEXTS: THE PROMISE AND PERIL OF RHETORICAL GENRE STUDIES

Catherine F. Schryer

Innis (1946), the polymath socio-economic and communications scholar, declared that working from the margins, whether those margins be disciplinary, political or economic, produces exemplary innovative work. In this essay I suggest that Rhetorical Genre Studies (RGS) have been making and have the capacity to make a significant contribution to writing research precisely because RGS researchers work at the interstices of various disciplines. In fact, RGS researchers often, to quote Wenger (1998), "broker" or translate between different fields in order to accomplish their projects, projects that typically involve investigating texts in their social contexts. In order to investigate written or spoken texts in their social contexts, genre researchers have to weave together theoretical and methodological perspectives that permit them to investigate the way that texts interact with and co-construct their social networks. In the following I will outline my own journey to craft together a working model to accomplish the projects that I think are required if researchers take seriously the call to investigate texts in their social contexts. The journey begins with rhetorical genre theory, travels through applied linguistics, traverses through social theories, and winds up with some current theories on learning. At each stage, I will point to some implications for research on genre and more generally on writing research. The trip concludes with a retrospective look at some of the promises and perils of doing such research.

RHETORICAL GENRE THEORY

Uniting much of the current research in RGS is a commitment to a central insight found in Miller's (1984) reworking of the concept of genre. Essentially, Miller established the basic framework to claim text types or genres had to be investigated in their social contexts. Building on Campbell and Jamieson's (1979) discussion of genre, Miller asserted that genres were, in fact, forms of social action – that they functioned to coordinate the work of organizations or to accomplish some kind of significant task. Miller based this argument on Campbell and Jamieson's insight that "a genre does not consist merely of a series of acts in which certain rhetorical forms recur.... Instead a genre is composed of a constellation of recognizable forms driven by an internal dynamic" (p. 21). As Miller explains, this sense of an "internal dynamic" is crucial because it conveys the sense that these language events emerge as fusions of substantive and stylistic features in response to specific situations. Using Bitzer's (1968) notion of "exigence," Miller suggests that people in their social networks over time recognize the need to respond (exigence) to specific situations, typify those situations and develop communicative resources to respond effectively. So, for example, my own research on healthcare communication (Schryer, 1993; Schryer, Lingard, & Spafford, 2003; Schryer, Lingard, & Spafford, 2005; Schryer & Spoel, 2005; Schryer, Campbell, Spafford, & Lingard, 2006) has identified genres that have emerged to respond to healthcare professionals' needs to record their observations of patients, consult with experts, and transfer information about patients. Over time these practitioners developed ways to handle these needs, and these strategies evolved into recognizable text-types or oral speech events such as patient records, consultation letters and case presentations. These already existing structures, fusions of content, style and organization, now facilitate practice in these settings, and newcomers have to learn how to wield them in order to get their work done.

In short, Miller's reconceptualization of genre as a theoretical concept paved the way for professional communication researchers to investigate texts in their social contexts. Researchers who operationalized and refined Miller's insights include Winsor (2000) and Artemeva (1998) in engineering, Schryer (2000), Smart (1993), and Yates and Orlikowski (1992) in business communication, Spinuzzi (2003) in software development, and Bawarshi (2003) and Devitt (2004) in composition studies. In healthcare research, genre perspectives have assisted in identifying the communicative implications of specific documents such as policy documents or manuals (Berkenkotter, 2001; Spoel & James, 2003), records (Schryer, 1993), and clinical talk (Dunmire, 2000; Schryer et al., 2003; Segal, 2001). Two conferences and their related publications have also been of particular importance for genre researchers in North America. The first conference and publication (Freedman & Medway, 1994) acknowledges the value of genre research in professional contexts; the second conference and publication (Coe, Lingard, & Teslenko, 2001) offers more critical perspectives on genre research.

Another important source for the renovation of genre theory was the work of Bakhtin (1981, 1986) and his circle including Volosinov (1986/1929). Although Bakhtin developed his ideas during the 1920s and into the 1930s (and mostly in reaction to de Saussurean linguistics and literary formalism) his dynamic ways of thinking about language did not enter into the North American academy until the 1970s and even the 1980s. Rhetoricians (Bialostosky, 1992; Kent, 1991; Klancher, 1989; Schuster, 1985), anthropological linguists (Hanks, 1987), and professional communication researchers (Berkenkotter & Huckin, 1993; Schryer, 1993, 1994) recognized the relevance of Bahktin's insights for investigating texts in their contexts. As Dentith (1995) notes, central to Bakhtin's thought is the basic principle "that communicative acts only have meaning, only take on their specific force and weight, in particular situations or contexts" (p. 3). Once again, the implication for RGS researchers, or any researcher interested in oral or written communication, is that texts only have significance in relation to specific social contexts.

Two key terms—utterance and speech genre—evoke Bakhtin's dynamic way of conceptualizing language and constitute his major contribution to genre theory. As he explains, the primary unit of communication is not the sentence or the word but the utterance. The utterance is "individual" and "concrete" and generated by participants in the "various areas of human activity" (1986, p. 60). The utterance inherently, he suggests, addresses and responds to another person or collective of people. This understanding of language stands in direct opposition to traditional linguists (such as de Saussure) who see language as an objective system with classifiable elements (langue) that the writer or speaker operationalizes. Instead, Bakhtin sees that as we speak or write we are always shaping our language for real or imagined others.

This profoundly situated understanding of language might suggest that, for Bakhtin, communication is indeterminate and chaotic. However, in "The Problem of Speech Genres" the concept of speech genre provides a balance. He suggests that, although utterances are individual, "each sphere in which language is used develops its own *relatively stable types* of these utterances" which he calls "*speech genres*" (p. 60). He indicates that genres are heterogeneous and range from "short rejoinders of daily dialogue ... to the fairly variegated repertoire of business documents" and include the "diverse forms of scientific statements and all literary genres" (pp. 60-61). Bakhtin's theory can accommodate this diversity because he posits that speech genres exist in both primary and secondary forms and are both centrifugal and centripedal. A primary genre is a simple, usually brief utterance such as a command (Go) or a negation (No). A secondary genre is a complex oral or written text which encompasses other primary and even other secondary genres. Thus, a complex genre can incorporate other text types. For example, a doctor's consultant report exists as a secondary genre because it encompasses other genres such as tests results The centrifugal quality of utterances or speech genres refers to the forces of change that occur within text types; whereas the centripetal quality refers to the social forces that attempt to keep an utterance stable (Bakhtin, 1981). An important feature of Bakhtin's thought is that both actions (stabilizing and destabilizing) co-occur within utterances.

Bakhtin's insights into genre shifted the ground for communication researchers in several important ways. First, his work extends concepts of genre far beyond literary texts into examining powerful written genres such as records, reports, and letters that constitute our social worlds. Secondly, his insights, like those of Miller's, offer a way to theorize the process of classifying utterances. It really matters how social agents classify their text types or speech events. These classifications tell researchers a great deal about what a group values and recognizes as assisting in accomplishing its social purposes. At the same time, however, these same utterances are not simply instances of a category. Because each occurrence of a genre is addressed to a different context, audience, and time, it evokes a different set of strategies within an acceptable (to participants) range. In effect, genres are abstractions or ever changing sets of socially accepted strategies that participants can use to improvise their responses to a particular situation. As I (1993) suggested in a study of veterinary medical records, genres are "stabilized-for-now or stabilized enough sites of social and ideological action" (p. 200). This definition expresses the sense that genres are just stabilized enough so that agents can accomplish their social purposes but that genres are constantly evolving. Finally, Bakhtin's work suggests that utterances or genres are the socially situated ways that we learn to communicate. Rather like a singer who learns to sing by singing songs, we all learn to communicate through these constellations of resources.

APPLIED LINGUISTICS

Applied linguists have also used the concept of genre and contributed to research into written texts, especially in areas related to second language learning, literacy, and pedagogy. One group, associated with English for Specific Purposes (ESP), has provided detailed descriptions of the moves or "schematic structures"

(Hyland, 2002, p. 116) within genres as diverse as the research article (Swales, 1990), grant proposals (Connor, 2000; Connor & Mauranen, 1999), and business letters (Bhatia, 1993; Upton & Connor, 2001). Many of the analytic tools used by these researchers derive from systemic functional linguistics (Halliday, 1994). To focus carefully on texts, a communication specialist needs specific definitions and tools in order to do a fine grained analysis. Systemic functional linguistics (SFL) provides particularly useful tools as it centers on function or how language both affects and is constrained by specific social contexts. In a study, for instance, of consultant letters and reports that travel between optometrists and ophthalmologists, my own research group (Schryer, Gladcova, Spafford, & Lingard, forthcoming) focused on the ways these communicators used modality to negotiate issues of competency and responsibility. Fortunately software such as Wordsmith (2005) exists that can facilitate textual analysis across the large data sets that genre researchers often want to investigate in order to identify a range of strategies evoked by a particular genre. Another group of linguists (Cope & Kalantzis, 1993; Martin 1992, 2001) who have contributed to genre research has focused on the pedagogical implications of genre research. Often called the Sydney School, this group asserts that the often tacit rhetorical and linguistic choices within powerful genres need demystification for those with less access to privileged forms of education. Like many sociocultural theorists (Bourdieu, 1991; Gee, Hull, & Lankshear, 1996), members of the Sydney School accept that the discourse practices of traditional schooling reflect upper or middle class Western-style discourse practices. Children born into families that use these discourse practices have a distinct advantage. Consequently, these scholars call for more overt teaching of genres in order to resolve this inequity.

The Sydney School critiques RGS research on two counts. They note that North American genre researchers, through their dependence on qualitative studies, have focused on exploring social context rather than texts and that RGS has failed to link genre research to pedagogical issues. RGS advocates, on the other hand, have critiqued the Sydney School, for abstracting genres from their social contexts and attempting to codify them (Freedman & Medway, 1994). The pedagogy associated with this type of research, they suggest, fails to address issues related to situated learning.

Gee and colleagues (1996) effectively dramatize the debate by pointing to the discourses associated with law school. They point out that law students are not directly taught the strategies associated with legal discourse. Rather they are subjected to an immersion program wherein they learn "inside the procedures, rather than overtly about them" (p. 13). This immersion program works for two reasons. First, as Gee and colleagues point out, trying to spell out the rules of the game involved in doing law would only offer a "panacea" (p. 12). They assert that, "All that goes into thinking, acting, believing, valuing, dressing, interacting, reading, and writing like a lawyer cannot be put overtly into words" (p. 12) and the attempt to codify all these strategies produces stilted, unconvincing performances. Secondly, learning inside procedures ensures that a learner "takes on perspectives, adopts a worldview, accepts a set of core values and masters an identity without a great deal of critical and reflective awareness" (p. 13). Such an immersion is necessary for apprentices. No field or organization wants its newcomers to question its basic values as such questioning would undermine the kinds of "fluent and fluid performances" (p. 13) that mark a speaker as a member of a field. However, Gee and others (Casanave, 2002) also note that these kinds of immersion experiences work to exclude those not prepared to deal with these discourse expectations or their attendant ideological commitments. Of course, Gee and colleagues suggest that field-specific discourses should be critiqued but not during the process of acquiring them.

The implications of this debate for researchers committed to investigating texts in their social contexts are two-fold. To focus on texts, we need to profit from linguistic concepts that take into account social contexts (see Giltrow, 2002; Hodge & Kress, 1993; Hyland, 2000; Stillar, 1998; and Swales, 1990). At the same time the pedagogical implications of RGS research or any project that focuses on communication must be acknowledged for two reasons. First, results from such research can move into classroom practice in sometimes decontextualized ways. Secondly and more importantly, as theories of situated learning assert (Wenger, 1998), social contexts are, by their very nature, learning spaces, and text-types or genres often exist at the heart of these spaces. As we will see, communication researchers who investigate texts in their social contexts need a theorized account of learning in order to understand these social spaces.

SOCIAL CONTEXT THEORIES

Because RGS researchers explore texts in their contexts, they need ways to conceptualize social contexts (theories) and ways to navigate that context (methods). RGS researchers (Dias, Freedman, Medway, & Paré, 1999; Schryer, 2000; Yates & Orlikowski, 1992) have profited from the theoretical and methodological insights developed by theorists such as Giddens and Bourdieu. Central to Giddens' (1993) work is his insistence on the "mutual dependence of structure and agency" (p. 122). Giddens rejects structuralist and functionalist notions that conceptualize social structures as abstract systems outside of time. Such accounts describe agents as either fully in control of their own operations or as fully subject to their social contexts. For example, in de Saussurean linguistics, language users are conceptualized as fully in control of their language systems; whereas in Levi-Straussian structuralism, agents are at the mercy of systems (such as systems of myths) which compel them to articulate essentially the same structure (despite discrepant details). Neither account explains, in Giddens' view, the complex and nuanced way that human agents are affected by and reproduce their social environments. Rather, Giddens suggests that temporality is always present in social contexts. Agents bring with them their memories of past experiences and/or they use already existing structures—genres such as reports, meetings, memos, patient records et cetera—to guide them in their interactions with other social agents. These already constructed social structures are filled with "rules" or the resources and constraints that enable and constrain the constant reproduction of social life. However, as Giddens explains, these "rules" are not like the rigid rules present in a game of chess. Rather they are more fluid, emergent and dependent on the collective agreement of those involved in the interaction (pp. 118-120).

Giddens' insights help explain how relationships exist between texts and their social contexts. Giddens, like genre researchers, is particularly interested in recurring structures, and text types fall into this category. In fact, genres function as structured structures that structure (Schryer et al., 2003, p. 66). In other words, genres pre-exist their users. They are filled with rules and resources that both constrain and enable the performance of their cases. For example, in our research on case presentations, my research group (Schryer et al., 2003) never observed case presentations that used exactly the same resources even though all participants labeled these events as case presentations.

Giddens also offers a methodological stance of importance to genre researchers. He parallels his focus on agency with an insistence that agents "are able to explain most of what they do, if asked" (p. 93). Researchers need to include participant information in their data collection because social agents have access to both discursive and practical knowledge about their routine activities. Social agents, according to Giddens, are reflexively monitoring their own activities and have valuable explanations (discursive knowledge) of their practices. At the same time agents have "practical knowledge" or "knowledge embodied in what actors 'know how to do'" (p. 126) in their daily activities. This practical knowledge, however, is often tacit and, consequently, researchers need to develop methodologies that capture this knowledge.

Another social theorist, Bourdieu (1991; Bourdieu & Wacquant, 1992), has contributed significantly to the theoretical and methodological development of much genre research. Like Giddens, Bourdieu acknowledges temporality in both social agents and their chosen professions or fields. Unlike

37

Giddens, however, Bourdieu emphasizes the role of power in social life. In fact, for Bourdieu, the most important aspect of social agents is that they are social or inhabited by "habitus." Bourdieu (Bourdieu & Wacquant, 1992) defines habitus as "socialized subjectivity" (p. 126). As Wacquant, one of Bourdieu's main collaborators, explains, the habitus "consists of a set of historical relations 'deposited' within individual bodies in the form of mental and corporeal schemata of perception, appreciation and action" (Bourdieu & Wacquant, 1992, p. 16). Habitus, thus, is not a passive kind of socialization; it produces an active engagement wherein social agents, because of their prior experiences, recognize how to respond appropriately and even strategically to "fields" (p. 14) or specific social contexts. To respond, agents must have a range of resources that predispose them to react appropriately, and, in fact, these predispositions emerge within social contexts or fields. Thus, for example, healthcare fields accept students from academic programs that predispose them to work within healthcare paradigms. These professions or fields then further shape students to perceive, communicate and behave in professional or acceptable ways.

The concept of 'field,' or 'market,' or 'game' is central to Bourdieu's way of conceptualizing disciplines, organizations, or social systems and their relationship to power. For Bourdieu, society is not a seamless totality, but, rather an "ensemble of relatively autonomous spheres of play" (Bourdieu & Wacquant, 1992, p. 17). A game, market, or field is a "structured space of positions in which the positions and their interrelations are determined by the distributions of different kinds of resources or capital" (Bourdieu, 1991, p. 14). The position of agents within a field is determined by their access to three different forms of power or capital: economic (material wealth), cultural (knowledge, skills) and social (accumulated prestige or honor) (Thompson, 1991, p. 14). Bourdieu's model highlights the workings of power between and within different social spaces or fields.

In other words, agents are structured by their experiences within a field. At the same time, they also structure or reproduce those fields but not in purely reductive ways. Rather, because agents occupy different positions within their fields (and thus have different access to power) and because fields themselves occupy different positions in relation to each other, agents enact different strategies (although only within a specific range). Bourdieu calls these regulated, improvisational strategies, triggered by the interaction between habitus and field, "the logic of practice" (as cited in Robbins, 1991, p. 112). Much of my own research has been dedicated to exploring the logics of practice articulated within genres such as insurance writing (Schryer, 2000) and healthcare communication (Schryer et al., 2003; 2005).

Integral to habitus is linguistic habitus, or agents' improvisational and communicative "feel for the game" (Bourdieu & Wacquant, 1992, p. 129), or the communication strategies that agents can access in order to enhance and distinguish their own position and thus play the game successfully. Language, particularly that aspect of language called style, is deeply implicated in this struggle to succeed. Bourdieu observes that "style exists only in relation to agents endowed with schemes of perception and appreciation that enable them to constitute it as a set of systematic differences" (p. 39). Furthermore, this process of differentiation, or style production is deeply implicated in the reproduction of symbolic power. Bourdieu notes that

> This production of instruments of production, such as rhetorical devices, genres, legitimate styles, and manners and, more generally, all the for mulations destined to be "authoritative" and to be cited as examples of "good usage", confers on those who engage in it a power over language. (p. 58)

As instruments of production, some genres, especially those enacted by well-positioned agents in well-positioned fields such as medicine or law, can reproduce forms of symbolic power that can literally shape their receivers' views of the world. These genres are, in Bourdieu's terms, "symbolic structures" (p. 166).

Bourdieu, like Giddens, provides a useful methodological stance for genre researchers who wish to examine texts in their social contexts. He recognizes the "logic of practice" possessed by all participants within their fields. But researchers themselves also have their own logic of practice—one that is distinct from the groups that they study. In fact, Bourdieu suggests a methodology that combines two types of analyses in order to uncover the structures that maintain and reproduce power. His methodology, called "social praxeology" (Bourdieu & Wacquant, 1992, p. 11), consists of two crucial steps: "First, we push aside mundane representations to construct the objective structures ... that define the external constraints bearing on interactions and representations. Second, we reintroduce the immediate, lived experience of agents in order to explicate the categories of perception and appreciation" (p. 11).

Several of my projects, but also those of other researchers (Hyland 1999, 2000), have included first, a close reading (objective) of specific texts to describe and critique the strategies evoked within these discursive events, and second, interviewing participants and asking them for explanations for their strategies and problem-solving techniques. This interview data can provide richer views of the social context that surround texts. As Bourdieu makes clear, although both steps are necessary, the first step takes priority. In other words, disciplinary forms of analysis are crucial and lead to what he calls "objectivist" (p. 11) analysis. However, Bourdieu is not invoking the objective paradigm of truth and validity to which feminist researchers and postmodernists have so rightly objected. Bourdieu sees disciplinary forms of analysis as situated language practices that themselves require reflection to see what values and ideologies they espouse.

Bourdieu also insists researchers must analyze agents' practical knowledge, or "phronesis" (Bourdieu &Wacquant, 1992, p. 128) for two reasons. First, in order for researchers to understand what passes for common sense, or decorum, or "the way we do things around here," this intuitive "feel for the game" set of improvisational strategies must be articulated (p. 128). And, second, when the operations of the logic of practice are articulated, agents can sometimes acquire "tools for distinguishing zones of necessity and of freedom, and thereby for identifying spaces open to moral action" (Bourdieu & Wacquant, p. 49). This moment of reflexivity occurs when social agents themselves can become more aware of the social within them and more capable of controlling their own categories of thought and action. Needless to say this commitment to investigating participants' "practical knowledge" also involves a commitment to qualitative data analysis techniques (see Strauss & Corbin, 1998) greatly facilitated by data analysis software programs such as NVIVO.

Several implications of importance to communication research emerge from these structuration theorists. Both Giddens and Bourdieu provide a theorized way to conceptualize the dynamic, dialogical ways that texts and their social contexts interact. Their understanding of the rich nature of social improvisation provides a way to explain the ways that structure and agency are not dialectically opposed poles of opposition but rather in a state of constant co-construction. Bourdieu also provides not only a critical perspective on power within social groups but also a balanced methodology – a way to justify doing textual analysis using linguistic disciplinary resources together with qualitative studies that explore with research participants the reasons for their language choices. Finally, Bourdieu's insights offer a rationale for interdisciplinary projects. After all, how can researchers gain insights into the tacit realm of the "logic of practice," unless they bring members of the group they are studying into the research team? In fact, practices associated with qualitative data analysis—locating, defining and refining themes—in my experience, can lead to the moments of reflexivity to which Bourdieu alludes.

Although, in my view, Giddens and Bourdieu provide the basis for conceptualizing social context, Activity Theory (AT) adds additional insights to explain the complex agents and their social structures, especially with respect to the role of learning and the role of technologies. Vygotsky (1978) and Leont'ev (1981) opposed simplistic notions of socialisation which either envisioned individual agents as self-contained pre-formed entities (psychological model) or as entities totally at the mercy of their environments (behaviorist model). Instead, as noted elsewhere (Schryer et al., 2003), they envisioned agents as learning through using tools in purposeful, goal directed activities. They saw that these tools, both physical (hammers, pencils) and cultural (language), pre-exist their users and mediate the interaction between agents and their social environments. By using tools, human agents internalized the values, practices and beliefs associated with their social worlds. At the same time as they become experienced users, agents can, in the midst of purposeful activity, affect their social contexts or even modify their tools. Certainly in our research, we saw that, by using the mediating tool of case presentations, healthcare students were internalizing the values and practices while involved in purposeful activities that would lead to their own ability to affect future social contexts (i.e., their ability to deal with their own future patients or clients).

Engeström (1987, 1999) and other researchers (Cole, 1999; Scribner, 1985; Wertsch, 1981) have extended Vygotsky and Leont'ev's work into a model for the analysis of complex interactions between agents and social structures in professional and workplaces settings. While retaining the concepts of tools mediating the socialization of agents, they have expanded the analytical concepts within the notion of system to account for more of the dialectical, or rather dialogical, interactions that occur between social agents and between social agents and their settings. Engeström (1993) defines an activity system as a system "that incorporates both the object-oriented productive aspect and the person-oriented communicative aspect of human conduct," and he suggests that a human activity system "always contains the subsystems of production, distribution, exchange and consumption" (p. 67).

Furthermore, activity system theorists have developed interesting approaches to help account for change and the ways that agents themselves, while internalizing their social tools affect their social settings. Most workplace settings are characterized by multiple and even overlapping activity settings. As participants in those systems, agents can and often do bring rules and resources from one system into another and in this way can introduce change or innovation into a system. Furthermore, according to Engeström (1987; 1999), activity systems are characterized by contradictions, and change sometimes enters systems because of those contradictions. In his work on a health clinic, Engeström (1993) noted the internal contradiction that physicians experience as "gatekeepers and cost-efficient producers ... and as healers or consultants" (p. 72).

In more recent research, Engeström, Engeström, and Vähääho (1999) introduced the concept of Knotworking to describe work situations that require the "active construction of constantly changing combinations of people and artefacts over lengthy trajectories of time and widely distributed space" (p. 345). The metaphor of the knot describes the unstable, distributed and collaborative nature of many workplace settings. Communication, technologies and especially communication technologies are essential to mediate this unstable collective activity system. Part of this collectivity, as Engeström and colleagues make clear in their illustrative example of a mental patient being forced into care, are "mediational means" (p. 355). Mediational means include genres such as healthcare records and technologies such as handcuffs, each of which represents an activity system. In a knotworking situation, in fact, representatives from activity systems (in their illustrative case—healthcare providers, social workers and the police) have to improvise ways to co-operate with each other in order to accomplish their task (dissolve the knot).

Several important implications, especially for future work in genre and communication studies, emerge from AT. As researchers we need to attend to the role that technologies play with respect to communication. As tools, technologies change the nature of the genres that we use daily. Electronic reports are not the same as paper reports. Online healthcare records differ substantially from paper-based records. Most importantly, genres and technologies exist in complex human communication networks. As Bazerman (1994) and others (Spinuzzi, 2003) have noted, genres are not solitary entities and neither are technologies. We need research prepared to investigate the complex interactions of texts and their social, technological contexts. Finally, AT is a theory about learning. As social agents learn to use tools, whether symbolic such as genres or technological such as software programs, they are learning the practices and values of their social settings.

LEARNING THEORIES

From the perspective of AT, the problematic of simply importing lessons learned about specific workplace genres into class room settings is clear. For instance, Dias, Freedman, Medway, and Paré (1999) in their thought provoking comparison of writing practices in the workplace and the academy, claim that the school genres of the academy are "worlds apart" (p. 3) from workplace genres. Reflecting the purposes of schooling, educational genres typically create the circumstances wherein "epistemic" or knowledge-making tasks are evaluated on an individual basis (p. 44). As Dias and colleagues explain, "Within the classroom context each paper is graded in comparison to all others, and the institution has a vested interest in a quality spread" (p. 62). Workplace genres, on the other hand, mediate the interactions of agents in different ways. In workplace settings managers will intervene in writing processes as "the institutional goal is to elicit the best possible product from each employee each time writing is undertaken" (p. 62). In fact, Dias and colleagues conclude that the activity systems of education and workplaces differ so radically, that educational institutions cannot claim to be teaching workplace communication. This perspective, of course, is deeply troubling to educators in professional communication who claim that the strategies that students learn in professional communication classrooms translate into useful practices in workplace settings. (See Fahnestock, 1993 and Freedman, 1993a, 1993b for a succinct debate on this issue.)

Much of Dias and colleagues' arguments stem from their realization that the activity systems of the workplace and education have inherently different purposes. However, their insights were also shaped by current research into learning theory, particularly the concept of "communities of practice" (COP) as developed by Lave and Wenger (1991), and later refined by Wenger (1998). Lave and Wenger describe a COP as "a set of relations among persons, activity and world, over time and in relation with other tangential and overlapping communities of practice" (p. 98). Wenger later expands this definition to suggest that a COP consists of three elements. First, a COP consists of people involved in "mutual engagement" (p. 73). They have formed a complex network of relations to accomplish their work. Second, the group is involved in a "joint enterprise" that requires negotiated expertise and involves accountability and local interpretations. Finally, the group has a "shared repertoire," or resources such as discourses, tools, style, concepts and genres. A COP could consist of insurance assessors (Wenger, 1998), workplace teams (Gee et al., 1996), or any group such as agency-based social workers or healthcare providers involved over time in a set of practices to accomplish a specific kind of work. Lave and Wenger and their many supporters insist that learning is a natural and ubiquitous phenomenon and that it occurs most naturally and effectively within COPs through the process of "legitimate peripheral participation" (p. 34). As Lave and Wenger explain, "learning is an integral part of generative social practice in the lived-in world" (p. 35) and occurs naturally and constantly in groups consisting of expert and inexpert members. Less expert members learn through their involvement in legitimate (recognized by the group) practices. At first this involvement is peripheral (by observing, by being assigned part of the task, by being supervised) but eventually less expert members assume full participation in the group's activities.

For educators, this position on learning has several implications. Dias and colleagues' recognition of the value placed on "situated learning" within COPs puts educational programs into question. How can such programs, separated as they often are from practitioners, create COPs wherein their students can acquire "legitimate" practices? As Brown, Collins, and Duguid (1989) point out, students need to be in "cognitive apprenticeships" (p. 38) where they can legitimately steal knowledge. This last observation also echoes a value placed on tacit knowledge. Brown and Duguid (1996) state that "In being explicated, the implicit loses its value as implicit knowledge ... and that, in fact, "implicit aspects of practice have a dynamism by virtue of their implicitness" (p. 50). Less expert members learn through involvement in discourses and practices not necessarily by analysing and abstracting those same practices. This value placed on tacit knowledge offers challenges to educators. What should experts' role be in a COP or in apprenticeship situations? One traditional role has always been to develop concepts, procedures or rules that attempt to codify practice. But Brown and colleagues (1989), as well as Lave and Wenger, insist that evolving practices and knowledge always exceed codification and that implicit knowledge is more valued anyway. Another response has merged from Vygotsky's notion of the "zone of proximal development" (ZPD) and the notion of "scaffolding" that emerged in response to Vygotsky's work. In fact, Bruner and Sherwood (1976) saw the implications of ZPD and the role of the mentor/expert in Vygotsky's work and developed the notion of "scaffolding "to describe the ways that effective mentors interacted with learners. For this group of researchers, the ZPD refers to the distance between what learners can do on their own and what they can do with assistance. An expert who intervenes in a legitimate task and provides scaffolding by reframing or reinterpreting the novices' words or deeds into the terms and processes of the activity system can assist in the internalizing of the system's practices.

Lave and Wenger also insist that COPs exist in overlapping networks of other COPs, some of which have more power than others. They also suggest that we all belong to many COPs (work groups, church affiliations, volunteer programs, etc.). Wenger (1998) notes as well that some individuals find themselves "brokering" between COPs, that is, working at the margins of different communities bringing resources (or problems) from one group to another (pp. 108-110). Quoting the work of Bowker and Star (1999), he also suggests that some documents or tools can function as "boundary objects" or reifications that can move between COPs and coordinate their work (pp. 105-108).

The research on situated learning has several implications for genre researchers. The notion that workplaces are inherently learning spaces puts recurrent text types or genres at the heart of many workplace practices. As symbolic structures or sets of improvisational resources that users invoke in order to address recognizable (to them) issues or problems, genres should be at the centre of written or oral communication research. In fact, the point at which they should be studied is at the point when they are being learned. During the learning or training process is one of the few times that tacit strategies become more overt and when the nature of situated expertise also becomes more transparent. Much of the critical work of genre researchers should consist of studies that undcover these tacit sets of resources, not just to make them more visible, but also to open them up for critique. As Gee and colleagues (1996) note in their study of the discursive practices associated with law, these practices need critique. These practices seem like "common sense" to their users, but once they are opened up for critical reflection, then even their users might want to challenge some of their practices and attendant ideological values. Genre researchers working in interdisciplinary teams using a text-in-social context approach are well positioned to offer such a balanced critique—one that combines discourse analysis with social agents' explanations of their language choices.

In fact, such teams can function as "brokers" and possibly create "boundary objects" that traverse different communities of practice. For instance, the interdisciplinary team in which I am involved has published its findings in fields as diverse optometry (Spafford, Lingard, Schryer, & Hrynchak, 2004, 2005), medical education (Lingard, Garwood, Schryer, & Spafford, 2003; Lingard, Schryer, Spafford, & Garwood, 2003), social work (Spafford et al., 2007) and professional communication (Schryer et al., 2003, 2005; Varpio, Spafford, Schryer, & Lingard, 2007). These publications, in my view, constitute "boundary objects," because in each instance the findings which they articulate have been negotiated across these fields of practice. Furthermore, the writers themselves have functioned as "brokers" articulating their own field concerns but also forming a community of practice in which expertise can be explored, challenged and negotiated.

This "brokering" role is also one that communication instructors can adopt in their classrooms. Dias and colleagues are correct in asserting that classroom activity systems cannot replicate the activity systems present in workplace settings and they should not claim to do so. Rather, classroom instructors can create communities of practice within their courses that focus on some of the resources present in workplace writing. After all, genres consist of sets of resources and some of those resources (such as the judicious use of the passive voice) can be taught. As instructors we can also teach our students to be savvy genre readers. After all, even the academic essay has a history and consists of a plentitude of resources (see Giltrow, 2002; Hyland, 2000). Teaching students to negotiate and then challenge this genre can help them to understand other texts that they will encounter and that also envelop themselves in the mantle of common sense. We can and should contribute to our students' developing linguistic habitus—but in ways that make them critically aware of their genre choices.

So the working model that I have been journeying towards begins with genre as an overarching concept. This concept allows me to analyze instances of texts as fleeting performances that pull together strategies from a repertoire of available but also evolving strategies. Many of these strategies can be tacit and all reflect deeply shared social values. My job as a researcher is to map, as best as I can, these shifting resources by examining them through two lenses: discourse analysis and qualitative data gathered through interviews and observations. These maps, these boundary objects, then can become accounts that instructors or practitioners can use to query discursive practices in the classroom or in their own fields. However, like all texts, my accounts are participating in generic resources and as such also have their blind spots or areas of common sense.

PROMISE

In an admonition to communication researchers, Sarangi and Roberts (1999) observed that we need "thick description" that "reaches down to the level of fine-grained linguistic analysis and up and out to broader ethnographic description and wider political and ideological accounts" (p. 1). RGS researchers are particularly well placed to heed this admonition. We take the injunction to investigate texts in their social contexts seriously and thus, in our different ways, continue to identify the theoretical resources and methodological skills needed to conduct the kinds of studies that Sarangi and Roberts require. I think, too, that as an enterprise we have a useful, considered approach to pedagogy. We study sites of situated learning in workplace settings and therefore know that our findings cannot be codified into strict rules. They can only be used as accounts or maps to make traversing workplace terrains a little less mysterious.

PERILS

However, some perils do exist. Investigating texts in their social contexts often means creating two large data sets: one dedicated to analyzing a set of texts, and the other focused on analyzing interview data. These two different kinds of demands mean that such projects can be lengthy and expensive and can require combinations of expertise that exceed the typical humanity's style research project. Furthermore, careful planning and design are needed to get the results from the two data sets to talk to each other. Again, researchers need to think about the time and money needed for such planning. As noted earlier, such projects also often require an interdisciplinary team in order to provide the insider knowledge needed to understand the "logic of practice." Brokering between fields can be challenging, especially if that brokering concludes with published research studies. In what fields should these studies be published? Is it possible that such a diversity of fields and audiences means that a community of practice around genre studies might not stabilize?

Needless to say, despite these perils I believe that RGS and other communication researchers who seriously investigate texts in their social contexts are on the right track. These studies are producing the innovative, exemplary work that Innis (1946) suggests can only come from the margins, the interstices between disciplines.

REFERENCES

Artemeva, N. (1998). The writing consultant as cultural interpreter: Bridging cultural perspectives in the genre of the periodic engineering report. *Technical Communication Quarterly,* 7, 285-299.

Bakhtin, M. M. (1981). *The dialogic imagination: Four essays.* (C. Emerson & M. Holquist, Trans.). Austin, TX: University of Texas Press.

Bakhtin, M. M. (1986). *Speech genres and other late essays.* (V. W. McGee. Ed., C. Emerson, & M. Holquist, Trans). Austin, TX: University of Texas Press.

Bawarshi, A. (2003). *Genre and the invention of the writer: Reconsidering the place of invention in composition.* Logan, UT: Utah State University Press.

Bazerman, C. (1994). Systems of genres and the enactment of social intentions. In A. Freedman, & P. Medway (Eds.), *Genre and the new rhetoric* (pp. 79-101). London: Taylor and Francis.

Berkenkotter, C. (2001). Genre systems at work: DSM-IV and rhetorical recontextualization in psychotherapy paperwork. *Written Communication,* 18, 326-349.

Berkenkotter, C., & Huckin, T. (1993). *Genre knowledge in disciplinary communication: Cognition/culture/power.* Hillsdale, NJ: Erlbaum

Bhatia, V. J. (1993). *Analyzing genre: Language in professional settings.* London: Longman.

Bialostosky, D. (1992). Bakhtin and rhetorical criticism: A symposium. *Rhetoric Society Quarterly,* 22(4), 1-28.

Bitzer, L. F. (1968). The rhetorical situation. *Philosophy and Rhetoric,* 1, 1-14.

Bourdieu, P. (1991). *Language and symbolic power.* (G. Raymond & M. Adamson Trans., J. B. Thompson, Ed.). Cambridge, MA: Harvard University Press.

Bourdieu, P., & Wacquant, L. (1992). *An invitation to reflexive sociology.* Chicago: University of Chicago Press.

Bowker, G., & Star, L. (1999). *Sorting things out: Classification and its consequences.* Cambridge, MA: MIT Press.

Brown, J. C., Collins, A., & Duguid, P. (1989). Situated cognition and the culture of learning. *Educational Researcher,* 18(1), 32-48.

Brown, J. C., & Duguid, P. (1996). Stolen knowledge. In H. McLellan (Ed.) *Situated learning perspectives* (pp. 47-56). Engelwood Cliffs, NJ: Educational Technologies Publishers.

Bruner, J. S., & Sherwood, V. (1976). Peekaboo and the learning of rule structures. In J. S. Bruner, A. Jolly & K. Sylva (Eds.), *Play: Its role in development and evolution* (pp. 277-285). Harmondsworth, England: Penguin Books.

Campbell, K. K., & Jamieson, K. H. (1979). Form and genre in rhetorical criticism: An introduction. In K. K. Campbell, & K. H. Jamieson (Eds.), *Form and genre: Shaping rhetorical action* (pp. 9-32). Falls Church, VA: Speech Communication Association.

Casanave, C. P. (2002). *Writing games: Multicultural case studies of academic literacy practices in higher education.* Mahwah, NJ: Lawrence Erlbaum.

Coe, R. M., Lingard, L., & Teslenko, T. (Eds.). (2001). *The rhetoric and ideology of genre: Strategies for stability and change.* Cresskill, NJ: Hampton Press.

Cole, M. (1999). Cultural psychology: Some general principles and a concrete example. In Y. Engeström, R. Miettinen, and R.-L. Punamaki (Eds.), *Perspectives on activity theory* (pp. 87-106). Cambridge: Cambridge University Press.

Connor, U. (2000). Variation in rhetorical moves in grant proposals of United States humanists and scientists. *Text,* 20, 1-28.

Connor, U., & Mauranen, A. (1999). Linguistic analysis of grant proposals: European Union research grants. *English for Specific Purposes,* 18(1), 47-62.

Cope, B., & Kalantzis, M. (1993). How a genre approach to literacy can transform the way writing is taught. In B. Cope, & M. Kalantzis (Eds.), *The powers of literacy: A genre approach to teaching writing* (pp. 1-21). London: Falmer.

Dentith, S. (1995). *Bakhtinian thought: An introductory reader.* London: Routledge.

Devitt, A. J. (2004). *Writing genres.* Carbondale, IL: Southern Illinois University Press.

Dias, P., Freedman, A., Medway, P., & Paré, A. (1999). *Worlds apart: Acting and writing in academic and workplace contexts.* Mahwah, NJ: Erlbaum.

Dunmire, P. (2000). Genre as temporally situated social action. *Written Communication,* 17, 93-138.

Engeström, Y. (1987). *Learning by expanding: An activity-theoretical approach to developmental research.* Helsinki, Finland: Orienta-Konsultit.

Engeström, Y. (1993). Developmental studies of work as a testbench of activity theory: The case of primary care medical practice. In S. Chaiklin & L. Lave

(Eds.), *Understanding practice: Perspectives on activity and context* (pp. 63-103). Cambridge: Cambridge University Press.

Engeström, Y. (1999). Activity theory and individual social transformation. In Y. Engeström, R. Miettinen, & R. Punamaki (Eds.), *Perspectives on activity theory* (pp. 19-38). Cambridge, MA: Cambridge University Press.

Engeström, Y., Engeström, R. and Vähääho,T. (1999). When the center does not hold: The importance of knotworking. In S. Chaiklin, M. Hedgaard, & U. J. Jensen (Eds.), *Activity theory and social practice* (pp. 345-374). Aarhus, DK: Aarhus University Press.

Fahnestock, J. (1993). Genre and rhetorical craft. *Research in the Teaching of English,* 27(3), 265-271.

Freedman, A. (1993a). Show and tell? The role of explicit teaching in the learning of new genres. *Research in the Teaching of English,* 27(3), 222-251.

Freedman, A. (1993b). Situating genre: A rejoinder. *Research in the Teaching of English,* 27(3), 272-281.

Freedman, A., & Medway, P. (Eds.). (1994). *Genre and the new rhetoric.* London: Taylor and Francis.

Gee, J. P. (1999). *An introduction to discourse analysis.* London and New York: Routledge.

Gee, J. P., Hull, G., & Lankshear, C. (1996). *The new work order: Behind the language of the new capitalism.* Boulder, CO: Westview Press.

Giddens, A. (1984). *The constitution of society: Outline of the theory of structuration.* Berkeley: University of California Press.

Giddens, A. (1993). Problems of action and structure. In P. Cassell (Ed.), *The Giddens' reader* (pp. 88-175). Stanford: Stanford University Press.

Giltrow, J. (2002). *Academic writing: Writing and reading in the disciplines* (3rd ed.). Mississauga, Canada: Broadview Press.

Halasek, K. (1998). *A pedagogy of possibility: Bakhtinian perspectives in composition studies.* Carbondale: Southern Illinois University Press.

Halliday, M. A. K. (1994). *An introduction to functional grammar.* London: Edward Arnold.

Hanks, W. F. (1987). Discourse genres in a theory of practice. *American Ethnologist,* 14(4), 668-692.

Hodge, R., & Kress, G. (1993). *Social semiotics.* Ithaca, NY: Cornell University Press.

Hyland, K. (1999). Disciplinary discourses: Writer stance in research articles. In C. N. Candlin, & K. Hyland (Eds.), *Writing: Texts, processes and practices* (pp. 99-121). London & New York: Longman.

Hyland, K. (2000). *Disciplinary discourse: Social interactions in academic writing.* Harlow, England: Longman.

Innis, H. (1946). *Political economy in the modern state.* Toronto: Ryerson Press.

Kent, T. (1991). On the very idea of a discourse community. *College Composition and Communication,* 42(4), 425-445.

Klancher, J. (1989). Bakhtin's rhetoric. In P. Donahue & E. Quandahl (Eds.), *Reclaiming pedagogy: The rhetoric of the classroom* (pp. 83-96). Carbondale: Southern Illinois University Press.

Lave, J., & Wenger, E. (1991). *Situated learning: Legitimate peripheral participation.* Cambridge: Cambridge University Press.

Leont'ev, A. N. (1981). *Problems of the development of mind.* Moscow: Progress.

Lingard, L., Garwood, K., Schryer, C. F., & Spafford M. M. (2003). A certain art of uncertainty: Case presentations and the development of professional identity. *Social Science and Medicine,* 56(3), 603-616.

Lingard, L., Schryer, C. F., Spafford, M. M., & Garwood, K. (2003). Talking the talk: School and workplace genre tension in clerkship case presentations. *Medical Education,* 37, 612-620.

Martin, J. R. (1992). *English text: System and structure.* Amsterdam: Benjamins.

Martin, J. R. (2001). A context for genre: Modeling social processes in functional linguistics. In R. Stainton & J. Devilliers (Eds.), *Communication in linguistics* (pp. 1-41). Toronto: GREF.

Miller, C. (1984). Genre as social action. *Quarterly Journal of Speech,* 70, 151-167.

Robbins, D. (1991). *The work of Pierre Bourdieu: Recognizing society.* Milton Keynes, England: Open University Press.

Sarangi, S., & Roberts, C. (Eds.). (1999). *Talk, work and institutional order: Discourse in medical, mediation and management settings.* Berlin, New York: Mouton de Gruyter.

Schryer, C. F. (1993). Records as genre. *Written Communication,* 10(2), 200-234.

Schryer, C. F. (1994) The lab vs. the clinic: Sites of competing genres. In A. Freedman & P. Medway (Eds.), *Genre and the new rhetoric* (pp. 105-124). London: Taylor and Francis.

Schryer, C. F. (2000). Walking a fine line: Writing 'negative news' letters in an insurance company. *Journal of Business and Technical Communication,* 14(4), 445-497.

Schryer, C. F., Campbell, S. L., Spafford, M. M., & Lingard, L. (2006). You are how you cite: Citing patient information in health care settings. In A. Freedman & N. Artemeva (Eds.), *Rhetorical genre studies and beyond* (pp. 143-187). Winnipeg: Inkshed Press.

Schryer, C. F., Gladcova, O., Spafford, M. M., & Lingard, L. (Forthcoming). Co-management in healthcare: Negotiating professional boundaries. *Discourse and Communication.*

Schryer, C. F., Lingard, L., & Spafford, M. (2003). Structure and agency in medical case presentations. In C. Bazerman & D. Russell (Eds.), *Writing selves/writing societies: Research from activity perspectives* (pp. 62-96). Fort Collins, CO: The WAC Clearinghouse and Mind, Culture, and Activity. Retrieved from http://wac.colostate.edu/books/selvessocieties/

Schryer, C. F., Lingard, L., & Spafford, M. (2005). Techne or artful science and the genre of case presentations in healthcare settings. *Communication Monographs,* 72(2), 234-260.

Schryer, C. F., & Spoel, P. (2005). Genre theory, healthcare discourse, and professional identity formation. *Journal of Business and Technical Communication.* 19(3), 249-278.

Schuster, C. I. (1985). Mikhail Bakhtin as rhetorical theorist. *College English,* 46(6), 594-607.

Scribner, S. (1985). Vygotsky's uses of history. In J. V. Wertch (Ed.), *Culture, communication and cognition: Vygostkian perspectives.* New York: Cambridge University Press.

Segal, J. Z. (2001). Problems of generalization/genrelization: The case of the doctor-patient interview. In R. Coe, L. Lingard & T. Teslenko (Eds.), *The rhetoric and ideology of genre: Strategies for stability and change* (pp. 171-184). Cresskill, NJ: Hampton Press.

Smart, G. (1993). Genre as community invention. In R. Spilka (Ed.), *Writing in the workplace: New research perspectives* (pp. 124-140). Carbondale and Edwardsville: Southern Illinois University Press.

Spafford, M. M., Lingard, L., Schryer, C. F., & Hrynchak, P. K. (2004). Tensions in the field: Teaching standards of practice in optometry case presentations. *Optometry & Vision Science,* 81, 800-806.

Spafford, M. M., Lingard, L., Schryer, C., & Hrynchak, P. K. (2005). Teaching the balance act: Integrating patient and professional agendas in optometry. *Optometric Education,* 33(1), 21-27.

Spafford, M. M., Schryer C. F., Campbell, S. L. & Lingard, L. (2007) Towards embracing clinical uncertainty: Lessons from three healthcare fields. *Journal of Social Work,* 7(2), 155-178.

Spinuzzi, C. (2003). Compound mediation in software development: Using genre ecologies to study textual artifacts. In C. Bazerman & D. Russell (Eds.), *Writing selves/writing societies: Research from activity perspectives* (pp. 97-124). Fort Collins, CO: The WAC Clearinghouse and Mind, Culture, and Activity. Retrieved from http://wac.colostate.edu/books/selvessocieties

Spoel, P., & James, S. (2003). The textual standardization of midwives' professional relationships. *Technostyle,* 18(2), 3-29.

Stillar, G. G. (1998). *Analyzing everyday texts: Discourse, rhetoric and social perspectives.* Thousand Oaks, CA: Sage.

Strauss, A. L., & Corbin, J. M. (1998). *Basics of qualitative research: Techniques and procedures for developing grounded theory* (2nd ed.). Thousand Oaks, CA: Sage.

Swales, J. M. (1990). Genre analysis: English in academic and research settings. Cambridge: Cambridge University Press.

Upton, T., & Connor, U. (2001). Using computerized corpus analysis to investigate the textlinguistic discourse moves of a genre. *English for Specific Purposes,* 20(4), 313-29.

Varpio, L., Spafford, M. M., Schryer, C., Lingard, L. (2007). Seeing and listening: A visual and social analysis of optometric record keeping practices. *Journal of Business and Technical Communication,* 21(4), 343-375.

Volosinov, V. N. (1986/ 1929). *Marxism and the philosophy of language.* Cambridge, MA: Harvard University Press.

Vygotsky, L. S. (1978). Mind in society: The development of higher psychological processes. Cambridge, MA: Harvard University Press.

Wenger, E. (1998). *Communities of practice: Learning, meaning and identity.* Cambridge: Cambridge University Press.

Wertsch, J. V. (Ed.). (1981). *The concept of activity in soviet psychology.* Armonk: M. E. Sharpe.

Winsor, D. (2000). Ordering work: Blue-collar literacy and the political nature of genre. *Written Communication,* 17(2), 155-84.

Wordsmith. (2005). Version 4.0. Oxford University Press.

Yates, J., & Orlikowski, W. (1992). Genres of organizational communication: A structurational approach to studying communication and media. *Academy of Management Review,* 17, 299-32

3 "CURIOUS GENTLEMEN": THE HUDSON'S BAY COMPANY AND THE ROYAL SOCIETY, BUSINESS AND SCIENCE IN THE EIGHTEENTH CENTURY

Janet Giltrow

Genre has been a concept useful to—even identified with—the study of professional communication. Miller's (1984) oft-cited "Genre as Social Action" while synthesising and advancing principles from 15 years of rhetorical reasoning about genre, also illuminated these principles in applying them to technical communication. Miller's work mobilised professional-writing researchers to productive inquiry over the next two decades, improving our understanding of both workplace writing and the phenomenon of genre itself.

Workplace contexts also highlighted aspects of genre which might have been, in other contexts, less provocative to theory. While we might ask of any genre, *how do people learn* to recognise rhetorical situations, and learn to respond to them in writing which others recognise as fitting and functional, the genres of professional writing bring this question to a point, owing to institutional investments in that learning. Generations of post-secondary students in applied and professional programmes have taken courses in technical communication, these courses going ahead on the assumption that people could be taught the *writing* independently of their having experience of the *situation*. Giving situation priority over form, new-rhetorical genre theory questioned this assumption.[1]

This chapter re-visits the question of how people learn a genre by presenting the rhetorical history of one writer: an 18th-century trader for the Hudson's Bay Company (HBC). At the same time, this rhetorical history may also call into question assumptions about the uniqueness of our "information age," for, as we will be reminded by this trace of an era of overseas trade and scientific initiative, the 18th century was also a period of "information explosion" and long-distance transmission of data. Amongst our assumptions about our own "global" and informationally-explosive age, there may be some which both invite and constrain applications of new-rhetorical genre theory. While, compared to the study of professional writing, research in computer-mediated communication (CMC) has seen only a few applications of new-rhetorical genre theory, CMC researchers have nevertheless found in genre some opportunities for understanding the promise and challenge of information technologies. CMC researchers have appreciated the role of communities of language users and local situations in making the efficiencies of genre: its ready recognitions and responses. Toms (2001), for example, warns that Web design can put genre efficiencies at risk by imposing a "cookie-cutter" format.[2] But the CMC research context is such that *form* overtakes *situation* in reckoning the global span of information technologies. In surveying problems of information retrieval, CMC theorists propose sorting information by genres—by means of *formal* markers (Crowston & Williams, 2000; Kwasnik, Crowston, Nilan, & Roussinov, 2001). One theorist (Beghtol, 2000) recognizes the cultural contingency of text types—that is, genres' local motives—but sees the need for, in light of "globalization," a culturally neutral typology: a universal, sociohistorically transcendent one. From the perspective of this discipline, with its interest in managing organisational behaviours, standardised form secures functional communication across global contexts. Also spanning global contexts, 18th-century trade and science may tell a different story, one which privileges local situation as much as a standardising centre.

The brief history presented in this chapter will suggest that rhetorical motive—the experience of *exigence* (Bitzer, 1968), the feeling that a certain sort of writing *should* be done, *now*—derives not so much from perception of single, narrowly contained "purpose," as from the articulation of multiple scenes of activity, these articulations themselves capable of linking across great distances, social and spatial. Further, the rhetorical history of this trader-writer is, inescapably, the history of his colleagues and acquaintances, too, for his ways of writing can be shown to be the outcome of social interaction, rather than schooling, or compliance with convention. As products of and contributions to social interaction, these ways of writing are not approaches to an ideal type but contingent replications, resilient but unenforceable opportunities, and incentives to other, unforeseen speech. Although attended to by headquarters, writings from the trade outposts were only sporadically or indirectly or incidentally standardised by the centre, and, being thus unmanageable, were responsive to local contexts, and versatile rather than regular in being so.

OBSERVATIONS ON HUDSON'S BAY

Here are some passages from *Observations on Hudson's Bay*, composed in the winter of 1742-1743 by James Isham (1949/1743), trader, Factor and Chief Factor for the Hudson's Bay Company at York Fort and Prince of Wales Fort.

This is how the local people look

> The men are for the most part tall and thin streight & clean Lim'd Large bon'd and full breast'ed, their is Very few crooked or Deform'd persons amongst them but well shap'd.... both men & women are for the most part round Visag'd with their nose flatt between the Eyes not unlike a negro ... their Eyes Large and Grey yet Lively and Sparkling. (p. 79)

These are their mortuary practices

> If one of a family Dies their nearest friend or Ralations Burries them Very oft'n with most of their Effects when Done is;—They put a pile of wood Like unto a faggott, round the graves, then they make an offering, putting a painted Stick up, some with a cross hanging a hatchet, Bayonett, or Ice Chissel. (p. 93)

Here are some of the berries found around the Fort—gooseberries, currants, and a sort of raspberry

> Goose Berries Very plenty but never see any but the black when ripe, some Grow's as high as in England, other's which grow's at this Barren and Rocky place are not above 6 inches high spreading along the Ground.

> Currans both Red and black the same in other parts,—Cranberries Very plenty, as also Huckle berries, or Dew berries.

> A Yellow Berrie Grow's here (alias) Borocatomenuck whici is Like unto a Rasberrie for bigness, and tast, but grows on a plant not above 5 inches from the ground, also a Red berrie which in taste Like a Rasberry and also Grows Low. (p. 133)

Here are the birds to be seen, and their feathers

> Grey Geese there is a pretty many in the marsh's and fen's in England the same sort as these to the best of my Rememberance, the Natives style's these (Neishcoock) they are grey featherd, black feathers in their wings, some few white feathers in their tail, a white Circle round their Neck, white breast and Belly, with brown Les and feet, and of a Different Call from the weyweys, and much Larger being the Size of an English goose. (p. 121)

There are fish to be found, salmon and others, in their season

> Tickomegg which is Like a herring is also Very Numerious, Catching with a Setting net, in the Summer season, when they come from the sea into the Rivers to spawn, some hundreds, and with a sean some thousands at one haw'l, they are a Very soft fish but god Eating, we preserve them with salting as also jack pike trout & perch for the winter time,—perch here is the same as in England, Carp and tench very plenty, silver trout and Sammon trout Very Numerious, and Large, Sammon here is at this river and long the North Coast some Year's Very plenty for ab't 3 months (vizt. From the 1 June to the Last of augt.). (p. 169)

Isham sent his manuscript to London in 1744, addressing it to his employers, "The Honourable the Governour Deputy Governour and Committee of the Hudsons Bay Company London." Presenting images of distant places to a European audience, Isham's *Observations* is an instance of a genre well known at the time, and also documented in today's scholarship. Much of this scholarship is conducted by post-colonial literary study. While not the most recent example of such scholarship, Pratt's (1992) *Imperial Eyes* is one of the most influential. Neither Isham particularly nor the "Northwest" generally are considered in Pratt's survey, but her study would locate Isham at the mid-18th-century "Linnaean watershed" (Pratt, 1992, p. 39)—the pitch of taxonomic enthusiasm, which, colourfully described by Pratt, inspired "botanizing" or "herborizing gangs" to go to the ends of the earth in their searches and researches, involved in the "obsessive need" of the metropolis "to present and re-present its peripheries and its others continually to itself" (p. 6). From the summit of peak texts—the perspective, that is, of literary study—we get a view of "herborizing" expeditions traipsing through alien lands past surprised locals, and such endeavour could indeed seem obsessive. But a rhetorical perspective offers different views, and the endeavour appears not so much a pathology—or even an automated convention: less an obsession or a convention even at this moment of standardising taxonomy, than a continuum of everyday experience and multiple motivations. For a rhetorical approach to genre also finds that the epoch-making shift to scientific observation is not a lurch forward or an interruption, but a merger of life-times, career-paths, and institutional collegiality.

TRADE TALKS

Using methods other than literary-critical ones, we find Isham's writings not obsessive but practical: that is, sensible business writing. Isham is talking business when, for example, he tells how the Cree typically arrive at the Fort, in organisational formation—"A Captn. or chief comes with a gang of Indians, in this gang they Divide themselves into severall tents or hutts, where their is an ancient man, belonging to Each family, who is officers under the Chief (alias) Uka maw" (p. 82)—and with organisational information—the chief getting an invitation to a preliminary meeting in the Fort to give "Information, of the Strength of his Little army, or Gang of Indians" (p. 84). On the day following the arrival, a round of trade talks begins, for which "they give notice they want to come into the fort to Smoak, in the Callimutt &c." (p. 84), going in and settling according to a protocol in which the Company rep has a recognised role:

> [T]he chief is complimented with a chair, where he plasses himself *by the factor*, the rest sitting upon their Brich round the table [...]- in this manner they sitt Very Demur'r, for some time, not speak a word, tell the Ukemau, Break's Silence, - he then takes one pipe or Callimutt and *presents itt to the factor*, who Lights itt, having a Young man to hold itt as before mention'd, - when Light *the factor takes the Callimutt* by the midle, and points the small End first to the sun's Rising, then to the highth or midle of the Day, then at the suns setting, then to the Ground, and with a round turn presents itt again to the Leader, when they all and Everyone cry ho! (which signifies thanks) [...] tell the pipe is Exhausted, they then *Deliver itt again to the factor*, who is to turn it as before observ'd according to their country three or four times round his head, by the midle of the callimutt, then Lay itt Downe upon the skin, when the whole Assembly makes the Room Ring with an Ecco of thanks. (pp. 84-85, emphasis added)

Setting out trade demands, the chief reminds the factor of previous agreements—"'You told me Last year to bring many Indians, you See I have not Lyd. Here is a great many young come with me, use them Kindly!'" (p. 85)—and of competing trade opportunities – "'we come a Long way to See you, the French sends for us but we will not here, we Love the English'" (pp. 85-86). The chief also complains about the previous year's trade goods: the powder was in "short measure and bad, I say!" (p. 85), leading to great want in the winter. The chief specifies the quality of guns to be received in trade ("'Light guns small in hand, and well shap'd, with Locks that will not freeze in the winter'"), the design of kettles to be traded, and he complains of short measure of the cloth received previously (p. 86). The chief recommends his people for fair and generous dealing: "The young men Loves you by coming to see you, take pity, take pity I say! – and give them good, they Love to Dress and be find, do you understand me!" (p. 86).

As well as being a job description for factors, the account answers business interest at every point. Although the Company enjoyed exclusive trade rights across wide territories, this was a domain in principle only without its substantiation in commercial activity, a flow of goods from London to the "Northwest" and back again. The exchange of valuable furs for nearly worthless trinkets—beads or other frippery—is legend, but the actual terms of trade were more onerous. Many scholars emphasise how quickly aboriginal people became economically and culturally dependent on European goods, and how quickly they became discriminating consumers of firearms, iron utensils, and textiles—as well as decorative or amusing items. Already we see that Isham's descriptions of the trade-meeting genres are, for all their openness today to literary interpretations as "othering," or as steps preliminary to what Pratt calls "planetary consciousness," finely tuned to commercial exigence. How was the market responding to the goods on offer? The Company needed this information to specify manufacture and to calculate optimum cargoes, to maximise investment in the best years, to avoid ruin in the worst. As Innis' (1962/1930) monumental *The Fur Trade in Canada* demonstrates in its exhaustive publication of bills of lading, account books, and financial statements, even commodities relatively cheap near their point of manufacture accrued value in their expensive transport. And even a monopoly could not guarantee a profit: the wrong trade goods, or defective ones, shipped at great cost to an indifferent market or to a market disappointed in previous purchases, could cancel the advantages of monopoly, and rack up losses rather than profits.

Besides, the Hudson's Bay Company's monopoly was only national. The French enjoyed trade relations with many aboriginal groups and were often able to offer more appealing goods and terms—opportunities for comparison shopping—and also diplomatic assurances in the politics of aboriginal nations' interrelations. So Isham's description of trade talks including mention of "the french" answers immediate policy concerns and also political ones, for the Company's monopoly was under attack in this period, as London financial interests hostile to the Company stoked controversy over the seriousness of the Company's territorial efforts.

The Company's agents were under instructions to treat their indigenous trading partners with leniency and mildness, to benefit the Company's investment by encouraging trust. Isham's long report of trade talks demonstrates the trader's address—ease, attentiveness, rhetorical command of a complex situation—and also his alertness to his employers' interest. Even the reports of the leave-taking disseminate information useful to the Head Office. When the actual trading has been done, the Chief addresses "his gang of Indians," giving instructions and urging unity and accord—"'Do not Quarrell or Leave one another'"—stipulating a rendezvous location, and engaging the hunters to meet him again at the fort in the spring, to trade once more, in light of the fair treatment they have enjoyed so far. This report of speech offers a glimpse of the indigenous system of distribution and wholesaling of goods, an economic geography beyond the company's trade offices. With trade-driven increases in hunting activity, beaver populations declined: chasing these dwindling numbers, European traders needed to know about aboriginal groups ever more remote from the first installations. The established forts were a world away from the London investment milieu, but locations of hunters with access to the receding beaver populations were even further away. Information about these locations could be extrapolated from published "voyages" or "travels," but more reliably it came from indigenous people: what they had seen, or heard of—spaces beyond the narrow scope of tenuously provisioned forts in a country far from the familiar scene of metropolitan investment and shareholding. Report of the Cree traders' speech may send the metropolis a sense of its Other, but it also offers intelligence of an unknown hinterland, informing both geographical and capital speculation.

Calculating risk and opportunity, the Company's London committee required extensive reporting from their factors, to correct the Committee members in their assumptions, and to inform their decisions (Rich, 1949). In the field, the traders wanted to write, and they wanted the Committee to read—to span the distance from field to Head Office. Without the organisational genres which queried and instructed, and those which answered, the trade was impossible. Neither could go on without the other.

So other sections of the *Observations* describe snares for deer, traps, snowshoes, canoes . All these are links in the contact between Europeans and North Americans: aboriginal people hunted and harvested for the traders, provisioning them locally; they manufactured snowshoes and canoes for them. We have seen Isham's catalogues of berries and fishes: these also answered questions about reducing cost by local provisioning. But the contact zone is not restricted to only immediate commercial concerns. Descriptions of indigenous games and adornments, matrimonial customs and fertility, the sweat lodge, the construction of a cradle board ("They have no Notion of cradles for children as the English has, but use other methods, which seem's much better ... " [p. 105])—all these can be read as answers to the Committee's standing question: who are our trade partners?

Still, though, the cradle-boards might begin to seem a bit surplus to business concerns—as does some other information. It is good to know, for example, about geese when local provisioning is an issue, but does the Committee need to know that the birds are "grey featherd, black feathers in their wings, some few white feathers in their tail, a white Circle round their Neck, white breast and Belly, with brown Legs and feet" (p. 121)? The surplus is perhaps most evident in Isham's description of the beaver—the main article of trade. In the published version of the *Observations,* the beaver gets more than seven pages of scrutiny of its size ("they are Very Large with the wester'n Indian's, having seen some of Large as an ordinary Calves skin, and to the Northwd. they are very small ... " [p. 143-144]); colour ("for the most part brown, some black, and some few white" [p. 144]), glands ("the oyly stones or two small bladders ... Contains an oyly Substance, which they style (wetuappaca) these Lyes next the Gendering stones the oyly Substance the Natives uses in trapping Rubbing the baits with itt, ... itt having a Very strong cent" [p. 144]); the construction of the lodges—including their fabulous architecture ("the inside is Spatious and Divided into 3 parts, one for their food, another for their Extrements, and the third where they Lye, having water under and Kep't as clean as any human person cou'd do" [p. 146]); and the techniques and economy of the beaver's capture: nets or traps; the rating of pelts by size ("Whole, ¾, ½, and ¼ beaver" [p. 147]); the distribution of the value of the hunt ("When Severall Indians is together, they have sett Rules to the right of the Beaver skin, which is;—if one finds a beaver house, all the Rest goes with and assists him to Kill them, he that found the house having all the skins, and the flesh Equaly Divided" [p. 147]) . Isham draws a detailed sketch, with 30 captions, of the beavers and their abode, and the customary activities of their human predators (pp. 148-149). Does central decision-making require all this information?

THE MAKING OF A "CURIOUS GENTLEMAN"

One way of addressing this question is to ask another: how did James Isham come to write this way? He was an "ordinary man" (Rich, 1949, p. lxvii), and "untrained" (Houston, Ball, & Houston, 2003, p. 12). Son of a London family of which there is apparently little record, Isham was apprenticed to the Hudson's Bay Company at 16 – "an obscure lad" (Houston et al., 2003, p. xiii) literate and educated enough to be a good candidate for training in accountancy, but without other "technical training" (p. lxviii), and without the literary experience of men from privileged positions. Typically, the Company recruited its agents from charitable institutions whose clients were the urban working classes—Grey Coat Hospital School, mainly, and Christ's Hospital School (Blue Coat)—and also from the Orkney Islands, from whose harbours the company's annual ships sailed, and whose eligible populations, while reliably educated to an adequate level, had lower wage expectations than the English or Irish (Houston et al., 2003; Houston & Houston, 2003; Innis, 1962/1930; O'Leary, Orlikowski, & Yates, 2002). Business historians have recently analysed the Company's management techniques as particularly effective in inspiring these boys to identify with Company interests and practices—loyalties crucial for the success of long-distance administration (O'Leary et al., 2002). (At the same time, in this period and later, the Company struggled with the problem of "private trading"—officers and employees in collusion with the Company's ship captains in carrying privately acquired trade goods, free-lance, back to European markets.)

In the field, the young recruits' education was up-graded with opportunities to learn accounting, map-making and surveying, and celestial observation (Houston et al., 2003). But these opportunities did not include instruction in ethnography or natural history. How did Isham—a child of the working classes sent to remote parts to live amongst small groups of men of similar background—come to know to write ethnographically, or in a naturalist's style—to compose beyond immediate commercial concerns? Or to know his employers' interest in such matters? There are traces of how this "ordinary man" came to the travel genre: how, unschooled, he came not only to know how to compose his *Observations* but also to know to do so—to experience exigence, and rhetorical motive.

Isham absorbed some of the rhetorical attitude of his mentor and predecessor, James Knight, who in 1714 took re-possession of York Fort from the French under the terms of the Treaty of Utrecht. Knight was an emphatic correspondent of the London Committee—demanding that his metropolitan employers take the trouble to read his dispatches if they wanted to overcome their ignorance: Isham's 20th-century editor says Isham's supervisor "set the tone" (Rich, 1949, p. xxxiii). As well as absorbing "the tone" from his co-workers, Isham was sometimes explicitly directed in his writing by the London Committee: "'your Several letter is not wrote in Paragraphs which you must not fail to observe for the future answering distinctly each Paragraph of our Letter'" (as cited in Rich, 1949, p. xxxvi). Factors were also directed by the Committee to "send home the roots of herbs, plants and shrubs, with seeds, berries and kernels, whilst the surgeons should identify them by their Indian names and list their qualities" (Rich, 1949, p. xxxvi). Isham sent four boxes of plants from York Factory in 1737, and again in 1738 (Houston et al., 2003). While the Committee did not tell their factor *how* to write his *Observations* in the winter of 1743, or *to* write them, and neither did his education school him to these efforts, Isham's Company journals, his Inward Letters, his accounting, his annotations on boxes of specimens, his correspondence with these worldly men at headquarters familiarised him with a quality of interest in the world.

In addition, Isham had at least two periods of friendly personal contact with Captain Christopher Middleton[3]—"a ship's captain who worked for the Company and who showed a genuinely scientific interest in Polar navigation and geography" (Rich, 1949, p. xlviii), a Fellow of the Royal Society who had read not only all the Company's reports on the topic but everything else he could find (p. lv). And, besides his collegial friendship with the scientifically-minded Middleton, there is Isham's ornithology. "I have made itt my Buisness" he writes, "to gaine the Names of all the different sorts and Kinds of fowl's in these parts" (p. 119). His ornithology was in part a collaboration with indigenous people. Describing, for example, what he says is called a "water crow" (p. 125), his information goes beyond his firsthand examination of the specimen to places and times he has not witnessed: "Long hairy feather's on the crown of the Head, I Never see but two of these crow's which was Brought me by upland Indian's, who gott itt at the back of this Island (York fort) wer'e they are but scarce" (p. 126). But Isham's notice of this bird was not simply a result of discussions with Cree traders or his own spontaneous interest in birds. It was a manifestation of the network which led to his contact with natural-history interests in London, especially with George Edwards, "Father of British ornithology" (Houston et al., 2003, p. 16), and "a friend of Linnaeus." Isham "probably first met George Edwards on [his 1745-1746] furlough" (Houston et al., 2003, p. 42), presenting Edwards with boxes of well preserved "'Furs of Beasts, and ... skins of ... Birds,'" earning the recipient's gratitude and recognition of him as a "'curious Gentleman'" (Edwards qtd. in Houston et al., 2003, p. 45). Isham was also "in touch" with Edwards in London again two years later. Edwards published seven volumes of natural history, including four volumes of *A Natural History of Birds*, the third volume including illustrations of thirty species, the specimens of which were provided by James Isham. Twelve specimens provided by Isham and painted by Edwards became the "official type specimens" for species then named by Linnaeus (Houston et al., 2003, p. 45).

This connection with the scientific élite, earning Isham personal credit for his astute observation and careful collecting, was not an eccentric hobbyism on his part. The Hudson's Bay Company was itself involved in the science of the times: founding members and several shareholders were fellows of the Royal Society (Houston et al., 2003). Exemplary of these dual memberships in the 18th century is Samuel Wegg—inheriting and purchasing Company shares; becoming a fellow of the Royal Society in 1753 and a member of the Hudson's Bay Company Committee in 1760, and deputy governor in 1774. While he served as Governor in 1782-1799, Wegg encouraged both the general reception of Company records by Royal Society members and, as well, individual correspondence by Hudson's Bay Company employees (Houston et al., 2003). So we find, for just one example, in the Royal Society's *Philosophical Transactions* of 1772, "An Account of the Birds sent from *Hudson's Bay;* with Observations relative to their Natural History; and *Latin* Descriptions of some of the most uncommon," by Johan Reinhold Forster, an eminent figure in scientific circles and official naturalist aboard Cook's second voyage. For all his travels, Forster never did visit the Bay himself, but derived his science from information making its way across great distances, dispatched by observers and collectors only indirectly instructed by the Linnaean standard. As Forster writes in a sequel, "An Account of some curious Fishes sent from *Hudson's Bay* ... in a letter to *Thomas Pennant,*" published in 1773, "The Governor and Committee of the Hudson's Bay Company presented The Royal Society with a choice collection of skins of quadrupeds, many fine birds, and some fish, collected by their servants at the several ports in Hudson's Bay; the Committee of the Royal Society, for examining and describing these curiosities, did me the honour to refer them to me for examination." Only indirectly informed of the standard of description and examination, the Company's employees were more directly schooled by their immediate social connections and proximities to institutional practice.

And what about Isham's reading—usually our first resort when we are tracing a writer's inspiration? What access did Isham, in his remote post, have to models of ethnographic or natural-history writing? While some other writer-traders are likely to mention their readings in natural history and travels, and Isham is less likely to do so, he was not unread. We know that he read Capt. Middleton's travel book (*Vindication of the Conduct of Captain Christopher Middleton* 1743), possibly in manuscript, for he quotes from it in his *Observations* (p. 72). And not only is Isham's *Notes and Observations on a Book Entitled A VOYAGE TO HUDSON'S BAY IN THE DOBBS GALLERY &C 1746 & 1747 Wrote by Henry Ellis* (1748)—composed as contribution to the Company's defense of its monopoly—the clearest possible evidence that he read Ellis' travels, he also criticises the book in terms which show that he is familiar with more than this one instance of the genre. "I observe its a common Rule," he begins, "with some persons that writes a history of Voyages &c. for want of a proper and just Subject to make a complete Book; they Enlarge upon things which is neither consistent with truth, justice, nor honour ... " (Isham, 1949/1743, n. p.), and proceeds, in the way of travel writers then and now, to correct the reports of others.[4]

Isham got to know a version of the travel genre presentable to his employers as it was instantiated in the intersections of metropolitan holdings, transit, and administration, directing his attention to the world in certain ways: singling out animals for comparison with known species, collecting seeds and cuttings in small boxes for transport, interrogating local people on territories and routes. This attention translated to the *Observations*. He sent specimens to natural historians in London, and had their reply, and was received by them in person. Like other traders, he kept accounts, wrote up his experiences for the Committee, and knew or corrected the assumptions which prompted their questions. There is no evidence that he was widely read, and its absence suggests that he was not as well read as some of his predecessors or successors. But the annual ships brought books, magazines, and newspapers. And Isham did know some instances of the travel genre, and was friendly with people who, like Captain Middleton, were well-versed.

Tracing the career of an "ordinary man" this way, we get a picture of genre knowledge as acquired through social interaction: through being involved with others in various ways in various activities. If we see genre emerging from such collegial but also fortuitous, intermittent, and interrupted social interaction, then genre must be a precarious phenomenon—and also robust, to survive such interruptions. A series of entries in Isham's *Observations* on effects of the cold climate can help us understand robustness in precariousness.

In his workplace on the shores of Hudson Bay, Isham was impressed by the cold: "Beer, wine, brandy spirits &c. sett out in the ope'n air for three or four hour's, will freeze to Solid Ice, not only so, but have known by the Extreamity of the cold, a two gallon Botle of water to freeze solid by the stove side, in the housses we Dwell in" (Isham, 1743/1949, pp. 69-70). He describes the permafrost ("in Dig'ing three or four foot downe in the ground in the midst of the summr. you shall find hard froze'n Ice" [p. 71]), and the effects of ice ("It's a most Surprizing thing and past belief to I'magine the force and Effects the Ice has in these parts" [p. 75]). Provoking surprise and disbelief, these reports could be attributed to general exigence which "marvels" answer: the rhetorical imperative in something so wonderfully out of the ordinary that it secures by contrast what is normal, or regular at home. Isham's recount of the effects of the cold on the living conditions of Company men could be read as a thrill for the sedentary: "Notwithstanding [the two-foot stone walls of the fort, the shuttered windows, and large, well fuelled stoves] in 4 or 5 hour's after the fire is out and the chimnly still close stop't, the inside wall of our housses are 6 to 8 inches thick of Ice, which is Every Day cutt away with Hatchetts" (p. 173). Marvellous as they are, however, these reports also contribute to practical debates about the architecture of the forts, and the cost of maintaining a commercial office in this distant place. And the measure of interest extends still further. Writing during the Little Ice Age, Isham and traders like him were not alone in their attention to the cold. Records of the Royal Society preserve many observations on the effects of cold, including experiments on freezing points, some of these experiments conducted by a later factor at York Fort. Isham's friend Captain Middleton reported on the arctic cold in the Society's *Transactions* ("The Effect of *Cold;* together with Observations on the *Longitude, Latitude,* and *Declination of the Magnetic Needle, at Prince of Wales's For,* upon *Churchill-River* in Hudson's Bay, North America," 1742). Climate was a topic of wide intellectual interest, reaching the bone-chilled personnel at the Bay. The Company's meteorological records, including Captain Middleton's own records for 1730, were submitted to and published by the Royal Society. Andrew Graham, Isham's friend and immediate successor, and author of his own *Observations,* was amongst those who reported their research into cold conditions, from both technical measures—"it appears by observations made at York Fort and Severn River the mercury on Farenheit's standard thermometer was oftentimes at 63° standard thermometer below the cipher" (Graham, 1969, p. 3)—material attempts: "I have ordered a hogshead full of water to be put out into the open air and in forty-eight hours it became solid ice and burst the cask" (Graham, 1969, p. 4). And here again, even as we can trace a scientific attitude in rhetorical response to the cold, a commercial practice shows up: by checking the freezing point of barrels of spirits, Company employees could report by how much the contents had been watered.

Equally, Isham's descriptions and inventory of creatures in the Company domain answer commercial questions about possible opportunities for trade in other furs and about local food sources which could alleviate the expense of provisioning the forts from London. Rabbits (Isham, 1949/1743), partridge, deer, eel and herring, salmon and shellfish, for example, are all accounted for in their abundance or seasonal scarcity, and in their palatability, and often in terms of their parallel to varieties known in England. But again the scope of interest extends beyond the practical questions about provisioning, and collating foreign fish and game with standards of an English diet. These animal species and their fluctuating populations also figure in Natural History: reports of them contributed to contemporary debates on bird and animal migrations and seasonal coloration.

Similarly the beaver information, in its science exceeding requirements for central decision-making but also indicating commercial practice, is a response to rhetorical exigence *overdetermined* by social experience: the trade, the science, the exotic encounter with marvels (a creature with a suite of rooms hygienically designed). If we want to know what makes people write—not only know how *to* write as they do, but know to write, feel that a certain sort of thing *should* be written *now,* now being for Isham the remote winter of 1743—then we can think of genre in terms of rhetorical motive springing from social experience overdetermined by multiple, interlacing scenes of activity: here, journey, trade, science. Genres answer not one immediate, contained purpose: this would not be enough to account for motive—the feeling that a certain kind of thing *should* be written, now, that it is proper to do it and the writer wants to do it, and gets credit for it. To be this kind of robust, conscientious action, genres have to be manifestations of consciousness overdetermined by multiple scenes of social interaction.

REPLICATED INFORMATION

Thorough and versatile in its reply to standing questions raised by multiple scenes of activity, the beaver information's surplus to decision-making can be measured not only in its extent but also in its replications. Just as Isham's reports on the cold are replicated elsewhere, his account of the beaver is far from the sole instance of the information. The method of capture is also reported in Ellis (1748) (and corrected by Isham, 1748). Like Isham, Andrew Graham reports size and colour; glands; the construction of the lodge—materials, fabulous architecture ("They have three apartments; one may be called the dining-room, another the bed-chamber, and the third is converted in to a necessary apartment which they frequently clean out, carrying the soil and filth to a considerable distance from the house"), and engineering of water level; and the techniques of capture (Graham, 1969, pp. 8-9), including the rating of the trapped animals by size and the means of distributing the value of the hunt . Other details, such as the beavers' diet and their felling of trees for construction, are also parallel. As Isham's successor and protégé, Graham probably had access to Isham's journals and possibly to drafts of his *Observations*, which, although submitted to the London Committee in 1744 was unpublished till 1949. Ellis, as agent for a faction hostile to HBC interests, could not so easily have known these documents—although the Company's practice of circulating and copying documents from the Northwest made a kind of quasi-publication which reached a larger audience than our idea of manuscripts suggests to us today. In any case,

Isham's interest in writing about the beaver in this way was not his alone: many others wrote about the beaver.[5] Digesting available information on the beaver and publishing in the Royal Society's *Transactions* in 1733, C. Mortimer in "The Anatomy of a *Female Beaver,* and an Account of the *Castor* Found in her" cites sources as early as 1684.

Although substantively similar, sometimes evidently derived or even copied from Isham's *Observations* or documents contributing to it, and certainly inspired by it, Graham's *Observations* presents information under more visibly orderly categories. His entries for birds, fishes, mammals, and plants are longer and more comparative than Isham's, and often refer to published research. For example, the sculpin ("Cowachemaycushshish, the Capelin") is examined for scales; the local whitefish ("Tickomeg, the Guiniad") is examined for "the lateral line," said in *British Zoology* to "consist of distinct dusky spots," and found to be lacking in the specimen examined (Graham, 1969, p. 122). Although we might take these differences as evidence of a genre perfecting itself or as instances approaching an ideal type, we might also take them as evidence of Graham's experience of social interaction being slightly different from Isham's. Whereas Isham enjoyed the company of Captain Middleton over at least two periods of contact—one when Middleton was master of the Company's annual supply ship to York Fort, one when he wintered at 1741 as master of the Dobbs expedition—Graham worked for years closely with Thomas Hutchins, surgeon at York Fort and Chief Factor at Albany. Graham's contacts with natural historians at home also seem to have been more regular or sustained: for example, he reports sending home salt for assay; presenting a beaver pelt to the Edinburgh Royal Society; having his identification of a fish ratified by the Royal Society. Wegg is said to have encouraged Andrew Graham to submit specimens directly to the Royal Society, and probably introduced him to Thomas Pennant, correspondent of Linnaeus and author of, among other volumes, *British Zoology* (1761-1766), *Arctic Zoology* (1784-1785), *The Genera of Birds* (1773) (Houston et al., 2003). Like Isham, Graham was "scantily educated" (Glover, 1969, p. xxvi), but ready for continuing education, learning names from *British Zoology* and other publications, and making his own *Observations* a nearly life-long project, continuing its preparation after his retirement to Scotland. Isham's career as both writer and company man was briefer: he died in 1761, at York Fort.

Graham's *Observations* in ten volumes, were deposited with the Company, the final volume, for which he received an honorarium of 10 guineas, arriving in 1793. We know these volumes today thanks to a 20th-century publishing event: in 1969, the Hudson's Bay Record Society selected one volume of Graham's *Observations* for editing and publication. Graham's editors, Glover and Williams, mention Isham as Graham's mentor and model. But Glover (1969) and Williams (1978) find the real story in their discovery that Thomas Hutchins got credit for natural-history observations which were actually, in their view, Graham's. Williams (1978) traces entries in manuscripts in Hutchins' own hand back to Graham, and also finds Pennant in his publication at first crediting Graham but then giving Hutchins full credit, and finds no attempt by Hutchins to correct the mis-attribution. By the time Hutchins had returned from the Bay to become Corresponding Secretary of the London Committee, his experiments with the freezing point of mercury had been published and praised by the Royal Society, and his status may have eclipsed Graham's simpler rank on his retirement from the Bay, as paymaster and purchasing agent for the Company in Scotland. Although Graham, long out-living the younger man, was evidently content with the published attributions, Glover and Williams are unforgiving in their exposé of Hutchins' plagiarism: his apparent representation of the Graham information to Pennant and others as his own, his circulation of the manuscripts in forms which did not identify Graham's authorship. The latest instalment in the controversy (Houston & Houston, 2003), however, interprets the evidence as collaboration rather than plagiarism: a blend of authorship, trader's experience and surgeon's technicality, a friendly cooperation. While these accounts take small notice of the substantive copying from Isham, they all show the role of social interaction, contacts in person and in print—institutional proximity—in shaping rhetorical motive. The Graham/Hutchins collaboration could be seen as an embodiment of articulated scenes—science and trade—each scene impinging on the other, for Graham the trader was coached in science and Hutchins the scientist was mentored in business, becoming a highly regarded trade manager. We have seen how the beaver information proliferated and replicated itself over this period, as each author conscientiously set out what could be known about this creature, rhetorically motivated by connected scenes of activity and interaction. Similarly, the information springing from the working relationship and companionable collegiality of Graham and Hutchins was taken up for circulation in the contiguous scenes of metropolitan science. In this interpretation—different from the plagiarism charge—scenes and situations motivate each writer to conscientious action. What looks nowadays like redundancy, if not plagiarism, was response to shared (but not identical) experience of exigence. These episodes of replicas may tell us that information is not simply the sending of knowledge from source to recipient but the expression of writers' quality of interest in the world, the terms on which they engage it, and the sociality of this engagement.

CURIOUS GENTLEMEN AT HOME AND AWAY

Tracing the writing life of one ordinary man, James Isham, through articulated and contiguous scenes, a little farther, following these transfers and recursive influences—from Isham to Graham to Hutchins to Pennant—we are drawn into the orbit of another circle of sociality, for Pennant is the addressee of 44 of the 100 letters of White's (1977/1788) famous *The Natural History of Selborne,* four of the total letters having been published in the Royal Society's *Transactions,* and the composition of Selborne deriving from decades of note-taking. Like Isham, White sent specimens to London, although the distance was abbreviated:

> This morning, in a basket, I packed a little earthen pot of wet moss, and in it some sticklebacks, male and female; some bull's heads; but I could produce no minnows. This basket will be in Fleet-street by eight this evening; so I hope Mazel will have them fresh and fair tomorrow morning. I gave some directions, in a letter, to what particulars the engraver should be attentive. (White, 1977/1788, p. 52)

Just as Isham received specimens from Cree traders, White was also a recipient, getting "many boxes and packages of plants and birds" sent to him by his brother from Gibraltar (p. 236). As Isham was directed in his paragraphing by the London Committee, White makes entries in a purpose-published "Naturalist's Journal." White has a livelier preference than Isham for the standard, encouraging others to record their observations according to the template in the "Naturalist's Journal", and imagining others prompted to proper observation of insects if provided with "some neat plates that should well express the generic distinctions of insects according to Linnæus" (p. 85). But the standard is perhaps only one expression of acertain subjectivity, that of the "'curious Gentleman,'" who is in *Selborne* a frequent presence. Sometimes he is hypothetical, "If some curious gentleman would procure the head of a fallow-deer, and have it dissected, he would find ... " (p. 42). Sometimes he is actual, "A gentleman curious in birds, wrote me word that his servant had shot one last January, in that severe weather, which he believed would puzzle me" (p. 37). The *curious* are distinguished from the *incurious,* who fail to appreciate, for example, the wonder of worms, and their part in the natural economy . In the scene of White's writing, the curious gentleman is an attitude, a capacity to take an interest, and to communicate the product of that interest to a circle of like-minded men. Even at a glance, *The Natural History of Selborne*, being letters, demonstrates the sociability of science, its substantiation in the personal exchange of information—recognition, "approbation" (p. 151), mutual regard, fraternity. While White recommends natural history for its contribution to the observer's "health," "cheerfulness," and "happiness," his ultimate recommendation of these practices is, in his own case, their leading him to "knowledge of a circle of gentlemen" and their "intelligent communication," "a matter of singular satisfaction and improvement" (p. 4). From the circle of interaction—not only models of address, but response and reply—springs the rhetorical motive for lifelong observation. Far away, Isham had also "made itt [his] Buisness to gaine the Names of all the different sorts and Kinds" (Isham, 1949/1743, p. 119) and was also a "curious Gentleman," a virtuous subject, identified by his writings and their address, his experience of exigence.

While the link from Isham on the shores of Hudson Bay to White in his Hampshire parish shows a subjectivity—a disciplined, sociable masculinity—frequenting scenes (home parish, foreign coasts) that become rhetorical situations, it also shows genre's overdetermination, its articulation in multiple scenes of activity. In contrast to the charitably educated Isham, White was a fellow of Oriel College, Oxford. *Selborne* offers not only some of its author's own verse, celebrating for example "THE GOD OF SEASONS" (White, 1977/1788, p. 213), but, much more prominently, his readings of Milton and the Bible, and of classical texts, especially Virgil and his mention of, for example, doves, frozen rivers, and the damaging effects of echoes on bees . Articulating with literary situations, White's natural history circles away from the scenes and situations experienced by Isham. Equally, while Isham's accounts of birds, berries, fishes, and temperatures answer commercial as well as scientific interest, White's observations project the position of the curious gentleman and also the practical one in a rural parish, with recommendations, for example, for appropriate cultivation around ponds, using gunpowder to reduce the abundance of crickets, planting to protect bushes from the effects of cold or heat, using a thermometer to know when to protect stored fruits and vegetables from freeze, or, most quaintly, building an obelisk so one will not only ornament one's grounds but also instruct oneself on the precise nature of the solstice . Articulating with rural husbandry, *The Natural History of Selborne* rotates, in its circle of interest, away from the horizon of interest of sub-arctic trade, even as it shares other scope with the trader-writers (like Graham and Hutchins, White watches thermometers [pp. 258, 261]; like Graham putting the cask of water out for testing, White uses an ear trumpet to test Virgil's opinion on bees [p. 205]). The connection between Isham and White is not a mis-match, or a crude approximation on the one side, and an ideal prototype on the other, but a demonstration of the multiple motivations of genre, genre's participation in multiple scenes of activity (Isham: travel, trade, science; White: sedentariness, literary practice, parochial husbandry, science) and the writer's motive springing from histories of interaction and career-path.[6]

GENRE AS CONSCIENTIOUS ACTION

For Isham to take up his pen unbidden in the forlorn winter of 1742-1743 and to write as he did (or for Graham to labour over ten volumes), he was moved by a condition more impressive than "convention," or even schooling. Rather, he was motivated by his experience of his position, his conscientious orientation to circumstances (the distance, the cold, the people approaching the fort, the beavers, the birds), roles in activities undertaken in the company of others. In turn, the position he takes is possible only by its rendering in language—wordings embedded in circumstance rather than free-standing convention or extant form, wordings infused with motive because they are attached to situation, social interaction being the way we learn language itself. When the situation expires—as Isham's long ago has done, or Graham's or Hutchins'—and the wordings survive, their motive drains away, and they may look "conventional"—apparently automatic form—and their replication can look like copying. Or their recurrence can look "obsessive," or scheduled by empire.

Or enforced by authority—but even if there were an official dictate to compliance, a centralising edict, there is little evidence of it in any success, for only a few traders did the kind of writing we see in Isham's *Observations,* or Graham's: only a few felt themselves thus called upon. Yet in this scarcity or scattering of response—the precariousness of genre's recurrence—is also genre's robustness. An obscure lad, charitably educated and indentured to an outpost, estranged from the centre by class and distance, and then re-connected by the contact zone and the Northwest trade, Isham is nevertheless occupied by their themes—both invested by them and interested in them. This occupation is his rhetorical motive, his identity and identification as a "curious Gentleman." In the career of James Isham, we do not see forces radiating from the centre to standardise expression, but a man at a distance, picking up intermittent signals locally and collegially, his translations of them (wordings, notes, specimens) then inserting themselves into the productions of the city. Isham's descriptions are no match for Pennant's or White's, or even for Graham's, which shows us not a failure of form but genre's versatility, its sensitivity to situations in their multiple articulations. Genre is robust *because* it is versatile and versatile *because* it is local, and *not* central and conventional—and also precarious because it is local: an opportunistic epidemiology rather than a standardisation, for who could have said who out there would become a "curious Gentleman"?

This brief rhetorical history suggests that what we today call professional—or technical or business—communication may not be so insular or chastely purposed as we sometimes think. Like documents from "the Bay," it may articulate with other scenes, may have other, multiple involvements. It would be interesting to know these. And, while we may be tempted by images of global transfers of information to design formal regularities—as some CMC researchers are tempted—to focus on standardisation or "conventional" aspects of communication may be to neglect the overdetermination of rhetorical motive, and its sources in social interaction. Even the Linnaean standard was a matter of conscientious motive, or an intimation relayed over many points of local contact.

NOTES

1. Some of the most impressive expressions of the question arise from the consortium of McGill/Carleton research in the 1990s, published as Dias, Freedman, Medway, and Paré, (1999), *Worlds Apart: Acting and Writing in Academic and Workplace Contexts,* and Dias and Paré, eds., (2000), *Transitions: Writing in Academic and Workplace Settings,* but also presaged by Freedman's (1994) bold statement of the issue.

2. A long article on Web design (Agre, 1998), with a serious account of genre theory, and the capacity of communities of language users to develop genres indigenously, at the same time implies that genres can be invented strategically and centrally—a possibility about which rhetorical theorists of genre might be sceptical.

3. Capt. Middleton made four voyages to Hudson's Bay Company posts in the decade preceding Isham's arrival at the Bay (1725, 1726, 1727, 1729) and made his last voyage to Hudson Bay for the HBC in 1737, five years into Isham's employment by the Company (*Eighteenth-Century Naturalists of Hudson Bay,* Appendix A "Sailing Ships to York Factory, 1716-1827). As master of the first Dobbs expedition—representing HBC rivals—he wintered at Churchill in 1741, during Isham's first year as Factor there.

4. Some topics on which Isham corrected Ellis: local medicinal practice; abundance of copper (vouched for by Ellis, doubted by Isham); gender roles; cannibalism; complaints of aboriginal trade partners (which Isham doubts Ellis was in a position to hear, and if he did hear such, would not understand).

5. In the twentieth century, Harold Innis begins *The Fur Trade in Canada* (1962/1930) with a natural history of the beaver surprisingly like Isham's (or Graham's). In his deep scholarly engagement in the world of the fur trade, he picks up and replicates the sound of the natural history of the beaver. Innis follows his own description of the beaver by noting how many such descriptions there are in the writings of those involved in the fur trade (p. 3).

6. Literary rather than rhetorical reading of the connection between the-Northwest and Selborne, between imperial expansion and parochial contraction, might pick up White's having heard from a friend about moose in the St. Lawrence ("the male moose, in rutting time, swims from island to island, in the lakes and rivers of North America, in pursuit of females. My friend, the chaplain, saw one killed in the water as it was on that errand in the river St Lawrence: it was a monstrous beast, he told me; but he did not take the dimensions" [p. 8]), or his having a "near neighbour, a young gentleman in the service of the East-India Company" (p. 247), or his notice that the eminent naturalist Scopoli is "physician to the wretches that work in the quick-silver mines" of Carniola (p. 123).

ACKNOWLEDGMENTS

This research was supported by the Social Sciences and Humanities Research Council of Canada. I am thankful for the inspired research assistance of Victoria Killington and Elizabeth Maurer, and the learned collegial comment of Alex Dick.

REFERENCES

Agre, P. (1998). Designing genres for new media: Social, economic, and political contexts. In S. Jones (Ed.), *Cybersociety 2.0: Revisiting computer-mediated communication and community* (pp. 79–81). Thousand Oaks, CA: Sage.

Beghtol, C. (2000). The concept of genre and its characteristics. *American Society for Information Science, 27*(2), 17-20.

Bitzer, L. (1968). The rhetorical situation. *Philosophy and Rhetoric, 1*, 1-14.

Crowston, K., & Williams, M. (2000). Reproduced and emergent genres of communication on the World-Wide Web. *The Information Society, 16*(3), 201-216.

Dias, P., Freedman, A., Medway, P., & Paré, A. (1999). *Worlds apart: Acting and writing in academic and workplace contexts.* Mahwah, NJ: Lawrence Erlbaum.

Dias, P., & Paré, A. (Eds.). (2000). *Transitions: Writing in academic and workplace settings.* Cresskill, NJ: Hampton.

Freedman, A. (1994). "Do as I say": The relationship between teaching and learning new genres. In A. Freedman & P. Medway (Eds.), *Genre and the new rhetoric* (pp. 191-210). London: Taylor and Francis.

Glover, R. (1969). Introduction. In *Andrew Graham's Observations on Hudson's Bay, 1767-1791*. London: Hudson's Bay Record Society.

Graham, A. (1969). *Andrew Graham's Observations on Hudson' Bay, 1767-1791*. London: Hudson's Bay Record Society.

Houston, S., Ball, T., & Houston, M. (2003). *Eighteenth-Century Naturalists of Hudson Bay*. Montréal & Kingston: McGill-Queen's University Press.

Houston, S., & Houston, M. (2003). The ten HBC manuscripts of Graham and Hutchins. In S. Houston, T. Ball, & M. Houston (Eds.), *Eighteenth-Century Naturalists of Hudson Bay*. Montréal & Kingston: McGill-Queen's University Press.

Innis, H. A. (1962/1930). *The fur trade in Canada*. Toronto: University of Toronto Press.

Isham, J. (1949/1743). *Observations on Hudsons Bay; Notes and Observations on a book entitled A VOYAGE TO HUDSONS BAY IN THE DOBBS GALLEY, 1749*. E. E. Rich and A. M. Johnson (Eds.). Toronto: The Champlain Society.

Kwasnik, B., Crowston, K., Nilan, M., & Roussinov, D. (2001). Identifying document genre to improve Web search effectiveness. *American Society for Information Science, 27*(2), 23-27.

Miller, C. (1984). Genre as social action. *Quarterly Journal of Speech, 70*, 151-167.

O'Leary, M., Orlikowski, W. J., & Yates, J. (2002). Distributed work over the centuries: Trust and control in the Hudson's Bay Company, 1670-1826. In P. J. Hinds & S. Kiesler (Eds.), *Distributed work* (pp. 27-54). Cambridge, MA: MIT Press.

Pratt, M. L. (1992). *Imperial eyes: Travel writing and transculturation*. London: Routledge.

Rich, E. E. (1949). Introduction. In J. Isham, *Observations on Hudsons Bay: Notes and Observations on a book entitled A VOYAGE TO HUDSONS BAY IN THE DOBBS GALLEY, 1749*. E. E. Rich & A. M. Johnson (Eds.). Toronto: The Champlain Society.

Toms, E. (2001). Recognizing digital genre. *American Society for Information Science, 27*(2), 20-23.

White, G. (1977/1788). *The natural history of Selborne*. Harmondsworth, Middlesex: Penguin.

Williams, G. (1978). Andrew Graham and Thomas Hutchins: Collaboration and plagiarism in 18th-century Natural History. *The Beaver, 308*(4), 4-14.

4 ELECTRONS ARE CHEAP; SOCIETY IS DEAR

Charles Bazerman

The most visible impacts of new communicative technologies are in the attention-grabbing and expressive potential of greater design control at the desktop, hypertext, and multimedia (graphics, animation, video, sound, haptics, and ultimately immersive virtual and augmented reality). Nonetheless, the most significant impacts of new communicative technologies are likely to be in the changing activities and communities facilitated by new potentials of transmission, storage, and accessibility that change time, space, memory, informational resources, and economy of social encounter. Beyond providing students with facility in design tools and multi-media rhetoric, teachers of rhetoric need to provide students with analytic tools to understand the changing locations and informational richness of encounters they will be creating, the larger knowledge, social, and activity environments that surround the particular encounter and activity spaces they are working in, and the ways in which communications will mediate transformed work, citizenship, and personal relations. Increasingly, to lead a full and productive life requires learning to navigate, maintain, and constantly reconstruct the built symbolic environment we share with others and which forms the basis of social cooperation in a knowledge society. And a core part of that learning is to understand how that communication, information, and cooperation can support humanly satisfying modes of social life.

Animals were social before they were communicative. Even coral requires a colony. Animals were social and communicative before they were symbolic; witness ants being led by each other's pheromones. Animals were social and communicative before they had language; bees dance to direct each other to pollen. Each of these developments in sociality extended the possibilities and range of interaction, cooperation, sharing, and intersubjectivity. Consider the complex and affectionate parent-child relations among advanced mammals, such as horses or chimps. Each of these developments also made activities more interesting, more complex, and more difficult to manage.

With language, our social groups extended beyond the family, flock, or pack to complex, differentiated tribes, villages, and cities. Levels of cooperation and task delegation increased for constructing dwellings, determining ownership, hunting, food growing and storage, domestication of plants and animals. Our arrangements for group security and aggression also grew, along with the technologies of metals and weapons.

Language, as well, fostered misunderstandings, disputes, assigning responsibility, blaming, adjudication, rules, and decrees. Force took on new roles in society as it was instigated, reinforced, and extended by threat and directed by language. Lore, tales, songs, and knowledge passed from generation to generation. Ancestry and genealogy became important for identity, status, and authority. Barter, deal making, distribution of property, as well as the need to adjudicate disputes and create collective will through words all increased the value of people who could wield words.

When humans, five thousand years ago, added literacy to our social tools, they further extended the boundaries of sociality across time and space. They also made possible the crafting of complex documents demanding high cognitive attention and contemplation, expanding the semi-private work in our heads we call consciousness. Writing brought accounts, ownership documents, aggregation of more wealth than you could keep an eye on, tax rolls, scribes, scribal schools, written laws, textually bound courts, lawyers, legal schools, religious scriptures, and interpretation, priestly classes, religious schools, apostasy, sectarian conflict, secular knowledge, and secular schools. Again, sociality became more extended, interesting, complex, and hard to manage.

With the increasing need for people of advanced language and literacy, so has the length of schooling increased. High schools were an invention of the nineteenth century, extending schooling in the middle, to prepare students for the new style of research, discipline-based university. Electronic production and distribution of text has opened a new chapter in the story. The first signs are that the plot will be the same—more extended, interesting, complex, and hard to manage—but we will return to that after an excursion inwards.

Though language has helped Humans become the most deeply and complexly social of beings, it has also made us, as best we can tell, the loneliest. Ants lead socially demanding and constraining lives, driven by each other's pheromones, but only an incurable anthropomorphizer would call it a life of quiet desperation, for as far as we know there is little depth of soul and individuality and aspiration in the ant. It appears that ants are perfectly content to be ants. Nor do wolves express a need to unburden the guilty depths of their violence-ravaged consciousnesses for violating the laws of god and tribe.

As language and literacy have expanded the complexity and potential of our lives, allowing us to live in relation to distant and complex bodies of thought, knowledge, and institutions, it has brought us interiority, individuality, and difference. We talk to different people and can read different books. A child not only can speak to strangers, but can abandon the scriptures of the parents for a competing church or a new philosophy learned in schools.

It was, after all, a novelist, a person of letters, a bookish person, who plaintively proclaimed, "Only connect." We have new possibilities of loneliness and difference, driven by our hunger for the stimulation of novelty and the practical possibilities of improving our lives. We are hungry for connection, making new connections, at greater and greater distances from the here and now where ants smell each other and horses nuzzle. Paradoxically, this hunger for connection of consciousness through communication makes us different and more distant from those most immediate to us, even though we have greater weight and complexity of perceptions, thoughts, puzzles, fantasies, and games to share.

The Internet has only exacerbated this paradox. A few centuries ago only a small number of scholars led quietly bookish lives, and even the expansion of publishing created only a limited market of novel readers and intellectuals, whose best friends were in their books. But this is nothing compared to those legions of teenagers with thousands of best friends on Facebook or the twenty-somethings who find fulfillment in their Second Lives. While these connections may seem to be pale shadows of those in embodied lives, seeking the easiest simulacra of gratification—witness the proliferation of porn on the Internet—yet people are drawn to these in a hunger for connection, a connection that will focus and activate our complex neural systems of meanings and emotions. Consider, too, the many academics and professionals who spend half the day on e-mail or preparing documents for electronic transfer, or telecommuting, working in a home office; they too are only connecting. They are all connecting with a pervasive intensity that was not previously available unless you worked in the city room of a busy urban newspaper.

Electrons, on the other hand, are pervasive, but happy to go to lowest state, even more than ants, for ants are still driven to explore for foods and build colonies. Electrons are easily organized, even self-organizing at lower energy levels, not really excited to be "excited." In fact, they need a lot of externally-provided energy to get them "excited." Yet humans have found machines to create energy differentials, organize the electrons, and make them work, despite their entropic natures. We have marshaled their energies to do human work—first mechanical energy for material work, but now we have them carry out communicative, symbolic work—helping us connect with each other through telegraph, radio, television, and now the Internet.

They excite us much more than we excite them. Yet our excitement has been focused largely on what we do to them and not what we do to ourselves, what we are trying to accomplish with each other, what new forms of social organization we are building, and how difficult it is to connect in meaningful activity. Rather, we have at first employed them within already existing social worlds. Some of the earliest activities that have driven the creation and proliferation of the Internet have been within well-developed social systems from the literate world that already have large institutional and economic presence.

The large economic stakes along with the complexity, stability, and power of those social systems mean that the technology gets designed to facilitate the existing work and arrangements, making it cheaper and quicker, but not disrupting it. Markets have intensified and sped up, and even reorganized some of their activities, eliminating some trading floors replaced by electronic queuing systems—even creating a low-cost trading system for day traders who no longer need a seat on the markets. Yet the underlying activity and market relationship is more robust than any technology, which has been bent to the needs of the robust social system and those groups that already hold power in these systems.

Similarly, legal reports were among the first documentary systems widely available electronically. Lexis/Nexis and Westlaw subscriptions eliminated expensive law libraries (though these services were not cheap, drawing profit from the same expensive law firms). Nonetheless, the legal process did not change much nor did the set of relationships among judge, lawyers, and clients. The publishers of information and other communicative resources serving the legal and market sectors carved out lucrative and even monopolistic niches, but they did not call the shots. Design followed the needs of the powerful clients and the social systems within which they maintained and exercised power.

An example of a much weaker system under much strain, more easily reorganized by technology, is personal relationships. While the biological impulses to mating, family, and friendship have remained constant and strong over millennia, urbanization, salary employment among strangers, social and geographic mobility, extended education, individualized economic resources, leisure, social heterogeneity, and other aspects of modernity have made the organization and management of personal relations a complex and fluid matter, very unlike the days when family, village, property, and agricultural ways of life limited one's social circle and reinforced local dependencies and bonds. For the last two centuries we have been caught up in the restless self-remaking and elective affinities of urban life, creating ad hoc systems of meeting, courting, and establishing longer-term arrangements. Forming and managing relationships is one of the great problems facing individuals living modern lives. The Internet with social network sites ranging from Craig's List to Match to MySpace has offered new sets of solutions and arrangements for personal life, extending the range of social contacts and possible mates, while bringing in whole new sets of dangers and contingencies.

It is unclear where this is going. Clever designers are finding ways of drawing people together into social networks that address all aspects of our personal needs, as we can see in the expanding range of activities on Second Life. News, spiritual advice, psychiatric counseling, homemaking tips, medical advice, cooking instruction—all are found on the Internet, sometimes provided by individuals connecting, but often enough by a smiling persona projected by entrepreneurial or large corporate organizations.

In the middle at risk are social systems that have some previously stable organizational presence, but lack the institutional, legal, or financial clout of markets or the legal profession. The introduction of new technology with new communicative designs is threatening existing arrangements in these cases. For example, the music and film entertainment industries have been cast into uncertain futures by the emergence of downloading and sharing technologies.

Even more at risk are newspapers—and current trends in television and internet news threaten even the newsgathering function. The technology has offered many new opportunities for defining, organizing, and commenting on the news. But these arrangements put at play such fundamental issues as who are journalists, who are commentators, who is professional and amateur, what is valid news, and who pays attention and when? At play as well is where we identify our citizenship, community knowledge, and the public sphere. While there are many issues of page design and information structure—how we organize the electrons in data bases and page displays—the deepest issues are what the vehicles for public participation will be and who participates with what knowledge. It is those that need most experimentation as well as careful rhetorical thought by communication designers.

Academic publishing is another domain caught in fluid instabilities of institutions, power, economics, and new potentialities of technology. While the economic stakes seem to be lower than in business markets or law, the high stake parts of academic knowledge such as medical biotech have tempted the same monopolistic information providers that control legal and market information to seek control of knowledge by sequestering it in their servers and selling it back at exorbitant rates. But here there are countervailing forces—like public health and public funding for research on one side, and improvisatory academic entrepreneurship made possible by technology on the other. At stake is whether we will be in a world of monopoly knowledge for a few elite institutions in rich countries or whether knowledge will flow freely for the good of all. No matter how this struggle plays out, the old academic publishing arrangements are breaking up.

At the same time the structure of disciplines and professional societies is at stake as their control over accreditation and distribution of knowledge built over the last century is up for grabs, as is their economic dependence on earlier modes of publication. Again, while page design and use of dynamic data bases and multimedia are always interesting, the real design issues concern identifying channels and connections to keep knowledge communities together, create new ones, provide infrastructural incentives, and identify economic resources. In the process, the forms and substance of what counts as knowledge and the products of disciplinary work may also be renegotiated, as they were in the printing revolutions of the fifteenth and nineteenth centuries.

Finally, educational social arrangements have been put up for renegotiation by new technologies, though it is unclear how well we are finding solutions and satisfactory arrangements. Schools in one sense are well-established government-funded institutions with enormous bureaucratic inertial force. Accordingly, providers are using new technologies to feed the existing bureaucracy with tests and materials, reinforcing and intensifying pre-existing dynamics. On the other hand, technology seems to hold the promise of just-in-time, convenient, high interaction, individualized educational experiences. Writing has been at the heart of this, as most of the models are based on the sending of texts back and forth, creating discussion boards, and similar written word media.

Virtuality provides special opportunities for education but also poses special problems. Writing itself is a virtual distance technology, but, typically, support for writing and learning to write has been local and personal—classroom teaching, editing, tutoring, peer group commenting. The transportable text may be sent out into the world, but production is also local—here and now. The thought, consciousness, affect, and sensibilities of the writer are here and now. They are located in the neuro-body and motor selves at the keyboard. It is not by accident that writing pedagogy is built on the local community of the classroom, the small group interaction, the in-class process, and even the communicative dyad—from the earliest emergent literacy experiences through the dissertation written in collaboration with and for the advisor and a small committee. These face-to-face interactions help us understand the sociality to be negotiated by the text as it moves through a social world at a distance.

Distance education has proved a puzzle because of social engagement issues of high dropouts, loss of motivation, weaker guidance, and a tendency towards objectification of other participants. A quick review of the journal *Comput-*

ers and Composition about experiences with online education reveals concerns about communal accountability and students' responsibility for each other. One author notes that facelessness makes it easy for students to silence each other and turn them into objectified "others." In response, the teacher needs new techniques to monitor and shape the character of the emergent community and the virtual space which contains it (Fleckenstein, 2005). Another study notes the failure of students in a virtual workshop to connect with the author as a real person and engage with dialogue about writing (Hirvela, 2007). Another interview study suggests the cause of high online dropout rates may be a lack of interpersonal rapport arising from a failure of the instructor to project trust, empathy, and credibility (Sapp & Simon, 2005). Another notes that in an online ESL class the identities and solidarities based on age, gender, and status forged in a face-to-face classroom are replaced by the textualized identities and authority systems afforded by the linguistic system (Matsuda, 2002). Despite these challenges to maintaining rapport and cooperative interaction, one study did notice that adding tools, such as a whiteboard, can affect an orientation toward task and idea generation, thereby positively changing the interaction (Hewett, 2006). This problem of virtuality challenging the learning relationship is not new, as Plato and Socrates pointed out 2,500 years ago. Somewhat more recently, it was the practice in humanist libraries to place busts of the great authors on the shelves so readers could feel the personal authorial presence.

E-mail and the Internet have particularly teased us with the possibility of offering personalized, individualized mentoring, without the inconvenience of moving bodies around. Mentoring is the quintessence of the sociality that sponsors learning to write, as Deborah Brandt's (2001) wonderful studies have reminded us. Mentoring is at the heart of Vygotsky's (1978) vision of learning within the Zone of Proximal Development. Resilience studies of those protective factors that allow young people to prosper despite adversity have identified mentoring as a key factor (Arellano & Padilla, 1996; Garza, Reyes, & Trueba, 2004). A recent study of students from homes where no English was spoken who became identified as excellent writers at college again notes the crucial role of mentorship (Singer, 2007).

A recent initiative seems to capture the essence of the promise of online mentoring. As we know, the concentration of scholarly publication in a few countries has lead to barriers of language, professional experience, and contact with knowledgeable colleagues for scientists whose primary language is not English. A group of senior scientists and editors of scientific journals are planning an online mentoring system called AuthorAid with the aim of increasing publication and professional development of international scholars (International Network for the Availability of Scientific Publications, 2006). This seems an enormous opportunity to ameliorate obvious inequities.

Those who have worked with universities where English is not the first language know that the need for faculty to publish internationally is a major perceived problem and one of the strong motivators of English language training. Following behind this are the many issues of English being used as the primary or supplementary medium of education. I have seen this configuration of need in projects I have been working on in Brazil, Mexico, and Nepal. On the European Association for the Teaching of Academic Writing (EATAW) list and the European Writing Center Association (EWCA) list, this topic has been a matter of great discussion. So, such a mentoring program at the highest level could strengthen academic language education at all levels.

Yet, mentoring is a deeply personal social relationship. We are lucky if we can, a few times in our lives, form the bonds of trust and interchange that allow us to learn deeply from a mentor. It is not clear what it would take to make this online mentoring system work beyond the level of a correction service. Such a superficial service is not likely to hold the attention or cooperation of experienced scientists for long; only a more satisfying sense that they are truly helping a younger colleague to be a more articulate and powerful scientist is likely to create an ongoing commitment to the project. Yet, such a satisfying experience of mentoring is hard to come by. The complex history of writing center practice, theory, and research has been in fact a testament to how much thought must be given to making mentoring work well, even within a face-to-face environment.

The fact that the mentoring will be carried out by senior scientists experienced in the ways of publishing will help in the knowledge they have to offer, as will their experience mentoring their own students. In addition, their authority would likely evoke respect and perhaps trust on the part of the mentees. On the other hand, that authority may also impose distances if the issue is learning and development, and not simply conforming to correction. The authoritative word must somehow merge with the internally persuasive word.

The growing literature about online mentoring provides some guidance about the importance of the interface design to mediate relationships, establish roles and expectations, shape participation, create task orientations, and establish or hinder collaborative interactions. But the literature also warns us that online interactions create distances and obstacles for an ethos of care and trust—especially when the mentees are adults where issues of roles, privacy, identities, feelings about work and competence, and the like touch on complex human sensibilities (Blair & Hiy, 2006).

The senior status of the professionals may also create challenges in providing the mentors guidance as to how to work best in an online environment across such physical and social distances. Again, the writing center literature has let us know, even in face-to-face settings, the value of tutor training, no matter how knowledgeable the tutor is about the subject. A study of training for online tutors suggests that online tutors whose entire relationship is mediated by text need to have even more specialized training, helping them understand the dynamics of text-only dialogue, to introduce them to text moves that encourage dialogue, to provide comment structures that advance serious inquiry and further articulation of thought (Breuch, 2000; Anderson, 2002). Traditional marginalia and editing comments and even electronic editing tools may disrupt the mentee's relationship to the text and sense of the meaning projected. More needs to be understood about the experience of submitting to such an online service and how the user interprets that experience.

In our own field, the Research Network Forum is also in the process of creating an online mentoring system as an extension of the face-to-face mentoring provided annually at the Conference on College Composition and Communication (www.rnfonline.com). Making the face-to-face version a success has had challenges, which have only been sometimes met—including providing a satisfactory enough experience so that the mentors as well as mentees keep returning. These challenges will be made even greater on the Internet. But I am sure in both cases, if we approach the issues with understanding, creativity, and the right intellectual tools, we will meet the challenge.

This returns me to my main message. Our challenges are not only in creating attention-grabbing design, but also, more fundamentally, in the mediation of information-rich social processes. It is this challenge we need to prepare our students for—to make deeply satisfying and socially advancing experiences, capable of supporting complex cooperative work and creating environments for human growth and sharing. Elsewhere I have talked about the challenge of the cyborg way of life, saying the challenge is not only in creating the technological enhancements, but our growth as people to interact with and act intelligently with and through those enhancements (Bazerman, 2007). But as cyborgs we are not just individual creatures, we remain social humans. So, society and our understanding of it must also grow to manage the new forms of enhanced communal intelligence that new forms of communication are making possible for us. The society of cyborgs has the potential for deeper interiorities, deeper loneliness—nonetheless it also has the potential of deeper sharing, deeper intelligence, deeper cooperation, and deeper connection.

REFERENCES

Anderson, D. (2002). Interfacing email tutoring: Shaping an emergent literate practice. *Computers and Composition,* 19, 71-87.

Arellano, A. R., & Padilla, A. M. (1996). Academic invulnerability among a select group of Latino university students. *Hispanic Journal of Behavioral Sciences,* 18(4), 485-507.

Bazerman, C. (2007). WAC for cyborgs: Discursive thought in information rich environments. In P. Takayoshi & P. Sullivan (Eds.), *Labor, writing technologies and the shaping of composition in the Academy* (pp. 97-110). Cresskill, NJ: Hampton.

Blair, K., & Hiy, C. (2006). Paying attention to adult learners: The pedagogy and politics of community. *Computers and Composition,* 23, 32-48.

Brandt, D. (2001). *Literacy in American lives.* New York: Cambridge University Press.

Breuch, L. K. (2000). Developing sound tutor training for online writing centers: Creating productive peer reviewers. *Computers and Composition,* 17, 245-263.

Fleckenstein, K. (2005). Faceless students, virtual places: Emergence and communal accountability in online classrooms. *Computers and Composition,* 22, 149-176.

Garza, E., Reyes, P., & Trueba, E. T. (2004). *Resiliency and success: Migrant children in the U.S.* Boulder, CO: Paradigm.

Hewett, B. (2006). Synchronous online conference-based instruction: a study of whiteboard interactions and student writing. *Computers and Composition,* 23, 4-31.

Hirvela, A. (2007). Computer-mediated communication and the linking of students, text and author on an ESL course writing listserve. *Computers and Composition,* 24, 36-55.

International Network for the Availability of Scientific Publications. (2006). AuthorAid@INASP. Retrieved from http://www.inasp.info/file/76f6645a4daa13a559dd43965d4ed483/authoraid.html

Matsuda, P. (2002). Negotiation of identity and power in Japanese online discourse community. *Computers and Composition,* 19, 39-55.

Sapp, D. A., & Simon, J. (2005). Comparing grades in online and face-to-face writing courses: Interpersonal accountability and institutional commitment. *Computers and Composition,* 22, 471-489.

Singer, J. (2007). Literacy sponsorship and first generation Latino college writers (Doctoral dissertation). University of California, Santa Barbara.

Vygotsky, L. (1978). *Mind in society: The development of higher psychological processes.* Cambridge, MA: Harvard University Press.

WRITING AS KNOWLEDGE WORK IN PUBLIC AND PROFESSIONAL SETTINGS

5 RISK KNOWLEDGE AND RISK COMMUNICATION: THE RHETORICAL CHALLENGE OF PUBLIC DIALOGUE

Philippa Spoel and Chantal Barriault

In 2001, the Ontario government released a soil survey report that defined levels of metal and arsenic contamination caused by mining activities in the Sudbury community of Northern Ontario. According to this report, "emissions from over 100 years of mining, smelting and refining have resulted in elevated levels of metals and arsenic in the soil over a large area" (Ontario Ministry of the Environment, 2003). Based on this report, a Human Health and Ecological Risk Assessment was initiated in 2003 to determine whether the levels of metals in the soil pose an unacceptable health risk to people or the environment. Although the risk assessment phase of the Sudbury Soils Study is nearing completion, final results have not yet been released to the public.

From our perspective as science communication and rhetoric researchers, the Sudbury Soils Study offers a valuable opportunity to examine the processes of public communication and dialogue at work within a community-based risk assessment. This chapter represents a first step in a larger case study of public communication in the soils study. Our purpose in this chapter is to develop a preliminary critical analysis of the main rhetorical processes and challenges involved in the study's public communication mandate and activities. To accomplish this purpose, we will begin with a selective literature review of relevant theory from the fields of science communication and risk communication; we will then apply key concepts from this theoretical review in an initial analysis of the study's main public communication activities and assumptions.

To date, the Sudbury Soils Study's risk assessment process has been shaped by a complex combination of public sector, private sector, scientific, and community interests and involvement. The "partners" (Ontario Ministry of the Environment, 2003) in the study include the provincial Ministry of the Environment, the regional health unit, the municipality, the federal health ministry's First Nations and Inuit Health Branch, and the two large mining companies that operate in the region. At the recommendation of the Ministry of the Environment, the assessment has been funded voluntarily by the two mining companies. Decision-making, however, rests with the Technical Committee, which was formed at the start of the risk assessment phase of the study "to provide overall management of the process" (Overview, n.d.). This committee includes representatives from each of the six partner organizations listed above. A primary responsibility of the Technical Committee has been to ensure the scientific validity and credibility of the study by making decisions about who is best qualified to undertake scientific and technical activities and by making sure that results are scrutinized through legitimate and respected processes of peer review.

Attending to the scientific credibility of the study's process is not the only priority of the Technical Committee. From the outset, public transparency, public involvement, and public communication have been stated priorities as well. On the Sudbury Soils Study's Web site, for example, prominent headers such as "The Sudbury Soils Study—An Open, Public Process" and "Public Input Part of an Open Process" (Overview, n.d.) emphasize this objective, while details on the public communication activities that have occurred demonstrate tangible ways in which this objective is being put into practice. We are told, for instance, that

> The Sudbury Soils Study is the most comprehensive assessment of its kind ever conducted in Ontario. The community will be kept informed of any possible risks these metals may pose to human health and/or the health of the environment. The study has already held three workshops and two public open houses, and released two community newsletters, as well as several news releases. In addition, there is a project Web site, and quarterly reports from the Independent Process Observer. (Overview, n.d.)

To date, the study's public communication and community dialogue activities have been diverse, frequent, and explicitly recognized as an important dimension of the study. Beyond the fairly typical modes and strategies of public communication listed above (e.g., open houses, newsletters, news releases, the Web site), the study has also attempted to integrate public participation and dialogue into the risk assessment process in a more central, structural way through the establishment of a Public Advisory Committee and an Independent Process Observer position.

Indeed, because of the apparent success of its efforts to create an "open, public" process, the Sudbury Soils Study is now being presented as a model for "community-based risk assessment" applicable to other places and other risk issues. In its description of community-based risk assessment, a recent federal report on "Non-Renewable Resource Development and Community Infrastructure in the Northwest Territories" identifies the Sudbury Soils Study as one of the best examples of this participatory process:

> Community-based participatory risk assessment is meant to influence the actions of local government, the private sector or others in order to address identified risks. The assessments use qualitative data collection and analysis, including consultations with those at risk, and mechanisms for self-reflection and community empowerment.... In Canada, the Sudbury Soils Study is one of the most interesting initiatives of this kind. (Infrastructure Canada, 2005, p. 2)

Given the Canadian government's identification of the Sudbury Soils Study as a leading model for community-based participatory risk assessment, as well as the study's own stated priorities, we want to look at its strategies for public communication and engagement from the perspective of recent discussions in science communication and risk communication scholarship. In particular, we are interested in the assumptions about communication and the role of the community in the study's public participation and dialogue efforts. To what extent have these efforts been successful in developing a truly dialogic, interactive process that foregrounds local knowledges and facilitates a meaningful exchange between expert and public perspectives?

Drawing on the theoretical framework established by a selective review of relevant scholarship on public participation and dialogue in the fields of science communication and risk communication, we explore several dimensions of public participation and dialogue within the study's risk assessment process to illustrate both the possibilities and limits of its approach to public communication and community engagement. This includes looking at the multi-faceted cluster of public communication activities that have been undertaken, the roles of the Public Advisory Committee and the Independent Process Observer within the study's organizational structure, as well as the preliminary plans for communicating risk assessment results to the public. Working from recent discussions of "consensus conferences" and "citizens juries" in science communication, in closing we suggest a possible future direction for constructing more meaningful modes of public engagement.

SCIENCE COMMUNICATION AND RISK COMMUNICATION THEORY: CONCEPTS OF PUBLIC ENGAGEMENT AND DIALOGUE

Science communication is an emerging field that focuses primarily on the public communication of science. Bryant (n.d.) defines science communication as "the processes by which the scientific culture and its knowledge become incorporated into the common culture" (para. 1) and further describes the Public Understanding of Science as "the comprehension of scientific facts, ideas and policies, combined with a knowledge of the impact such facts, ideas and policies have on the personal, social and economic well-being of the community" (para. 3). Burns, O'Connor, and Stocklmayer (2003) provide a good review of the evolving definitions and objectives of science communication, while Gross (1994) addresses the relationship between the fields of rhetoric and science communication. Journals in the field include *Science Communication, Public Understanding of Science,* and *SciDev.Net* (a web-based journal).

Risk communication, as Trumbo (2000) points out, can refer both to a field of research and a field of practice. As a field of research, risk communication covers a diverse and broad range of topics, including psychology-based research into risk perception, the cognitive processing of risk information, and the social amplification of risk; critical-cultural and sociological theories of the role of risk discourse in society; rhetorical criticism and theories of risk communication; and studies of risk communication as a mode of professional communication. Notably, those engaged in the study of risk communication include both scholars from a wide range of disciplines (e.g., psychology, sociology, rhetoric, professional communication, anthropology, policy studies) and professional researchers-practitioners from outside academe (e.g., those who work in government agencies, in public health, or as independent consultants to government and industry). Plough and Krimsky's (1987) review of the emergence of recent risk communication studies is still very helpful for understanding dominant tendencies in the field. They identify environmental issues and public health as two primary areas of focus, and they distinguish between "quantitative," and "technocratic" approaches to understanding risk communication and "cultural," socially contextualized approaches which they present as preferable (p. 8).

In recent years, public participation and dialogue have been increasingly valorized in the science communication field. This contrasts with earlier assumptions about science communication as primarily a one-way, top-down process of conveying pre-established scientific knowledge and information to the public in order to increase lay people's scientific literacy. Similarly, within the field of risk communication, researchers and practitioners are increasingly talking about the importance of public participation and dialogue, as opposed to previous transfer models of risk knowledge and communication.

What exactly do public participation and dialogue mean in the context of risk knowledge and communication? It is one thing to develop dialogue initiatives in the context of museums, science centres, or other informal educational venues where the public is a willing, non-adversarial participant in the science communication process; it is another to engage the public substantively and meaningfully in the potentially adversarial, highly charged contexts of making and communicating risk knowledge. As Plough and Krimsky (1987) note, "The communication of information about risks usually occurs within a context of fear and uncertainty" (p. 5).

SCIENCE COMMUNICATION: CONTEXTUAL-DIALOGUE MODEL

Within the past decade or so, "context" and "dialogue" have become central terms in science communication research and theory. This contextual-dialogue model of science communication counters assumptions and methods found within the earlier Public Understanding of Science movement. From the perspective of dialogue model proponents, this movement was limited in its assumption that lay people simply need to "learn the facts" about a scientific issue in order to understand, accept, and appreciate it. The improvement of scientific literacy was a primary goal of the Public Understanding of Science movement, a goal typically based on survey research indicating the general population's lack of knowledge of basic scientific facts (Miller, 2001a). Given this lack, the main purpose of public science communication was to convey or transmit expert, scientific knowledge to non-experts who did not possess this knowledge:

> Together, the name 'public understanding of science,' and the interpretation of early surveys of scientific literacy resulted in the so-called deficit model of public understanding of science. This model characterized the public as having inadequate knowledge, and science as having all the required knowledge. (Burns et al., 2003, p. 189)

The deficit model, as Gross (1994) states, "is asymmetrical: it depicts communication as a one-way flow from science to its publics" (p. 6). For Irwin and Wynne (1996), the epistemological-ideological assumptions about science and scientific knowledge that underlie the Public Understanding of Science movement's deficit model are especially problematic. These include the assumptions that "understanding" means faithful assimilation of the available scientific knowledges, including their framing assumptions and commitments; that public controversy over technical/scientific issues is created by inadequate public understandings rather than by the operation of science itself; that science offers a privileged view of the world that necessarily contributes to human improvement; and that science is a value-free and neutral activity (pp. 7-8).

Spurred by the critique of the Public Understanding of Science movement's deficit model, science communication scholars have more recently embraced the concept of a contextual, dialogic model of communication. This model is consonant with a rhetorical rather than transmission view of communication. As Burns and colleagues (2003) explain, this model accounts much better than simple linear or diffusion models do for the complex social negotiations of meaning that characterize all occasions of public science communication (pp. 195-96). For Gross (1994), the advantages of the "contextual model" are that it "depicts communication as a two-way flow between science and its publics. The contextual model implies an active public: it requires a rhetoric of reconstruction in which public understanding is the joint creation of scientific and local knowledge" (p. 6). The contextual approach, then, introduces a much more nuanced and rhetorically sound approach to the public communication of science, an approach that acknowledges the role of language and communication in creating, not simply conveying, scientific knowledge. This approach, claims Miller (2001b), is preferable to the Public Understanding of Science approach because it "sees the generation of new public knowledge about science much more as a dialogue in which, while scientists may have the scientific facts at their disposal, the members of the public concerned have local knowledge of, and interest in, the problems to be solved" (p. 117).

Not only science communication researchers, but likewise politicians and policy-makers are increasingly acknowledging the social, political, and ethical dimensions of scientific knowledge and the importance, therefore, of facilitating public participation and dialogue on scientific questions. In the words of the European Commission's 2005 Science and Society Forum,

> We need to recognise that the public is a key part of the thinking society, with particular interests, concerns and questions about science and technological innovations and how these

will shape the future of societies.... To address the new public of science the idea of a one-dimensional flow of information should be replaced by dialogue, engagement and participation. (Gaskell, 2005)

RISK COMMUNICATION: VIEWS OF PUBLIC INTERACTION

Like the field of science communication, studies in risk communication in recent years have begun to emphasize the importance of an interactive, dialogic approach to communicating with the public. The challenges for implementing this objective in potentially volatile, adversarial risk communication contexts may be greater than those in, for instance, contexts of informal, voluntary science learning. However, the importance of public engagement on ethically and politically charged issues of scientific research and policy (e.g., genetically modified foods, reproductive technologies, and climate change) is already being recognized, and strategies for facilitating this engagement in meaningful, effective ways have begun to be developed, as we shall discuss further at the end of this chapter.

The recent emphasis on dialogue and public participation in risk communication differs from earlier approaches whose assumptions aligned closely with those of the Public Understanding of Science movement and a linear model of communication. According to Bradbury (1994), "the focus of the linear model is the effect of communication on the receiver—essentially the goal is persuasion." In the context of risk communication, "the risk management agency is viewed as the communicator and groups of the public are the audiences" (p. 360). Implicitly, this model assumes a basic asymmetry between those who possess expert scientific knowledge and the lay public to whom this knowledge needs to be communicated. As Katz and Miller (1996) explain, in risk communication contexts,

> parties are often characterized as 'experts' on the one hand and citizens, laypeople, or the general public on the other. In decision-making contexts, risk communication developed as an attempt to overcome these differences by 'correcting' the public's 'risk perceptions' so that they would better match the 'risk analyses' made by the experts. The public's perceptions of risk are generally understood to be subjective, mistaken, emotional, and even irrational, whereas expert assessments are based on facts, knowledge, probabilities, and calculations. In this con-

ception, then, experts engage in risk communication to inform and educate the public, to improve and correct their perceptions, and to persuade them to change their behavior. (p. 116)

The growing critique of the assumptions that underlie the transfer-deficit model of risk communication has led rhetoric and communication researchers to develop more dialogic and participatory conceptualizations of the risk communication process. These conceptualizations foreground the principle that expert and lay perspectives should inform each other as part of a two-way process (Bennett, 1999). Waddell (1996), for example, proposes a "Social Constructionist Model" of environmental communication that understands information and knowledge as flowing in both directions, thus blurring the distinction between "expert" and "public," or "rhetor" and "audience" (p. 142). Bradbury (1994), for her part, notes the inherent incompatibility between a linear approach to risk communication and the ostensible commitment of regulatory bodies to "democratic dialogue" (p. 360). For example, she observes how the (American) National Research Council's 1989 publication Improving Risk Communication continues to use the terminology of linear communication despite its stated commitment to a more interactive, participatory process. She argues that a "Convergence Model" of risk communication needs to replace the "Linear Model." This convergence model "shows communication as an iterative, long-term process in which participants are mutual communicators rather than senders and receivers." Through this mutual communication, "participants share and create information, either diverging or converging on a common meaning or understanding" (p. 361).

The dialogic process of risk communication that these researchers propose likewise deconstructs the hierarchical separation of reason and emotion that the transfer-deficit model presumes. Instead, public responses to risk contexts are understood as having "a rationality of their own" (Bennett, 1999, p. 3). Katz and Miller (1996) emphasize the importance of treating the public's "emotional" responses to risk not as "irrational" but as, arguably, legitimate and logical—as evidence of "reasonable concern about and understanding of risk rather than ... as an irrational reaction to a controlled situation" (p. 131). Waddell (1996) stresses not only that the public's often-emotional responses to perceived risk may well have a "rationality" of their own, but also that values, emotions, and beliefs play just as significant a role in "expert" views of risk as they do in public perceptions. As he explains, in the social constructionist model, "risk communication is not a process whereby values, beliefs, and emotions are communicated only from the public and technical information is communicated only from technical experts.

Instead, it is an interactive exchange of information during which all participants also communicate, appeal to, and engage values, beliefs, and emotions" (p. 142). Bradbury's (1994) convergence model similarly recognizes and values different forms of rationality: subjective and social perspectives as well as the "objective," analytical approach of technical risk assessment (p. 362).

Based on this very brief, selective review of science and risk communication literature, we return now to the Sudbury Soils Study to look more closely at some of its methods for fulfilling its public communication and community engagement mandate. These methods include implementing a multi-faceted range of public communication activities and genres establishing a Public Advisory Committee and an Independent Process Observer as part of the risk assessment organizational structure, and developing preliminary plans for communicating the results of the assessment to the public. In relation to these methods, we are especially interested in looking at the assumptions about communication and the role of the community in the study in order to consider how effective its public communication efforts have been in developing a dialogic, interactive process of public engagement.

In conducting this preliminary analysis of the study's public communication mandate and activities, we are mindful of Katz and Miller's (1996) findings in their study of how a government authority approached public communication in an environmental risk context. In this context, Katz and Miller found that, despite constant emphasis on the importance of two-way communication with the public, public participation was in fact "a highly controlled process of information exchange" based on a restricted understanding of communication (p. 128). As they put it,

> For the Authority, communication may be a two-way process, but it occurs on one-way streets. In forums and situations that it selects and controls, the Authority receives comments, and through its public information program it disseminates information; in essence, the Authority and the public did not participate in the same communication process. (p. 128)

Despite important differences in the context of their study (a highly contentious decision-making process for identifying a nuclear waste disposal site) and the less volatile, adversarial context for our study, Katz and Miller's findings nonetheless suggest potentially problematic features that may be to some extent present in the Sudbury Soils Study's approach to "open" and "community-based" risk assessment.

PUBLIC COMMUNICATION ACTIVITIES

As we know from its Web site, the Sudbury Soils Study has made communicating with the public in diverse and frequent ways a central feature of its process. Indeed, the informative, friendly, and quite easily navigable Web site itself represents one of the most important ways in which the public can find out about the risk assessment process. The dominant voice of the Web site is clearly directed at a lay audience rather than an expert-technical one: explanations of the study's purpose, methods, and findings to date are written in an accessible way, and it is easy to navigate menus and links to find more information. Perhaps most strikingly, the first page that the reader encounters is an open invitation to attend the next meetings of the Public Advisory Committee and the Technical Committee. For those who want to delve beyond the general information sections, the Web site includes a substantive archive of materials produced throughout the study's duration, including news releases and media reports, the study's own newsletter, reports from the Independent Process Observer, minutes of Public Advisory Committee meetings (though not of Technical Committee meetings), and a link to the provincial government's 2001 soil survey. The Web site, then, is in itself a very significant mode of public communication, and it provides access to a number of other modes. However, despite its friendly, inviting persona, the Web site's primary mode of communication is unidirectional rather than interactive: it is, for the most part, a consumption-oriented Web site that approaches the Internet mainly as a medium for individual consumers to retrieve information rather than a community-oriented Web site that exploits the Internet's potential for creating and sustaining interactions and relationships among groups of individuals, as might, for instance, a web-based citizen discussion forum (Feenberg & Bakardjieva, 2004).

Other modes of public communication that have been initiated are somewhat more interactive: a hotline has been set up that members of the public can call if they have any questions or concerns about the study, and several open houses have been held as a way of providing the public with more information about the risk assessment process and allowing the community to talk with the experts involved in the project. This range of public communication activities clearly indicates the Sudbury Soils Study's desire and tangible efforts to be an "open, public" process.

However, it is also possible to see many of these activities as essentially part of a well-intentioned but rhetor-dominated public relations campaign. In other words, the majority of these materials and communication modes provide a reassuring view of the study: reassuring in terms of the information communicated and reassuring in the sense that the very act of engaging in a wide range of public communication activities (regardless of their specific content) contributes to an ethos of openness and accessibility. The range of information available through the Web site and other modes of public communication function as concrete proof to support this ethos. At the same time, however, keeping in mind that all communication constructs a selective (and hence deflective) version of reality (Burke, 1989), it is worth asking what restrictions there may be on the "amount and kind of information" (Katz & Miller, 1996, p. 126) to which the public has access (for example, the Public Advisory Committee minutes are easily accessible but the Technical Committee minutes are not). It is also worth considering how the official rhetoric of the Sudbury Soils Study works to create a publicly reassuring character for itself. Although the question is beyond the scope of this initial paper, our larger case study includes a close rhetorical analysis of specific public communication texts produced by the study in order to identify concrete ways in which this character (or ethos) is constructed and promoted. More generally, this kind of analysis of the rhetorical composition of the Sudbury Soils Study documents will provide a better understanding of the necessarily selective and value-laden version of reality that is being officially communicated.

Further, even though events such as open houses, hotlines, and meetings that are open to the public certainly do provide opportunities for people to ask questions and, to some extent, provide input, these events and their agendas are also, of course, managed by those in charge of the study. In that sense, they are not entirely "open" since the contributions of the public to the rhetorical exchange must be made within the terms established by the study team. One could say that an asymmetrical relationship exists between the rhetor (the study) and the audience (the public), in which the rhetor sets the agenda to which the public responds, deciding when and how the public speaks (Katz & Miller, 1996).

Despite the Soils Study's frequent appeal to public input and community dialogue and despite its tangible effort to make itself open and available to the public, a tension exists between this appeal/effort and the communication assumptions revealed by the language in which it describes public communication and involvement. For example, a recent presentation given by the Soils Study about the risk assessment process included a slide entitled "Community Involvement and Risk Communication" that identified the following "goals":

- Inform the community about the project and our goals
- Provide relevant and timely information
- Obtain input from varied stakeholders
- Communicate results in clear and concise language
- Address and incorporate community concerns (SARA Group, 2005)

Three of these goals (the first, second, and fourth) are based on a commonplace transmission model of communication, in which the soils study conveys information to the community through the vehicle of "clear and concise language." More encouragingly, the other two goals recognize the importance of listening to the audience, though the term "stakeholders" suggests (perhaps unintentionally) a more limited and privileged audience than "community." Further, rather than suggesting reciprocal dialogue with either or both of these audiences, the phrasing of these two goals also suggests a transmission model, with the study now positioned as the receiver (rather than the sender) but nonetheless in control of the communication circuit: from "stakeholders" they will "obtain input," while the community is reduced to a source of "concerns" that are to be addressed and incorporated by the study's leaders. This terminology, we suggest, reinforces rather than calls into question a standard view of public communication as primarily a "process of information transfer" (Katz & Miller, 1996, p. 129) from an authoritative source to a lay audience of receivers. In part, this tension between the appeal to public participation and the language of information transfer may emerge from a tension between competing senses of the term "open": does being "open" mean allowing the public to view, as through an open door or window, what is going on in the study, or does the term "open" mean inviting the public to come inside and actively participate in the conversation?

In the latter sense, there have been real opportunities for lay members of the community to contribute in substantive ways to the creation (not just reception) of risk knowledge. For example, as part of the study's efforts to construct an assessment that is responsive to local concerns and realities, the community has been invited to participate in "Have Your Say Workshops" about the ecological risk assessment as well as surveys and sampling of locally-grown and wild foods that are consumed by residents. Through these initiatives, local hunting and fishing groups, gardening groups and others from the community were involved in deciding which foods and plants should be included for analysis. This was to ensure that the study captures the reality of the community's diet, reflecting choices people make and food they eat. In this way, it is possible to say that the experts in charge of the study have actively sought to include local knowledge in the construction of scientific knowledge. In addition, these workshops and surveys have provided a valuable opportunity for the study's staff to interact with the public and share information about the assessment process.

THE PUBLIC ADVISORY COMMITTEE AND THE INDEPENDENT PROCESS OBSERVER

Generating diverse and numerous public communication materials and activities is not the only way the Sudbury Soils Study has attempted to address its public communication and community engagement mandate. Perhaps most importantly, the organizational structure for the risk assessment includes a Public Advisory Committee and an Independent Process Observer position. According to the study's Web site,

> The Public Advisory Committee has the responsibility of representing citizens' interests in the Sudbury Soils Study. Meeting quarterly, the members work closely with the Technical Committee and provide input on the process. As representatives of the community, they have the additional role of assuring the public that the study is an open, transparent process. (PAC overview, n.d.)

The role of the Independent Process Observer, meanwhile, is to "regularly review the study process, report to the public on a regular basis, and at all times represent the interests of both the general public and the environment" (Process observer: PO role, n.d.). The observer sits as a non-voting member on both the Public Advisory and the Technical committees. The terms of reference for this position further explain that "The purpose of the IPO is to oversee and report on the process used to conduct the HHRA [Human Health Risk Assessment] and ERA [Ecological Risk Assessment] to ensure that it is transparent to the community and that communication with the public is timely and effective" (Process observer: PO role, n.d.).

The decision to integrate the Public Advisory Committee and the Independent Process Observer within the Soils Study's basic organizational structure shows how concerned the project's leadership has been from the outset to ensure clear, established mechanisms for representing the public's interests in the process. As the language of the terms of reference for these two organizational components indicates, their purpose is not only to facilitate public input into the process, but just as importantly to assure the public that the process is transparent and that their interests are being represented.

In our view, the creation of the Public Advisory Committee represents an important way in which the Sudbury Soils Study has tried to make public participation a central, rather than simply peripheral, feature of the risk assessment process. From the outset, this committee has been recognized as an official part of the process responsible for advising the Technical Committee on "how best to communicate with and engage the public throughout this process" (Overview, n.d.). Because of its existence, the voice of the community has been granted an explicit, legitimate role in the process. All Public Advisory Committee meetings are open to the public who are invited to "express their concerns or ... ask questions about any aspect of the Sudbury Soils Study" (PAC overview, n.d.).

There are, however, noticeable constraints on the Public Advisory Committee's position and functions in the process. Most noticeably, the committee has no decision-making power; its role is purely advisory to the Technical Committee, whose members direct the study. In this sense, it is structurally subordinate to the Technical Committee rather than an equitable partner in the study. Likewise, the terms of reference for the Technical Committee suggest that it largely initiates and determines the advisory process of the PAC: the TC "will *seek* [emphasis added] comment and input from the PAC *on all relevant issues*" [emphasis added]" (Overview: Technical Committee, n.d.). Further, although the Public Advisory Commiteee is described as a mechanism for ensuring the public's engagement in the process, the nature of that engagement is conceived as essentially separate from the Technical Committee's areas of responsibility. The Public Advisory Committee, in other words, was constructed as a means for ensuring that issues relevant to the public had an official status in the process, but these issues are not seen as fundamentally the same ones for which the Technical Committee is responsible. The Web site's explanation of the Public Advisory Committee's inception reveals this separate-sphere framework based on the division of the risk assessment process into two goals:

> At the October 30, 2001 PLC [Public Liaison Committee] meeting it was agreed that the two goals of the PLC were to discuss and advise on technical issues, and to provide a forum for public consultation. It was felt that this process would be best served by two separate committees. The PLC evolved into the Technical Committee (TC), established for INCO and Falconbridge and the government stakeholders to discuss and advise on technical matters. A separate Public Advisory Committee (PAC) was established to address the concerns of the community at large. (PAC: PAC Terms of Reference, n.d.)

At its inception, then, the organizational structure for the risk assessment inscribed a hierarchical separation of expert and lay knowledge, with public contributions occupying a subordinate status outside the realm of "technical issues." The concerns of the community at large were assumed not to be technical, though in accordance with the Technical Committee's mandate and composition, we should understand "technical" in this case to include issues of policy and politics, too. By contrast, the Public Advisory Committee's terms of reference stipulate its responsibility to "provide opportunities for members of the public to express their concerns or to ask questions about any aspect of the Sudbury Soils Study, such as *questions related to scientific or technical matters* [emphasis added] or to process or procedural issues" (PAC: PAC Terms of Reference, n.d.). The public's interest in technical and scientific matters is presumed to be mainly a need for expert information rather than a desire for reciprocal knowledge exchange. Even the phrasing "community at large" suggests a community surrounding, impinging upon but ultimately outside the heart of the process—a community that needs to be addressed rather than a community engaged in reciprocal dialogue with the study team.

Interestingly, however, two subsequent modifications to the organizational procedures show the problem of functioning on the assumption of two separate, asymmetrically related spheres of knowledge and discussion. To some extent, the exclusion of the Public Advisory Committee from the realm of "technical issues" and of the public from direct contact with the Technical Committee, has been addressed over the course of the study. In late 2003 and early 2004, the Public Advisory Committee debated the need to have better access to scientific and technical information in order to support its own deliberations. As a result of this debate, the advisory committee clarified (for itself and for the Technical Committee) that it is entitled to solicit scientific information from the study's expert advisors whenever it wishes. As noted in the minutes of January 2004,

> The PAC deliberated and decided that they would not amend their Terms of Reference to include responsibility for review of technical/scientific issues. It was recommended that a statement be added to the Terms of Reference to clarify the opportunity to have the freedom to call upon Advisors at the cost of the TC, if it is deemed appropriate. It was noted that the two current Advisors are available to the PAC at any time. (Sudbury Soils Study Public Advisory Committee, 2004)

In 2003, the question of public access to Technical Committee meetings also surfaced. This issue was addressed in late 2003 by the Independent Process Observer, who noted in his report that "The public has a growing concern that they do not have access to the TC which is the key decision making body" (Mariotti, 2003). This "concern" indicates the public's clear awareness of the Public Advisory Committee's subordinate status in the process: if the public really wants its voice to be heard, this means addressing the decision-makers directly, not the designated public advisors. Indeed, this point raises the question of whether the advisory committee might be considered as much a mechanism for creating a mediating, distancing boundary (a kind of buffer zone) between the public and the Technical Committee as it is a mechanism for creating an open channel of communication between them. Subsequent to the recommendation of the Independent Process Observer, the Technical Committee did augment its accessibility to the public, building in an opportunity for the public to make presentations or ask questions at the start of each meeting, though the rest of the meeting remains in camera.

Although these procedural statements and modifications did not substantially alter the basic structural relationship between the public, the Public Advisory Committee, and the Technical Committee, we do see in these discussions, referenced in the advisory committee minutes, an awareness of some of the challenges involved in negotiating lay and expert knowledge boundaries, and in crafting organizational procedures that truly facilitate public engagement. We also note the significance of the Independent Process Observer's role, a role that arguably has more influence on the Technical Committee's decision-making and the overall conduct of the study than does that of the Public Advisory Committee: it was the Independent Process Observer's recommendation, and not that of the Public Advisory Committee, that initiated this procedural change to allow public access to Technical Committee meetings.

Our sense is that throughout the risk assessment process, the views and recommendations contained in the Independent Process Observer's quarterly reports have been taken more seriously by the Technical Committee than the advice offered by the Public Advisory Committee. This may not be surprising, given that the observer's role is essentially to oversee the appropriateness of the study's organizational procedures, including the proceedings of the Technical and Public Advisory committees. Within the procedural framework that the Sudbury Soils Study has established for itself, it is ultimately the observer's seal of approval that is taken to guarantee that the study's process appropriately "represents the interests of both the general public and the environment" and that it is "transparent to the community" (Process observer: PO role, n.d.). It is little wonder then that, in the interest of maintaining public trust in the proceedings, the Technical Committee appears to listen carefully to the observer's recommendations.

While both the Public Advisory Committee and the Independent Process Observer are mandated to "receive comment/input/complaints from the public" (Process observer: PO role, n.d.), the terms of reference for both emphasize their responsibility to communicate information from the study to the public. In other words, the language used to describe their responsibilities suggests their primary function as transmitters of information from the study to the community (and indeed, using the term "receive" to describe their relationship to public input reinforces this transmission model of communication; one may receive information without necessarily acting upon it). The Public Advisory Committee, for example, is supposed to "provide suggestions as to how to best facilitate the process of keeping the public informed"; it "will also act to communicate *to* [emphasis added] the residents of the City of Greater Sudbury on progress as well as issues and concerns that they identify" (Process observer: PO role, n.d.). One of the observer's main responsibilities, meanwhile, is to "Prepare a quarterly written report on the overall progress and direction of the work of the committees for *dissemination* [emphasis added] to the public" (Process observer: PO role, n.d.). Further, the purpose for creating these communication conduits to the public is not simply to make sure that citizens properly understand the study's risk assessment activities (a purpose consonant with a traditional Public Understanding of Research approach to science communication); it is also, and perhaps most importantly, from a public relations perspective to make sure that the Sudbury Soils Study is perceived by the community as an "open" and "transparent" process, thus contributing to an environment of trust rather than mistrust.

RISK COMMUNICATION PLANNING

As the preceding reviews of the Sudbury Soils Study's public communication activities and the roles of the Public Advisory Committee and Independent Process Observer show, communicating with (or to) the public throughout the risk assessment process has been an important goal and activity. From our rhetorical-epistemological perspective, this constitutes part of the study's overall risk communication: that is, we see risk communication as including what occurs during the process of constructing scientific and community-based knowledge about risk, rather than seeing risk communication with the public as something that occurs only once the scientific risk assessment has been completed. From the perspective of the Sudbury Soils Study, however, the latter view of risk communication is more applicable. Now that the scientific risk assessment is nearing its completion, the study's expert consultants, together with the Technical Committee and the Public Advisory Committee, have begun to plan for what is more typically understood as risk communication: namely, communicating to the public the study's findings about current and potential future risks to human health and the environment from metal contamination in the region. At this stage, risk communication is understood as what occurs after scientific knowledge has been constructed.

In support of its goal to develop effective risk communication (and to overcome "barriers" and "communication mistakes"), the Soils Study has hired a risk communication consultant. This step signals an appreciation on the part of the study team that not only scientific but also communication expertise is needed, even though this communication expertise is positioned as a final stage in the process and not as integral throughout. As Waddell (1996) notes, citing Lungdren, too often environmental communicators are brought in only at the end of a risk assessment process to "sell" the risk decisions, rather than being involved in the knowledge- and decision-making process from the outset:

> It is impossible for environmental communicators to simultaneously a) facilitate the social construction of environmental policy, and b) "sell" decisions that have been made by others. As with information development, environmental communicators need to be involved in—and need to involve the appropriate publics in—the process from the outset. (Waddell, 1996, pp. 15-16)

As we learned from a workshop that we attended with the Sudbury Soils Study's risk communication consultant, the main purpose of risk communication is not, in his view, simply to transmit expert information or knowledge to the public. Instead, his approach to risk communication foregrounds the importance of building trust and of acknowledging emotion as well as reason in the communication of risk knowledge; this approach identifies "dialogue" with the audience as a significant objective. His "goals for risk communicators," for example, include the following:

- Maintain and build trust and credibility
- Engage your audience in 'dialogue'
- Communicate early, often, and truthfully
- Legitimize the concerns of your audience
- Make commitments to communicate (Frontline, 2006, p. 5)

These goals indicate an awareness of the fundamental roles of trust and emotions in the risk communication process as well as the importance of validating the audience's views and engaging them in "dialogue." Rather than adopting a "pure" transmission approach to communication (along the lines of Waddell's "One-Way Jeffersonian" model, which assumes that the responsibility of experts and authorities is simply to "transfer" technical information to an uninformed lay audience), the approach of the Sudbury Soils Study's risk consultant resembles more closely the "Interactive Jeffersonian" model, which requires not only that "the public adjust to expert knowledge," but that "experts adjust to public sentiments" (Waddell, 1996, p. 9). This approach to risk communication reflects, we suggest, the kind of definition advanced by writers such as Covello and Sandman (2001): the current version of risk communication, they claim, is intended to address "the new partnership and dialogue of government and industry with the public" (p. 1). However, the nature and roles of the participants in this dialogue are quite different: risk communication is a rhetorical tool (a means of persuasion) to be used by government and industry in order to "calm people down," "provide reassurance," or "generate a sense of urgency" when public response is "one of apathy" (p. 1)—in short, it is a process that involves rational experts and authorities addressing the emotional public in order to achieve the rhetor's desired "outcomes" (p. 2). Although their critique is more than 15 years old, we think it is still possible to see some of the same basic assumptions operating in Covello and Sandman's more recent work.

Although the study's risk communication consultant identifies audience engagement and dialogue as desirable goals, the approach is still mainly rhetor-based: as Bradbury (1994) says, the risk assessment agency is viewed as the communicator and groups of the public are the audiences (p. 360). This coincides with Plough and Krimsky's (1987) critique of Covello and his colleagues as proponents of a "conventional" model of risk communication that restricts itself to the question of "how 'experts' inform others about the truth," rather than also considering the importance of "non-elites as risk communicators" (p. 7). In this view, the main reason for pursuing goals such as legitimizing the audience's concerns and engaging in dialogue with them is in order to maintain the rhetor's (i.e., the organization's) credibility and create a receptive audience for the message that the rhetor wants to convey. This is, we would argue, essentially a public relations strategy: understand your audience's perspective and establish rapport with them so that you can successfully craft and sell your message to them.

This approach to risk communication is also, we suggest, a defensive one: the rhetor is advised to be thoroughly prepared so that s/he can respond effectively to the audience's "fear," "outrage," and "emotional questions" (Frontline, 2006, p. 19). From this perspective, the public's emotional responses need to be acknowledged not because they have a "rationality of their own" (Bennett, 1999, p. 3) that deserves to be a substantive part of the conversation, but because these emotions need to be controlled and defused by the rhetor so that they do not become disruptive or threatening: The workshop materials list sample "emotional questions" such as "How will you deal with those who get sick?", "When were you first notified about this?", and "What can we expect?" (Frontline, 2006, p. 19). Labeling these "emotional questions" implicitly devalues them by suggesting that they are not logical or reasonable. Likewise, risk communicators who face a potentially emotional public are advised to maintain strict control over their communication by always sticking to "key messages" (Frontline, 2006, p. 16). In this way, they can defend themselves against being led astray into open, uncharted territory—or into dialogue steered as much by the audience as by the rhetor. We would argue that this defensive approach to effective risk communication is more about managing audience responses than about engaging the public in meaningful conversation.

Thus, although the Sudbury Soils Study is in the process of developing plans for risk communication as a final stage of its project, and although the principles of risk communication that underlie these plans recognize trust and emotion, as well as pure reason, as important ingredients in the communication process, the current defensive, rhetor-based approach does not, we think, engender a substantive dialogue model of risk communication—a model that recognizes the different knowledges and perceptions of experts and lay people as equally, though differently, valid; that understands that all participants in the communicative situation are motivated by complex clusters of values, interests, and emotions; and that engages participants in a mutual process of sharing and creating meaning (Bradbury, 1994, p. 361). In Waddell's (1996) terms, the model of risk communication currently being pursued by the study does not fully illustrate a Social Constructionist approach, that would see risk communication as "an interactive exchange of information during which all participants also communicate, appeal to, and engage values, beliefs, and emotions" (p. 9).

POSSIBILITIES FOR FUTURE PUBLIC PARTICIPATION AND COMMUNITY DIALOGUE

From one perspective, the upcoming communication of the risk assessment results to the public represents a final stage in the Sudbury Soils Study: the study's mandate to undertake a human health and ecological risk assessment of soil contaminants associated with mining in the region will have been completed. From another perspective, though, this is just the first step in a much larger process, namely the process of deciding what to do about soil contamination. In moving from a question of risk assessment to a question of risk management, the issue will shift from a stasis of definition (i.e., defining the nature of the risk) to a stasis of procedure (i.e., determining the best course of action to follow in light of the study's results). As this shift occurs, the questions of public dialogue and community engagement will remain equally if not more important than they were in the risk assessment stage.

In this closing portion of our paper, we want to present, briefly, two procedures for public participation in science communication that we think provide some valuable possibilities for facilitating a more meaningful process of community dialogue for the decision-making process of risk management. These are "consensus conferences" and "citizens juries."

"Consensus conferences" are a method for facilitating direct citizen participation in decision-making about science policy questions. They originated in the late 1980s in Denmark and have since been held in a number of countries, including Australia, Canada, New Zealand, Korea, and many parts of Europe. Consensus conferences work by bringing together 12-15 lay citizens to examine a controversial science or technology issue. This group of citizens engages in a deliberative process to identify key issue areas. The process interweaves lay and expert knowledges by providing citizens with access to experts of their own choosing, whom they can question on issue areas that concern them. In other words, citizens become not simply recipients of expert information, but instead they decide what kinds of knowledge and expertise they need to help them make decisions about the key issue areas they have identified. In Einsiedel, Jelsøe, and Beck's (2001) terms, citizens are authorized to "cross-examine" experts—and they are not relegated to doing so from the marginalized position of audience members at a public presentation controlled by expert authorities. In the final stage of the process, the citizen group arrives at a consensus position, and makes recommendations to the policy-makers and the public.

According to Allen, Du Plessis, Kilvington, Tipene-Matua, and Winstanley (2003), the consensus conference method of public participation in science issues has demonstrated that "those with little previous knowledge of a particular field of science can question experts and formulate recommendations that draw on their own ethical commitments, life experience and belief systems as well as information about the technologies" (p. 5). In essence, the consensus conference functions as a deliberative forum for citizens to participate directly in democratic decision-making on science and technology issues (for more on consensus conferences, see also Joss & Durant, 1999).

Similarly, "citizens juries" are a practical method for creating more meaningful public involvement in the negotiation of risk (Coote & Franklin, 1999, p. 189). Initiated in the 1990s by the Institute of Public Policy Research in Britain, citizens juries emerged out of a critique of more traditional approaches to public involvement. Coote and Franklin (1999) summarize some of these shortcomings,

> For example, a typical 'communications strategy' would all too often treat the public as passive recipients of information or opinion provided by experts—not withstanding recent recognition of the need for dialogue. A 'consultation exercise' would often bypass important stakeholders and leave no room for

genuine debate. A public meeting would provide a theatre for the rehearsal of fixed positions. An opinion survey would seek the views of the public but fail to provide any relevant information. A focus group would leave participants in the dark about how their contribution would be used in the future. And so on. (p. 190)

Citizens juries, by contrast, attempt to address at least some of these shortcomings by providing a method of public engagement that allows "scrutiny and deliberation" in a context that assures plenty of time and information for participants to consider complex science issues deeply and carefully (Coote & Franklin, 1999, p. 192). Like consensus conferences, citizens juries bring together a small group of ordinary citizens who meet for a number of days in order to address a controversial science issue. They receive extensive background information and they cross-examine expert "witnesses" and may request additional "evidence" (p. 190). Unlike consensus conferences, citizens juries do not have to reach a single "verdict" or group position; instead, the process may result in diverse conclusions (p. 190).

Both consensus conferences and citizens juries offer alternative models of public engagement that could, we think, be adapted to enhance the future participation of Sudbury's "ordinary citizens" in negotiating the meaning of the human health and ecological risks that the Sudbury Soils Study has been assessing. Coote and Franklin (1999) argue that the meaning of risk in public health contexts is becoming increasingly uncertain and unpredictable for all concerned—including the public, scientists, and government—yet decisions and policies on how to assess and manage risks still need to be made. In this kind of context, they claim, it is not enough to think about how to communicate with the public; it is necessary to engage in a process of negotiating what risks mean and how they should be addressed. Their preference for the term "negotiation" over "communication" is helpful, we think, for pointing out that the simple objective of public "dialogue" may not be enough: the nature and quality of the dialogue are crucial. As they explain, "while 'communication' implies (or should imply) a two-way conversation for sharing information and perspectives, 'negotiation' can be seen as a multiple engagement of diverse forms of knowledge and experience" (p. 187).

In the context of the Sudbury Soils Study, can consensus conferences and citizens juries provide possible mechanisms for ensuring that "ordinary citizens" participate directly—and with authority—in the long-term, unpredictable process of negotiating what the risks mean to the community and how they should be addressed? Can they help the study to live up to its citation by the Canadian government as a model of "community-based participatory risk assessment" that includes "consultations with those at risk, and mechanisms for self-reflection and community empowerment" as a means "to influence the actions of local government, the private sector or others in order to address identified risks" (Infrastructure Canada, 2005)?

CONCLUSION

By drawing on recent research and theoretical developments in the fields of science and risk communication, our analysis of public communication and community involvement in the Sudbury Soils Study has allowed us to identify both the tangible ways in which those in charge of the risk assessment process have attempted to facilitate an "open" public communication process and the limitations of these efforts. In particular, we have found that, despite a clear commitment to public communication and the establishment of diverse mechanisms to carry out this mandate, a limited and fairly traditional understanding of public communication still persists. We see this in the primarily unidirectional, informational nature of the Web site and the relatively controlled agenda of open houses and other public communication activities; we see it in the study's language, which describes public communication as implicitly a transmission rather than dialogic process; we see it in the hierarchical separation of the Technical Committee and the Public Advisory Committee in the study's management structure, as well as in the emphasis placed on the role of the advisory committee and the Independent Process Observer as transmitters of information; and we see it in the defensive, rhetor-based approach to risk communication that informs the study's preliminary risk communication plan.

For the most part, then, the Sudbury Soils Study has not (yet) developed a truly effective rhetorical approach for fostering a substantive, equitable process of dialogue with community members and ordinary citizens. Ideally, this is a dialogue that would recognize the values, beliefs, and interests of all who participate (including experts and authorities), respect and account for the diverse knowledges and perspectives of all participants, and facilitate the ongoing negotiation of meaning and knowledge-making about risk in this specific context and community. However, as the study shifts from being primarily a risk assessment to a risk management process, we think that new opportunities will present themselves for the development of a more substantive, interactive, and empowering process of public communication and community involvement.

For the fields of science and risk communication, our case study demonstrates the value of applying research-based models and theories to the analysis of specific rhetorical situations of risk communication. This application allows us to better understand the nuances and complexities of the particular situation being studied, thus generating findings that may be valuable to those directly involved in the situation as well as to researchers studying similar situations. The results of our case study likewise potentially contribute to the development of rhetorically informed models and theories in science and risk communication: for instance, by emphasizing the importance of attending to the local context and situational particularities of each risk communication process; by drawing attention to the diverse possible configurations of the relationship between rhetor and audience (or among rhetors) in risk communication contexts; by demonstrating how the language used to describe risk communication both reveals and shapes assumptions about the nature and purpose of that communication; and by reconfirming the integral but complex roles of trust and emotion in the making and communication of risk knowledge.

REFERENCES

Allen, W., Du Plessis, R., Kilvington, M., Tipene-Matua, B., & Winstanley, A. (2003). Consensus conferences: A model for engaging public in science and technology policy decisions. Excerpt from *Involving the public in science and technology decision-making: A review of national and international initiatives.* Retrieved from http://www.morst.govt.nz/Documents/work/sis/Involving-the-public-in-science-and-technology-decision-making.pdf

Bennett, P. (1999). Understanding responses to risk: Some basic findings. In P. Bennett & K. Calman (Eds.), *Risk communication and public health* (pp. 3-19). Oxford: Oxford University Press.

Bradbury, J. A. (1994). Risk communication in environmental restoration programs. *Risk Analysis, 14*(3), 357-363.

Bryant, C. (n.d.). *What is science awareness?* Retrieved from Centre for Public Awareness of Science: Australian National University Web site: http://cpas.anu.edu.au/science_awareness.php

Burke, K. (1989). Language as action: Terministic screens. In J. R. Gusfield (Ed.), *On symbols and society* (pp. 114-125). Chicago: University of Chicago Press.

Burns, T. W., O'Connor, D. J., & Stocklmayer, S. M. (2003). Science communication: A contemporary definition. *Public Understanding of Science, 12,* 183-202.

Coote, A., & Franklin, J. (1999). Negotiating risks to public health – models for participation. In P. Bennett & K. Calman (Eds.), *Risk communication and public health* (pp. 183-194). Oxford: Oxford University Press.

Covello, V., & Sandman, P. (2001). Risk communication: Evolution and revolution. In A. Wolbarst (Ed.), *Solutions to an environment in peril* (pp. 164-178). Baltimore: John Hopkins University Press.

Einsiedel, E. F., Jelsøe, E., & Beck, T. (2001). Publics at the technology table: The consensus conference in Denmark, Canada, and Australia. *Public Understanding of Science, 10*, 83-98.

Feenberg, A., & Bakardjieva, M. (2004). Consumers or citizens? The online community debate. In A. Feenberg & D. Barney (Eds.), *Community in the Digital Age* (pp. 1-28). New York: Rowman & Littlefield.

Frontline Corporate Communications Inc. (2006, January). *Risk communication: Building trust and credibility with the public.* [Workshop materials]. Sudbury, ON: Laurentian University.

Gaskell, G. (2005). Report of session 3: Toward a culture of science communication. *European Commission: Science in Society Forum,* Brussels, March 2005. Retrieved from http://ec.europa.eu/research/conferences/2005/forum2005/docs/report_session3_en.pdf

Gross, A. G. (1994). The roles of rhetoric in the public understanding of science. *Public Understanding of Science, 3*, 3-23.

Infrastructure Canada Research and Analysis Division. (2005). *Planning for a soft landing: Non-renewable resource development and community infrastructure in the Northwest Territories.* Retrieved from Infrastructure Canada, Our Results Web site: http://www.maca.gov.nt.ca/resources/INFC_Paper_plan_for_soft_landing(Nov10).pdf

Irwin, A., & Wynne, B. (1996). Introduction. In A. Irwin & B. Wynne (Eds.), *Misunderstanding science? The public reconstruction of science and technology* (pp. 1-17). Cambridge: Cambridge University Press.

Joss, S., & Durant, J. (Eds.). (1999). *Public participation in science: The role of consensus conferences in Europe.* London: Science Museum.

Katz, S. B., & Miller, C. (1996). The low-level radioactive waste siting controversy in North Carolina: Toward a rhetorical model of risk communication. In C. G. Herndl & S. C. Brown (Eds.), *Green culture: Environmental rhetoric in contemporary America* (pp. 111-140). Wisconsin: University of Wisconsin Press.

Mariotti, F. (2003). *Quarterly Report.* Fall (Vol. 2, no. 6). Retrieved from Sudbury Soils Study Web site: http://www.sudburysoilsstudy.com/EN/indexE.htm

Miller, J. D. (2001a). The acquisition and retention of scientific information by American adults. In J. Falk (Ed.), *Free choice science education: How we learn science outside of school*. New York: Teacher's College Press.

Miller, J. D. (2001b). Public understanding of science at the crossroads. *Public Understanding of Science, 10*, 115-120.

Ontario Ministry of the Environment. (2003). *Backgrounder: Sudbury soils study*. Retrieved from Sudbury Soils Study Web site: http://www.ene.gov.on.ca/envision /sudbury/soilsstudybg.htm

Overview: Technical committee—Terms of reference. (n.d.) Retrieved from Sudbury Soils Study Web site: http://www. sudburysoilsstudy.com/EN/indexE.htm

Overview: Why a study? (n.d.). Retrieved from Sudbury Soils Study Web site: http://www. sudburysoilsstudy.com/EN/indexE.htm

PAC overview. (n.d.) Retrieved from Sudbury Soils Study Web site: http://www.sudburysoilsstudy.com/EN/indexE.htm

PAC: PAC terms of reference. (n.d.) Retrieved from Sudbury Soils Study Web site: http://www. sudburysoilsstudy.com/EN/indexE.htm

Plough, A., & Krimsky, S. (1987). The emergence of risk communication studies: A social and political context. *Science, Technology, & Human Values, 12*(3/4), 4-10.

Process observer: PO role. (n.d.) Retrieved from Sudbury Soils Study Web site: http://www. sudburysoilsstudy.com/EN/indexE.htm

SARA Group. (2005). *Presentation to science communication graduate diploma program*. Science North, Sudbury, Ontario.

Sudbury Soils Study Public Advisory Committee. (2004). *Minutes: Meeting #12*. January 20, 2004. Retrieved from Sudbury Soils Study Web site: http://www.sudburysoilsstudy.com/EN/pac/minutes/01-20-04.htm

Trumbo, C. W. (2000). Risk, rhetoric, and the reactor next door. In N. W. Coppola & B. Karis (Eds.), *Technical communication, deliberative rhetoric and environmental discourse: Connections and directions*. (pp. 191-223). Stanford, CT: Ablex.

Waddell, C. (1996). Saving the great lakes: Public participation in environmental policy. In C. G. Herndl & S. C. Brown (Eds.), *Green culture: Environmental rhetoric in contemporary America* (pp. 141-165). Madison: University of Wisconsin Press.

6 THE EVOLUTION OF AN ENVIRONMENTALIST GROUP TOWARD PUBLIC PARTICIPATION: CIVIC KNOWLEDGE CONSTRUCTION AND TRANSGRESSIVE IDENTITIES

Diana Wegner

This study follows a local environmental group as it shapes a civic identity, before and after a municipal election, towards taking up a speaking position within the participation framework of city governance. This is an exploration and analysis of the tense co-existence of conflicting, oppositional identities, of marginality and power, in the context of local environmental conflict. The central question revolves around how this local group participates in the construction of civic discourse and community knowledge to build its political capital, and how, at the same time, it retains its activist discourse and marginal identity. It is hoped that this paper will contribute to current interdisciplinary scholarship on the issue of public participation in government decision-making and discourse studies on marginal identities and identity development. In this context, it is an effort to provide an analysis of how discursive rhetorical strategy functions in civic identity development and how the management of available discursive resources can enable citizen participation without disabling an activist identity.

Studies of public participation in environmental decision-making have found that local democratic political processes in environmental contexts are often dysfunctional. Such studies have, for the most part, yielded scenarios of unproductive processes of public participation, usually generating frustration among citizens, and deadlocking opposition between activists and government/industry. For example, in a study of the U.S. Forest Service's approach to public involvement, Walker (2004) found that, while the Forest Service propounded the importance of collaboration as a matter of policy, in practice it actually discouraged public engagement (p. 134). In a separate study of the Forest Service, Schwarze (2004) found that Forest Service management is over-preoccupied with the regulatory mechanisms for public discourse, with the result that there is now "a trained incapacity" among employees and management for addressing the question of legitimate public input (p. 154). In another study, Gregory (2001) found that citizens experienced the official body of the port authority as "not only elusive and unaccountable but also ... to be in the service of urban development policies promoting ... 'outside' economic interests of ... elites" (p. 143). Gregory concluded that these residents became shut out of public participation because the port authority ultimately "governed the political arena of neighborhood activism" and what was permitted to be "the politically sayable" in public debate (p. 167). Having studied a number of these cases, Depoe and Delicath (2004) concluded that public participation in environmental decision-making fails because community input often solicited by public officials is not allowed to affect "policy choices or regulatory outcomes" (p. 10). Similarly, based on her study of stakeholders in such processes of public input, Senecah (2004) found that they felt that their involvement was not "productive or meaningful" and that "the public had no voice" (p. 19). Indeed, those working in forest policy and research themselves have acknowledged the perception that community input has been futile in most processes of public participation:

> In the past, federal agencies like the Forest Service and the Bureau of Land Management have failed to successfully involve the public in natural resource planning and decisions. Community-based practitioners feel—after two decades of "public involvement" in which their comments have been synthesized, coded, counted, considered too late, or taken out of context—they have had little or no impact on what happens to the forests that surround them. (Gray & Kusel, 1998, p. 28)

Although not great in number, there are some encouraging stories of environmental activism. For example, Ingham (1996) reports on the rhetorical sophistication of the Beartooth Front Alliance and its consequent success in protecting the environment of the community of Red Lodge. Cooper (1996) applauds the successes of the Nature Conservancy and its efforts to include "both protesters and accommodators" in the process of environmental change (p. 256). Clearly, the rhetorical work of activists in these sensitive contexts need not always be thwarted by dismissive official processes or lead to deadlock and stalemate. This paper is intended to contribute to these studies and to deepen our understanding of how, in contexts of environmental conflict, productive knowledge building of accounts which are critical of government and lead to change may occur, and how it can occur without repudiating an activist identity. How do non-mainstream individuals and groups both effectively mobilize those features of a dominant discourse to receive recognition or acceptance by the dominant group, and, at the same time, sustain those transgressive features of discourse that are critical to their identity?

This question evolved as I studied the ongoing activities of a local environmental group over its third year of existence, from 2005 to 2006. The question owes much of its formulation to the work of Holland and Lave (2001), who ask how "people [can] act so as to foreground one kind of identity over others in local contentious practice, and at the same time act in ways saturated with other identity practices" (p. 26). By the end of the group's first two years (2005), my findings suggested that its members might become stuck with the dead-end effects of a polarizing activist discourse that precludes genuine public input. As the study proceeded into the group's third year, however, my findings began to suggest not a polarization but a co-existence of opposing discourses, inviting more focus on the constructive possibilities for such co-existence as an alternative to the usual scenarios of confrontation between activist citizens and their governments.

By the end of the third year, I found that the group's most effective strategy was its contributions to community knowledge-making. In the context of an election campaign, the group collaborated with other environmentalist groups to develop a community message that candidates would listen to. This message construction fostered the group's civic identity and its realization of the larger goal of entering civic discourse on environmental decision-making. In effect, as a basis for broader political support, the group contributed to the building of community knowledge that led to widespread awareness and concern over the mayor-in-council's cavalier dismissal of public input into land use decisions. Its efforts involved the strategic use of resources available from both activist and civic discourses to build community knowledge through the production and reproduction of certain community "sayings," and thereby to create its linguistic capital. This work entailed using the tactics of reported speech to produce linguistic expressions suitable for the linguistic market. The group's goal was to make its account of the city's "deafness" to public input on the development of natural areas prevail as community knowledge, and thereby achieve "acceptability" in the "market" of city politics (Bourdieu, 1991, p. 81). As a result, when the city's participation framework shifted with electoral change, the group became aligned with the new, salient account of events, and it had sufficient political capital to take up a speaking position afforded within this changed market. At the same time, the group protected a more transgressive discourse and hard-won activist identity, an identity that government representatives seemed to tolerate, and even accept, in meetings with the group. The group had fashioned a civic identity for itself and sustained its more activist identity and discourse.

To demonstrate how this group motivated and participated in the construction of community knowledge, and how it constructed its civic identity, I have adopted a theoretical framework that incorporates analyses of discursive conflict, identity development (Holland, Lachicotte, Skinner, & Cain, 1998; Holland & Lave, 2001), and knowledge construction as discursive formation (Foucault, 1972 a, 1972b). This framework is also applied to an analysis of how and why the group sustained its activist identity even as it achieved a civic speaking position. In what follows, I first provide a brief background of the group and the issues at stake, then elaborate the theoretical framework, describe my research methodology, and discuss the findings of the study. I have drawn on representative discursive events, both pre- and post-election, to illustrate the group's management of its civic identity, and the co-existing persistence of its activist identity.

BACKGROUND

The focus of this study is the third year of activity of the group, an umbrella organization for a number of environmentalist groups within a large Canadian city, now with 175 members. The group was organized by the project manager for the natural areas management plan and mandated by the city's natural areas management policy. This policy states that "A Commission natural area advisory committee should be formed to identify, promote, advocate and educate for, and about, natural areas and their benefits" (2003). Most members of the group have an activist history and long-time involvement in the community as volunteers and self-appointed, but welcome, stewards of the land. A number of them sit on other city advisory committees. The overriding purpose of the group is to advocate for natural areas, which have been undergoing rapid and questionable development with what many community members see as minimal or no public consultation. The city's growth continues at a rate of 800 people each month and as of May 2007 was over 410,000.

The group has acted independently but more often with other community groups and individuals to protest the destruction of specific sites of trees, streams, riparian corridors, and other environmentally sensitive areas taken for residential development. Often, by the time local residents realize what is happening, the developer has received approval and begun clearing the land. The group has initiated or participated in such activities as public meetings for input on new developments; meetings with the mayor, city managers and staff; interviews with the media; and writing letters to the mayor-in-council and regional governments, as well as numerous letters-to-the-editor to local newspapers. The group also holds its regular monthly meetings, frequently inviting guests—city staff and managers, wildlife and sustainability experts, and provincial civil servants—to discuss specific land development issues. Over 2005/2006, attendance at monthly meetings ranged from 7 to 20 members. Most communication among members and with other groups occurs through e-mail.

A recent example of the group's ongoing involvement with the local media, now a year subsequent to the period reported on in this chapter, shows the considerable challenge that the group continues to face in its advocacy for responsible land development. Days after another episode of unapproved tree-cutting, one local newspaper in July 2007 reported that "more than 30 tall conifers" were "cut down for a housing development." The article cites a member of the environmental group who is president of the local community association. She describes the areas as a "moonscape," and asks, "Are these the rules of the [city], has anything changed?" The article also reports that the president of the group itself was "troubled by a trend in [the city] of razing properties for development." A separate article in the same issue reports that "record residential development resulted in the loss of an average of 9,100 trees annually between 2001 and 2004," a figure that excludes one "huge cut in ... [a] business park which amounted to 14,000 protected trees lost." In spite of promises by the new mayor in 2005 to regulate and moderate the removal of trees in the city, and since the enactment of a new tree bylaw in 2005 and the inclusion of the environmental group as one of the mayor's community advisors, the rate of tree-cutting has continued to accelerate. The article refers to the president of the group as one "who helped put together [the city's] new tree protection bylaw" and reports her judgment that "the legislation doesn't appear to be having much of an effect." The article also reports the comments of the new mayor: "we've got to do a better job"; "more can be done to slow the number of trees coming down."

Initially, the project manager discouraged activist practices, reminding members periodically that the committee was sponsored by the parks and recreation department. In effect, they had been charged to advocate for the environment as a kind of satellite body attached to the periphery of the city through parks and recreation. However, after achieving recognition by the former mayor-in-council in its first year as an official delegation to city hall, it lost the city's support. In response to an incident that the city interpreted as face-threatening, the city severed its relations with the group. In its third year, the focus of this study, the group remobilized its efforts, working with other members of the community towards achieving public input in land use decisions. They used the pending municipal election in this effort, exploiting the resources available through candidates seeking a profile and heightened media interest to make their account of the city's dismissive attitude toward public input the official one in the community.

THEORETICAL FRAMEWORK

In this section, I describe the conceptual framework that is marshaled to understand the evolution of the group's civic identity. I first discuss the relationship between identity development, discursive knowledge construction, and positionality. This is followed by a discussion of transgressive discourse and marginal identities.

Identity, Discursive Formation, and Positionality

Ongoing work on the dynamics of conflicting discourses has focused on how marginal individuals and groups strategize to use available discursive resources to manage identities, yet resist being subsumed into a dominant or mainstream "normative" discourse (Bourdieu, 1991; Holland & Lave, 2001; Holland et al., 1998). Such a radical heterogeneity of identities necessarily entails both the achievement of power/knowledge and the play of non-sedimented power relations. On the one hand, agents engage in the rhetorical-discursive learning of the features of a dominant discourse as an exercise in discursive knowledge construction—and they come, consequently, to acquire authentic speaking rights through a repositioning within the dominant participation framework (Goffman, 1981) that aligns them with institutional power. On the other hand, they also maintain a marginal identity that neither threatens their public speaking rights nor loses itself to the dominant institutional structures.

Identity develops through a variety of rhetorical-discursive practices that reinforce the emergence or prior existence of a discursive formation. As practice, it is "the structuring of social existence ... in the lived activities of subjects who both participate in it and produce cultural forms that mediate it" (Holland & Lave, 2001, p. 4). In this study, "lived activities" include rhetorical strategizing, occupying certain speaking positions, attending meetings, and carrying out other advocacy activities. The "cultural forms" that agents produce and use are the socially recognizable genre performances they enact as they work towards their goal of being heard by the city, and of making their account of the city's attitude towards public input the account of others. As Holland and Lave assert, "[m]uch of what is contested in local struggles is the very meaning of what's going on" (p. 20). Marginal groups, thus, face the particularly difficult challenge of making their interpretation of events the official account; moreover, in their efforts to meet this challenge, they must use the cultural forms and "the language of the other" (p. 11): "any given struggle is partially formed in the taking up of the idiom of others" (p. 26). Holland and Lave further explain that "[t]he dialogic selves formed in local contentious practice are selves engaged with others across practices and discourses inflected by power and privilege" and that, although such selves may find these practices "uncomfortable" to adopt, "they cannot simply refuse" them (p. 18). In dialogical terms, in enduring struggles, the "answers made by the contentious others are authored in the cultural discourses and practices at hand" (p. 30); on the other hand, in the gap between transgression and reproduction there is space for innovation and generativity. In studying "culture in practice" as opposed to "culture as rules" (Holland et al., 1998, p. 278), improvisation comes into view as a significant feature of the scene of struggle. While such improvisation is limited by the type of space afforded for "authoring" (Holland et al., 1998, p. 279) and the available cultural forms, there is space for strategic play with the contingencies and uncertainties that develop in struggle, even if only temporarily.

As a discursive formation becomes attached to power and develops, so do opportunities for the identity development of marginal groups. Following Foucault (1972a, 1972b), I applied the concepts of discursive field and discursive formation to analyze conflicting discourses in relation to identity development. Such analyses help show how a discursive formation comes about through the strategic reiteration of certain sayings or statements, and how the salience of certain statements as the official account of events can be implicated in change and reconfigured speaking positions. Foucault (1972a) defines a discursive formation as the heterogeneous dispersal of a group of "statements" that form a unity through the "interplay" of certain "rules." A discursive formation is therefore characterized by its unique combination of rules and co-occurring objects, concepts, or themes. The interplay of rules "make[s] possible the appearance of objects during a given period of time" (pp. 32-33), as well as the appearance of certain concepts. For example, the accepted practices of citizen engagement with governments and the common practices of proponents of development make possible the emergence of objects and concepts such as sustainability, green growth, and community. The concepts that characterize a discursive formation, however, do not form a coherent set, but instead are significant to the discursive formation for "their simultaneous or successive emergence" (p. 35). For example, concepts such as democracy and nature emerge together in environmental conflicts. Similarly, a discursive formation can be characterized by a number of themes that provide, not stable meanings, but instead a "dispersion of the points of choice, and define prior ... to any thematic preference, a field of strategic possibilities" (p. 37). For example, the theme of environmental sustainability offers a number of positions and strategic possibilities, many of which may be incompatible with others, such as environmental protection and economic sustainability. In short, a discursive formation is a discourse: "a system of dispersion ... between objects, types of statement, concepts, or thematic choices" that constitute a "regularity (an order, correlations, positions and functionings, transformations)" (p. 38).

In Foucault's view, a discourse can be approached broadly or narrowly: in terms of "its general domain of all statements," "as an individualizable group of statements," or "as a regulated practice that accounts for a certain number of statements" (p. 80). All three approaches are incorporated in this study—a general approach for descriptions of conflicting discourses, and a narrower focus on both specific statements, as they are developed and become salient, and on the activist, political, and journalistic practices that reinforce these statements and attach them to power.

Identity development occurs through the strategic use of statements and regulated practices—cultural forms that are necessarily shared with or available through the dominant group. In exploiting these forms, the repeatability of the "statement," the primary building block of discursive formations, is a key resource. Foucault emphasizes the centrality of the "statement" in discursive formations. He attributes the statement's force to its "repeatability," its capacity for enunciative "duplications," its "possibilities of reinscription and transcription" (1972a, pp. 103–105). And, although Foucault explicitly brackets "the presence of authors" (p. 38), he presents the statement as a significant resource for speakers. Foucault posits "a field of stabilization" that derives from the attachment of the statement, in its repeatability, to power: "the statement ... appears with a status," "a certain modifiable heaviness" that "reveals the statement" as an object that speakers "produce, manipulate, use, transform, exchange, combine, decompose and recompose, and possibly destroy" (p. 105). The "statement" is a key resource in human struggles: "Thus, the statement circulates, is used, disappears, allows or prevents the realization of a desire, serves or resists various interests, participates in challenge and struggle, and becomes a theme of appropriation or rivalry" (p. 105).

Each reported version of an account offered by a marginal group thus has the potential to become the formulation of a statement. As instances of reported speech accumulate, they can become attached to power, thereby increasing the political capital of those who re-formulate and institutionalize the account. In dialogical terms, each formulation or "utterance" acquires something from each of its enunciative contexts and is therefore, a "hybrid construction ... that actually contains mixed within it two utterances, two ... 'languages,' two semantic and axiological belief systems" (Bakhtin, 1981, p. 304). As different speakers with different motivations strategically appropriate formulations into their different belief systems, reported speech can become progressively more salient. In belief systems or ideologies that successively afford greater power through repeated enunciations and institutional affiliation, these recontextualizations can lead to the formation of a "statement," bringing with it, for speakers, the affordances of more legitimate speaking positions within the enunciative field of the statement.

The statement provides the conditions of possibility for the emergence of certain objects, discourses, sentences, and speaking positions, such that "the position of the subject can be assigned" (Foucault, 1972a, p. 95). These are subjects who have acquired political capital through their utterances of an influential statement, so that even marginal subjects may become legitimized by the statement and be assigned or come to occupy speaking positions within the statement's enunciative field. The work of developing a discourse and identity out of the resources of the dominant discourse enables subjects to be called into or "interpellated" by an institutional structure. Group members may then participate with agency in the forces of change.

The enunciative field of a statement develops in what Bourdieu (1991) calls the "linguistic marketplace." In his introduction to Bourdieu, Thompson (1991) explains that, in practice, participants do not act upon, but in relation to, their social context—a "field of action" or "market" (p. 14). The market is "a structured space of positions in which the positions and their interrelations are determined by the distribution of different kinds of resources or 'capital,'" such as economic, cultural, symbolic, linguistic, political, and so on (p. 14). Within this marketplace, linguistic or symbolic power can be transformed into political power as participants develop a suitable "habitas" or "set of dispositions" (p. 15). As Thompson summarizes, Bourdieu's "linguistic utterances" are "the product of the relation between a linguistic habitas" made up of "dispositions acquired ... to speak in particular contexts," and "a linguistic market" (p. 17). The market is always a site of struggle where "different speakers possess different" capacities "to produce expressions" suitable to the "particular market" and where "the distribution of linguistic capital is related ... to the distribution of other forms of capital

... which define the location of an individual within the social space" (p. 18). It is in this sense that a "suitable expression" carries the weight of a "statement."

The next section takes the broader view of discourse, moving beyond the phenomenon of specific linguistic expressions and statements, to examine the relationship between transgressive discourse and marginal identities.

Transgressive Discourse and Identity

The persistence of transgressive discourses, existing alongside those of mainstream discourses, has become an arresting object of investigation in studies of conflicting discourses. The features of transgressive discourses can function as evidence and reinforcement of a hard-won identity. In some cases, these features can come to be tolerated and even validated by those with speaking positions within dominant discourses. Such tolerance is in direct opposition to more traditional, dismissive attitudes that treat transgressive discourse as non-rational, and, therefore, irrelevant—often a default response that only intensifies mistrust of political authority (Wynne, 1992, p. 278). Allowing for (and perhaps endorsing) the non-rational is not an endorsement of relativity; it is, however, an acknowledgment of the indeterminacy of a post-modern world that, according to Wynne, has displaced "the modernist paradigm of singular unconditional rationality" and the corresponding "concept of social identities as unproblematic and completed" (Wynne, 1992, p. 295). Therefore, a more explanatory concept of social actor would include both types of social identities, those that are discursively constructed in situations of social dependence on a more powerful "other," and "alternative social identities," conveyed through dialogically generated, transgressive discourses that constitute "answers" to messages of hegemonic power and deafness to marginal identities. In this view, the social actor is therefore, reflective of "a complex existence within different social worlds" (Wynne, 1992, p. 296).

In their explanation of the persistence of transgressive identities, Holland and Lave (2001) refer to "intense" addressivity whereby one is addressed with heightened provocation. They adapt Bakhtin's premise that "sentient beings—alone and in groups—are always ... in a state of being 'addressed' and in the process of 'answering'" (Holland & Lave, 2001, pp. 9–11). "In answering (which is the stuff of existence) the self 'authors' the world—including itself and others" (Holland et al., 1998, p. 173). In being intensely addressed, especially when negatively addressed, a group may answer by authoring itself as radical. Holland and Lave (2001) cite the case of IRA women prisoners who responded to punitive strip searches by reasserting their political identities as committed members of the IRA (p. 16). They adopted the practice of publicly rehearsing the common experience of being subjects of strip searches. So, a transgressive identity may become a group's *raison d'etre,* with its practices of identification serving to reinforce its transgressive self). As people identify themselves with unacceptable objectifications of themselves, they construct a rationale for resentment and further resistance (Holland et al., 1998, p. 143). While this often reinscribes a marginal identity, which can further distance a group from the center, it is the necessary ground for action. In this sense, transgressive discourse can circulate as a necessary force for re-motivating resistance to power at the institutional level and re-affirming a marginal identity that exists contiguously with a more institutional identity.

METHOD

My research methodology has been ethnographic and qualitative. It includes the development of a participant-observer relationship with a municipal parks and recreation department, which provided a basis for the interpretation of both contextual and textual data. My involvement with the department began as a member of an urban forest advisory committee and then as a consultant hired to help revise the natural areas management plan in 2000-2001. Subsequent to working for the department I began the research project, studying the internal collaborative development of the natural areas management plan (2001), the staff/community collaboration to develop policy from the plan (2002–2003), and the activities of the advocacy group, which was mandated by the policy (2003–ongoing).

Like other ethnographers of social practice, I have focused on relevant "local practices" and "cultural forms," such as monthly meetings and public hearings: as objects of investigation, these are "starting points" in the effort to show how, at the local level, enduring struggles "are structured by and structuring of state and civil institutions" (Holland & Lave, 2001, p. 9).

The primary method of data collection has been recording observations at the group's monthly meetings from June 2005 to May 2006. Notes were taken at all meetings; with the exception of two meetings, discussion was audio taped and transcribed in simplified form (with minimally detailed phonological markings). This data has been interpreted in the context of written documents that help explain the oral data: minutes of the meetings, numerous e-mails and letters, newspaper articles and letters-to-the-editor (from three local newspapers), and a number of foundational city documents.

The focus on a local manifestation of an enduring struggle is conceptually and methodologically supported by similar studies whose motivations are both research-based and social. Holland and Lave's (2001) inquiry is primarily research-based, though implicitly socially motivated: they explore enduring struggles and the cultural production of identity, "beginning from situated participation" in order to illuminate "the generative, conflictual participation of persons in practice" (p. 5). Their work examines local conflict in order to show how it mediates both the "broader structural forces" of enduring struggles and the agency and identity of individuals and groups (p. 9). Others, like Williams and Matheny (1995), who investigate public participation in environmental decision-making, explicitly combine research and social goals. They hope to discover, through studies of local citizen engagement, "a pathway to reconstructing citizenship" at the federal and state levels (p. 10). Through the findings that follow here I analyze one group's strategies to assert their citizenship as agents with a speaking position within the structures of city governance.

FINDINGS

Reconstructing a Civic Identity through Mainstream and Community Affiliations

Addressees and Answers: Responding to the City's "Deafness". As described earlier, this umbrella group was created in 2003 through parks and recreation policy, but lost the city's support a year later. Since then, it has tried to recoup its lost speaking rights and political capital. In the run-up to the city's Fall 2005 election, the recurrent theme in the group's deliberations, and in the discourse of a significant number of members of the community-at-large, was the perceived "deafness" of city hall to public input on land development proposals. A typical comment comes from a group member at their July 2005 meeting: "And it doesn't matter if you have a public hearing or not because they just do what they want." The theme persists at subsequent meetings. For example, members had provided solicited written input to the city in response to a proposal to develop part of a large park into a golf course. The city had surveyed the public for its response to the proposal with a set of questions. Group members provided their responses, including comments that went beyond the specific questions. These additional contributions were not included in the city's corporate report presented by council at the following regular council meeting, yet members believed they should have been:

> Member 1: I started to do some more reading on this corporate report, and ... I still haven't found those areas where I proposed things that weren't in the questions.

Member 2: And I didn't see any mention ... of the comments that I made about the need to have development permit areas as a tool ...

Member 3: So ... if it wasn't in the questions that parks staff, planning staff devised, then ... the public input didn't get recorded. (July 28, 2005)

The theme of "deafness" has also been ongoing in local newspapers in letters-to-the-editor from both citizens-at-large and group members. These letters capture the perceived indifference of council to public input in depictions of council members as "cardboard cutouts," a "mayor who won't listen to those who elected him," and "these people" who have ignored "all" of the recommendations stipulated in city-commissioned environmental assessments:

Most of the council could have cardboard cutouts of themselves at these hearings, and no one would know the difference. (letter-to-the-editor, April 27, 2005)

I urge everyone to lift a pen or phone to protest what is happening to our section of the world. If our mayor won't listen to those who elected him, it's time to find someone who will. (letter-to-the-editor, July 6, 2005)

There's the city's own critically important 1996 Environmental Assessment Report that ... classified the area [already under development] as ESA1, or most sensitive. There's also the ... Wildlife Assessment (2003) and the two ... Bio-Inventory reports (1996, 2001) on aquatic and terrestrial habitats... Among the many recommendations in the reports were: Sparing the mature forest areas and ... tributaries of [a local river] ... expanding riparian zones... To date all of these recommendations have been ignored. Acres of mature forest have been leveled; ponds and wetlands filled in; original streams trenched up ... Councilors have stated they were not apprised of this before voting for the project [the creation of an industrial park] in 2003. How can this happen ... Citizens of [the city] have an opportunity to hold these people to account come November. Make sure your voice is heard. (letter to the editor from a group member, Aug. 3, 2005)

A number of newspaper articles take up the same theme; for example, "[h]uge parcels of land centred around [a green corner in a quiet neighborhood] have been cleared of trees and leveled to create building sites and that's got environmentalists crying foul.... [the mayor] did not return calls for comment before the [newspaper's] press deadline" (Sept. 7, 2005).

Eventually, the theme is taken up by the rival mayoral candidate who appropriates it as part of his platform. He states that people's "voices or concerns" are not "heard at city hall," that "they feel shut out" by the city's "culture of control." His statements are reproduced here from a newspaper account:

> "People don't feel that their voices or concerns are heard at city hall," [he] said ... [He] said the problem extends to development in the city and residents often feel decisions are made before council sits down to publicly debate issues. "There has to be a balance and process where people feel they are heard. Right now, they feel shut out. A culture of control ... has developed at city hall under [the mayor]." (Oct. 8, 2005)

Reported speech, such as these reformulations, involves the repetition of certain sayings, which can be recontextualized in more powerful arenas (like the press) until, in the Foucauldian sense, they acquire the salience and social force of statements. The community's "statement," asserting the city's deafness to its citizenry, becomes the basis for its response, which is to expose the mayor's apparent indifference to the electorate. Since one is "always in a state of being 'addressed' and in the process of 'answering'" (Holland & Lave, 2001, pp. 9-11), the mayor's message of indifference has the effect on citizens of an intensely hostile addressivity. In perceiving itself to be so negatively addressed (blatantly non-addressed), the environmentalist group, along with others in the community, develops a correspondingly intense answer in formulations of a counter-statement.

As Senecah (2004) found in studies of public participation in civic issues, citizens frequently experienced a lack of access to civic decision-making space, or a lack of standing—a speaking position from which to be heard. In the absence of either or both, Senecah found that citizens "become frustrated, angry, and increasingly antagonistic and aggressive in creating the space" where they "can claim ... access or standing" (p. 25). Lacking "civic legitimacy," groups like those studied by Senecah may revert to transgressive expressions of opposition. They can "act dramatic, loud, obnoxious, emotional, and even threatening" in an effort to "creat[e] their own standing by creating media events, bolstering their organization, appealing to other citizens to join them, and trying to intimidate officials into thinking of further repercussions" (p. 31). To some extent, this is how the advocacy group began to construct its answer to the city. And, to the same extent, this is how the features of its transgressive identity came to serve its objective at the initial stage of its response strategy.

In response to this deafness, the group came to form two collaborations: one with a national, more mainstream environment group, "The Green Group," and the other with other community groups who, together, hosted an all-candidates meeting. The success of these collaborations depended upon, among other conditions, the strategic use of cultural forms that were available and "at hand." These turned out to be the genres of "report cards," newspaper ads, all-candidates meetings, and newspaper reports.

Building Identity through Mainstream Affiliation. In the first collaboration, the two groups canvassed candidates with environmentally related questions and published the results in two local newspapers. The exercise was an opportunity for the group to participate in the shaping of a civic discourse that would address candidates and other members of the community. The group developed the questions, with guidelines set by the Green Group advisor. For example, the advisor indicated early on that "there might be some questions that [The Green Group] would feel ... uncomfortable asking ... and other questions that would be in line with [their] mission statement." He justified this gate-keeping based on the Green Group's monetary contribution: "because we're paying for the ad and our logo is all over it, we'll have a say" (August 23, 2005). A month later, he evaluates the questions—"Maybe I can just share with you some examples of ... ones that I thought worked, and then make a recommendation and then hear back from you." He also sets a key criterion that the questions should be general instead of site-specific: One of the things I was looking at were ... questions that, um ... were non-site specific ... so that we really appealed to a general public ... as opposed to just the people who lived around a particular neighbourhood" (Sept. 20, 2005).

This strategy, as others have noted, aims for identification across a community, a kind of common ground that environmental activists often lose in their focus on site-specific issues. As Gregory (2001) explains, a focus on "place-based identities" offers "ineffective subject positions from which to formulate needs, interests, and strategies in relation to regional political and economic processes" (p. 151). As the advisor thus guides the group, he tutors them in strategies for addressing institutional players, and, for the most part, members defer to his expertise. For example, on the issue of who should contact the candidates, there is agreement that the Green Group would be more appropriate because it "is seen as very non-partisan" (Sept. 20, 2005), an indication that there is a shared consciousness that the group's more activist and marginal position may be a liability:

> Member: Will you be sending the emails to the candidates?
>
> Advisor: Well, we can ...
>
> Member: Under your name?
>
> Advisor: We can talk about that. I think, um ... in someway, well, yeah.
>
> Member: I think that would be best.
>
> Advisor: I kind of think it would be best as well.
>
> Member: Yeah.
>
> Advisor: Just because [the Green Group] is seen as very non-partisan.
>
> Member: Exactly. Yeah.
>
> Advisor: And we'd be very clear that we're partnering with [the group] on ... this ... and be very clear that we're printing their responses. (Sept. 20, 2005)

Members continue to assess their profile in this collaboration and find it satisfactory. For example, at the next meeting, from which the advisor is absent, one member who was involved in developing the questions reports on their progress. He sums up the content of the advisor's latest e-mail, reporting first that the advisor has been deliberating their strategy at the head office: "the pow-wow he's talking about is with his communications team in Toronto." He also reports that the communications team has decided to "go with the report card format" with "both our ... logo and the [Green Group's] logo ... at the top of the report card" (Oct. 18, 2005). At the subsequent meeting, four days before the election, mutual thanks are exchanged, and, taking the advisor's lead, general satisfaction is expressed with the report card ad and the candidates' responses to their questions. The president of the group, who also chairs the group's meetings, reiterates the advisor's positive assessment of the process and the advisor points to future uses of the results of the survey in holding candidates accountable to their responses:

> Advisor: Well, it was a really good process.

> President: And, I think, as you've said, it's our first time we've had a chance, and next time it'll be better.
>
> Advisor: And I think the responses ... I don't know how much is ... you know, candidate-speak at the forum, but ... I think ... they were put on the spot ... it holds them accountable, so now ... we have a lot of yeses and details now to play with ... to go back and say, you know, you were very public with this, and if they don't deliver .... (Nov. 15, 2005)

At the end of the meeting, the advisor reinforces the affiliative effects of this general satisfaction with their mutual effort by inviting the group to participate in future events, attaching to the invitation a request for a letter of support from the group, and offering to provide a template of the letter. As an available cultural form, the template offers the group another opportunity to shape its discourse and identity with the material of a more mainstream idiom, that of the bureaucracy in which the national group participates. In exchange for writing the "form" letter, the group has received funding and guidance towards its immediate goals.

In addition to their yes/no responses, the candidates' longer comments were published on the Green Group's Web site. Notably, among the responses is the rival mayoral candidate's promise of a "culture of environmentally aware development," a phrase standing in for his earlier critical reference to the current "culture of control." His statement yokes this projection into office with an appropriation of the community's message to improve the process of public input on development from groups like the environmentalist group:

> As I believe in balanced growth, I believe that it is important to continue to *develop* but that it is done in an *environmentally aware manner*.... One of the biggest problems currently is that *public consultations* are not taken seriously by *council*.... The *culture of environmental awareness* must be led first and foremost by the elected political chief amongst them *the Mayor*. (Nov. 17, 2005 [emphasis added])

Formulations of this statement have appeared in many earlier incarnations from a number of citizens, including a letter-to-the-editor from the group's president. The need for public input to ensure good development is the key message: "Natural areas ... are necessary. We are not opposed to development. We advocate for *quality development* ... we believe *council* should hold a *public hearing* to allow people to *express their concerns directly to council*" (April 29, 2005 [emphasis added]).

The mayoral candidate's formulation of the issue is also apparent in his comments drawn from an interview and published in a local newspaper:

> "I'm hearing on a fairly regular basis that *residents don't feel their voice is being heard,* that land-use issues have already been decided before ever hearing the community's concerns," [he] said this week. "We need to make sure there's *a process in place for dealing with development applications,* in that there is *no interference from the mayor's office* or senior managers." (November 12, 2005 [emphasis added])

All agents who reproduce this statement invest it with their own motivations. Following Foucault (1972a), "according to the position, status and role of one formulation among others ... the way in which other statements are present in the mind of the subject will not be the same" (p. 98). The mayoral candidate's appropriation of this statement likely occurs in the context of his electoral ambitions and is endowed with his political motivations. For environmental advocates, one could speculate that formulations of the statement emerge from the context of land protection and green development and are endowed with ostensibly altruistic motivations.

Building Identity through Local Affiliation. Throughout the process, group members have met with key candidates, and, in a second collaboration, they have teamed up with a number of community groups to host an all candidates meeting focused on "sustainability" (which the incumbent mayor did not attend). Group members extended the report card strategy by using the results as a basis for their questions at the meeting. This strategy was suggested by a member of the group in an e-mail:

> [An all-candidates meeting] would be more effective if coordinated with the publishing of the ... questionnaire responses—a couple of nights later strikes me as potentially very effective as it would offer a chance for candidates to expand on their ... answers ... citizens would have these responses in hand and be able to further grill candidates on how they answered. (Oct. 7, 2005)

This strategy is endorsed by three other groups that made up the coalition hosting the all-candidates meeting. The Green Group advisor also participates, supporting the extension of the report card strategy at the public meeting, as a way of "continuing outreach/education around the election" (Oct. 13, 2005). This view is echoed by the president, who suggests building on the report card strategy by adding "questions that relate to sustainability. Not necessarily similar to those we are asking for our ad" (Oct. 14, 2005). In preparation for the meeting, the president asks for the advisor's feedback in an e-mail, for example, on a question about an acquisition budget for natural areas: "I thought that a question relating to the amount that [the city] is setting aside for natural areas parks ... would be good. In '04 [the incumbent mayor] ... lowered that amount to 50% without any explanation ... There is not now a designation or acquisition budget for natural areas parks" (Nov. 6, 2005).

Shaping their discourse again, the advisor responds by e-mail with suggestions for revision, to give the questions more focus and punch. Replacing the president's language, he offers a series of pointed questions: "There is a ton of good info in your [question]. Why not zero in on some of that? For ex. 'Why does [the city] NOT have an acquisition budget for natural area parks, and would candidates put one in place? If so, how much is the city willing to invest in securing natural areas ... ?'" (Nov. 7, 2005). His advice cuts through the details and expressions of blame. In his e-mail, he also advises the president to "check out the web for the detail[ed] responses by some of the candidates" that were insufficiently "concrete," and "to try to nail the candidates down to some solid idea" (Nov. 7, 2005). His advice on rhetorical and research strategies, thus, helps put the group on a more even discursive field with the candidates. It helps build the group's public profile and identity as a credible player in the election campaign.

"The Community Livability All-Candidates Meeting" was attended by more than 150 people from all areas of the city and the local media. It was moderated by the editor of one of the local newspapers, who was known to be critical of the city's development processes, and whom the coalition had invited to take on this role. Newspapers carried the meeting's collective message, not surprisingly reifying the key content, or "statement," of the expressed concern that natural areas are being developed without public input: "The ... majority on council has silenced critics, shut down committees and suppressed reports in its zeal to speed development at the cost of green space and wildlife, challengers charged at an all-candidates forum Nov. 9" (Nov. 16, 2005). The process of developing the questions, publishing the results, and exploiting them at the all-candidates meeting was part of an accumulation of expressed discontent and growing political capital among environmentalist and other groups in the community. Just as the mayoral candidate, who is pro-development, formulates this statement of blocked public input to garner votes, by emphasizing the need for public input for "good" development, local newspapers formulate the statement to stir up controversy by emphasizing the current mayor's abrogation of democratic processes that would ratify public input. This statement becomes critical content and a forceful node of knowledge/power. It constitutes the elements of discourse that agents have repeated and reproduced, through strategy and opportunism. Participants who re-formulate these linguistic expressions can build knowledge by shaping the statements that will become the prevailing account of events in the community. If favorable events occur, this built account can be synchronized with, and incorporated into, a change in the linguistic marketplace. As part of the pre-election momentum, the group can be seen shaping an identity and discourse in preparation for a possible change in city governance, and an accompanying shift in participation framework and speaking positions. This possibility is realized through the incumbent mayor's defeat.

Taking Up a Speaking Position within a Reconfigured Participation Framework

The structural changes at the institutional level, brought on in this case by the election, as "an exercise in power" (Gregory, 2001, p. 146), rewarded the risk of uncertainty and afforded the group a positioning opportunity on which it was then able to capitalize. As Holland and Lave (2001) conclude, "the structuring of social existence" is a "historical process": "both the continuity and the transformation of social life are ongoing, uncertain projects" (p. 4). They emphasize the productive role of uncertainty in this process, pointing out that it is "the generativity of cultural practices" that creates "alternative subjectivities" which "introduce uncertainty—wild cards of a sort—into the careers of local contentious practice" (p. 9). The group had fashioned itself an identity and network of city connections that helped create the conditions of possibility for a stronger speaking position. With the election, it was positioned then to "fit" productively into the new participation framework of civic politics. The group thus achieved "acceptability" in the new "market" of city politics (Bourdieu, 1991, p. 81): having achieved sufficient political capital, when the city's participation framework shifts, it strategically attuned its identity work to find a speaking place within the changed market. It was also able to structure its social existence so as to retain the continuity of its activist identity even through its evolving civic identity.

The election, in fact, changed the footing possibilities not only for the group but also for the city staff, allowing both more latitude for expressing dissent and providing input into land use decisions. For example, after the election some city staff were uncharacteristically forthright about their own lack of influence under the previous mayor. Before the election, members of the group had been harshly critical of city staff for their silence and compliance with the mayor-in-council. In a typical comment at the time a member decried a known city engineer's public comments on protecting wildlife: "He's got an engineering degree ... he is saying things that he has to know is [sic] wrong," to which another added, "It's either do that, or lose his job" (July 28, 2005). Three months after the election, however, at one of the group's own meetings, invited engineering staff (including the engineer referred to above) acknowledged the repressive political climate of the former mayor's regime. They reported that they had always wanted to include consideration of fish and streams in their work with developers, but had not been permitted to do so: "We've been arguing this for years ... but basically we've been told what to do" and "We just have to follow the rules, so to speak" (February 21, 2006). They referred to "what the previous council did" (excluding riparian areas regulations from developer permits) and divulged that "there were some weird deals [with developers] ... some things got done that shouldn't have gotten done" (February 21, 2006).

The group itself now also has more official input into city initiatives. For example, the president reports that the engineers have incorporated the group's written recommendations into a memo to the new mayor-in-council; "I found out that they in fact have agreed to what we were suggesting in the letter" (April 18, 2006). Their new footing with the engineering department also disposes the group to sometimes curb its extreme positions. For example, at the same meeting, when one member suggested verifying this input by trying to obtain the memo in question through a "freedom of information request," another member counseled against such an action: "if we go making a fuss about the memo then we will destroy any trust which is built up between him [the engineer] and us" (April 18, 2006). Such desire for and recognition of the importance of "trust" is a significant move for the group, for it signals a change from the usual public skepticism of institutional authority. The group seems to be engaged in a central element of organizational learning, which Wynne (1992) describes as "the developing identity of the organization itself, through deeper appreciation of relations with others" (p. 293).

The group's growing influence on decision-making is also evident in the city's official invitations to provide input at public hearings and other meetings. The ground for this change had been laid during the run-up to the election, as group members met the mayor-to-be at public meetings, and established good relations with three environmentally friendly councilors who were re-elected. With other community groups, the group was later invited to attend public meetings on new development projects. For example, in February 2006, the group was invited to city hall, as one of 40 community groups, to present revisions to a stronger tree bylaw, which council finally approved. While one member is still privately skeptical, cautioning, "Let's see if they're willing to implement it fully at the council level" (February 22, 2006), he also expresses public optimism in a regular column he writes for one of the local newspapers, in which he praises this "encouraging and praise-worthy administrative change" (April 22, 2006).

Group members also expressed their sense of being part of a positive shift in city politics. At the March 2006 meeting, for example, comments included the following: "[the mayor—by first name] seems to be taking a new approach about ... new development"; "A light went on"; and "We might make it to the twentieth century." A local newspaper also reports that a councilor, who was part of the former mayor's team, voted against the old team "on a controversial commercial development" so that the remaining team members were "stranded by the new councilors, who sided with ... the [new] mayor." The article reports that "[the councilor] believes gone are the days of block voting on issues, and while the party remains pro-development, it will be 'good development' that gets his support" (May 13, 2006).

The change in the group's speaking rights is signaled in other ways as well. Its official input on development projects is also now duly recorded by the media. For example, local newspapers reported on its stance on a major bridge and residential development proposal: "[The group] is calling for an independent study showing if in fact congestion would be relieved by the [bridge expansion]" (March 29, 2006). Moreover, the new mayor invites the group to become a member of the first Mayor's Community Association Advisory Committee. The invitation is, at least ostensibly, recognition of the increased value of the group's political capital. The mayor registered their value in the letter of invitation: "As a community group you are closest to the issues that affect your community. Your involvement has provided you with a thorough and unique understanding of the history, issues and people at the grass-roots level" (April 25, 2006). He wrote that he would like them to "keep [him] apprised of" and to "advise [him]" on "action" to address "public concerns" (April 25, 2006).

Multiple Discourses and Identities

A particularly significant finding of this study is that this civic identity does not eclipse the group's more extreme language, which is still frequent and persistent. It is alive and well, especially in the back regions of their meetings, where group members do not censor activist expressions, even when the presence of guests at its meetings renders their remarks public. The theme of councilors' disinterest also persists in comments like "it's exactly as if you'd never been there at all" and "I think [the questionnaires] go to the shredder," as follows:

> Member 1: Public hearings, these displays, poster boards. They listen to what you have to say and say, thank you very much.
>
> Member 2: And do what they want.

Member 1: And tomorrow it's exactly as if you'd never been there at all.

Member 2: They DNP it. They document ... and then they proceed. They document what the public says to them and then they proceed.

Member 1: And ... they ask you to fill out questionnaires. And so, what happens to those questionnaires. I think they go to the shredder or something [laughter]. (March 22, 2006)

The co-existence of these identities is now sometimes a tolerated feature of language in discussions with government representatives. At a post-election monthly meeting, for example, two invited representatives of the provincial Ministry of Transportation clearly came prepared to listen and respond to confrontational expressions and questions from the group, which they negotiated with humor, respect, and patience. They were giving a presentation on a major highways project, which included the bridge expansion, during which many members became confrontational towards the Ministry representatives. In response to a Power-Point slide showing an "artist's concept" of a nine-lane bridge, one member interjected: "Why don't you show it realistically" with the "congested cars" and "pollution" instead of "all the green?" (May 16, 2006). He accused the Ministry representatives of "green washing" the project, and added sarcastically, "nice paint job" (May 16, 2006). Perhaps members felt entitled to adopt such discourse in the back region of their own meeting place, but in this case it was being offered for wider public consumption.

CONCLUSION

The features of activist discourse apparent in members' comments occur even as they are making serious efforts to shape their public discourse for civic presentability, and they are permitted increasingly greater speaking rights with the city staff, councilors, and mayor. The anger, cynicism, ridicule, and humor that accompany members' complaints about not being heard persist as features of activist discourse. Like many environmentalist groups, they see themselves as mavericks (even saviors of the environment), lone heroes on the frontiers of the environmentalist versus development battle, advocates for a pristine and victimized nature, and entitled to their anger. For example, at a post-election executive meeting, members discuss the final public hearing on the new tree bylaw that has just taken place. In the process, they clearly enjoy vilifying and ridiculing the head of city planning:

> Member 1: That's the problem. [The planner] and his living documents.
>
> Chair: Yes. [laughs]
>
> Member 2: He's so pleasant when you talk to him, isn't he?
>
> Member 1: Yeah.
>
> Member 2: He's a weasel. [laughter]
>
> Member 1: That's a very good description of him, actually.
>
> Chair: Weasel.
>
> Member 1: I was trying to put my finger on it. (March 7, 2006)

Such aspersions are a common ritual of bonding and identity affirmation. They belong here to the master narrative of the environmentalist world and are important for the group's sense of identity and for their motivation and hope, even when they continue to express cynicism and question the point of their actions.

Eruptions of activist discourse, thus, often function to sustain an activist identity and the investment of passion in a cause. Such responses can reinforce the environmentalist mythos and reinvigorate identification with the passion and belief in their cause. They are an important "assertion" of a different set of relations of symbolic power, a "linguistic counter-legitimacy" expressed in a "space" where "dominant individuals are ... excluded, at least symbolically" (Bourdieu, 1991, p. 98). Eruptions of activist discourse are also often legitimate expressions of the "public disquiet" (Eden, 1996, p. 196) that is stirred by reports of environmental destruction and government inaction. They are a response to institutional inertia and deafness—a response that manifests as mistrust and urgency at the local level. These explanations may, in part, account for why there can be, in enduring struggles, the tense co-existence of both activist and civic discourses. They may also point to the critical role of marginal identities in postmodern change and to the valuing of the activist expressions of transgressive identities, which reflect a subversive and differently valued state of relations of symbolic power.

The risk for the group is that, in its struggle for the environment, as it reconstitutes itself in a changed participation framework, reconstructions of its activist identity may in turn, paradoxically, serve to contain its oppositional nature. The risk is that by reinforcing its activist identity as "difference," its marginality will become reinscribed, for example, in the mayor's words, as a "grass-roots" group. The risk is that such identifiers can become inserted in the expression of a political, unitary discourse, at once drawing the speaker's legitimacy from the group and performing an act of re-subjugation (Bourdieu, 1991, p. 129). As Kearney (2001) reminds us, the reproduction of difference arises not only through "institutions of inequality (the state and its agencies)" but it is also self-generated due to "the habitual actions of persons in their resistance to such structured inequality" (p. 261). The challenge for such groups is to "moderate the dialogic process" to achieve a net gain in the linguistic and political marketplace (Kearney, 2001, p. 276). Managing these identities involves the careful deployment of rhetorical-discursive strategies that maximize the gains derived from an institutional speaking position and minimize the losses incurred through the expressions of a transgressive discourse.

REFERENCES

Bakhtin, M. M. (1981). *The dialogic imagination: Four essays.* (M. Holquist, Ed.). Austin: University of Texas.

Bourdieu, P. (1991). *Language and symbolic power.* (J. B. Thompson, Ed.). Cambridge: Harvard University Press.

Cooper, M. (1996). Environmental rhetoric in the age of hegemonic politics: Earth First! and the Nature Conservancy. In C. G. Herndl & S. C. Brown (Eds.), *Green culture: Environmental rhetoric in contemporary America* (pp. 236-260). Madison: University of Wisconsin Press.

Depoe, P., & Delicath, J. W. (2004). Introduction. In S. P. Depoe, J. W. Delicath, & M. Aepli Elsenbeer (Eds.), *Communication and public participation in environmental decision making* (pp. 1-12). Albany: State University of New York Press.

Eden, S. (1996). Public participation in environmental policy: Considering scientific, counter-scientific and non-scientific contributions. *Public Understanding of Science, 5,* 183-204.

Foucault, M. (1972a). *The archaeology of knowledge.* A. M. Sheridan Smith, Trans. New York: Pantheon Books.

Foucault, M. (1972b). The discourse on language. Appendix to *The archaeology of knowledge* (A. M. Sheridan Smith, Trans.) (pp. 215-238). New York: Pantheon Books.

Goffman, E. (1981). *Forms of talk.* Philadelphia: University of Pennsylvania.

Gray, G., & Kusel, J. (1998, Winter). Changing the rules. *American Forests,* 27-31.

Gregory, S. (2001). Placing the politics of black class formation. In D. Holland & J. Lave (Eds.), *History in person: Enduring struggles, contentious practice, intimate identities* (pp. 137-170). Santa Fe: School of American Research Press.

Holland, D., Lachicotte, W., Jr., Skinner, D., & Cain, C. (1998). *Identity and agency in cultural worlds.* Cambridge: Harvard University Press.

Holland, D., & Lave, J. (2001). History in person: An introduction. In D. Holland & J. Lave (Eds.), *History in person: Enduring struggles, contentious practice, intimate identities* (pp. 3-36). Santa Fe: School of American Research Press.

Ingham, Z. (1996). Landscape, drama, and dissensus: The rhetorical education of Red Lodge, Montana. In C. G. Herndl & S. C. Brown (Eds.), *Green culture: Environmental rhetoric in contemporary America* (pp. 195-212). Madison: University of Wisconsin Press.

Kearney, M. (2001). Class and identity: The jujitsu of domination and resistance in Oaxacalifornia. In D. Holland & J. Lave (Eds.), *History in person: Enduring struggles, contentious practice, intimate identities* (pp. 247-281). Santa Fe: School of American Research Press.

Schwarze, S. (2004). Public participation and (failed) legitimation: The case of forest service rhetorics in the Boundary Waters Canoe Area. In S. P. Depoe, J. W. Delicath, & M.-F. A. Elsenbeer (Eds.), *Communication and public participation in environmental decision making* (pp. 137-156). Albany: State University of New York Press.

Senecah, S. (2004). The trinity of voice: The role of practical theory in planning and evaluating the effectiveness of environmental participatory processes. In S. P. Depoe, J. W. Delicath, & M.-F. A. Elsenbeer (Eds.), *Communication, and public participation in environmental decision making* (pp. 13-34). Albany: State University of New York Press.

Thompson, J. B. (Ed.) (1991). Editor's introduction. In P. Bourdieu, *Language as symbolic action* (pp. 1-31). Cambridge: Harvard University Press.

Walker, G. B. (2004). The roadless areas initiative as national policy: Is public participation an oxymoron? In S. P. Depoe, J. W. Delicath, & M. F. A. Elsenbeer (Eds.), *Communication and public participation in environmental decision making* (pp. 113-136). Albany: State University of New York Press.

Williams, B., & Matheny, A. R. (1995). *Democracy, dialogue, and environmental disputes: The contested languages of social regulation.* New Haven: Yale University Press. Wynne, B. (1992). Risk and social learning: Reification to engagement. In S. Krimsky & D. Golding (Eds.), *Social theories of risk* (pp. 275-300). London: Praeger.

7 MAKING LEGAL KNOWLEDGE IN GLOBAL DIGITAL ENVIRONMENTS: THE JUDICIAL OPINION AS REMIX

Martine Courant Rife

As a highly social knowledge-making practice, writing depends on the ability of authors to draw on, question, critique, build on, advance, or in other ways "remix" work produced by other writers. Accordingly, writing has long been a highly regulated social practice, with copyright laws striking a balance between the rights of authors and publishers to protect and benefit from their intellectual property on the one hand and their right to use existing work by other writers in order to produce their own work, that is, their right to the fair use of copyrighted works, on the other hand. In any society, much depends on this balance: Creativity, innovation, and knowledge production directly depend on both the rewards and recognition authors receive for their work and the extent to which they can access and build on existing work (DeVoss & Porter, 2006; Lessig, 2008; Rife, 2008).

In digital environments, however, writing undergoes important change because the current balance inscribed in existing copyright law is upset by the ease with which the Internet, as a set of global technologies, allows for the sharing and copying of files (DeVoss & Porter, 2006; Lessig, 2008; Rife, 2008). The ease with which files can be copied and shared allows for new forms of writing and, specifically, new ways of drawing on, combining, or "remixing" existing work in new ways and for new purposes. Although people have always drawn on each other's work to advance knowledge and to produce new cultural expression, digital technologies allow for new ways of bringing existing works together and making them speak to each other for new purposes, thus enabling new forms of creativity, cultural expression, and knowledge production (DeVoss & Porter, 2006; Lessig, 2008; Rife, 2008).

At the same time, concerns about legal repercussions for copyright infringement triggered by remix writing are growing exponentially (CCCC, 2009; Center for Social Media, 2009; DMCA Rulemaking, 2009; Lessig, 2008). In particular, the content industry, whose business model has long rested on holding the copyright to the creative and other work it distributes, has viewed the ease of file sharing enabled by digital technologies as a threat to its business model. As a result, the balance between the rights of copyright holders and those of users are being recalibrated in each national context—a highly contested and complex process of local legal knowledge making in response to global technological change.

As such, this process also raises an important question about the role of writing as a knowledge-making practice in legal settings: How does legal discourse work to arrive at the knowledge necessary in order to develop opinions and judgments in local jurisdictions when responding to the contestation surrounding global digital technologies? To address this question, this chapter examines the judicial opinion that justified Canada's Supreme Court ruling in CCH Canadian Ltd. v. Law Society of Upper Canada (2004), a case in which a group of publishers of legal materials, including the publisher CCH Canadian Ltd., sued the Law Society of Upper Canada, which maintains the Great Library of Toronto, for copyright infringement over the copy machines it provided for patron use as well as over copies of legal materials the library mailed out to patrons on request.

The case is of particular relevance for the question examined here for a number of reasons. To begin with, the case addresses the very question of how the balance between copyright protection and fair use, a balance that is critical to writing as a knowledge-making practice, is being renegotiated. The case is particularly important because, while originally concerned with copy machines, it has had wide-reaching implications for the regulation of file sharing through peer-to-peer technologies. For this and a number of other reasons, the case is widely considered a landmark case in copyright and fair dealings regulation in Canada and possibly worldwide. As Geist (2006) remarks, the unanimous court decision was "one of the strongest pro-user rights decisions from any high court in the world, showing what it means to do more than pay mere lip service to balance in copyright." Although the focus and the stature of the case alone render it highly relevant for analysis, as I illustrate in this chapter, the case most importantly demonstrates how legal writing—in this case, the judicial opinion—relies on innovative forms of global remixing by drawing on related legal cases, statutes, and regulations in other national jurisdictions in order to arrive at the globally informed but locally situated legal knowledge that underlies the court's decision to redefine Canadian fair dealing rights in a way that meets the needs of Canadians for the sharing, remixing, and collaborative creation of knowledge. In short, the case is important for examining not only how law shapes writing, but also how writing shapes law.

For this purpose, I first provide a context for the CCH decision, highlighting key developments in both U.S. and Canadian copyright and fair use regulation as they pertain to the case. I then provide a brief overview of the case, outlining some of its main achievements in striking a balance between copyright and user rights to fair dealings with copyrighted materials. To show how the court arrived at the knowledge needed to attain this achievement, I then briefly sketch the theoretical framework of intertextual analysis and remix writing that then informs my analysis of Justice McLachlin's judicial opinion. I conclude with considerations for legal writing as a knowledge-making practice in response to global digital technologies as well as with implications for the teaching of writing.

COPYRIGHT AND FAIR USE OR FAIR DEALING IN CANADA AND IN THE U.S.

In both Canada and the U.S., copyright law has long given exclusive rights to copy, distribute, perform, display, and make derivative works to the copyright holder for all types of writing, including literature, user manuals, creative nonfiction, as long as that writing is "original" and "fixed." While copyright law gives exclusive rights to copyright holders, in both Canada and the U.S., exceptions to copyright law are provided by way of fair dealing and fair use, respectively. These exceptions allow for limited uses of copyrighted work under certain conditions without the copyright holder's permission. Traditionally, however, Canada and the U.S. have taken different approaches to fair use. The U.S. provided a broad definition of fair use while Canada developed its fair dealing doctrine on a case-by-case basis.

In the United States, the fair use doctrine was introduced in Section 107 of Title 17, United States Code (U.S.C.) as part of the Copyright Act of 1976. Fair use in Section 107 contains what is commonly referred to as the four-factor test. This test serves as a heuristic that is applied to individual situations, allowing one to determine whether or not a use is "fair" and therefore potentially to avoid copyright infringement. In the U.S., the four factors include the "purpose and character of the use," the "nature of the copyrighted work," the "amount and substantiality" of the portion used in comparison to the work as a whole, and the impact the use has on the copyright holder's "potential market" (Section 107, Title 17, U.S. Code).

Importantly for the purpose of this chapter, although not explicitly acknowledged, the U.S. fair use doctrine very closely reflects the UK opinion on the issue of fair use from a few years earlier: Hubbard v. Vosper (1972). Hubbard v. Vosper involved the case of Mr. Cyril Vosper, who, after becoming disillusioned with his indoctrination into the Church of Scientology, wrote a book critiquing Scientology. The criticism involved incorporating lengthy passages of Scientology literature, but the Hubbard court nonetheless found fair use. In 1972, the U.S. had not yet created the fair use doctrine in Section 107, since that statute was part of the Copyright Act of 1976. Prior to that time, the U.S. relied on U.S. case law to define fair use. The UK's Hubbard analysis therefore preceded Section 107, and appears to have been leveraged in the drafting of Section 107, although the U.S. statute offers no attribution to Hubbard or the UK. Of course, attribution is not normally a component of statutes or legislation, so it would be difficult to prove or disprove empirically whether or not the Hubbard opinion was expressly referenced without completing a full-study of the legislative record, to the extent such legislative record exists. This kind of deep research into the origins, history, and cross-cultural influence within a country's law and judicial opinions is an area of study and one that seems to be expanding (see for example Black, 2008). The Hubbard opinion states,

> It is impossible to define what is 'fair dealing'. It must be a question of degree. You must consider first the number and extent of the quotations and extracts. Are they altogether too many and too long to be fair? Then you must consider the use made of them. If they are used as a basis for comment, criticism or review, that may be a fair dealing. If they are used to convey the same information as the author, for a rival purpose, that may be unfair. Next, you must consider the proportions. To take long extracts and attach short comments may be unfair. But, short extracts and long comments may be fair. Other considerations may come to mind also.

Section 107 echoes much of the Hubbard analysis: Hubbard's "number and extent" connects to the U.S. "amount and substantiality." The "use made of them" maps onto Section 107's "nature of the use." "Rival purpose" connects to 107's "effect on market." While not stated in this passage, important to the Hubbard court was the nature of the copyrighted work. In this case, the Scientology literature contained material that raised public safety issues. Therefore the Hubbard court found a public interest in exposing these issues. In addition to drawing upon the Hubbard opinion in shaping its fair use statute back in 1976, the U.S. also appropriated and remediated the English term "fair abridgement" from a line of English cases of the 1700's (Duhl, 2004), localizing the concept into its doctrine of "fair use" (see also Rife, 2007). The point is that even the U.S.'s fair use doctrine has been internationally influenced, although it might not appear so from simply reading the statute.

Canadian copyright and fair use regulation differs in important ways from that in the U.S. For example, Canada maintains a private copyright exemption—balanced by collecting a tax on media products that is used to compensate copyright holders. Having the foresight to realize that private copying by users could not be stopped with a mere law, in 1997 Canadian law via parliamentary effort formally made private copying legal (Copyright Act Part VIII). In return for consumers' right to make private copies, a levy is added to blank recording materials such as CDs and cassette tapes.

Moreover, in contrast to the U.S., Canada originally developed a piecemeal approach to fair dealing by crafting detailed copyright exceptions for various uses. Defined in great detail in the Canadian Copyright Act of 1985, user rights were localized in a list of exceptions to copyright protection characterized as a "ragbag of simple instances" and a "piecemeal approach" (Geist, 2006; Vaver, 2004). Pre-CCH rights to fair dealings in copyrighted work were an exhaustive list of exceptions continuing on (and on) for several pages, listing extremely specific exceptions and then subjecting them to a multitude of limitations. For example, excepted from copyright infringement are educational uses involving dry-erase boards, flip charts, overhead projectors, communicating or performing copyrighted materials for purposes of testing, and various other kinds of live performances on the premises of the educational institution, but they are subject to a variety of additional limitations. The piecemeal approach was complicated, and it remained difficult for Canadian users to know whether the copying and use of educational materials was legal or infringing. This piecemeal approach likely developed as exceptions were continually needed in light of the development and dissemination of new technologies.

The regulation of these new technologies is of particularly great concern to the content industry, including publishers, the music industry, and the motion picture industry, whose business model depends on holding the copyright to creative works for distribution, a model that is challenged by the ease of distribution of such work in digital environments (DeVoss & Porter, 2006; Lessig, 2008; Rife, 2008). Accordingly, the industry, with its associations, such as the Motion Picture Association of America and the Recording Industry Association of America, has engaged in massive efforts to influence the regulation of these technologies—as Bazerman (this volume) notes, to "bend" these technologies back in line with established business models—to make peer-to-peer (P2P) file sharing illegal in the U.S. These efforts have included a wide range of strategies, including legislative lobbying as well as massive lawsuits with the goal of having file sharing technologies declared illegal, lawsuits whose judicial opinions then have wide ranging precedent both for how legislation is interpreted and applied as well as for how future lawsuits are decided. Key examples of U.S. cases involving P2P filesharing technologies are the cases of Napster and Grokster (A&M Records v. Napster, 2001; Metro-Goldwyn-Mayer Studios Inc., et al. v. Grokster, 2005). The Napster court basically said that because a centralized server was used, the technology producer had actual or constructive knowledge that illegal file sharing was taking place. So, that judicial opinion created a possible loophole for file sharing technologies that did not use a centralized server. This is what Grokster tried to accomplish. Grokster users used the Grokster file sharing technology by downloading the software and then sharing from computer to computer rather than through a centralized server. However, in Grokster the court said the technology producer/distributor cannot purposely turn a blind eye to illegal activity just to evade the law. So, that type of file sharing software was made illegal as well. Following Grokster, there was a legal loophole because, of course, U.S. courts have jurisdiction only over their own territories, for the most part, and so the P2P innovation just moved to Canada or offshore (Samuelson, 2004; for a detailed analysis of the P2P file sharing cases in the U.S., see Rife, 2006).

Ultimately, the judicial opinions of Napster and Grokster did not accomplish their goal, which was to eliminate technologies that permit "illegal" file sharing. Illegal file sharing is still occurring. Because in cyberspace geographical locations do not matter as much, the producers of dual-use technologies (i.e. technologies that can be used for both illegal and legal activities, like copy machines) just move to offshore locations, or in this case, to Canada. All that Napster accomplished was to spur innovation of file sharing technologies that avoid the reasoning in Napster. All that Grokster did was move P2P innovation to Canada or offshore. People are still engaging in what the U.S. deems "illegal" file sharing. It is "illegal" in the U.S., but not in Canada.

These efforts by the content industry to influence the regulation of the copyright and fair use balance continue worldwide. Example international treaties/organizations covering this area include TRIPS (Trade-Related Aspects of Intellectual Property Rights, 1994) and WIPO (World Intellectual Property Organization). However, Canada has not imitated some of the more corporate-friendly/copyright holder-friendly legal stances that the U.S. has. For example, Canada has not yet implemented a law similar to the DMCA (Digital Millenium Copyright Act, 1998), illustrating what is perceived by many to be Canada's more pro-user rights stance (as compared to the U.S., for example). Just recently, Canada was placed on the U.S.'s priority watch list in the "Annual 301 Report"

(Geist, 2009; Viana, 2009), an annual report unilaterally evaluating U.S. trade partners' intellectual property regulations by the Office of the U.S. Trade Representative, with implications for possible trade sanctions against Canada. The pressures from lobbying influences continue to increase for Canada. And it is in light of these developments that the CCH case becomes even more interesting in that it shows how the judicial opinion has worked to protect Canadian rights for sharing knowledge despite the interests of the U.S. content industry.

CCH CANADIAN LTD. V. LAW SOCIETY OF UPPER CANADA (2004).

In CCH, the publishers CCH Canadian Ltd., Thomson Canada Ltd., and Canada Law Book Inc. (CCH) sued the Law Society of Upper Canada, a professional society that regulates the legal profession in Ontario and maintains the Great Library in Toronto, for copyright infringement. The publishers, all publishing legal materials, filed a lawsuit because the Great Library, as is common practice in many libraries both in the U.S. and in Canada, provided self-service copy machines in the library and sent out copies of select texts (articles, chapters, case summaries) on the request of patrons to improve public access to the law. The publishers argued that the Great Library's practices of providing copy machines and of copying and distributing copyrighted texts were both direct copyright infringement and authorization for library patrons to commit copyright infringing behaviors. Specifically, the publishers argued that the Law Society expressly acknowledged the infringing use of the copy machines through posting a notice with the copy machines indicating that the Law Society was not responsible for copyright infringing uses. According to section 27(1) of the Canada Copyright Act (1985), "It is an infringement of copyright for any person to do, without the consent of the owner of the copyright, anything that by this Act only the owner of the copyright has the right to do," such as reproducing the work. The publishers argued that since the Great Library maintained copy machines, it violated the copyright act because it authorized users to infringe on the copyrights of others. The Law Society denied liability, arguing that providing a copy machine in the library was not an authorization for others to infringe and that copying texts for research purposes in these limited circumstances was fair dealing. After the lower courts struggled with this issue (holding mainly in favor of the publishers), the Canadian Supreme Court ruled in favor of the Law Society.

The CCH ruling was a landmark case in Canadian copyright legislation, with far reaching implications for fair use not only in Canada, but also worldwide. Although there are many ways in which the ruling was revolutionary, for the purpose of this chapter, three reasons stand out in particular: First, in its holding, the CCH court made a critical policy statement about the purpose of Canadian copyright law as that of "balance[ing] the public interest in promoting the encouragement and dissemination of works of the arts and intellect and obtaining a just reward for the creator" (p. 16). In line with this purpose, the CCH court localized its definition of fair dealing by dramatically broadening the concept away from Canada's former statutory piecemeal approach as well as exceeding fair use standards in other jurisdictions, specifically in the United States. The CCH court stated that the fair dealing exception is "always available," again pushing against a construct of fair dealing as a list of narrow and limited exceptions, or a ragbag of user rights. The user must only show two elements in order to be within fair dealing: that the purpose of the use was for research or private study and that the use was fair.

Second, the court addressed the vital question of whether the provision of a technology (in this case, the copy machine) that can be used in dual ways, that is both in legal ways—i.e., for copying under the exceptions for fair dealings—and in copyright infringing ways, automatically constitutes the authorization of users to infringe on copyright and thus makes the provider of the technology responsible for copyright infringement. This question is an important focus for the content industry in its effort to ban technologies that challenge its established business models as attempted in its lawsuit against Grokster. In Grokster, software was provided, which, according to the U.S. Supreme Court, "induced" users to infringe; in CCH, the suspect technology was the copy machine sitting in the library. The Canadian trial court had not decided the issue and the Federal Court of Appeals, relying on an Australian case, decided in favor of the publishers holding that "the Law Society implicitly sanctioned, approved or countenanced copyright infringement of the publishers' works by failing to control copying and instead merely posting a notice indicating that the Law Society was not responsible for infringing copies made by the users of these machines" (CCH, 2004, p. 32). The CCH court rejected the Federal Court of Appeals' holding and acted wisely in limiting the definition of authorization. The CCH court argued that rather than assuming illegal behavior, technology providers and courts should equally be able to assume legal behavior:

> 38. "Authorize" means to "sanction, approve and countenance": ... Countenance in the context of authorizing copyright infringement must be understood in its strongest dictionary meaning, namely, "[g]ive approval to; sanction, permit; favour, encourage": see The New Shorter Oxford English Dictionary (1993), vol. 1, at p. 526.... a person does not authorize

> infringement by authorizing the mere use of equipment that could be used to infringe copyright. Courts should presume that a person who authorizes an activity does so only so far as it is in accordance with the law: Muzak, supra. This presumption may be rebutted if it is shown that a certain relationship or degree of control existed between the alleged authorizer and the persons who committed the copyright infringement .... (p. 31)

The court further argued that rather than presuming illegal behavior, "courts should presume that a person who authorizes an activity does so only so far as it is in accordance with the law" (p. 31). This is the opposite assumption to that in Grokster. In Grokster, the court implied that the burden was on the dual use technology producer/distributor to show that there was at least some legal use. In contrast, the CCH court said that regarding one who authorizes an activity which could potentially be copyright infringing (i.e. copying at a library), the assumption should be that the authorized use is meant to be legal unless there is evidence otherwise.

Third, the CCH ruling was significant through its considerable legal force as a judicial opinion. As defined by *Black's Law Dictionary* (1979), a judicial opinion is "the statement by a judge or court of the decision reached in regards to a cause tried or argued before them, expounding the law as applied to the case, and detailing the reasons upon which the judgment is based" (p. 985). Judicial opinions differ from legal opinions, which are crafted by an attorney in response to a client request and serve to assess the possible legal liabilities for a client's future behaviors. A judicial opinion, in contrast, is crafted by a judge or court in deciding the outcome of a legal case or trial. Supreme Court judicial opinions in both the U.S. and Canada are particularly powerful regulatory documents because they set precedent for their respective country's lower courts as these must follow the holdings espoused via writing in the higher court opinions. In addition, they dictate the rules that must be followed by the citizens they govern. Judicial opinions extend and refine legislation by interpreting it and by determining how it is to be understood and applied in the lower courts.

The knowledge produced in judicial opinions therefore often has far reaching consequences, since the law defers to precedent. That is, in order to prevent laws from changing too quickly, a court in Canada and/or the U.S., will look to the decisions made by previous courts (within its jurisdiction) on the same particular issue. Unless a court can distinguish the current litigants' fact situation from that of previous cases, the court will follow previous court holdings because of the importance of following precedent. The CCH judicial opinion, for example, laid the foundation for BMG Canada Inc. In BMG Canada Inc. v. John Doe

(2004) the largest members of Canada's recording industry brought a motion seeking disclosure from five ISPs (Internet service providers) of the 29 identities of users downloading copyrighted music files by way of P2P file-sharing services offered by KaZaA and iMesh. The court held in favor of "John Doe," denying BMG the right to discover the names. Judge Finckenstein stated that simply making available a folder or file that others might share is not enough to meet the heavy intent required to make private copying illegal under CCH. Addressing the issue of authorization, Judge Finckenstein stated, "Before it constitutes [the affirmative act of authorizing] distribution, there must be a positive act by the owner of the shared directory, such as sending out the copies or advertising that they are available for copying" (BMG Canada Inc. v. John Doe, 2004). Judge Finckenstein followed CCH by creating a presumption that an "authorization" of an activity, such as file sharing or the provision of copying machines, is legal unless proven otherwise. He states,

> I cannot see a real difference between a library that places a photocopy machine in a room full of copyrighted material and a computer user that places a personal copy on a shared directory linked to a P2P service. In either case the preconditions to copying and infringement are set up but the element of authorization is missing. (BMG Canada Inc. v. John Doe, 2004)

The Canadian stance here, then, is in contrast to the U.S. Grokster decision because the BMG case held that private file sharing of music by users is not copyright infringement. As Tabatabai (2005) points out, this decision was particularly remarkable in light of Canada's previous focus on protecting copyright holder rights.

Because of their strong regulatory force, judicial opinions often also receive both considerablescholarly and media attention nationally and internationally, thus often becoming paradigmatic locations where they may not be precedential. For example, when P2P technologies were made virtually illegal in the U.S., Canada opened its doors with BMG. As the Napster case was decided, the headlines across Canada noted that under BMG, file sharing was legal in Canada (Borland, 2004; McFarland, 2004; Online, 2004; Webb, 2004).

Accordingly, the knowledge created in a written judicial opinion often serves (on the global level) as a non-precedential paradigm, open to appropriation by allies or competing sovereign entities. When the U.S. produced Napster and Grokster opinions, holding that file sharing service providers were indeed secondarily liable for the copyright infringing behavior of users, they provided examples for other jurisdictions. When Canada churned out the CCH opinion, it provided an example for other jurisdictions as well. Canada's CCH opinion was particularly significant as there currently is no international fair use doctrine, and many countries do not currently have such a doctrine for their local jurisdiction. Having produced one of the most important user-rights oriented fair-dealings statements, the CCH opinion provides a particularly powerful example of addressing the ways in which global digital technologies upset the existing balance. Perhaps more importantly, because judicial opinions reflect the ideology of their originating jurisdiction (Bowrey, 2005), the CCH opinion also makes an important statement in affirming the rights of Canadian citizens to fair dealings for sharing knowledge, thus resisting the long-standing pressures of the content industry on Canada to establish a copyright regime similar to that in the United States.

The considerable significance of the CCH judicial opinion raises the question of how the opinion worked to arrive at the knowledge necessary for this achievement. As I argue, the CCH judicial opinion relies on remix, a judicious process of considering, rejecting, and weaving together legal texts from other jurisdictions. To analyze and illustrate how this process unfolds in CCH, I draw on Lessig's (2008) notion of remix as well as on the concept of intertextuality as articulated by Bazerman (2004).

REMIX AND INTERTEXTUALITY

As Lawrence Lessig (2008) points out,

> [Remix] is the essence of good writing in the law. A great brief seems to say nothing on its own. Everything is drawn from cases that went before, presented as if the argument now presented is in fact nothing new. Here again, the words of others are used to make a point the others didn't directly make. Old cases are remixed. The remix is meant to do something new. (p. 52)

Writing in legal contexts has always depended on the techniques of remix, but that fact has become more visible with the attention to remix writing afforded by digital environments. Due to the digital age, those specializing in writing are acknowledging the remixed nature of most texts, especially since the Internet allows quick access to information and others' work.

> However, much [digital] writing is done ... collaboratively, across time and space and documents ... remix [is] a key practice for invention and composing. That is, writing by appro-

> priation—taking bits, pieces, and ideas and compiling and remixing them in new and innovative ways. Sometimes these acts of appropriation ... are in a spirit of sharing and within an environment where this use is expected. (Rife & DeVoss, in press

As Lessig (2008) points out, with the history of judicial opinions "plagiarizing" attorney briefs, it appears that these acts of appropriation may be "in a spirit of sharing" and in a discourse community where such uses are expected. In non-legal digital-writing environments, the theory around how to understand appropriation and textual sharing is still being developed (as is clear from the scholarly attention to student plagiarism and remix—See Rife & DeVoss, in press, for example).

Remix is a term used with respect to digital writing, but it is connected to our understanding of intertextuality. Intertextuality is a term that was mainly developed for use with respect to alphabetic texts. As Bazerman (2004) explains, "almost every word and phrase we use we have heard or seen before ... We create our texts out of the sea of former texts that surround us, the sea of language we live in ... The relation each text has to the texts surrounding it, we call intertextuality" (pp. 83-84). By taking "bits, pieces, and ideas and compiling and remixing them in new and innovative ways" (Rife & DeVoss, in press), writers create an end product that is intertextual because that end product, such as the judicial opinion, is in relationship to the texts surrounding it. As Lessig (2008) points out, legal writing is remix writing, and always has been, because it draws from the "sea of former texts," those precedents and documents, those opinions, that have come before (see also Prior, 2004).

In examining the extent to which a piece of writing is remixed, one needs to trace the textual origins of that writing. Tracing the origins of writing, or from where a piece of writing derived, is "intertextual analysis" (Prior, 2004, p. 168) due to the fact that such tracing will provide a snapshot of that particular text's "intertextual" nature.

Judicial writing practices as impacted by remix culture can be productively researched by examining the similarities and differences between the texts/laws drawn upon, i.e. their intertextuality. By definition, remix writing takes the old, the existing, and mixes it in with the new in order to create something novel. Both the past and the present appear simultaneously in a judicial opinion—simultaneously, the remix has an element of anticipation—anticipating the future (Rife, 2008).

In digital spaces like creative commons, it often remains visible that many authors have contributed to a text. In describing a story of remixing sound tracks in the creative commons Web site, Lawrence Lessig (2008) details how it is clearly visible that the remixed track that is eventually created is authored by many: "People were asked to upload tracks. As those tracks got remixed, the new tracks would keep a reference to the old. So you could see, for example, that a certain track was made by remixing two other tracks. And you could see that four other people had remixed that track" (p. 16). In judicial opinions written in standard alphabetic prose (or in statutes and legislation as I mentioned earlier), that multi-authorship is not visible unless a citation is expressly given. It is commonly known that U.S. opinions "plagiarize" attorney briefs in a major way (See Durscht, 1996). Because U.S. courts have access to many countries' judicial opinions and because these issues are now widely covered by media watchdog groups such as the Intellectual Property Watch and Global Voices Online, it is simply not possible that such forces have no bearing on the knowledge produced in U.S. judicial opinions.

REMIX AND INTERTEXTUALITY IN THE CCH JUDICIAL OPINION

In CCH the court remixed the laws of several nations, and moved closer to Section 107, the U.S. fair use clause (Geist, 2006; Gervais, 2004; Scassa, 2004; Tabatabai, 2005; Vaver, 2004), while distancing itself from the U.S. stance on authorization and inducement.

Remixing Fair Dealing

The CCH opinion refers to and takes bits and pieces of the "law in the United States" in crafting an open-ended definition of fair dealing, setting forth an analysis, remixing the four-factor test of the U.S. fair use law contained in Section 107. In CCH, the court explained its new vision of fair dealing in Canada. Drawing upon U.S. fair use, the opinion states that examinations for fair dealing should include examining the purpose, character, and amount of the dealing plus alternatives to the dealing, the nature of the copyrighted work, and the "effect of the dealing on the work" (CCH Canadian Ltd. v. Law Society of Upper Canada, 2004). As Figure 1 shows, the CCH analysis of fair dealing literally maps onto the U.S. fair use analysis, illustrating the intertextuality between U.S. fair use and the new version of fair dealing in Canada.

As illustrated in Figure 1, the first and second factors listed in CCH map onto the first factor in Section 107, while the third CCH factor, amount of dealing, maps onto the third factor listed in 107. There is no "alternatives to the dealing" factor listed in Section 107, but CCH's sixth factor maps onto the fourth factor in Section 107. While "alternatives to the dealing" might initially appear to map onto U.S. market effect issues (is legal licensing available?), instead the CCH opinion makes clear that the availability of licensing should not be a factor

Canada's Fair Use Factors per CCH	United States Fair Use Four Factors per §107
(1) the **purpose** of the dealing;	(1) the **purpose** and **character** of the use, including whether such use is of commercial nature or is for nonprofit educational **purposes**;
(2) the **character** of the dealing;	(2) the **nature** of the copyrighted **work**;
(3) the **amount** of the dealing;	(3) the **amount** and substantiality of the portion used in relation to the copyrighted **work** as a whole; and
(4) alternatives to the dealing;	
(5) the **nature** of the **work**; and	
(6) the **effect** of the dealing on the **work**.	(4) the **effect** of the use upon the potential market for or value of the copyrighted **work**.

Figure 1: The Canadian fair use analysis maps onto the U.S. fair use analysis.

when considering "alternatives." The opinion states the availability of licensing is not relevant to a fair use interpretation because otherwise, the copyright holder's limited monopoly over use of material would extend too far in scope against the need to protect user rights. Canada's version of fair dealing and the U.S. version of fair use are now intertextual because Canada has remixed the U.S. fair use statute and created something drawing upon Section 107, but at the same time, created something specific for Canada.

With respect to library staff copying material for patrons and the provision of self-serve copy machines in the library, the court said because many library materials did not circulate and patrons lived outside the Toronto area, if copying was not permitted, patrons would have to do all of their research and note taking at the library at great inconvenience. The court found this was not reasonable, and therefore alternatives to the dealing were not viable. This particular consideration is fairly unique to Canada in a U.S.-Canadian comparison. But overall, the two fair dealing/fair use analyses fold in together almost completely and are thus intertextual; words in common are "purpose," "character," "amount," "nature," "work," and "effect" in addition to the numerals in parentheses and the use of semi-colons between factors. This is a prime example of remix writing techniques used by Judge McLachlin; the CCH judicial opinion remixes, or identifies with U.S. law, but simultaneously differentiates itself from Section 107 by making changes and additions, thus crafting something new and innovative.

However, the CCH court openly references not just the United States, but also British and Australian law for examples. And so, this explicit mentioning and stitching together of other countries' cases and rules-of-law might be illustrative of not so much a power imbalance, but instead the innovative Canadian judicial practice of openly and honestly acknowledging the collaborative nature of writing, the unavoidable "remixing" process that takes place when new laws are written, even at the Supreme Court level. As many writing specialists in non-legal settings are now developing an understanding about remix writing through research, so too, the Canadian CCH opinion seems to embrace the idea that all writing is collaborative, even if in some cases attribution is not appropriate or expected.

The Canadian approach in CCH is unique in comparison to U.S. approaches in that the Canadian court openly references paradigms of fair use/fair dealing from other countries. In the research I have conducted specifically in the area of U.S. copyright law over the last five years, as well as in the legal opinions I have read since I graduated from law school almost 25 years ago, I have not noticed the U.S. courts, in copyright or other contexts, citing the laws of other countries as openly as the CCH court did. This is one reason why my first impression of the CCH opinion was astonishment at how open the court was in its strategy of drawing upon and evaluating the laws of other countries. U.S. Supreme Court Judge Scalia has made it a political point to openly state how inappropriate it is, in his opinion, to look at foreign law in the context of U.S. Constitutional interpretation (Dodge, 2006). However, the willingness of the U.S. Supreme Court to draw upon foreign laws is certainly an important area for further research (See Black, 2008), and especially so now that Barack Obama has been elected and may change the political shape of the U.S. Supreme Court through appointments. Clearly, the issue of whether or not U.S. Supreme Court judicial opinions should cite foreign law is a political topic that has been around since the early days of the United States. The current Supreme Court judges do not agree on this point. Here is an excerpt on this debate from a speech given by Justice Ginsberg in 2006. She explains,

> Justice Scalia counsels: The Court "should cease putting forth foreigners' views as part of the reasoned basis of its decisions. To invoke alien law when it agrees with one's own thinking, and ignore it otherwise, is not reasoned decision making, but sophistry."
>
> Another trenchant critic, Seventh Circuit U.S. Court of Appeals Judge Richard Posner, commented not long ago: "To cite foreign law as authority is to flirt with the discredited ... idea

of a universal natural law; or to suppose fantastically that the world's judges constitute a single, elite community of wisdom and conscience." (Ginsberg, 2006)

Admitting that Judge Posner is correct in that foreign judicial opinions are not precedential in the sense that they are not authoritative for U.S. judges, Ginsberg argues that foreign laws can serve as examples and paradigms. Ginsberg states,

> They can add to the store of knowledge relevant to the solution of trying questions. Yes, we should approach foreign legal materials with sensitivity to our differences, deficiencies, and imperfect understanding, but imperfection, I believe, should not lead us to abandon the effort to learn what we can from the experience and good thinking foreign sources may convey. (Ginsberg, 2006)

It appears that the CCH strategy sides more with Ginsberg's outlook on this issue than with Scalia's.

After identifying with U.S. approaches to fair use/fair dealing, CCH then differentiates its own position, creating a fair dealing doctrine that is uniquely Canadian. However, the differentiation in CCH also leaves telltale signs of what might be a power imbalance between copyright regimes in the U.S. and Canada. In the opinion the word "U.S." appears five times, "American" three times, and "United States" three times either in reference to U.S. case law, or as Judge McLachlin explicitly compares her moves to those in the U.S. In other words, the U.S. presence in CCH looms large. This issue is worthy of further exploration since I have read innumerable U.S. legal opinions over the last couple decades and found almost no mention of Canadian laws, nor the laws of other countries (of course in early U.S. opinions English law is often cited).

REMIXING AUTHORIZATION AND INDUCEMENT

As mentioned earlier, Canada's legal term "authorization" maps onto the U.S. term "inducement." By looking at the laws and practices of other countries, the Canadian judge implicitly acknowledged the inherent social construction and collaboratively-authored nature of all texts. Ultimately the court created something new in its remix by reshaping the law. It rejected the Australian stance on authorization, stating that it went too far in shifting the balance favoring copyright holders as opposed to user rights. It qualified its holding by noting that no evidence showed actual infringing use of copy machines and therefore the presumption that copyrights were being infringed was equal to the presumption that they were not. Finally, in a discussion similar to the Grokster discussion of vicarious liability, the CCH court noted that the Law Society and the Great Library had no duty to control the actions of patrons. Ultimately, CCH came to a different conclusion than the Grokster court. In Grokster, the peer-to-peer software provider was held secondarily liable. In CCH, the library was not held liable for patron actions. The CCH court rejected the Federal Court of Appeals' holding that the posting of a notice above the copy machine requesting users not to infringe acted as "express acknowledgment" that copyright infringement was occurring. Thus, Canada took a clear stance in opposition to U.S. media-industry interests.

While the Canadian court's discussion of "authorization" of copyright infringement is similar to the U.S. development of secondary liability examinations in copyright infringement contexts such as expressed in Grokster, the CCH court did not look to U.S. law in its discussion, but did create a remix in its opinion by openly referring to Australian case law and British practice, along with previous Canadian holdings. Not only did Canada adopt and surpass U.S. fair use, the Canadian court strategy here again is innovative. The Canadian courts appear to carefully consider legal measures around the world, and then select, stitch together, and remix the very best parts.

This remix approach allowed the CCH court to anticipate carefully possible future conditions under the effect of globalization when it narrowed what was considered "authorization" of another's infringing behaviors. Instead, the CCH court could have limited its definition of authorization to just copy machines in libraries, but was smart by leaving the notion of "authorization" a little uncertain and open-ended, thus leaving more room for interpretation of future events under the effect of globalization and in light of the affordances of digital writing environments. By creating something novel in its definition of authorization, the Canadian court was innovative by openly considering the legal measures in other sovereign states in order to inform its own decisions.

CONCLUSION—IMPLICATIONS FOR LEGAL WRITING AS A KNOWLEDGE-MAKING PRACTICE AND FOR THE TEACHING OF WRITING

Law, and specifically legal writing, has a role in regulating writing as a knowledge-making practice in global digital environments. Writing shapes law. Regardless of the form it takes, all writing involves some level of remix, and legal writing is no exception. The CCH judicial opinion is innovative in both its willingness to adapt to a new age, and in the creative way it pieces together the laws and ideas from other countries to craft something uniquely Canadian.

They say that history repeats itself. If copyright machines were outlawed, I imagine we might revisit the times of monks and medieval scribes. In the Middle Ages, even though the church was heavily involved in the production of knowledge via the written text, "The copying of books was also slow, tedious, and very time-consuming" (Yu, 2006, p. 7). It took years for a scribe to complete a "fine" manuscript that included colored initials and art work. Yu (2006) writes,

> When Bishop Leofric took over the Exeter Cathedral in 1050, he found only five books in its library. Despite immediately establishing a scriptorium of skilled workers, his crew managed to produce only sixty-six books in the twenty-two years before the bishop's death in 1072. Likewise, although the Library of

> Cambridge University had a remarkable collection of 122 books in 1424, it labored for a half-century to increase the number to 330. (p. 7)

This example is a small illustration that collapses time, giving context to how integral technology, like copy machines, is to the production of knowledge. CCH contains this wisdom. Not only has Canada adopted and even exceeded U.S. protection of user rights via CCH, but, in contrast to the U.S., Canada deems private use not copyright infringing.

Like the court in CCH, judges working in networked environments must be able to craft language and texts that anticipate effects of globalization, fast information streams, changing technologies, language and texts that are not too open-ended and not too specific (piecemeal). This is a challenge to all judges who remix laws from other countries in order to create something new.

Because the issues decided in CCH are at the heart of education, research, and writing, like authors such as DeVoss and Porter (2006), I argue that writing teachers should maintain awareness of current copyright developments and should also make their students aware of these issues. Also, as we move forward in the digital age, mapping some of our understandings and research in the area of intertextuality and intertextual analysis onto our developing theories of remix writing might prove generative. As I have illustrated in this chapter, by meshing these two concepts and using this frame to think about remix writing and intertextuality in the context of internationally circulating judicial opinions, new understandings and new knowledge may develop. Certainly, there are political issues that arise when one considers why one court might openly attribute another, and why another court might have reservations about doing so (as evidenced, for example, by the debate between Ginsberg and Scalia). These issues in the context of legal writing may inform how we understand remix writing, attribution, and intertextuality in more local settings, such as our writing classrooms.

Using comparative techniques to teach differences and similarities between new texts and old texts, to examine the process of remix, to examine intertextuality in new contexts including legal forums, and to raise the issue of power and politics in the strategies of remix writing itself, gives students an awareness of how complicated digital writing might be from a legal standpoint (see also Yancey, 2009). In gaining increased awareness of these issues, it is generative for composition teachers to explore judicial opinions using the tools that they always have—examining rhetorical turns taken by judges. Such explorations provide opportunities to examine the power of writing.

Copyright law and fair use/fair dealing are important to writing teachers and their students in the digital age because these legal concepts shape knowledge-making practices (Rife, 2007). Copyright law, law that deals specifically with writing, shapes our classroom practices as well as how (and whether) field knowledge is constructed, whether we acknowledge this or not (Durack, 2006; Westbrook, 2006).

Copyright law is important to writing teachers and researchers because such law attempts to control the process and product with which we are most concerned: writing. For educators, fair dealing/use is crucial in order to teach and in order to encourage student learning. It follows then that copyright should be taught in writing classes, and along this trajectory, it will also be productive to examine the law itself as writing, and how the law-as-knowledge is constructed by writing, thus illuminating the power that can be achieved through the remix, creation, and circulation of texts such as judicial opinions, in global contexts.

REFERENCES

A&M Records, Inc. v. Napster, Inc, 239 F. 3d 1004 (9th Cir. 2001). Retrieved from http://www.law.cornell.edu/copyright/cases/239_F3d_1004.htm

Bazerman, C. (2004). Intertextuality: How texts rely on other texts. In C. Bazerman & P. Prior (Eds.), *What writing does and how it does it: An introduction to analyzing texts and textual practices* (pp. 83-96). Mahwah, NJ: Lawrence Erlbaum.

Black, R. C. (2008, January). *A cosmopolitan U.S. Supreme Court? Analyzing foreign law citation in the court's written opinions.* Paper presented at the annual meeting of the Southern Political Science Association, Hotel Intercontinental, New Orleans, LA.

Black, H. C. (1979). *Black's law dictionary with pronunciations* (5th ed.). St. Paul, MN: West Publishing Co.

BMG Canada Inc. v. John Doe, 3 F.C.R. 241 (Trial Div.) (Can. 2004). Retrieved from http://www.canlii.org/en/ca/fct/doc/2004/2004fc488/2004fc488.html

Borland, J. (2004, Mar. 31). Judge: File sharing legal in Canada.CNET News.com. Retrieved from http://news.com.com/2100-1027-5182641.html

Bowrey, K. (2005). *Law & internet culture.* Cambridge: Cambridge University Press.

Canada Copyright Act, C-42 (1985). Retrieved from http://laws.justice.gc.ca/en/ShowFullDoc/cs/C-42//20090615/en

CCCC. (2009). The remix: Revisit, rethink, revise, renew. Annual Conference. Retrieved from http://www.ncte.org/cccc/conv

CCH Canadian Ltd. v. Law Society of Upper Canada, SCC 13, 30 C.P.R. (4th) 1 (2004).

Center for Social Media. (2009). Remix culture: Fair use is your friend. Retrieved from http://www.centerforsocialmedia.org/videos/fair_use_is_friend/

DeVoss, D. N., & Porter, J. E. (2006). Why Napster matters to writing: File-sharing as a new ethic of digital delivery. *Computers and Composition, 23*(2), 178-210.

Digital Millennium Copyright Act, 112 Stat. 2860 (1998). Retrieved from http://www.copyright.gov/legislation/dmca.pdf

DMCA Rulemaking. (2009). U.S. Copyright Office. Retrieved from http://www.copyright.gov/1201/

Dodge, W. S. (2006, Februrary 22). Justice Scalia on foreign law and the constitution [Web log post]. Retrieved from http://lawofnations.blogspot.com/2006/02/justice-scalia-on-foreign-law-and.html

Duhl, G. E. (2004). Old lyrics, knock-off videos, and copycat comic books: The fourth fair use factor in U.S. Copyright Law. *Syracuse Law Review, 54,* 665-738.

Durack, K. T. (2006). Technology transfer and patents: Implications for the production of scientific knowledge. *Technical Communication Quarterly, 15*(3), 315-328.

Durscht, J. S. (1996). Judicial plagiarism: It may be fair use but is it ethical? *Cardozo Law Review, 18,* 1253–97.

Geist, M. (2006, April). What could Tory copyright look like under Harper government?. *The Hill Times.* Retrieved from http://www.thehilltimes.ca/html/index.php?display=story&full_path=/2006/april/3/geist/&c=1

Geist, M. (2009). U.S. targets Canada over copyright in special 301 report. Retrieved from http://www.michaelgeist.ca/content/view/3911/125/

Gervais, D. J. (2004). Canadian copyright law post-CCH. *Intellectual Property Journal, 18,* 131-167.

Ginsberg, R. B. (2006). "A decent respect to the opinions of [human]kind":The value of a comparative perspective in constitutional adjudication Constitutional Court of South Africa. Retrieved from http://www.supremecourtus.gov/publicinfo/speeches/sp_02-07b-06.html

Hubbard v. Vosper, 2 Q.B. 84, 1 All E.R. 1023 (C.A. 1972). Retrieved from http://uniset.ca/other/cs3/vosper.html

Lessig, L. (2008). *Remix: Making art and commerce thrive in the hybrid economy.* London, Bloomsbury.

McFarland, J. (2004, April 1). Ruling deals blow to music industry. *Globe and Mail* (Toronto). Retrieved from http://www.theglobeandmail.com

Metro-Goldwyn-Mayer Studios Inc., et al., Petitioners v. Grokster, Ltd., et al., 545 U. S. (June 27, 2005).

Online music swapping legal: Court. (2004, March 31). *CBC News.* Retrieved from http://www.cbc.ca/canada/story/2004/03/31/download_court040331.html

Prior, P. (2004). Tracing process: How texts come into being. In C. Bazerman & P. Prior (Eds.), *What writing does and how it does it: An introduction to analyzing texts and textual practices* (pp. 167-200). Mahwah, NJ: Lawrence Erlbaum.

Rife, M. C. (2006, Spring). Why *Kairos* matters to writing: A reflection on our intellectual property conversation and developing law during the last ten years. *Kairos, 11*(1). Retrieved from http://english.ttu.edu/kairos/

Rife, M. C. (2007). The fair use doctrine: History, application, implications for (new media) writing teachers. *Computers and composition an international journal, 24*(2), 105-226.

Rife, M. C. (2008). Rhetorical invention in copyright imbued environments (Doctoral dissertation). Michigan State University, East Lansing, MI.

Rife, M. C., & DeVoss, D. N. a DigiRhet.net Project. (in press). Teaching plagiarism: Remix as composing. In A. M. Stockdell-Giesler, T. A. Morse, R. Ingalls, M. Donnelly, & J. Castner (Eds.), *Understanding Plagiarism: Discussions for Students and Teachers,* Cresskill, NJ: Hampton Press.

Samuelson, P. (2004, Winter). Intellectual property arbitrage: How foreign rules can affect domestic protection. T*he University of Chicago Law Review, 71.* Retrieved from http://www.ischool.berkeley.edu/~pam/papers/IP%20arbitrage%20duke.pdf

Scassa, T. (2004, July). Recalibrating copyright law? A comment on the Supreme Court of Canada's Decision in *CCH Canadian Limited et al. v. Law*

Society of Upper Canada. Canadian Journal of Law and Technology, 3, pp. 89-100. Retrieved from http://cjlt.dal.ca/vol3_no2/pdfarticles/scassa.pdf

Shimbun, A. (2009). Japan considers fair-use clause based on U.S. copyright law. *Anime News Network.* Retrieved from http://www.animenewsnetwork.com/news/2008-05-28/japan-considers-fair-use-clause-based-on-u.s-copyright-law

Tabatabai, F. (2005, April). A tale of two countries: Canada's response to the peer-to-peer crisis and what it means for the United States. *Fordham L. Rev. 73*(5), pp. 2321- 2382.

TRIPS. (1994). Retrieved from http://www.wto.org/english/docs_e/legal_e/27-trips_01_e.htm

U.S. Copyright Act. (2006, April). Retrieved from http://www.copyright.gov/

Viana, L. P. (2009). US special 301 process acclaimed by industry, assailed by public interest groups. *Intellectual Property Watch.* Retrieved from http://www.ip-watch.org/weblog/2009/05/02/special-301-process-acclaimed-by-industry-assailed-by-public-interest-groups/

Vaver, D. (2004). Canada's intellectual property framework: A comparative overview. Retrieved from http://strategis.ic.gc.ca/epic/site/ippd-dppi.nsf/vwapj/01-EN%20Vaver.pdf/$file/01-EN%20Vaver.pdf

Webb, C. L. (2004, April 1). Canada puts Arctic chill on music industry. *The Washington Post.* Retrieved from http://www.washingtonpost.com/ac2/wp-dyn/A41679-2004Apr1?language=printer

Westbrook, S. (2006). Visual rhetoric in a culture of fear: Impediments to multimedia production. *College English, 68*(5), 457-480.

Yancey, K. (2009). Writing in the 21st century: A report from the National Council of Teachers of English. Retrieved from http://www.ncte.org/library/NCTEFiles/Press/Yancey_final.pdf

Yu, P. K. (2006). Of monks, medieval scribes, and middlemen. *Legal Studies Research Paper Series* Research Paper No. 03-25. Michigan State University. Retrieved from http://papers.ssrn.com/sol3/papers.cfm?abstract_id=897710

8 UNDERSTANDING AND SUPPORTING KNOWLEDGE WORK IN SCHOOLS, WORKPLACES, AND PUBLIC LIFE

William Hart-Davidson and Jeffrey T. Grabill

In this chapter, we take up the issue of what knowledge (writing) work looks like and what it means for writing researchers and teachers to support this work. Supporting knowledge work across domains is important for technical and professional writing programs in particular, largely because contemporary social and institutional contexts are dependent on high-quality symbolic work. To put the issue differently, the activity of citizenship, as well as the activity of professionals working in organizational settings (including technical writers), is knowledge work that is either supported by writing or embodied as writing.

We are researchers and co-directors (two of three) of the Writing in Digital Environments (WIDE) Research Center at Michigan State University. The Center has taken up the problem of how to study writing given new and changing digital and networked information technology tools and environments. We study how the use of digital technologies changes the processes, products, and contexts for writing—particularly composing processes in organizational contexts. Fundamental to our approach is the development of information and software tools as a deliverable of our research. The development of software tools, in particular, might seem unusual as a research deliverable. Computers and writing researchers, in the early years of that field's development, often made software to support then new computer supported writing processes. We understand WIDE as part of that tradition. But more substantively, we see software as either a way to test developing theories of writing or as useful responses to needs we see emerging from research—and sometimes both. These tools and resources, generally speaking, leverage functionality associated with social computing systems, including information visualization and unified content management architectures to enable and support writing. WIDE's goal is to take theories and research methods that have served the community of writing researchers and place them into the hands of writers in a range of contexts (school, workplaces, and public domains). These intellectual tools, embodied in the function as well as the "content" of information systems, will become useful for writers in a variety of contexts who, like students, have a stake in reflecting on and improving writing as an important piece of improving their work overall.

We orient to writing in particular ways as well. We study writing as a verb, which means that we are interested in the activity, not precisely the object. Studying writing as an activity also entails asking how we can best do it and how we can help others to do it better. We understand the activity of writing to be carried by a variable semiotic (e.g., multiple media), and we understand the activity of writing to be epistemologically productive—that is, we situate ourselves within a rhetorical tradition that understands writers as producing new knowledge as part of acts of composing (this becomes thorny and more interesting when the writers in question are not readily understood as "experts"). We are interested, in other words, in what writing does, not in what it means; in the social and organizational functions and impacts of writing, not in the interpretation of the texts themselves. As this perspective concerns "knowledge work," we are interested, simply, in the work that writing (and writers) does. Finally, we tend to be much more interested in how groups write rather than in how individuals write.

Our point in sharing this institutional and conceptual background about the Center and ourselves is to frame the approach we take in this chapter. We provide here an understanding of what we think writing (knowledge) work looks like and why it matters to support it, and we do so by focusing on the digitally mediated activities of groups. We offer for consideration and critique, then, both our focus and approach. We are making an argument for how writing researchers might usefully orient to the study of writing. In what follows, we will first unpack what it means to understand writing and (as integral to) knowledge work. We then move to some visualizations of writing work and their possible interpretations. We conclude by moving toward implications for rhetorical theory.

WRITING AND/AS KNOWLEDGE WORK

Perhaps the most significant idea connecting our work and animating the work of the WIDE Center is the notion of "knowledge work." Knowledge work is typically understood as "analytical" and thus requiring problem-solving and abstract reasoning, particularly with (and through) advanced information technologies. Johnson-Eilola (2005) notes that knowledge work is also typically concerned with the production of information, as distinct from the production of material goods, and he also usefully points out that increasing numbers of us do not just work with information, we inhabit it because the very environments in which we work are information immersive (his favorite example is the digital sound editing software-studio interactions of musicians). Thus knowledge work, or what Johnson-Eilola calls symbolic production, is the making of largely discursive performances that, quite literally, do work. The concept of knowledge work has tremendous cultural capital right now, and we fully admit to an interest in the language for that reason. But the concept that "knowledge work" glosses is poorly understood in our view. This is a statement that demands qualification. There is a significant amount of work in management studies that seeks to understand knowledge work (e.g., Orlikowski & Yates, 1994; Pentland, 1995). But we are interested in a fine-grained understanding, and we are interested in understanding the activity of knowledge work and in rendering that activity visible to those who are engaged in that activity. When visible, we suspect that knowledge work looks like writing (indeed, is writing) or is substantively supported by writing. Writing is how knowledge work carries value in organizations.

Our claims about knowledge work, value, and writing demand some justification. To make visible these claims about writing and knowledge work, we turn to vignettes drawn from a series of small studies conducted with organizations that we understood to have knowledge work problems. We will then propose a model for group writing that is descriptive of some of the dynamics that emerge from the vignettes. We will close with a discussion of a fourth project that illuminates opportunities in the model for supporting writing as knowledge work.

Career Services and Placement

Michigan State's office of career services and placement came to us with a common problem: we need a new Web site. At first we did not fold this project into the workflow of the Center. Instead, Jeff taught a year long independent study class with five students who planned and completed a research and development project that eventually led to a new Web site (http://www.csp.msu.edu).

What became quickly apparent to Jeff and his students was that the key problem for Career Services and Placement (CSP) was a writing problem. With their previous way of working, many people within the organization wrote their Web site—sometimes as individuals, sometimes as part of small teams. They did so without a clearly marked workflow, and they did so within a basic html architecture: no style sheets controlling design; no content management system supporting the writing. As a result, when writers within the organization updated the Web site, they often broke it. Given the lack of standardization, the site evolved into a tangled web of links, cul-de-sacs, and inconsistent and sometimes conflicting content.

The CSP project was one of the first in which we posed two simple but powerful questions to that organization: who are you (together); and who writes? The first question is designed to help people figure out how they cohere in terms of their identities, organization, and work (what is their groupness). And the second question is designed to help them to see that what they do with and through their Web site is write together, and, therefore, to ask themselves who should be doing that writing. This realization is by no means obvious or without controversy. None of the individuals who literally wrote the CSP Web site understood themselves as "writers." The eventual solution was the use of a content management system, in this case Plone, to support the writing of three people within the organization charged with coordinating CSP's work with and through their Web site. Adapting a content management system to become a writing environ-

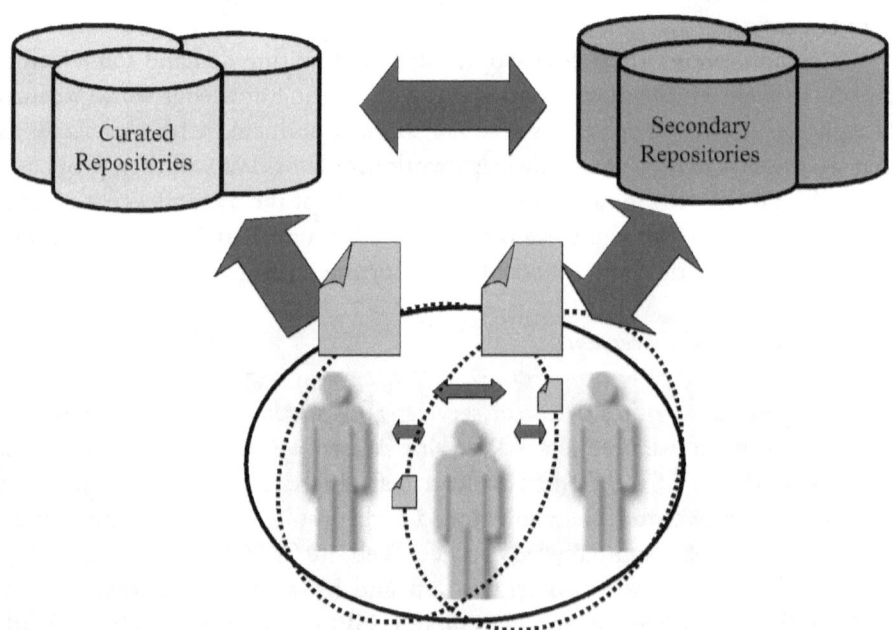

Figure 1. A macroscopic view of writing activity in social groups.

ment is no small task. We continue to work on this problem. But the point we want to make with this example is simple: the key moment in this project was when the people of CSP were able to see themselves as writing together when they were "doing" their Web site. Once CSP understood itself as an organization that writes—and individuals and groups within that organization began to see themselves in this way—then the project shifted dramatically from one focused on helping the organization "get" a new Web site to one focused on developing effective and explicit writing processes (imagine a writing center tutorial with an organization rather than an individual). A new Web site happened, but it was a product of writing research, or a writing process (change), and of a shift in organizational culture.

Teachers for a New Era

"Teachers for a New Era" (TNE) (2004) is the title of a multi-year initiative undertaken by the School of Education at Michigan State University with support from the Carnegie Foundation of New York. The aim of the TNE project is to create and disseminate teacher knowledge standards that would guide the education and professional development of future teachers. When the TNE team approached us in September 2005, we agreed to conduct a study to determine how the "Teacher Knowledge Standards" (TKS) developed by the TNE project team could best be delivered to its intended users—that is, "MSU students preparing for teaching careers, all faculty involved in their disciplinary and pedagogical preparation, K-12 teachers and administrators, and public officials responsible for educational policy" ("Teacher Knowledge Standards," November 2004, p. 1).

In Fall 2005, the WIDE team conducted its study. We adapted an interviewing method known as contextual inquiry (see Beyer & Holtzblatt, 1997) with the aim of discovering, in a practical and detailed way, how teachers and teacher educators reported using the standards and integrating them into their work practices. Participants were interviewed about the use of standards information in their day-to-day work as teachers and/or teacher educators. We asked to meet the participants in the places where they actually worked so that we could see as much of their working environment as possible. In many cases, meeting them in their office or with their computer nearby meant that we could ask them to show us how they performed certain types of routine tasks such as preparing lesson plans or evaluating student work. By prompting participants to show us examples of work routines, we were better able to discover tacit uses of standards in the participants' practice by noting where and when they accessed, referenced, or made direct use of standards language in their own work products.

We contacted approximately seventy potential participants from the Teacher Education literacy team and interviewed twenty-two teachers and teacher educators who volunteered for the study. Eleven of the interviewees represented the elementary grades, and 13 represented the middle and secondary grades. A variety of roles were represented in the participant group as well, including four undergraduate TE students and teacher interns, three mentor teachers, six subject area leaders, eight field instructors, 12 content-area instructors (some participants, as the role totals indicate, served in more than one role).

Each interview lasted approximately 60 to 90 minutes. We took field notes as our primary method of data gathering. We also audio recorded the interviews as a backup. We did not make full transcripts of the audio recordings, but we did listen to them to flesh out the notes for each interview. We also gathered sample artifacts—documents representing typical work product or guidelines for work—from the participants when possible.

We analyzed the interviews in an effort to construct comparable accounts of teachers' use of standards information, paying particular attention to the combinations of information (texts), technologies, and strategies used. We did this by constructing lists in response to questions such as "what kinds of terms did people use to refer to 'standards'?" or "what uses for standards information were mentioned?" We then identified individual cases that tended to be typical or atypical, using these as the basis for more detailed questions about motives and rationales for the use of standards.

In reporting on how they used standards, teachers and teacher educators revealed that they would re-appropriate the standards for their own purposes. One example from our final report focused on a mentor teacher acting in the role of department chair. When describing how she used standards, the mentor teacher talked about her experience as a department chair working with her colleagues. More precisely, each department in her high school was charged with collaboratively creating a unit that ties back to the district standards. This teacher used the standards and a shared document called the "Understanding by Design" planning model to "coordinate [their] work together by talking through it all." Once her department decided on a text to use, they took the following steps:

- Considered outcomes
- Identified appropriate assessments
- Created classroom activities
- Identified all the possible standards associated with this task
- Decided which standards to foreground

The teacher reported that she did not view the standards as a starting point, but rather as something to help her refine her outcomes, assessments, and activities. While she believed student standards helped her to "focus and justify the things I want to do," she also feared that standards may be used to show how students are failing, rather than how they are succeeding. Thus, this teacher seemed to use standards as a way to talk with her colleagues, to aid in her planning process, and to address the concerns of other stakeholders, such as parents, policy makers, and administrators. In other words, the standards were reappropriated to do a kind of work that is important for a department chair to do: build consensus among her colleagues and other stakeholders. But this is delicate work, not least because the same standards might get used in ways that the teacher is not willing to support.

Based on patterns of reappropriation illustrated in the previous example, we recommended to the TNE team that standards be presented as a means for empowering users—teachers and teacher educators—and helping them to do their work, rather than as another set of mandates foisted upon them. Our detailed recommendation took the form of a new software tool that eventually came to be called the Literacy Resource Exchange (http://tne.wide.msu.edu). The system allows teachers and teacher educators to share commonly-used materials such as lesson plans, syllabi, rubrics, and other "working genres" in an environment where links between these materials and teacher knowledge standards can be made explicit. In other words, the system supports the kind of writing that teachers need to do in both formal and informal social collectives (e.g., as members of departments, as members of affinity groups). Much of the day-to-day practice of teaching is made up of writing that requires teachers to adapt materials drawn from other sources in the service of knowledge-work tasks such as creating lessons, documenting curricular decision-making, and evaluating students.

Capital Area Community Information

The Capital Area Community Information (CACI) project is an attempt to design with "users" (citizens) information communication technologies that will support their knowledge work in communities. The claim that the work of citizenship is knowledge work is more fully developed in Grabill (2007), but the claim itself rests on the observation that when groups of people are working for community change of any kind, the work that they must do—and the first part of this argument is to understand citizenship as work—is a form of rhetorical labor that requires the use of advanced information technologies (searching; use of databases; making databases) and a great deal of writing (letters; proposals; reports; Web sites; iMovies; flyers; and on and on). All of this work is focused on assembling participants around issues (i.e., organizing), keeping projects focused and on-target (i.e., management), and achieving change (persuasion).

The CACI project is a study of an existing initiative called CACVoices (http://www.cacvoices.org), a public Web site that hosts databases and public information related to public health, crime, parks and recreation, including as well Web sites for small community and neighborhood organizations. While the CACVoices resource is valued by community-based organizations in the Capital Area, there were usability problems with interfaces and database tools. Web sites like CACVoices exist in communities all over the world, particularly in the developed world. Originally they were the byproduct of digital government initiatives or attempts to close digital divides and even urban and regional planning efforts. In most instances, the narrative supporting the development of Web sites such as CACVoices tells a story of increased community activity, enhanced information technology capacity, and a more robust and informed citizenry. In the communities served by CACVoices, there is little evidence that the information tools have enabled citizen productivity or that they have led to the social transformation expected by both sponsors and users.

Like many data-rich tools, CACVoices provides an array of options and languages for non-expert users to navigate the Web site, access databases, and create Web sites by using built-in development tools. Once users find and access specific database tools, they are confronted with interfaces and language that demand expert users. For instance, to access crime data for one's neighborhood, a user without any training or documentation must use a Geographic Information Systems (GIS) tool developed for professional geographers. In our usability evaluation of this tool, users often did not even recognize the default map of their community (represented visually in terms of a network of roads, rivers, and county lines) as their community. The problems suggested by these interfaces are substantial, both at the interface and in terms of their implications for what users can do with the information. That is, the usability problems associated with this site, such as failures to navigate to critical information and databases that were opaque to users (problems that have since addressed), are problems only because they prevent the ability of people in communities to engaged in the knowledge work that is necessary. Bad interfaces and tools that do not support complex work are disabling technologies. But even here usability as an approach is inadequate, because usability only allows us to see and solve problems at the surface layer of interfaces; writing and other complex activities are "deeper" both in terms of the intellectual activities required of users and the system interactions required to support users. Citizens writing to change communities need to do much more than navigate clearly and cleanly. They must have sophisticated interpretive skills, both for text and visuals and data displays. They must also be able to produce complex documents—reports, letters, issue summaries, digital video. Very few individuals have these literacies. But groups of people do, and they can be highly effective if they have tools smart enough to support how they write together.

GROUPS BEING GROUPS: WRITING AND SOCIAL COLLECTIVES

What emerges from these three projects is a model of writing as central to group activity. And despite the differences among the groups represented in each project, we can identify some common features of this group model of writing. Whether formally or informally, explicitly or tacitly, the work of groups writing together involves the crucial interplay of communication with others in the group, with curated repositories of information, and with secondary repositories of information. As our two previous examples help to illustrate, this dynamic is increasingly a pattern for living, working, and participating in day-to-day activity in the context of an emerging global knowledge society (Castells, 1999; Zuboff & Maxmin, 2004).

Curated repositories are those that have a community of editors, reviewers, and possibly merchants looking out for the quality of materials, providing a standard for organizing these (e.g., metadata standards, search tools), and providing means to access the materials. These could be free (as in a library) or fee-based, as in a proprietary collection of bioinformatics research data. Secondary repositories are user-driven schemes that add value to content in curated repositories by providing a bottom-up set of materials that sit alongside the curated content and help users access, understand, and use it. Reviews and comments are two familiar genres in secondary repositories, which can also include "derivative works" that build on materials in a curated repository. Secondary reposito-

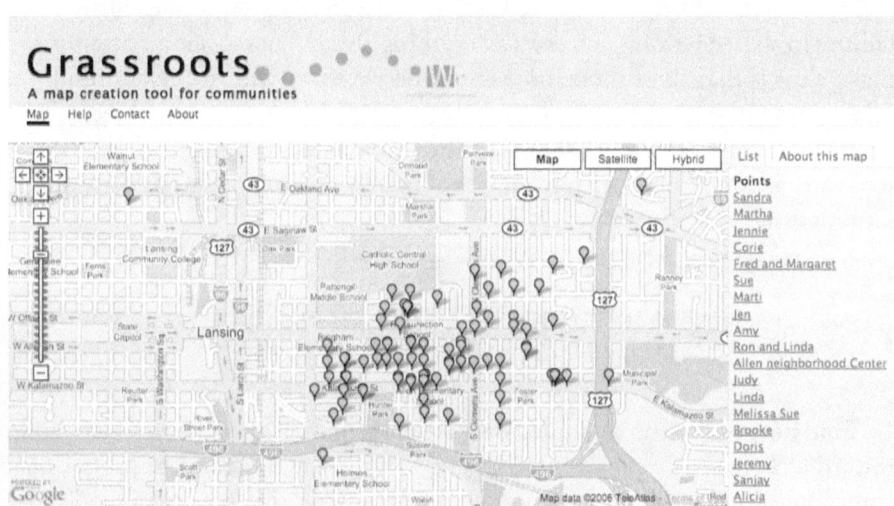

Figure 2. Distribution of Farmer's Market yard signs.

ries may also have robust metadata schemes, search tools, and other resources, though there is no centralized top-down control of these (because when there is, they become curated repositories). Secondary repositories are often a function of user activity, and much of that activity is what we might usefully understand as writing. User-created product reviews on sites like Amazon.com, for example, are created by users for other users. Their status as secondary repositories, then, is a function of the fact that they are user activity that is not curated—so imagine the conversation Amazon.com representatives had to have with their retail partners about this fairly radical concept: "the only reviews of your product on the site might be negative ones ... we just can't say for sure ... because we will not edit what users write."

But what drives sales on Amazon.com is exactly what drives the system represented in Figure 1: the activity of users interacting with one another, doing their own work on their own terms. Much of this work relies upon and results in texts of various kinds, and so while we would understand it as "writing," users may not experience their work in this way. This "disconnect" between user experience and activity is a key theme in our shared work. Just as lawyers rarely see themselves as expert professional writers, teachers in the TNE project did not see the work of teaching as thoroughly discursive, and the people we worked with on the CACI project rarely saw the writing that they did. Therefore, the participants in the projects described above, for example, were more focused on delivering placement services to undergraduate students, working for change in their communities, or preparing course materials. Failures in workflow—in the ability to work effectively and successfully—are, in our view, just as likely to be failures in shared writing processes as anything else. What our model attempts to make clear is that all of these interactions derive from, and frequently result in, information objects that users create: documents, forms, learning objects. That is, users are makers, not consumers. When they access information, they do so to create, adapt, remix, and reuse it ... not merely to read, digest, or consume it. Groups write.

UNDERSTANDING AND SUPPORTING RHETORICAL ACTIVITY

One purpose of the examples we have presented in this chapter is to build toward a claim regarding the meaning of writing, the functions of professional communicators, and the role of writing research. If writing is a distributed activity at the very core of knowledge work in a broad array of domains and organizations, then a key function for professional communicators (and writing researchers) is to support the writing work of others. This does not mean, of course, that professional communicators are done writing themselves—quite the opposite, in fact—but our claim does mean that we have some work to do to understand writing work differently than we have in the past in an effort to support this work more effectively.

To flesh out this argument, we will utilize relatively recent work from Latour (2005) and another example from the work of the Center. To begin, it is first important to move one step beyond our assertion that groups write and focus somewhat differently on who and what constitutes a group. In other words, to focus on what is required to get writing work done. In this regard, we understand writing as a collective social activity, and when we treat writing in this way, we understand

- that writing requires infrastructure
- that the texts and technologies (and other elements of practice and standards) that comprise infrastructure are participants—they are part of the collective

We would go on further to claim

- that the purpose of rhetoric is to serve as a type of connection between participants
- that we ought to be engaged in making—and facilitating the making—of those connections

There are a number of important issues embedded in this list. The concept of "infrastructure" we take from Starr and Ruhleder (1996), who write that "infrastructure is something that emerges for people in practice, connected to activities and structures" (p. 112). The commonplace notion of infrastructure as largely material and foundational is certainly part of what Starr and Ruhleder mean by the concept, but their notion of infrastructure is at once broader and more social and cultural. They write, "Computers, people, and tasks together make or break a functioning infrastructure," underlining the contingent meanings that can be attached to a concept (infrastructure) that is material, institutional, cultural, and social at the same time. In other words, just as a tool is not an artifact with "pre-given attributes frozen in time" but rather given meaning as a tool by specific users working on particular problems in specific situations, so too does the meaning and value of an infrastructure emerge. An infrastructure's meaning and use are not stable. They are a product of ongoing processes of use.

The value of a concept like infrastructure is that it gives us a heuristic for seeing the required elements of a productive writing infrastructure. Infrastructure, after all, is notoriously difficult to see, particularly when it works well. We are also better able to name its participants. So, in the case of this bit of writing work, we can name "Bill" and "Jeff" as participants, but we also need to be able to name "computer" and "network" and "time" and "shared office space" and "smart, supportive editor" as a few of the other participants enrolled in the work at hand. Given this, what distinguishes those collectives that are highly effective at knowledge work from those that are not? This is an essential question, of course, and one we might very well spend a few years examining. But here is where we see a role for rhetorical theory and practice because certain forms of rhetorical theory might enable us to see collectives in particular ways (or at all), understand how best to assemble them, and how best to support them. Our sense of rhetoric, then—and therefore our sense of the core activities of writing and writers—is that it serves as a particular type of connection between things that are not rhetorical and that good writers create and maintain those connections. We close this chapter by attempting to explain this last sentence in two ways.

The first way that we find it useful to explain rhetoric as a type of connection between things that are not rhetorical, is to refer to a commonplace of technical and professional writing that we have discussed in various ways previously in this chapter: the difference between professional writers and professionals who write. We know that professionals (knowledge workers) write all the time—it is a key competency and activity in their jobs. However, as the examples above illustrate, few if any of these professionals understand their activity as writing. They understand themselves to be accounting or lawyering or managing. All non-rhetorical things (when an economist is analyzing data, she is doing economics, not rhetoric). But to do the work of an economist, eventually that economist must assemble what Latour (2005) would call participants (what we have characterized as elements of infrastructure). These acts of assembly and connectivity and the redeployment of these participants toward new ends are rhetorical and require a tremendous amount of writing. For instance, our economist is certainly analyzing data for some purpose and in response to some exigency. However, that exigency may not be shared, or it may not be shared as widely as is necessary to achieve some end—to act on the analysis in particular ways. What our economist must do in the lexicon of Latour, therefore, is assemble participants around a matter of concern, an issue that brings people together precisely because it divides them. This is rhetorical work saturated by concrete acts of writing, and it is basic to effective knowledge work. Our economist must propose, persuade, enroll, analyze, build relationships and assemble all of the elements of infrastructure required to act effectively. She is no longer a discrete economist but a participant in a larger association doing economics.

Similarly, the job of the professional writer is to become an expert in assembling participants to achieve rhetorical goals, and then to care for these assemblies over time (it might be the particular expertise of writers to care for assemblies). To write effectively, to recall an earlier example, CSP needed both to understand itself differently as an organization and assign specific individuals to assemble the organization around the goal of communicating. In addition, CSP was required to change the culture of the organization—and reconfigure its infrastructure—to care for this new assembly (of texts, people, machines, and so on) that was "doing" its new Web site.

The second way we like to explain rhetoric as a type of connection is to talk about Grassroots, an asset mapping tool that we helped to assemble as part of the Capital Area Community Information project. Through that project, one of the most common forms of writing we observed concerned the making of maps and the use of maps in making other sorts of arguments and documents. Currently in our community, there are lots of GIS tools that allow people to make maps of data. But none of these tools allow people to map data that they create or that is of interest to them. Instead, maps can be made based on databases typically collected by government agencies, which focus on problems in the community. Grassroots is intended to enable communities to name, locate, and thereby create maps of their communities using variables of their choosing. This impulse is supported by a large body of literature that is generally known as an asset-based approach to community development (e.g., Kretzmann & McKnight, 1993). Because the use of mapping tools is a fundamental inventional activity for many community-based organizations, Grassroots is both writing software and an important participant in the rhetorical activity of a number of organizations. Grassroots is also a prime example of what is happening to "writing" as powerful digital tools become more deeply immersed in knowledge work. "Writing" involves much more than tools (participants) capable of making black marks on white screens and paper.

Figure 2 represents a typical use of Grassroots. What is represented in the map is the location of yard signs advertising a farmer's market sponsored by a neighborhood-based organization. We like this map not because it is meant for display to the public on a Web site or in a report or brochure. We like this map—this use of Grassroots—because this map is not meant for a public audience or for wide distribution. Rather, this map is a working document within the organization that enables it to track where its signs are and to tell itself a set of stories about the distribution of signs in a given area. This map supports other forms of activity; this type of mundane writing is important to the organization in ways that would be rendered invisible if we were only studying texts as artifacts or writing as separate from other forms of activity. As digital writing, however, this simple map is even more powerful. This is an organization that regularly uses maps. Some are electronic, but others are paper maps hanging on walls. The existing electronic tools that they have will not permit them to create the sorts of maps shown in Figure 2. And the paper maps are not editable and reusable in other electronic documents.

While the use shown in Figure 2 is a simple example, we like it because it shows clearly how a tool like Grassroots can support more complex rhetorical work by groups. Grassroots as a writing tool represents an attempt to make the construction of a complex genre more accessible for ordinary citizens. In addition, perhaps the most exciting feature of Grassroots is how it enables the sharing of maps within and across groups, teams, or communities. Drawing on the value of reuse, every map created by a Grassroots user can be the basis for another map. Therefore, groups of users can collectively create and edit maps by giving others the ability to add or change things about the map's contents or its features (e.g., zoom level). In this way, for example, a group might choose to use a map to augment other information they already publish and maintain, thereby turning a map into a database. Furthermore, in order to make maps easy to find once they have been created, users can add descriptive "tags" using a system called a "folksonomy" that depends on aggregation and variation among descriptive keywords to create an alternative to a controlled-vocabulary taxonomy. A folksonomic structure allows users to apply highly-idiosyncratic, even personal terms to characterize maps for the sake of making the map findable to their specific group. A group might tag a map with their organization's name, for example, or with an acronym. At the same time, other users can tag the same map with more general keywords like "pizza." Aggregation of tags allows the common descriptors to influence factors such as the placement of a map in search results lists. The use of metadata in this way provides a rich source of descriptive information to enable the searching and grouping of maps. Each of these features and functionalities enables group writing, collective intelligence, and the rhetorical practices of organizations. In the language that we have been using in this last section of the chapter, Grassroots enables writers to make connections between other participants (data, geocodes, images, people, audiences) in a rhetorical situation. But just as importantly from our point of view, Grassroots itself is a connection. Grassroots connects us (and our Center) with other participants, and these participants are then connected to others. With Grassroots we have assembled participants and enabled the assembly of others. Sometimes rhetoric produces more than texts, speeches, and other well-known performances. Sometimes rhetoric makes software.

We began this chapter by saying that we were interested in what knowledge (writing) work looks like so that we might help imagine effective ways to support this work. As we hope to have demonstrated in this chapter, visualizing writing in this way can be complex, and the implications of these visualizations have been—for us at least—challenging to how we have typically understood writing, writers, and our own roles as teachers and researchers. We have turned increasingly to a Latourian understanding of writing and knowledge work in an effort to theorize what we have observed in ways that are conceptually coherent yet dynamic. We find ourselves, therefore, starting to build rhetorical theory that begins with the understanding that writing as knowledge work is done to make, remake, and unmake associations. Written artifacts and writing-as-action are both concrete tracings of associations. Digital environments are especially exciting to us because in these environments actions leave traces that are ephemeral in offline settings. Life is textualized in digital environments.

The conceptual approach we have sketched in this chapter is not without problems, of course. One that continues to concern us is that despite the efforts of many writing researchers to render visible writing in the making of associations, matters of concern, and in work of many kinds, writing itself (as artifact or action) only occasionally rises to the level of visible infrastructure. We wonder if the approach that is emerging from the work of the WIDE Center will have better luck. Still, it is up to us as writing researchers to a) pay attention to, and b) leverage both the relatively well-known tracings of associations available in texts and the newly-afforded opportunities to trace association building in writing-as-action in online spaces for the sake of supporting knowledge work. It turns out that when we do this, we do not limit ourselves to describing or prescribing support in a textual account (e.g. an article or book); rather, we can also build our findings into the very environments that users inhabit in order to mediate their work directly. The act of making Grassroots is a statement about how we might best express, test, and verify our theories about writing and knowledge work. More generally, we hope this chapter makes clear why we see writing as fundamental to understanding knowledge work and why we see knowledge work as a useful descriptor for the group activities we see in all sorts of contemporary organizations. The problem is that writing is perhaps the paradigm case of invisible work. Like most elements of infrastructure, we only notice it when it breaks. We suggest, then, that a key political as well as intellectual act of writing research is to make writing visible, particularly to those doing the writing. Only then can we develop notions of rhetorical work that correspond to the complexity of that work and build better infrastructures for supporting this essential work in schools, in workplaces, and in the diverse knowledge work contexts of everyday life.

REFERENCES

Beyer H., & Holtzblatt. (1997). *Contextual design: A customer-centered approach to systems designs.* San Francisco: Morgan Kaufmann.

Castells, M. (1999). *The rise of the network society.* Cambridge, MA: Blackwell.

Grabill, J. T. (2007). *Writing community change: Designing technologies for citizen action.* Cresskill, NJ: Hampton Press.

Johnson-Eilola, J. (2005). *Datacloud: Toward a new theory of online work.* Cresskill, NJ: Hampton Press.

Kretzmann, J., & McKnight, J. (1993). *Building communities from the inside out: A path toward finding and mobilizing a community's assets.* Chicago, IL: ACTA Publications.

Latour, B. (2005). *Reassembling the social: An introduction to actor-network theory.* Oxford: Oxford University Press.

Orlikowski, W. J., & Yates, J. (1994). Genre repertoire: The structuring of communicative practices in organizations. *Administrative Science Quarterly, 39,* 541-574.

Pentland, B. T. (1995). Information systems and organizational learning: The social epistemology of organizational knowledge systems. *Accounting, Management and Information Technologies, 5*(1), 1-22.

Starr, S. L., & Ruhleder, K. (1996). Steps toward an ecology of infrastructure: Design and access for large information spaces. *Information Systems Research, 7*(1), 111-134.

Teachers for a New Era. (2004). Teacher knowledge standards. Retrieved from http://www.msu.edu/~tne/

Zuboff, S., & Maxmin, J. (2004). *The support economy: Why corporations are failing individuals and the next episode of capitalism.* New York: Penguin.

THE ROLE OF WRITING IN THE PRODUCTION OF KNOWLEDGE IN RESEARCH ENVIRONMENTS

9 RHETORIC, KNOWLEDGE, AND "THE BRUTE FACTS OF NATURE" IN SCIENCE RESEARCH

Heather Graves

What is the relationship between rhetoric and reality in the creation of scientific knowledge? This question has caused considerable debate among rhetoricians and philosophers in the last twenty-five years. During this debate, only limited consideration has been given to views from scientific practice. This chapter considers the question from the perspective of such views, from scientific investigation itself, by examining examples drawn from research in experimental and theoretical physics. For this purpose, I begin by outlining some of the background theory relating to this discussion: the role of rhetoric in the creation of scientific knowledge and the ways in which one rhetorical figure in particular—metonymy—creates meaning. Drawing on this theoretical grounding, I then analyze several examples of the role of metonymy, the rhetorical figure that substitutes an attribute for the thing itself, in the construction of knowledge claims in experimental physics. I investigate how two experimental physicists used the rhetorical trope of metonymy as an argumentative strategy when revising a paper for publication to persuade the referee to accept their claim that a particular method of fabrication created good quality amorphous silicon thin films. Two additional examples from these physicists illustrate how metonymy works to bridge ontological realms of things and concepts in drawing conclusions from an experiment. Finally, I analyze one example from theoretical physics, specifically string theory, to explore how recent work in that field has tended to collapse the traditional distinctions between what is science and what is rhetoric. The chapter closes with a brief consideration of the implications of string theory for the question about the relationship between rhetoric and reality in the creation of scientific knowledge.

RHETORIC AND ITS ROLE IN THE CREATION OF SCIENTIFIC KNOWLEDGE

The relationship between arguments and facts, especially in science, has been a matter of extensive debate over the last fifteen or twenty years by scholars in rhetoric of science. Some scholars have shown how scientists have adapted and used rhetoric, that is, techniques of persuasion, to present and argue for new knowledge claims based on their research (Moss, 1993; Myers, 1990; Rymer, 1988; Scott, 1976, 1993; Prelli, 1989; among others). Some of these same scholars, and others, have argued that in addition to contributing to the presentation of new insights, rhetoric has also aided scientists in actually generating new insights in the first place (e.g., Graves, 2005; Gross, 1990, 1991, 2006; Little, 2000, 2008;). With recent publications, this discussion has moved well beyond disputing whether or not rhetoric contributes to the generation of knowledge in science (epistemology) to assessing the extent to which rhetoric helps to constitute the entities that science studies in its research (ontology).

Questions about the relationship between rhetoric and ontology (existence) were first raised by Gross in 1991, although few scholars in rhetoric of science have addressed them since. During an exchange with McGuire and Melia (1991) in *Rhetorica* about the relationship between rhetoric and reality, Gross (1991) argued that scholarship in the rhetoric of inquiry "has insert[ed] itself into the inner sanctum of epistemological and ontological privilege," and this activity had strengthened "the case for the rhetorical construction of *all* [emphasis added] knowledge" (p. 285). In these statements, Gross (1991) argues that rhetoric mediates not only the development of knowledge in all disciplines, including science, but also the existence of entities upon which this knowledge is developed.

In response, McGuire and Melia (1991) argue that Gross's claim about rhetoric's contribution to developing knowledge "replace[s] scientific discovery with rhetorical invention" (pp. 303-4). They reject his claim that all science is rhetoric, and they propose a more moderate position: they suggest that the "facts" that make up reality may be both discovered (in other words, the facts exist prior to human experience) and constructed (that is, human effort brings them into existence). However, those facts must also exist independent of human perception. They warn that although rhetoricians may seek evidence of the "rhetoricity of scientific facts, 'the brute facts of nature' will turn out to be just those products of science that appear to be beyond rhetorical analysis" (p. 304). They insist on preserving some vestige of a reality outside of language (and rhetoric) that constitutes the source of facts about nature/science.

To shed light on this debate, I focus here on the role of style in the creation of scientific knowledge, because if we study the language that scientists use to conceptualize their objects of study (for example, how they use metaphor, metonymy, and analogy), we can gain insight into the role that rhetoric plays in both the epistemology (creation of knowledge about facts) and the ontology (existence of "facts") of science, principally in physics. In conventional wisdom, style, like rhetoric itself, has often been viewed as ornament—that is, the words chosen to express a thought have often been considered separate from the thought itself, especially in discussions of scientific fact and theory. Conventional wisdom dictates that the words used to describe a theory can change without changing the theory itself. In this chapter, I complicate these ideas about style by showing how the use of the rhetorical trope of metonymy by two physicists contributes to the process of knowledge creation in science, and, in fact, the generation of the brute facts of nature that become scientific knowledge.

A number of rhetoricians have studied the use of figurative language in science (Fahnestock, 1999; Graves, 2005; Little, 2000, 2008; Prelli, 1989) to describe the ways in which tropes such as metaphor and analogy serve an epistemic function in scientific discovery. For analytical perspectives on the tropes themselves (in other words, how metonymy functions to create meaning), recent work in cognitive linguistics offers some useful tools. Lakoff and Johnson (1980), and Lakoff and Turner (1989) have shown that metaphor should no longer be considered just ornamental or a captivating turn of phrase: it is, in fact, foundational to human experience of the world. Without metaphor, they claim, humans cannot communicate. More recently, Radden and Kövecses (1999), and Croft (1993) (and others) have explored the role of metonymy in human language. Similarly, Gentner (1988) and Gentner and colleagues (1997) have studied how analogy contributes to scientific discovery and insight. This research in cognitive linguistics suggests that rhetorical tropes and figures are not "just" stylistic devices. It argues that the words selected to express an idea actually shape that idea; using different language ultimately changes the idea, however subtly.

The work of these scholars supports that of rhetoricians, such as Fahnestock (1999), as well as my own work in *Rhetoric in(to) Science*, which argue that rhetorical tropes, such as metaphor or metonymy are useful in "extending language to represent new and innovative ideas" (Graves, 2005, p. 42). In other words, rhetorical tropes can contribute to the development of new ideas, not just describe the ideas after they are developed. Indeed, scholarship in rhetoric and cognitive linguistics has shown how metaphor and metonymy can and do serve as central tools in the development and creation of new ideas. For example, in theoretical physics, string theorists use the metonymy of a single string to stand in for the multitude of strings in the multiverse to help them build insight into individual string behaviour. It seems reasonable to assert that a stylistic trope such as metonymy does contribute to the development of scientific knowledge and ideas.

THE RHETORICAL TROPE OF METONYMY

Several scholars have tried to account for how metonymy creates meaning. Burke (1969) argued that metonymy is a metaphorical substitution, where a concept from an abstract realm of being is reduced or made concrete by comparing it with an entity from a less complex realm of being. He uses the example of "the heart" to refer to the "emotions," for example, "my heart bleeds for you"—in other words, I feel badly for you. Research in an experimental physics laboratory has shown the physicists using metonymy as a way to reduce complex processes to single words or phrases (Graves, 2005). Other specialists fill in the background theory that the phrase evokes to comprehend immediately a complex idea.

Pointing to the difference between metaphor and metonymy, Croft (1993) explains that metaphor maps two concepts from different domains, while metonymy maps two concepts within a single domain matrix. For example, one of the physicists in my study referred to a "virgin sample," meaning one that had not had any tests done to it. This metaphor maps from the domain of human sexual experience to the domain of a new thin film sample to illuminate the significant aspect of the film—that it is untested. In contrast, metonymy remains within one domain as illustrated by this use of metonymy (and metaphor) by a physicist to explain the concept of a quantum well:

> A quantum well is a one-dimensional well (imagine the furrows in a ploughed field where the individual furrow extends indefinitely in either direction, but is bounded on either side by the adjacent furrows) in which a particle or electron is trapped in the well with infinite boundaries (the length of the furrow) and infinite barriers (the adjacent furrows). The particle (or electron) can move along the plane of the well, but it cannot move through the barrier.... [But] if the barrier has a finite height and width, the quantized particle can tunnel or move through the barrier, rendering it transparent. (Graves, 2005, p. 212)

This physicist's use of metonymy maps the domain of a three-dimensional well (an oil or water well) onto the domain of a one-dimensional well (an area where electrons are trapped). Listeners are expected to apply what they know about three-dimensional wells to the new situation to grasp the concept of a one-dimensional well.

According to Radden and Kövecses (1999), however, metonymy is not just a substitution of one term for another but interrelates two terms to "form a new, complex meaning" (p. 19). As the authors argue, metonymy creates meaning by relying on idealized cognitive models (ICMs) that encompass both encyclopaedic (the sum of our experience with a word or idea) and cultural models. In their description, idealized cognitive models comprise three different realms of being or existence: 1) the world of reality, which has to do with things and events; 2) the world of conceptualization or concepts; and 3) the world of language, which they call "forms." They argue that all three of these realms of existence are equally "real": the external world of things and events; how humans build concepts from their physical and intellectual experience of things and events; and how they use language to express and describe those concepts.

Metonymy creates meaning when we take an entity from one of these ontological realms and apply it to one of the other ontological realms. For example, the quantum well metonymy relies on listener knowledge of three-dimensional wells from the world of things when it applies this knowledge to the theoretical concept of the one-dimensional quantum well. Listeners understand the quantum well as holding something that cannot easily escape its container. The metonymy allows listeners to move intellectually from the world of things to the world of concepts when they apply their knowledge of the idealized cognitive model of a well to the new concept of a quantum well. It allows listeners to consider the existence of a quantum well based on their prior knowledge of the existence of an oil or water well. In the situation where the quantum well metonymy is introduced, the physicists do not know whether their measured data is evidence of a quantum well in their multilayered thin films or whether it is produced by some other unexplained phenomenon. As they deliberate over an explanation for these results, the physicists move back and forth between the realms of things and events, of concepts, and of forms. Through their use of metonymy, it is not always clear to which realm they are referring. In this way, the physicists develop arguments and evaluations that help them to decide whether the entity in question really exists or whether another more mundane explanation for the results is valid (ot was).

THE ROLE OF METONYMY IN EXPERIMENTAL PHYSICS

MacDonald and Tzu, two experimental physicists, had conducted basic research into the properties of different combinations of amorphous silicon (disordered, rather than crystalline silicon—the basis of the computer industry) semiconductors. They produced films using different methods and then examined the electrical and optical properties to make claims about the quality of the films and the usefulness of the methods of fabrication. Their research involved a series of experiments with a-SiN:H (hydrogenated amorphous silicon nitride) superlattices (multilayered thin films) with the goal of determining whether amorphous silicon semiconductors show evidence of a quantum mechanical effect referred to as confinement (this example contrasts the example discussed at the start of this chapter which studied single-layer non-hydrogenated amorphous silicon nitride thin films). The physicists wanted to determine whether they could observe quantum confinement in an amorphous semiconductor (quantum confinement was already well documented in crystalline superlattices). For this purpose, the physicists created superlattices with alternating layers of amorphous silicon that had different concentrations of nitrogen. These alternating layers could theoretically create a quantum well if the layers with a higher concentration of nitrogen formed the barrier layers and the layers with a lower concentration of nitrogen created the well layers. One of the experiments done to evaluate the properties of the superlattice was a measurement of the photoconductivity of the film, that is, the ability of the thin film to conduct electricity based on the intensity of light rays (infrared or visible light) being absorbed in it.

At one point in the course of their experiments, Tzu and Macdonald encountered persistent photoconductivity in a series of their thin film samples of a-SiNx. Persistent photoconductivity occurs when high levels of photoconductivity continue to be measured after the light source is removed from the film. Usually, the level decreases to its dark values as soon as the photons are no longer available for the semiconductor to absorb. As Tzu and MacDonald are trying to figure out the reason, MacDonald reads two sentences from a draft of an experimental article that Tzu has written (and MacDonald is revising) and then he thinks aloud about the ideas contained in the draft. In the draft and in the verbal explanation, both Tzu and MacDonald are using the metonymy of mechanism to describe the measurement of photoconductivity. Mechanism is a metonymy in this example because it refers to a single example of this degradation phenomenon to represent both the molecular structure of the film and the process that results in the measured change in photoconductivity. These are much larger and more complex entities, which the physicists have reduced to a single example as a way to conceptualize what might be taking place in the film to produce the measurements they have obtained. First, MacDonald reads the two sentences:

> Although hydrogen may play a role in the degradation mechanism [he is referring here to the decrease in the photoconductivity of the film], the former study suggests that it does not. In addition, the same degradation noted in the superlattice structures and the single layer films suggests that neither interface states nor carrier confinement in the wells influence the degra-

dation mechanism very much. (Graves, 2005, p. 75)

Second, he explains the thinking behind the written text:

> I guess this [passage] is speaking to the [degradation] *mechanism* [emphasis added]. I guess ... the impression you've then made on the reader's mind is that, first of all, the mechanism is probably a characteristic of the silicon nitride [rather than some other effect], and the presence of these thin layers, or the barrier potentials, or the effect that occurs there doesn't seem to change that [degradation] *mechanism* [emphasis added] at all. The *mechanism* [emphasis added] is occurring in ... both the well layers and the barrier structures. (Graves, 2005, p. 75).

In this explanation, MacDonald describes how he intends readers to interpret the textual discussion about the degradation mechanism—they should conclude that structural characteristics of the silicon nitride caused the decrease in photoconductivity (rather than other possibilities like the presence of hydrogen or the width of the well or barrier layers).

From the perspective of metonymy, in this passage MacDonald is using mechanism as what Radden and Kövecses (1999) call an "Action ICM" (idealized cognitive model) of the result being substituted for the action and the action for the result. That is, mechanism stands for the result or cause (the physical object) and for the whole activity or action (the process). In this particular instance, mechanism also functions as a concept metonymy, taking the formula formA-conceptA for formA-conceptB, in which mechanism, the word, refers to mechanism, the physical object, and then mechanism, the word, shifts to stand for mechanism, meaning the process. Radden and Kövecses note that this type of metonymy is lexically polysemous, meaning "two senses of a word-form are relatable within the same ICM" (p. 27). The polysemous nature of mechanism in this example cuts across the ontological realms of things/events and concepts. The metonymy then infers the existence and operation of the process from the existence of the physical cause of the decrease measured in the film's photoconductivity. This concept of metonymy obscures the ontological status of the actual physical cause of PPC by proposing the mechanism as both a thing (thing/event) and a process (concept). It is difficult to determine, therefore, whether this phenomenon, which traverses the ontological space between an idea or theory and a physical entity, should qualify as real, that is, a "brute fact of nature."

This example shows that it can be difficult to distinguish between entities that are real (i.e., those "brute facts of nature") and those that are linguistic constructions (i.e., theoretical concepts), at least on the basis of studying the linguistic practices of working scientists. The difficulty of distinguishing at least opens the door to supporting Gross's contention (1991) that all knowledge is rhetorically constructed. At the same time, science has proceeded over the last 2000 years by seeking an accurate description of the natural world, a basis that assumes there is a "real world out there."

Another example, MacDonald and Tzu's efforts to revise a rejected manuscript based on their work, shows how the physicists' skillful use of metonymy works to persuade reviewers that their good-quality pure amorphous silicon nitride films do indeed exist. A referee for *Physical Review Letters* had objected to the evidence MacDonald and Tzu had offered for their claim that the fabrication method (ion beam assisted reactive deposition [IBAD]) produced good quality pure amorphous silicon nitride films. The referee demanded proof that using an ion beam actually did eliminate the dangling and wrong bonds, as well as the cracks and microvoids between atoms, to create a good quality film. Such proof of the improved quality was not available or even possible with the technology that MacDonald and Tzu had available at the time. Nor did they want to conduct additional tests, since the experiments had been concluded and Tzu was working on a different project.

Instead, they had to use a different tactic to persuade the referee of their films' improved quality: argument. In the first submission to the journal, they did not argue strongly for the improved quality of their films because they believed such a conclusion was obvious. The referee's response convinced them otherwise. They decided to present the pieces of evidence they had that suggested a certain conclusion and then to argue in defense of that conclusion. MacDonald treated the pieces of evidence metonymically, that is, as smaller parts of a larger puzzle that, when assembled, gave a clear picture of their films with fewer structural defects than other pure amorphous silicon nitride single-layer films. Through constructing a metonymic argument, MacDonald hoped to change their claim for this referee from an argument into a fact.

In fact, this is what MacDonald decided to do in revising his and Tzu's submission for *Physical Review Letters:* use rhetoric, in the form of argument, to change the referee's perception of their good quality pure amorphous silicon nitride films from non-existent to existing. MacDonald offered the referee two pieces of evidence, neither of which was particularly strong by itself, but together made a stronger argument than in their original draft. The first piece of evidence was an arithmetical calculation, T_0/T, drawn from Mott's variable range hopping theory (a theory about the movement of electrons under certain conditions in a film), that showed that the higher the nitrogen content in the film, the lower the density of defects in it. After Tzu calculated and graphed the density of states for their film, MacDonald used the graph to show that the density of states (or number of structural defects) was lower in their pure amorphous silicon nitride films made using IBAD than in the same types of films made using other fabrication methods. The graph was meant to act as a metonymy: in depicting the relationship between higher nitrogen content and lower conductivity, it constituted an attribute of films with a reduced number of structural defects. This attribute supported MacDonald and Tzu's argument that IBAD improved the quality of the films it produced.

MacDonald's revisions to the paper in this analysis show one way in which the so-called reality outside of language (i.e., the actual quality of the pure amorphous silicon nitride films made with IBAD) is called into or out of existence based on his use of language. In fact, the actual quality of the film exists in spite of the referee, but unless MacDonald and Tzu can persuade him to acknowledge or verify its existence through their use of argument and evidence, its actual quality does not matter to the larger scientific community because it will never see MacDonald and Tzu's unpublished letter.

The second piece of evidence that MacDonald included in his revision had to do with the type of conductivity (the movement of electrons through the film when it is illuminated) that Tzu measured in the films. Of the two types of transport—carriers hopping from one gap state or defect in the material to another or activated conductivity at high temperatures—Tzu had measured only the second type, activated conductivity, which can only be measured in films with fewer defects. By emphasizing in their argument that "*all* [they] saw were activated energies, but [they] only saw them at high temperatures" (Graves, 2006, p. 237), MacDonald assigned a metonymic function to this second piece of evidence as well: activated conductivity at high temperatures is an attribute of high-quality films. As noted, the quality of these thin films remained the same throughout the drafting and revision of this article. Until MacDonald and Tzu constructed a persuasive argument backed by convincing evidence, the referee refused to believe in its existence. However, MacDonald's skillful use of metonymy as an argumentative strategy conferred existence or ontological presence onto the high-quality pure amorphous silicon nitride films.

The issue of the unchanging existence of the quality of the thin films fits neatly into McGuire and Melia's (1991) phrase about "the brute facts of nature." This understanding of reality is based on a Newtonian view of physics and science, one that assumes that reality is separate and independent of the observer. This view of a stable reality assumes that the "properties of elementary particles are eternal and set by absolute law[s]" (Smolin, 2006, p. 62), but developments in early twentieth century physics suggested that elementary particles (those most basic ingredients of "the brute facts of nature") are contingent, varying with the history and environment in which they occur. Smolin (2006), a theoretical physicist at the Perimeter Institute for Theoretical Physics in Waterloo, ON, confirms this point. In *The Trouble With Physics,* Smolin (2006) explains that "the properties of elementary particles depend in part on history and environment .... [They] are contingent and depend on which solution of the laws is chosen in our region of the universe or in our particular era" (pp. 61-62). If we extrapolate from these insights about the properties of elementary particles, that the characteristics of elementary particles may change in different regions of the universe, or even over time, then our concept of reality is not necessarily independent and separate. Several scholars, including Barad (2000), a scientist, and Desilet (1999), a rhetorician, have explored the relationship between reality and the brute facts of nature from Bohr's perspective in Barad's case and Einstein's perspective in Desilet's case; their theories of agential realism and rhetorical ontology take into account the fact that the observer influences the observed. In agential realism, Barad calls for scientists to articulate the conditions surrounding an experiment to provide a fuller context for the observations and conclusions. She argues against science's conventional use of "constructed objectivity" in reporting experiments because this style obscures the mutually affecting relationship between the observer and the observed.

THE ROLE OF METONYMY IN THEORETICAL PHYSICS

String theory, the major focus of efforts in theoretical physics for the last thirty years, provides a fascinating new direction for questions about the relationship between rhetoric and reality. String theory grows out of 20th century experiments with particle accelerators. Between 1930 and 1960, physicists accumulated a great deal of data from accelerators about what happened when various kinds of strongly interacting particles collided. Analysis of this data yielded an interesting insight into the physical representation. According to Smolin (2006),

> particles could not be seen as points .... Instead, they were 'stringlike,' existing only in a single dimension, and they could be stretched, like rubber bands. When they gained energy, they stretched; when they gave up energy, they contracted—also just like rubber bands. And like rubber bands, they vibrated. (p. 103)

Based on this data, string theory argues that elementary particles are not point-like but the vibrations of strings.

Obviously, theoretical physicists have made extensive use of analogy and metaphor to develop string theory. The particles are not strings or rubber bands, but their properties indicate that they behave similar to strings or rubber bands. And once the analogy is accepted, the idea quickly passes into metaphor, as in "string theory" where the metaphor is conceptualized as a literal description for the purposes of making progress in understanding the ideas.

In describing the central components of string theory, Smolin uses metonymy in much the same way that MacDonald did in the PPC example. While there are an indeterminable number of strings (or entities that have been described as strings), the physicists refer to a single string as they try to conceptualize the architecture and the processes that give rise to the theory. A single, archetypal string stands in for all the others which are presumed to behave identically in the theory.

In describing the two constants associated with string theory, the string tension and the string coupling constant, Smolin (2006) notes this interesting point about the string coupling constant:

> Actually the string coupling constant is not a free constant but a physical degree of freedom. Its value depends on the solution of the theory, so rather than being a parameter of the laws, it is a parameter that labels solutions. One can say that the probability for a string to break and join is fixed not by the theory but by the string's environment—that is, by the particular multidimensional world it lives in. (pp. 108-109)

In this passage, Smolin refers to the behaviour of one particular string as a way to describe what is happening among the whole universe or dimension of strings. He also makes a fascinating point about the way that the string coupling constant is linked not only to an abstract idea but also to a facet of the particular environment in which the string exists. This concept of the string coupling constant clearly breaks down the barriers that we think of as existing between the world of ideas and the world of things and events because it is both theoretical and real.

As we have just noted, the theory itself shifts between ontological realms, and, following the passage just quoted, Smolin goes on to note this point: "This habit of constants migrating from properties of the theory to properties of the environment is an important aspect of string theory" (p. 109). This use of language that shifts and obscures the separation between the entity and the idea about the entity is a characteristic of this theory in theoretical physics, according to Smolin.

The result of metonymic language use seems to be that eventually the users see the theory or concept as evidence of the existence of the "real" thing or event. This has, in fact, happened in the discipline of theoretical physics, where many string theorists believe that their theory is true, even though they have not been able to test much of it, nor have they been able to use the theory to predict new aspects that can then be tested through experiment. These are some of the baseline requirements for a theory in science to be plausible. However, string theorists are talking about changing our understanding of science to reflect their belief in the validity of their theories (there seem to be approximately 10,500 different string theories—not infinite but close). Smolin (2006) summarizes the dilemma as follows:

> [String theory] has failed to make any predictions by which it can be tested, and some of its proponents, rather than admitting that, are seeking leave to change the rule so that their theory will not need to pass the usual tests we impose on scientific ideas. (p. 170)

Interestingly, string theorists adhere faithfully to their belief in its validity—even though it fails to meet the basic requirements of a valid theory in science, that of making predictions, being falsifiable, and being confirmable. So faithfully, in fact, that they propose redefining science as a field. String theorists might, therefore, be described as proposing to turn science into rhetoric. Science becomes rhetoric when rhetorical tropes such as metaphor and metonymy, as well as mathematical equations (i.e., analogies), provide the primary ways to affirm the existence of the reality described by string theory. While transforming science into rhetoric might be one solution to the dilemma proposed earlier in this chapter, it is not necessarily a satisfactory one from a number of perspectives. For example, in *The Trouble with Physics,* Smolin (2006) calls for a shift in financial and institutional support away from string theory and towards alternative research programs that will preserve science as science. He also calls on theoretical physics to develop a new philosophical stance beyond realism that takes into account how quantum physics has changed the relationship between the observer (human perception) and the observed (the real world). Both Barad (2000) and Desilet (1999) have proposed a version of this type of philosophy with their theories of agential realism and rhetorical ontology, but there is a great deal more work to do to expand these proposals into workable philosophies.

CONCLUSION

From the perspective of rhetorical studies, the claim that all science is rhetoric misses the mark. An accurate description of the relationship between rhetoric and reality will likely turn out to be far more complex, interesting, and illuminating than simply collapsing the fields of study into one another. Recent research in the rhetoric of science shows that rhetoric does play a central role in the creation of knowledge in science, and it can also make possible the perception of the entities that may become what we think of as the "brute facts of nature."

Let us revisit the warning issued by McGuire and Melia in their rebuttal to Gross in *Rhetorica* in 1991: that although rhetoricians may seek evidence of the "rhetoricity of scientific facts, 'the brute facts of nature' will turn out to be just those products of science that appear to be beyond rhetorical analysis" (p. 304). In this chapter, I have shown how the brute facts of nature can, in fact, be subject to rhetorical analysis without definitively resolving the issue.

REFERENCES

Barad, K. (2000). Reconceiving scientific literacy as agential literacy, or learning how to intra-act responsibly with the world. In R. Reid & S. Traweek (Eds.), *Doing science and culture* (pp. 221-258). New York: Routledge.

Burke, K. (1969). *A grammar of motives*. Berkeley: University of California Press.

Croft, W. (1993). The role of domains in the interpretation of metaphors and metonymies. *Cognitive Linguistics, 4,* 335-371.

Desilet, G. (1999). Physics and language—Science and rhetoric: Reviewing the parallel evolution of theory on motion and meaning in the aftermath of the Sokal Hoax. *Quarterly Journal of Speech, 85,* 338-360.

Fahnestock, J. (1999). *Rhetorical figures in science*. New York: Oxford University Press.

Gentner, D. (1988). Structure mapping: A theoretical framework for analogy. In A. Collins & E. E. Smith, (Eds.), *Readings in cognitive science: A perspective from psychology and artificial intelligence.* San Mateo, CA: Morgan Kaufman.

Gentner, D., Ferguson, R., Markman, A. B., Levidow, B. B., Wolff, P., & Forbus, K. (1997). Analogical reasoning and conceptual change: A case study of Johannes Kepler. *The Journal of the Learning Sciences, 6,* 3-40.

Graves, H. B. (2005). *Rhetoric in(to) science: Style as invention in inquiry.* Cresskill, NJ: Hampton Press.

Gross, A. (1990). *The rhetoric of science*. Cambridge: Harvard University Press.

Gross, A. (1991). Rhetoric of science without constraints. *Rhetorica, 9,* 283-299.

Gross, A. (2006). *Starring the text: The place of rhetoric in science studies*. Carbondale: Southern Illinois University Press.

Lakoff, G., & Johnson, M. (1980). *Metaphors we live by.* Chicago: University of Chicago Press.

Lakoff, G., & Turner, M. (1989). *More than cool reason: A field guide to poetic metaphor.* Chicago: University of Chicago Press.

Little, J. (2000). Analogy in science: Where do we go from here? *Rhetoric Society Quarterly, 30,* 69-92.

Little, J. (2008). The role of analogy in George Gamow's derivation of drop energy. *Technical Communication Quarterly, 17,* 220 - 238.

McGuire, J., & Melia, T. (1991). The rhetoric of the radical rhetoric of science. *Rhetorica, 9,* 301-316.

Moss, J. D. (1993). *Novelties in the heavens: Rhetoric and science in the Copernican controversy.* Chicago: University of Chicago Press.

Myers, G. (1990). *Writing biology: Texts in the social construction of scientific knowledge.* Madison: University of Wisconsin Press.

Prelli, L. (1989). *A rhetoric of science: Inventing scientific discourse.* Columbia: University of South Carolina Press.

Radden, G., & Kövecses, Z. (1999). Toward a theory of metonymy. In K. Panther & G. Radden (Eds.), *Metonymy in language and thought* (pp. 17-59). Philadephia: John Benjamins.

Rymer, J. (1988). Scientific composing processes: How eminent scientists write journal articles. D. A. Jolliffe (Ed.), *Writing in academic disciplines* (pp. 211-251). Norwood: Ablex.

Scott, R. L. (1976). On viewing rhetoric as epistemic: Ten years later. *Central States Speech Journal, 18,* 258-266.

Scott, R. L. (1993). Rhetoric is epistemic: What difference does that make? In T. Enos & S. C. Brown (Eds.), *Defining the new rhetorics* (pp. 120-136). Newbury Park: Sage.

Smolin, L. (2006). *The trouble with physics: The rise of string theory, the fall of a science, and what comes next.* Boston: Houghton Mifflin.

10 DISCIPLINES AND DISCOURSES: SOCIAL INTERACTIONS IN THE CONSTRUCTION OF KNOWLEDGE

Ken Hyland

The view that academic writing is persuasive is now widely accepted. Exactly how this is achieved, however, is more contentious, and raises a number of important issues, not least of which are those concerning the relationship between reality and accounts of it, the efficacy of logical induction, and the role of social communities in constructing knowledge. These topics have been debated for years in epistemology and the sociology of science, and in the past decade applied linguists have also entered the fray.

Corpus linguists have been particularly active in emphasising the importance of rhetoric in academic persuasion, and, in this chapter, I bring my own small contribution to the discussion. In particular, I look at what differences in disciplinary discourses tell us about the ways academic knowledge is socially constructed, focusing on interpersonal features of language. I am interested in what this tells us about writers' ideas of appropriate writer-reader relationships and how this, in turn, contributes to knowledge-making in the disciplines (Hyland & Bondi, 2006).

ACADEMIC DISCOURSE AND SCIENTIFIC EXPLANATION

I want to begin with a few words about academic persuasion. Academic discourse is a privileged form of argument in the modern world, offering a model of rationality and detached reasoning. It is seen to depend on the demonstration of absolute truth, empirical evidence or flawless logic, representing what Lemke (1995) refers to as the discourse of "Truth" (p. 178). It provides an objective description of what the natural and human world is actually like, and this, in turn, serves to distinguish it from the socially contingent. We see this form of persuasion as a guarantee of reliable knowledge, and we invest it with cultural authority, free of the cynicism with which we view the partisan rhetoric of politics and commerce.

This view is most strongly represented by the natural sciences. The label "scientific" confers reliability on a method and prestige on its users. It implies all that is most objective and empirically verifiable about academic knowledge. As a result, it has been imitated by other areas of human inquiry that are often considered softer and more rhetorical in their forms of argument. Underlying this realist model is the idea that knowledge is built on experiment, induction, replication, and falsifiability. Scientific papers are seen as persuasive because they communicate truths which emerge from our direct access to the external world. The text is merely the channel through which scientists report observable facts. This is, in fact, probably why writing is marginalized in universities as it is just seen as reporting more important things that go on elsewhere.

But scientific methods provide less reliable bases for proof than commonly supposed. Although we rely on induction in our everyday lives—believing that the bus we take to work will pass by at 8 a.m. tomorrow if it has passed at 8 a.m. every day for the past week—it has been criticized by philosophers of science. They argue that induction offers probabilities rather than proof, and by moving from observations of instances to general statements about unobserved cases, scientists introduce uncertainty. Nor is the widely accepted alternative, Popper's 'Falsification' model, which puts theories through experimental testing and replaces those that are defective with more verifiable ones, any more reliable. It is simply not possible to conclusively falsify a hypothesis because the observations that form the basis for the falsification must be expressed in the language of some theory, and so will only be as reliable as that theory.

The problem for scientific knowledge, then, is that interpretation always depends on the assumptions scientists bring to the problem (e.g., Kuhn, 1970). That is, all reporting occurs within a pragmatic context and in relation to a theory which fits observation and data in meaningful patterns, so there is no secure observational base upon which any theories can be tested. As the Nobel physicist Hawking (1993) notes, "a theory may describe a range of observations, but beyond that it makes no sense to ask if it corresponds to reality, because we do not know what reality is independent of a theory" (p. 44).

In other words, there is always going to be at least one interpretation for research data and the fact that we can have these competing explanations shifts attention to the ways that academics argue their claims. We have to look for proof in the textual practices for producing agreement.

SOCIAL PRACTICES AND DISCIPLINARY CONVENTIONS

Because writers can only guide readers to a particular interpretation rather than demonstrate proof, readers always have the option of refuting their interpretations. At the heart of academic persuasion, then, are writers' attempts to anticipate possible negative reactions to their claims. To do this, they must display familiarity with the persuasive practices of their disciplines, encoding ideas, employing warrants, and framing arguments in ways that their potential audience will find most convincing. They also have to convey their credibility by establishing a professionally acceptable persona and an appropriate attitude, both to their readers and their arguments. In sum, persuasion in academic articles, as in other areas of professional life, involves the use of language to relate independent beliefs to shared experience. Writers galvanise support, express collegiality, resolve difficulties, and negotiate disagreement through patterns of rhetorical choices which connect their texts with their disciplinary cultures.

Persuasion, then, is accomplished with language. But it is language that demonstrates legitimacy. Writers must recognize and make choices from the rhetorical options available in their fields to appeal to readers from within the boundaries of their disciplines.

RESEARCH METHOD AND CORPUS

Academic corpora have begun to offer some useful insights into the ways this is done. I will report a series of investigations I have conducted over the last decade into the role of interaction in academic persuasion using a corpus of 240 research articles and interviews with academics. The corpus was compiled to represent a broad cross-section of academic practice and comprises 30 research papers from each of eight disciplines in the sciences, engineering, social sciences, and humanities, and a total of 1.4 million words (Table 1). The journals were nominated by discipline informants for being among the leading publications in their fields, and the articles were chosen at random from current issues. The corpus has been used to study a range of features including citations (Hyland, 2001a), directives (Hyland, 2002a), questions (Hyland, 2002b), authorial pronouns (Hyland, 2002c), and engagement features (Hyland, 2001b).

Table 1. Text Corpora.

Disciplines	Texts	Words	Disciplines	Texts	Words
Molecular Biology	30	143, 500	Sociology	30	224, 500
Mechanical Eng	30	114, 700	Philosophy	30	209, 000
Electronic Eng	30	107, 700	Marketing	30	214, 900
Magnetic Physics	30	97, 300	Applied Linguistics	30	211, 400
'Hard' fields	120	463, 200	'Soft' fields	120	859, 800

The value of a corpus is that it gives us information about the frequency of items and how they are used. This information points to systematic preferences in the ways members of different disciplines use language in their arguments. These preferences, in turn, tell us something about how writers see their readers and their disciplines.

The texts were searched for specific features seen as initiating writer-reader interactions using a commercial text analysis programme. A list of 320 potentially productive search items was compiled based on previous research into interactive features (e.g., Biber & Finegan, 1989; Bondi, 1999; Hyland, 2000, 2005), from grammars (Biber, Johansson, Leech, Conrad, & Finegan, 1999; Halliday, 1994), and from the most frequently occurring items in the articles themselves. All cases were examined to ensure they functioned as interactional markers and a sample was double-checked by a colleague working independently. The interviews were conducted with experienced researchers/writers from the target disciplines using a semi-structured format. These employed open-ended interview prompts that focused on subjects' own and others' writing, but allowed them to raise other relevant issues. Subjects could therefore respond to texts with insider community understandings of rhetorical effectiveness, while also discussing their own discoursal preferences and practices.

INTERACTIONS IN ACADEMIC WRITING

My argument is that academics do not just produce texts that plausibly represent an external reality. They are not just talking about garlic proteins, stress fractures or brains in vats. Instead, they use language to acknowledge, construct and negotiate social relations. The notion of interaction, and especially the ways writers convey their personal feelings and assessments, has become a heavily populated area of research in recent years. This research has been conducted under various labels, including "evaluation" (Hunston & Thompson, 2000), "intensity" (Labov, 1984), "affect" (Ochs, 1989), "evidentiality" (Chafe & Nichols, 1986), "hedging" (Hyland, 1998), and "stance" (Biber & Finegan, 1989). The expression of evaluation and stance in academic research writing has been especially productive (e.g., Bondi, 1999; Hyland, 2005).

Interaction in academic writing essentially involves "positioning", or adopting a point of view in relation to both the issues discussed in the text and to others who hold points of view on those issues. In persuading readers of their claims, writers must display a competence as disciplinary insiders, which is, at least in part, achieved through a writer-reader dialogue which situates both their research and themselves, establishing relationships between people, and between people and ideas. Writers therefore seek to project a shared professional context which only partly depends on domain knowledge, as meanings are ultimately produced in the interaction between writers and readers in specific social circumstances. In other words, claims for the significance and originality of research have to be balanced against the convictions and expectations of readers, taking into account their likely objections, background knowledge, rhetorical expectations and processing needs. All this is done within the broad constraints of disciplinary discourses.

STANCE AND ENGAGEMENT

I suggest that interactions are accomplished in academic writing by making choices from the interpersonal systems of stance and engagement. Stance refers to the writer's textual "voice" or community recognised personality, an attitudinal, writer-oriented function which concerns the ways writers present themselves and convey their judgements, opinions, and commitments. Engagement, on the other hand, is more of an alignment function, concerning the ways that writers rhetorically recognise the presence of their readers to actively pull them along with the argument, include them as discourse participants, and guide them to interpretations (Hyland, 2001a). Together they recognise that statements need to both present the writer and his or her ideas as well as anticipate readers' possible objections and alternative positions, incorporating an appropriate awareness of self and audience.

Stance and engagement are two sides of the same coin, and, because they both contribute to the interpersonal dimension of discourse, there are overlaps between them. Discrete categories inevitably conceal the fact that forms often perform more than one function at once because, in developing their arguments, writers are simultaneously trying to set out a claim, comment on its truth, establish solidarity and represent their credibility. In addition, the marking of stance and engagement is a highly contextual matter as writers can employ evaluations through a shared attitude towards particular methods or theoretical orientations which may be opaque to the analyst. Nor is it always marked by words at all: a writer's decision not to draw an obvious conclusion from an argument, for example, may be read by peers as a significant absence (Swales, 2004). The present study is restricted to grammatical devices that express stance and engagement, identifying predominant meanings to compare the rhetorical patterns in different discourse communities. The key resources by which these interactional macro-functions are realised are summarised in Figure 1.

Together these resources have a dialogic purpose in that they refer to, anticipate, or otherwise take up the actual or anticipated voices and positions of potential readers (Bakhtin, 1986). Distinguishing between these two dimensions is a useful starting point from which to explore how interaction and persuasion is achieved in academic discourse and what these can tell us of the assumptions and practices of different disciplines.

STANCE AND WRITER-ORIENTED INTERACTION

Stance concerns *writer-oriented features* of interaction and conveys different kinds of personal feelings and assessments, including attitudes that a writer has about particular information, how certain they are about its veracity, how they obtained access to it, and what perspective they are taking to it and to the reader. It conveys three broad meanings:
- *Evidentiality,* or the writer's expressed commitment to the reliability of propositions and their potential impact on readers;
- *Affect,* or personal and professional attitudes towards what is said;

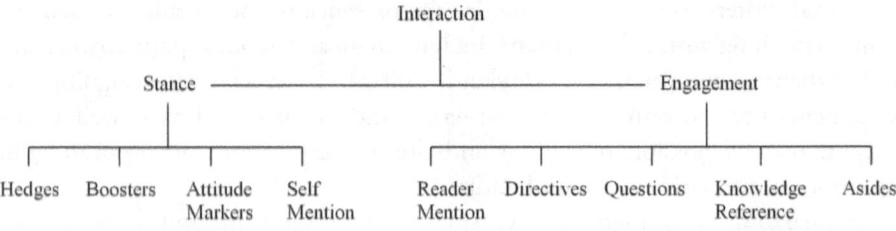

Figure 1. Resources for expressions of stance and engagement.

- *Presence,* or how far writers choose to project themselves into a text

Briefly, it is comprised of *hedges, boosters, attitude markers,* and *self mention.*

Hedges are devices which withhold complete commitment to a proposition, allowing information to be presented as an opinion rather than fact (Hyland, 1998). They imply that a claim is based on plausible reasoning rather than certain knowledge and so both indicate the degree of confidence it might be wise to attribute to a claim while allowing writers to open a discursive space for readers to dispute interpretations. This is an example from biology:

> (1) There are several possible reasons for this: (1) pressures increase upon freezing and thus may force bubbles back into solution at the time of thaw; (2) since xylem water is degassed by freezing there is a tendency for bubbles to redissolve at the time of thaw; and (3) xylem water may flow in advance of ice formation and could refill some of the previously embolized vessels. (Bio)

Boosters (like, definitely, sure, prove, etc.), on the other hand, allow writers to express certainty in what they say and to mark involvement with the topic and solidarity with readers. While they restrict opportunities for alternative voices, they also often stress shared information and group membership as we tend to get behind those ideas which have a good chance of being accepted. Like hedges, they often occur in clusters, underlining the writer's conviction in an argument:

> (2) Of course, I do not contend that there are no historical contingencies. On the contrary, the role of contingencies should be stressed. On this point, we must definitely stop following Hegel's intuitions. Nobody can foretell that tomorrow totalitarian regimes will not reappear and eventually spread over the planet. (Soc)

Attitude markers indicate the writer's affective attitude to propositions, conveying surprise, agreement, importance, frustration, and so on, rather than commitment. This is affect, not epistemology. This allows writers to both take a stand and align themselves with disciplinary value positions. Attitude is most explicitly signalled by attitude verbs, sentence adverbs, and adjectives, and this marking of attitude in academic writing allows writers to both take a stand and align themselves with disciplinary-oriented value positions. This example is from Applied Linguistics:

> (3) Certainly, I find it remarkable that even as proficient a non-native user as Yao should have introduced such an unexpected, subtle and self-evaluative question about her writing into the discussion. (AL)

Self mention refers to the use of first person pronouns and possessive adjectives to present information (Hyland, 2001b). Presenting a discoursal self is central to the writing process (Ivanic, 1998), and we cannot avoid projecting an impression of ourselves and how we stand in relation to our arguments, discipline, and readers. The presence or absence of explicit author reference is a conscious choice by writers to adopt a particular stance and disciplinary-situated authorial identity.

> (4) Our investigation of writing at the local government office comprised an analysis of the norms and attitudes of each individual. We asked the different employees about their norms concerning a good text and a good writer. We also asked them about their attitudes toward writing at work. What we found interesting about this context, however, is the degree of uniformity of their norms and attitudes. (Soc)

ENGAGEMENT AND READER-ORIENTED INTERACTION

Unlike stance, the ways writers bring readers into the discourse has been relatively neglected in the literature. Engagement seeks to build a connection with readers to both stress solidarity and position them by anticipating possible objections and guiding their thinking. Based on their previous experiences with texts, writers make predictions about how readers are likely to react to their arguments and craft their texts to explicitly address them at certain points (Hyland, 2001a). Engagement markers include reader pronouns, personal asides, references to sharedness, directives, and questions.

Reader pronouns offer the most explicit ways of bringing readers into a discourse, but we almost never find "you" in academic writing, perhaps because it implies a separation between writer and reader, rather than seeking connections. Instead there is enormous emphasis on binding the two together through the use of inclusive "we." There are several reasons for using this form, but, most centrally, it identifies the reader as someone who shares similar interests or ways of seeing to the writer as a member of the same discipline. At the same time as expressing peer solidarity, however, it also anticipates reader objections, presuming mutual understandings while weaving the potential point of view of the reader into the argument.

> (5) In carrying out such a "meta-analysis", moreover, we should try to minimize the possibilities of self-authorization of our own pragmatic theories. (AL)

> If we acknowledge folk psychology's value-anchoring role we can see the moral importance of greater representational complexity. (Phil)

Directives are mainly expressed through imperatives and obligation modals and they direct readers to engage in three main kinds of activity:
- textual acts: direct readers to another part of the text or to another text (*see Smith, 1999; refer to table 3,* etc.)
- physical acts direct readers how to carry out some action in the real-world (e.g., *open the valve, heat the mixture*).
- cognitive acts instruct readers how to interpret an argument, explicitly positioning readers by encouraging them to *note, concede* or *consider* some argument or claim in the text.

Personal asides allow writers to address readers directly by briefly interrupting the argument to offer a comment on what has been said. By turning to the reader in mid-flow, writers can initiate a brief dialogue that adds more to the writer-reader relationship than to propositional development:

> (6) And - as I believe many TESOL professionals will readily acknowledge - critical thinking has now begun to make its mark, particularly in the area of L2 composition. (AL)

> He above all provoked the mistrust of academics, both because of his trenchant opinions (often, it is true, insufficiently thought out) and his political opinions. (Soc)

Appeals to shared knowledge are explicit signals asking readers to recognise something as familiar or accepted. These constructions of solidarity ask readers to identify with particular views and in so doing construct readers by assigning to them a role in creating the argument, acknowledging their contribution while moving the focus of the discourse away from the writer to shape the role of the reader:

(7) Tillage as a form of soil disturbance is well known to disrupt hyphal networks and reduce colonization by arbuscular mycorrhizas. (Bio)

Obviously, such unsymmetric process geometry would cause the unbalanced rolling. (Mech Eng)

Questions are a key strategy of dialogic involvement, inviting participation, encouraging curiosity and leading readers to the writer's viewpoint (Hyland, 2002b). Questions perform a range of functions in academic writing and can have a different authoritative impact from the naïve puzzlement of limited knowledge to the confident anticipation of reaching an answer. In all cases, though, they invite direct collusion because they address the reader as someone with an interest in the issue the question raises and the good sense to follow the writer's response to it:

(8) Why did impoverished and almost defenseless shantytowns emerge as the center of resistance to authoritarian rule? Why did shantytown residents risk arrest, torture, and even death to fight a regime they seemed to have so little chance of defeating? Why did protests center in some shantytowns, but not others? (Soc)

Table 2. Stance and Engagement features in the research articles.

Stance	Items per 1000 words	% of total	Engagement	Items per 1000 words	% of total
Hedges	14.5	46.6	Reader pronouns	2.9	49.1
Attitude markers	6.4	205.	Directives	1.9	32.3
Boosters	5.8	19.2	Questions	0.5	8.5
Self mention	4.2	13.7	Shared knowledge references	0.5	8.2
			Asides	0.1	1.9
Totals	30.9	100		5.9	100

Now, in making choices from these systems of stance and engagement the writer is involved in a process of audience evaluation. So texts tell us something about how writers see their readers and therefore how language is related to specific institutional contexts.

DISCIPLINARY VARIATIONS IN STANCE AND ENGAGEMENT

Overall there were about 200 stance and engagement features in each paper, about one every 28 words. Table 2 shows that stance markers were about five times more common than engagement, and hedges dominated the frequencies. Questions, knowledge references and aside were less common.

We can get an idea of the significance of these frequencies by comparing them with other common features. Biber and colleagues (1999), for instance, record 18.5 cases per thousand words for passive voice constructions and 20 per thousand words for past tense verbs in a large corpus of academic writing. So these are major items in academic writing which do not always get the attention they deserve in EAP courses. More interesting, however, are the disciplinary distributions. Table 3 shows the density of features in each discipline normalised to a text length of 1,000 words. As can be seen, the more discursive 'soft' fields of philosophy, marketing, sociology and applied linguistics contained the highest proportion of interactional markers with some 75% more items than the engineering and science papers.

It is clear that writers in different disciplines represent themselves, their work and their readers in different ways, with those in the humanities and social sciences taking far more explicitly involved and personal positions than those in the sciences and engineering (Hyland & Bondi, 2006). In broad terms, rhetorical practices are inextricably related to the purposes of the disciplines. Natural scientists tend to see their goal as producing public knowledge able to withstand the rigours of falsifiability and developed through relatively steady cumulative growth (Becher, 1989). The fact that this research often occupies considerable investments in money, training, equipment, and expertise means it is frequently concentrated at a few sites and commits scientists to involvement in specific research areas for many years. Problems, therefore, emerge in an established context so that readers are often familiar with prior texts and research, and that the novelty and significance of contributions can be easily recognised.

Readers are often familiar with prior texts and research, and so a strong interpersonal element is not so necessary in the sciences. Writers are able to rely more on shared background and proven methods. The people who read those papers are often working on the same things and are familiar with the earlier work. They have a good idea about the procedures used, whether they have been properly applied, and what results mean. This helps reinforce a view of science as an impersonal, inductive enterprise and allows scientists to see themselves as discovering truth rather than constructing it.

The soft-knowledge domains, in contrast, produce discourses which often recast knowledge as sympathetic understanding, promoting tolerance in readers through an ethical rather than cognitive progression (Hyland, 2000). They have to spell things out, and work harder to establish their credibility and to create an understanding with readers. Personal credibility, getting behind your arguments, plays an important part in creating a convincing discourse in the humanities and social sciences.

Table 3. Stance and engagement features by discipline (per 1,000 words).

Feature	Phil	Soc	AL	Mk	Phy	Bio	ME	EE	Total
Stance	42.8	31.1	37.2	39.5	25.0	23.8	19.8	21.6	30.9
Hedges	18.5	14.7	18.0	20.0	9.6	13.6	8.2	9.6	14.5
Attitude markers	8.9	7.0	8.6	6.9	3.9	2.9	5.6	5.5	6.4
Boosters	9.7	5.1	6.2	7.1	6.0	3.9	5.0	3.2	5.8
Self mention	5.7	4.3	4.4	5.5	5.5	3.4	1.0	3.3	4.2
Engagement	16.3	5.1	5.0	3.2	4.9	1.6	2.8	4.3	5.9
Reader ref	11.0	2.3	1.9	1.1	2.1	0.1	0.5	1.0	2.9
Directives	2.6	1.6	2.0	1.3	2.1	1.3	2.0	2.9	1.9
Questions	1.4	0.7	0.5	0.3	0.1	0.1	0.1	0.0	0.5
Shared knowledge ref	1.0	0.4	0.6	0.4	0.5	0.1	0.3	0.4	0.5
Asides	0.2	0.2	0.1	0.1	0.0	0.0	0.0	0.0	0.1
Totals	59.1	36.2	42.2	42.7	29.9	25.4	22.6	25.9	36.8

AUTHORIAL INVOLVEMENT IN KNOWLEDGE CONSTRUCTION

Now I will turn to look at what this model tells us about knowledge construction in the research article corpus, examining stance first.

Both hedges and boosters are more common in the humanities and social science papers with about 2½ times as many devices overall and hedges particularly strongly represented. This is mainly because the soft-knowledge fields are typically more interpretative and less abstract than the hard sciences and their forms of argument rely more on a dialogic engagement and more explicit recognition of alternative voices. Research is influenced far more by contextual factors, there is less control of variables, more diversity of research outcomes, and generally fewer unequivocal bases for accepting claims. Writers in the soft fields cannot, therefore, report their research with the same confidence of shared assumptions. They must rely far more on focusing readers on the claim-making negotiations of the discourse community, the arguments themselves, rather than relatively unmediated real-world phenomena. This means that arguments have to be expressed more cautiously by using more hedges:

> (9) Wilson leaves us disappointed, it seems to me, in the sense that his theory is far from being general. (Soc)
>
> We tentatively suggest that The Sun's minimalist style creates an impression of working-class language, or restricted code. (AL)

The fact that methods and results are more open to question also means that writers in the social sciences and humanities also work harder to establish the significance of their work against alternative interpretations. In particular, they restrict possible alternative voices by using boosters. Two comments from informants typify this view:

> It's often a good idea to present ideas confidently so that people take you seriously. I'm very much aware that I'm building a façade of authority when I write, I really like to get behind my work and get it out there. Strong. Committed. That's the voice I'm trying to promote, even when I'm uncertain I want to be behind what I say. (Soc interview)
>
> You have to be seen to believe what you say. That they are your

> arguments. It's what gives you credibility. It's the whole point. (Phil interview)

This kind of commitment is evident in these extracts:

> (9) It is certainly true that many arguments involve multiple premises. (Phil)

> This particular result is undoubtedly attributable to the impending incorporation of Hong Kong into the People's Republic of China. (Mk)

In the hard sciences, positivist epistemologies mean that the authority of the individual gets subordinated to the authority of the text and facts are meant to 'speak for themselves' (Hyland, 2005). Writers often disguise their interpretative responsibilities behind linguistic objectivity. The less frequent use of hedges and boosters is one way of minimising the researcher's role, as is the preference for modals over cognitive verbs, such as think, believe and suspect. Modals can more easily combine with inanimate subjects to downplay the person making the evaluation. So instead of

> (10) I think this would be a mistake. (Soc)

we suspect that the type of product used in this study may have contributed to the result (Mkt), we tend to find:

> (11) The theory given above simply provided some insight into the various mechanisms that might or might not yield a polarimetric effect. (Phy)

> For V. trifidum, ANOVA showed a significant increase from L to L' and FI, which could be interpreted as reflecting the dynamics of fungal colonization. (Bio)

> The deviations at high frequencies may have been caused by the noise measurements ... (EE)

Two scientist informants commented on this kind of use:

> Of course, I make decisions about the findings I have, but

> it is more convincing to tie them closely to the results. (Phy interview)

> You have to relate what you say to your colleagues and we don't encourage people to go out and nail their colours to the mast as maybe they don't get it published. (Bio interview)

Self mentions are also less common in the sciences for similar reasons, as writers often downplay their personal role to suggest that results would be the same whoever conducted the research. They are concerned with generalisations rather than individuals and with strengthening the objectivity of their interpretations. By subordinating their own voice to that of nature, they put greater burden on the methods, procedures, and equipment used. As this biologist told me,

> I feel a paper is stronger if we are allowed to see what was done without "we did this" and "we think that." Of course we know there are researchers there, making interpretations and so on, but this is just assumed. It's part of the background. I'm looking for something interesting in the study and it shouldn't really matter who did what in any case. (Bio interview)

In contrast, in the humanities and social sciences the strategic use of self-mention allows writers to strongly identify with a particular argument and to gain credit for an individual viewpoint. Through first person they can claim authority by expressing their convictions, emphasizing their contribution to the field, and seeking recognition for their work (Hyland, 2001b; Kuo, 1999). It sends a clear indication to the reader of the perspective from which statements should be interpreted, distinguishing the writer's own work from that of others. It is not surprising therefore that some 69% of all cases of self-mention were in the humanities and social science papers, with an average of 38 per article, compared with only 17 per paper in science and engineering. Successful communication in the soft fields depends far more on the author's ability to invoke a real writer in the text. Personal reference is thus a clear indication of the perspective from which a statement should be interpreted, enabling writers to emphasize their own contribution to the field and to seek agreement for it.

> (12) I argue that their treatment is superficial because, despite appearances, it relies solely on a sociological, as opposed to an ethical, orientation to develop a response. (Soc)

> I bring to bear on the problem my own experience. This experience contains ideas derived from reading I have done which might be relevant to my puzzlement as well as my personal contacts with teaching contexts. (AL)

So, in the humanities and social sciences, self-mention can help construct an intelligent, credible, and engaging colleague by presenting an authorial self, reflecting an appropriate degree of confidence and authority:

> Using 'I' emphasizes what you have done. What is yours in any piece of research. I notice it in papers and use it a lot myself. (Soc interview)

> The personal pronoun 'I' is very important in philosophy. It not only tells people that it is your own unique point of view, but that you believe what you are saying. It shows your colleagues where you stand in relation to the issues and in relation to where they stand on them. It marks out the differences. (Phil interview)

PARTICIPANT RELATIONSHIPS AND INTERPERSONAL ENGAGEMENT

In addition to creating an impression of authority and credibility through stance choices, writers also highlight or downplay the presence of their readers in the text through the use of engagement devices. As we saw in Table 3, engagement devices were far less frequent than stance items, but showed similar variation across disciplines.

Reader pronouns were the most frequent engagement items in the corpus and over 80% of these occurred in the soft disciplines where they appealed to scholarly solidarity. Here writers emphasised mutual, discipline-identifying understandings linking writer and reader:

> (13) Adopting a reflexive and continuously critical approach towards ourselves and our sociological practices is especially necessary because our profession is an all-embracing calling that penetrates our self and collective identities, and serves for many of us as a functional equivalent of ideology or civil-religion. (Soc)

Claiming communality is important to writers in the discursive fields, as several of my informants noted:

> I suppose "we" helps to finesse a positive response—we are all in this together kind of thing. I use it to signal that I am on the same wavelength, drawing on the same assumptions and asking the same questions. (Mkt Interview)

> It helps to locate you in a network. It shows that you are just doing and thinking what they might do and think. Or what you would like them to, anyway. (Soc interview)

But these pronouns claim authority as well as collegiality. They not only appeal to disciplinary solidarity but address readers from a position of confidence, taking on their potential point of view to guide them through an argument and towards a preferred interpretation, as can be seen here:

> (14) Now that we have a plausible theory of depiction, we should be able to answer the question of what static images depict. But this turns out to be not at all a straightforward matter. We seem, in fact, to be faced with a dilemma. Suppose we say that static images can depict movement. This brings us into conflict with Currie's account. (Phil)

> Although we lack knowledge about a definitive biological function for the transcripts from the 93D locus, their sequences provide us with an ideal system to identify a specific transcriptionally active site in embryonic nuclei. (Bio)

Several of my informants were well aware of this more Machiavellian purpose:

> Part of what you are doing in writing a paper is getting your readers onside, not just getting down a list of facts, but showing that you have similar interests and concerns. That you are looking at issues in much the same way they would, not spelling everything out, but following the same procedures and asking the questions they might have. (Bio interview)

> I often use 'we' to include readers. I suppose it brings out something of the collective endeavour, what we all know and want

to accomplish. I've never thought of it as a strategy, but I suppose I am trying to lead readers along with me. (ME interview)

Questions. There was an even greater disciplinary imbalance with the use of questions, which we almost exclusively find in the soft fields. But over 80% of questions in the corpus were rhetorical, presenting an opinion as an interrogative, but often answering the question immediately, simultaneously opening and closing the dialogue to present a claim:

> (15) Does the Brain-in-a-vat thereby succeed in including the relation in which it stands to its environment "the delusive relation"? There are, I think, compelling reasons to say that it does not. (Phil)
>
> What do these two have in common, one might ask? The answer is that they share the same politics. (AL)

The fact that they reach out to readers was seen as a distraction by my science informants:

> Questions are quite rare in my field I think. You might find them in textbooks I suppose, but generally we don't use them. They seem rather intrusive, don't they? Too personal. We generally prefer not to be too intrusive. (ME interview)
>
> I am looking for the results in a paper, and to see if the method was sound. I am looking for relevance and that kind of dressing is irrelevant. People don't ask questions as it would be seen as irrelevant. And condescending probably. (EE)

In contrast, the soft knowledge writers saw them as an important way of relating to readers:

> In my field that's all there are, questions. Putting the main issues in the form of questions is a way of presenting my argument clearly and showing them I am on the same wavelength as them. (Phil interview)
>
> Often I structure the argument by putting the problems that they might ask. (Mkt interview)

Finally, *directives* were the only interactive feature which occurred more frequently in the science and engineering papers than in the humanities and social sciences. Generally, explicit engagement is a feature of the soft disciplines, where writers are less able to rely on the explanatory value of accepted procedures, but directives are a potentially risky tactic as they instruct readers to act or see things in a certain way. As a result, most directives in the soft fields were textual, directing readers to a reference or table rather than telling them how they should interpret an argument.

> See Steuer 1983 for a discussion of other contingencies' effects. (Mkt)

> Look at Table 2 again for examples of behavioristic variables. (Mkt)

> For transcription conventions refer to the Appendix. (AL)

Two of my respondents noted this in their interviews:

> I am very conscious of using words like 'must' and 'consider' and so on and use them for a purpose. I want to say 'Right, stop here. This is important and I want you to take notice of it'. So I suppose I am trying to take control of the reader and getting them to see things my way. (Soc interview)

> I am aware of the effect that an imperative can have so I tend to use the more gentle ones. I don't want to bang them over the head with an argument I want them to reflect on what I'm saying. I use 'consider' and 'let's look at this' rather than something stronger. (AL interview)

Argument in the hard knowledge fields, in contrast, is formulated in a highly standardised code. Succinctness is valued by both editors and scientists themselves and directives allow writers to cut directly to the heart of matters. This helps explain why cognitive directives, potentially the most threatening type, were overwhelmingly predominant in the natural science corpus. These explicitly position readers by leading them through an argument or emphasising what they should attend to:

> (17) Consider a sequence of batches in an optimal schedule.

> (EE)
>
> A distinction must be made between cytogenetic and molecular resolution. (Bio)
>
> What has to be recognised is that these issues ... (ME)

This facilitates succinctness and an economy of expression highly valued by space-conscious editors and information-saturated scientists, as several informants noted:

> I rarely give a lot of attention to the dressing, I look for the meat—the findings—and if the argument is sound. If someone wants to save me time in getting there then that is fine. No, I'm not worried about imperatives leading me through it. (EE interview)
>
> I'm very conscious of how I write and I am happy to use an imperative if it puts my idea over clearly. Often we are trying to work to word limits anyway, squeezing fairly complex arguments into a tight space. (ME interview)

CONCLUSIONS

These different features, taken together, are important ways of situating academic arguments in the interactions of members of disciplinary communities. Induction and falsification are not proofs. Because we do not have direct access to the world and our understandings can only be mediated by a theory to interpret it, knowledge has to be seen as a rhetorical construct. I hope to have shown that effective academic writing depends on interactions and I have suggested a model which attempts to show how writers deploy linguistic resources to represent themselves, their positions, and their readers. These resources represent relatively conventional ways of making meaning and so elucidate a context for interpretation, showing how writers and readers make connections, through texts, to their disciplinary cultures.

In other words, discourse conventions are persuasive because they carry the epistemological and social beliefs of community members. The regularities I have highlighted are influenced by the types of inquiry and understandings of different knowledge domains. Reference to the writer or the reader sends a clear signal of membership. It textually constructs both the writer and the reader as people with similar understandings and goals. This not only helps writers persuade their colleagues of their claims, but puts writing at the heart of knowledge creation and teaching. It also helps us to understand something about disciplinary communities and the ways they construct knowledge.

REFERENCES

Bakhtin, M. (1986). *The dialogic imagination: Four essays*(M. Holquist, Ed., C. Emerson & M. Holquist, Trans.). Austin: University of Texas Press.
Becher, T. (1989). *Academic tribes and territories: Intellectual inquiry and the cultures of disciplines*. Milton Keynes, UK: SRHE/OUP.
Biber, D., & Finegan, E. (1989). Styles of stance in English: Lexical and grammatical marking of evidentiality and affect. *Text, 9*(1), 93-124.
Biber, D., Johansson, S., Leech, G., Conrad, S., & Finegan, E. (1999). *Longman grammar of spoken and written English*. Harlow: Longman.
Bondi, M. (1999). English across genres: Language variation in the discourse of economics. Modena: Edizioni Il Fiorino.
Chafe, W. L., & Nichols, J. (Eds.). (1986). *Evidentiality: The linguistic coding of epistemology*. Norwood, N. J.: Ablex.
Halliday, M. A. K. (1994). *An introduction to functional grammar* (2nd ed.). London: Arnold.
Hawking, S. (1993). *Black holes and baby universes and other essays*. New York: Bantam.
Hunston, S., & Thompson, G. (Eds.). (2000). *Evaluation in text*. Oxford: Oxford University Press.
Hyland, K. (1998). *Hedging in scientific research articles*. Amsterdam: John Benjamins.
Hyland, K. (2000). *Disciplinary discourses: Social interactions in academic writing*. London: Longman.
Hyland, K. (2001a). Bringing in the reader: Addressee features in academic writing. *Written Communication, 18*(4), 549-574.
Hyland, K. (2001b). Humble servants of the discipline? Self-mention in research articles. *English for Specific Purposes, 20*, 207-226.
Hyland, K. (2002a). Directives: Power and engagement in academic writing. *Applied Linguistics, 23*(2), 215-239.
Hyland, K. (2002b). What do they mean? Questions in academic writing. *Text, 22* (4), 529-557.
Hyland, K. (2002c) Authority and invisibility: Authorial identity in academic writing. *Journal of Pragmatics, 34*(8), 1091-1112.

Hyland, K. (2005). *Metadiscourse*. London: Continuum.

Hyland, K., & Bondi, M. (Eds.). (2006). *Academic discourse across disciplines*. Frankfort: Peter Lang.

Ivanic, R. (1998). *Writing and identity: The discoursal construction of identity in academic writing*. Amsterdam: Benjamins.

Kuhn, T. (1970). *The structure of scientific revolutions* (2nd ed.). Chicago: University of Chicago Press.

Kuo, C.-H. (1999). The use of personal pronouns: Role relationships in scientific journal articles. *English for Specific Purposes, 18*(2), 121-138.

Labov, W. (1984). Intensity. In D. Schiffrin (Ed.), *Meaning, form, and use in context: Linguistic applications* (pp. 43-70). Washington, D. C.: Georgetown University Press.

Lemke, J. (1995). *Textual politics: Discourse and social dynamics*. London: Taylor and Francis.

Ochs, E. (Ed.). (1989). *The pragmatics of affect* [Special issue]. Text, 9.

Swales, J. (2004). *Research genres*. Cambridge: Cambridge University Press.

11 KNOWLEDGE AND IDENTITY WORK IN THE SUPERVISION OF DOCTORAL STUDENT WRITING: SHAPING RHETORICAL SUBJECTS

Anthony Paré, Doreen Starke-Meyerring, and Lynn McAlpine

As knowledge moves centre stage in all sectors of society, governments around the world have identified the development of new researchers as one of the most critical infrastructure issues in knowledge-intensive societies (Canadian Association for Graduate Studies, 2005; Council of Graduate Schools, 2007; European University Association, 2007). Doctoral graduates are increasingly seen as "advanced knowledge workers" (Lee & Boud, 2008, p. 18), whose roles include the education of future generations of knowledge workers and researchers as well as the production and dissemination of original knowledge. In short, doctoral education is increasingly seen as a critical factor in spurring innovation, economic growth, and national prosperity.

For their research productivity, doctoral students, like all researchers, depend on their ability to write not only their dissertations, but, increasingly, also peer-reviewed publications as well as scholarship and grant applications. Indeed, as Hyland (2004) remarks, researchers rely on their writing "as a means of funding, constructing, evaluating and negotiating knowledge" (p. 5). Although often taken for granted, research writing is a highly specialized and discipline-specific social practice critical to knowledge making and to (re)producing disciplinary membership and identity (Bazerman & Prior, 2005; Green, 2005; Hyland, 2004, this volume; Horne, this volume; Kamler & Thomson, 2006; Prior, 1998; Tardy, 2009).

In this chapter, we draw on a larger longitudinal study of doctoral education in two Education faculties to shed some light on the knowledge and identity work that constitutes doctoral education. Although the formation of disciplinary subjects is, as Green (2005) argues persuasively, best "conceived ecosocially, as a total environment within which postgraduate research activity ('study') is realised" (p. 153), here we are interested in the role supervision of doctoral student writing plays in enacting the knowledge and identity work of doctoral education. As we illustrate, the transformation that occurs during doctoral education involves the formation of rhetorical subjects capable of participating in the discourse practices that produce the specialized knowledge of their research communities. We are particularly interested in the rhetorical nature of this work—that is, the ways in which students find their location or position in the rhetorical situations that produce a community's knowledge. More specifically, we would like to understand how students learn to participate in the highly situated, interested, contingent, and constantly evolving process of knowledge production in their fields. And we want to understand the role that supervisory sessions play in the formation of the rhetorical subject. Finally, we are curious about if and how the rhetorical nature of knowledge-making emerges in the conversation between students and supervisors about dissertation writing.

We explore these questions by considering recorded excerpts of those conversations. The comments reveal the extent to which supervisors' feedback is designed to help doctoral students locate themselves appropriately and effectively in the rhetorical situations that produce their discipline's knowledge. We hope our illustration opens up new opportunities for considering the role a rhetorical understanding of knowledge and identity work can play in making these acts of location and subject formation subject to critical exploration.

For this purpose, we begin by considering the particular role of doctoral education, and, specifically, the apprenticeship relationship between supervisors and doctoral students in the reproduction of the academic workplace and its practices. In doing so, we exploit the advantages a workplace learning perspective has for our understanding of doctoral supervision and its role in introducing students to that workplace. We then draw on rhetorical genre theory to conceptualize the specific knowledge and identity work that constitutes doctoral education. Next, framed by this rhetorical understanding, we present excerpts from doctoral supervision sessions as well as interviews with participants in order to trace some of the ways in which supervision sessions locate students in their research communities and shape them as rhetorical subjects. We conclude by exploring opportunities that arise from an understanding of doctoral writing as a deeply rhetorical and epistemic practice for a critical examination of disciplinary knowledge and identity questions as well as for the future of doctoral education in a knowledge-intensive society.

UNDERSTANDING DOCTORAL WRITING THROUGH THE LENS OF WORKPLACE LEARNING

Because the doctoral education cycle focuses on original knowledge production, doctoral students play a very different role in universities than do undergraduate or even Master's students. Unlike undergraduate students and many Master's students, doctoral students must ultimately be able to participate in the ongoing knowledge-making endeavors of their research communities. Although some of them may pursue careers outside of academe, they seek membership in a research community in order to be able to contribute to that community's knowledge-making goals. In many ways, PhD students are newcomers in the academic workplace, serving an apprenticeship under the guidance of oldtimers whose task it is to help move students towards competent participation in the ways of producing knowledge that are appropriate to a particular academic community. Accordingly, we feel that the interactions between supervisors and doctoral students are best examined in the context of workplace learning (e.g., Engeström & Middleton, 1998; Lave & Wenger, 1991; Wenger 1998), and particularly the learning of workplace writing (e.g., Bazerman & Paradis, 1991; Dias, Freedman, Medway, & Paré, 1999; Dias & Paré, 2000; Odell & Goswami, 1982, 1985; Spilka, 1993; Winsor, 1996). As we have argued elsewhere (Paré & Le Maistre, 2006a, 2006b), mentorship within organizations is often a distributed affair, with direction and instruction coming from many sources; nonetheless, in academia as in other contexts, the supervisory dyad remains a key relationship in the induction process. Examining this relationship through the lens of workplace learning gives us a number of advantages for understanding the ways in which supervisors help move students toward competent participation in their research community's knowledge-making practices.

To begin with, we hope that treating university departments as workplaces will help us de-mythologize the PhD process by knocking some of the ivory off the tower and making the doctorate a transition to working life rather than an initiation into some kind of secret society. It is not that we want to equate doctoral education to widget production, but we do want to acknowledge that some part of it is—or could be—a training in practices and procedures that are straightforward and teachable, though they are often learned by awkward (and sometimes painful) stumbling, trial and error, or imitation rather than direct instruction. Often constituting a kind of "invisible curriculum," these practices are an academic community's knowledge-making activities. They involve the implicit (and tacit) regularities and routines of the discipline as well as the rifts, affiliations, allegiances and other divisions that characterize disciplines and help construct the subjectivities of new members (Green, 2005). They are usually learned, but not taught, enacted, but not articulated.

In addition, a workplace perspective on doctoral writing helps us uncover some of the unique characteristics of the academic workplace, two of which are particularly relevant for our study: first, in the academic workplace, researchers engage in their core activity, the making of knowledge, largely outside of their immediate organizational contexts—that is, outside of their departments and universities, within their far-flung disciplinary communities. In fact, the value they bring to their immediate organizational contexts is largely determined by the extent to which peers in those dispersed disciplinary communities accept and cite their knowledge claims, support their research proposals, recommend their articles for publication, or propose their work for research awards or their names for prestigious positions in their disciplinary communities and beyond. For doctoral students, this characteristic of the academic workplace represents particular challenges because disciplinary practices are not as easily observable in their daily physical spaces as knowledge-making practices might be in workplaces in other types of organizations. Instead, aside from occasional conferences, these practices are observable predominantly in the form of written discourse—in print, whether on paper or on the screen.

And this is the second key characteristic of the academic workplace: because knowledge is made in research communities that tend to be widely distributed, much social interaction happens in writing, be it proposing one's research, publishing one's work, reviewing the research of other colleagues for peer-reviewed publications and conferences, and more. As a result, the academic workplace is probably one of the most highly writing-intensive workplaces imaginable. For doctoral students, the challenge here is that social interaction and practices are not only difficult to observe, but that the written forums where they can be observed have been taught in a largely arhetorical way throughout their education—that is, as a matter of mere "information" or "sources." Accordingly, until they begin their doctoral education, students learn to think of articles and books as "sources" of information and facts for research projects. Hardly ever are they taught to regard written discourse as forums for social interaction, where knowledge claims are staked out, tested, questioned, suppressed, ignored, relegated to footnotes, defended, negotiated, accepted, or advanced; where scholarly reputations are built, negotiated, or destroyed; and where scholars align themselves with or against their colleagues, depending on their various epistemological, ideological, or ontological commitments. That is, the deeply rhetorical, interested, and situated nature of knowledge-making has remained shrouded or unspoken throughout much of their education.

In addition to helping us de-mythologize the PhD process and foregrounding key characteristics of academic settings, the workplace learning lens also provides us with the analytic power of contemporary theories of workplace and situated learning, including the developmental sequence predicted by Lave and

Wenger's (1991) notion of legitimate peripheral participation. That trajectory describes the learner moving toward competent practice through participation in a series of authentic and ever-more difficult workplace tasks under the direction and guidance of workplace veterans. So, for example, we might track a graduate student's progress from teaching assistant to seminar leader to undergraduate course instructor and, finally, as a new professor, to instructor and supervisor at the graduate level, where newcomer becomes oldtimer. Or, following a progression more relevant to the study reported here, we might trace development from course essay to comprehensive examination to dissertation and journal article.

Similarly tracing the trajectory of graduate student community membership, Prior (1998) identifies three modes of graduate student participation: "passing," "procedural display," and "deep participation" (pp. 100-103). Although he is careful to point out that these modes are not "a general stage model" (p. 100), Prior does suggest that the three modes "do capture ... some important patterns of participation in school-based disciplinary enculturation" (p. 101). In our own discussions, we have also considered three types of participation, which we see as characterizing an increasing sense of membership or disciplinary identification: undergraduate roles are often those of eavesdroppers, listening in on the disciplinary conversation and reporting it back to the professor (an actual member); Master's students' roles are, in Bakhtinian terms, often those of ventriloquists, able to sound like participants, but really only channeling the voices of actual members; doctoral students—if they are fortunate—find themselves increasingly involved as participants in work that matters, in work that will be public and that might affect others. Even more, as Golde and Walker (2006) suggest, they may come to see themselves as "stewards of their discipline." Their access to and engagement in the range of practices that constitute the community's work result in the "deep participation" to which Prior refers. That transformation marks the beginnings of membership and participation and is accomplished largely through writing as knowledge and identity work.

DOCTORAL WRITING AS KNOWLEDGE AND IDENTITY WORK: A GENRE PERSPECTIVE

To understand the knowledge and identity work at the heart of this membership trajectory, we have depended on rhetorical genre theory (e.g., Artemeva & Freedman, 2006, this volume; Bawarshi & Reiff, 2010; Bazerman, 1988; Bazerman, Bonini, & Figueiredo, 2009; Campbell & Jamieson, 1978; Coe, Lingard, & Teslenko, 2002; Devitt, 2004; Freedman & Medway, 1994; Giltrow, 2002, this volume; Miller, 1984; Paré, 2005; Schryer, 1993, this volume), one manifestation of a perspective in the study of language that sees writing not as a set of portable skills, but as situated social practices. Genre theory assumes that repeated textual practices arise in human collectives because they produce material, intellectual, ideological, and/or relational outcomes valued by the collective or a sub-group within the collective. These practices have, at their core, hard copy or electronic texts that display similarity across instances of their production. Such typical texts are what we used to call genres—that is, documents that, over time, exhibit similar patterns in linguistic, lexical, structural, topical, and intentional features.

More recently, beginning with Campbell and Jamieson (1978) and Miller (1984), genre theorists have expanded their focus out from that physical text to the regularized outcomes, actions, or consequences of generic literate practice, as well as the contextual and conceptual regularities that shape the production of standardized texts: the institutional and intellectual processes by which participants identify and assemble appropriate resources and arguments, the collaborative activities—such as meetings, co-authoring, peer reviewing—through which texts develop, as well as the patterns and habits associated with the distribution, consumption, and archiving of texts. For example, the repeatedly occurring need for developing new researchers in a given field has predominantly been met through the genre of the dissertation, which over time has developed a somewhat stabilized appearance in that field—certain similarities in structure, types of argumentation, ways of positioning claims, ways of citing others—as well as regularized social processes involved in the production of a dissertation, such as supervision meetings and exams, that have become expected, valued, and normalized in a given disciplinary and institutional location.

For the purposes of our study, three insights from genre theory are particularly pertinent: First, genres maintain and regularize the production of certain kinds of knowledge outcomes valued in a given research community; in short, genres are epistemic. That is, genres regularize who can participate in a genre and in what role; what is appropriate to be said, what not, in what order; what kind of previous knowledge can or must be included or excluded (e.g., how practitioner knowledge or knowledge from different disciplines is to be handled, etc.); what kinds of knowledge claims can be made, how, based on what evidence; what makes an argument credible; how data can or must be generated, justified, and discussed; or what disciplinary orthodoxies must be reproduced and which ones can be questioned. As Graves (this volume) illustrates, for example, researchers depend on understanding the kinds of arguments that will persuade colleagues to accept their knowledge claims—that certain facts do indeed exist. Or as Hyland (this volume) illustrates, researchers depend on shared practices of social interaction that have evolved over time to enable their collective knowledge-making endeavors. In short, genres provide the spaces that assemble, enable, and constrain knowledge production in ways that have evolved in research communities through repetition over time in order to meet a given community's knowledge-making goals.

Second, genres inscribe, enable, and constrain not only a range of particular knowledge-making practices and outcomes, but also the identities (Bazerman, 2002; Green, 2005; Kamler & Thomson, 2006; Paré, 2002, 2005) that make the production of specialized knowledge in a given field possible. In Bazerman's (2002) words, "genre shapes intentions, motives, expectations, attention, perception, affect, and interpretive frame" (p. 14). For example, through writing a dissertation, participants learn the extent to which they must distance themselves from their knowledge claims through the use of the passive voice, for instance; or conversely, they learn the extent to which they must reflect on their role as researchers in the knowledge-making process in order to render their knowledge claims less open to questioning and perhaps more credible in a given research community. Or in literature reviews, which Kamler and Thomson (2006) describe as "the quintessential site of identity work" (p. 29), doctoral students learn to align themselves on contested terrain with certain disciplinary groups or factions by adhering to and reproducing certain disciplinary patterns, regularities, and assumptions (Kamler & Thomson, 2006). From a genre perspective, therefore, writing is deeply implicated in the development of identities: it is through their participation in genres that writers gradually learn to (re)produce certain types of disciplined knowledge as well as the identities that make the production of this disciplined knowledge possible. Accordingly, completion of a dissertation in anthropology will produce researchers with disciplined ways of thinking that allow for the production of the kind of knowledge that is valued in anthropology by identifying with and adhering to specific disciplinary paradigms; completion of dissertations in physics or social work or any other field will likewise produce different types of thinkers and thinking, including the kinds of epistemological stances that are valued in those research communities. In other words, rhetorically, the process of identity or subject formation involves the act of locating oneself in an ongoing disciplinary knowledge-making endeavor.

Part of this disciplinary identity formation and location involves producing and reproducing what Sullivan (1996) calls disciplinary "orthodoxies" (p. 227). According to Sullivan, these orthodoxies include four kinds of disciplinary knowledge: The first type of knowledge, a discipline's "narrative knowledge," explains the current overall ways of viewing the world—why the things being studied are the way they are according to current disciplinary lore. The second kind of knowledge involves assumptions about the ways things are done (methodologies, ontologies, and epistemologies) in the discipline—the way the disciplinary group goes about the business of research, which includes both the explicit rules of methodologies and the underlying tacit assumptions (about the world, about what we can know and how) on which they rest. The third kind of knowledge is knowledge about the "system of social and power relationships" (p. 229) in the disciplinary group: a territorial map of who's who in a given field—who should be credited with what accomplishment, who can or should be cited with whom, who should not be cited and why not, and who should not be cited together (e.g., which researchers do not make good bedfellows conceptually) and why not. Finally, the fourth kind of knowledge is "doctrinal knowledge" (p. 230), which involves explanations of specific instances, artefacts, or events. They constitute, in Sullivan's words, "episodic narratives" (p. 230).

As Sullivan notes, for researchers to have their knowledge claims accepted (i.e., to claim a contribution), researchers must allege innovation in the fourth kind of knowledge—knowledge about specific instances—and sometimes in the area of methodologies (though rarely about the tacit assumptions underlying these methodologies). Knowledge claims that question the overall conceptual narrative of the field, the assumptions underlying its ways of doing things, or even disciplinary hierarchies, are much riskier and therefore relatively rare. And omissions on the disciplinary landscape may be highly political statements of epistemological or ideological alignment or contestation. Given that new researchers begin with their previous conceptualization of academic discourse as "sources of information," how, then, do they develop disciplinary subject positions that allow them to participate in these disciplinary knowledge-making practices? As Green (2005) notes, this development of a disciplinary subject position that allows for the production of disciplinary knowledge is much of what doctoral work and supervision are about: "Supervision ... must be seen as a (pedagogic) practice producing subjects, as directly and actively implicated in the socio-symbolic work of subject formation, or the discursive construction of subjectivity: the constitution of the academic subject" (p. 152). And as we illustrate below, that process of subject formation is a deeply rhetorical process, and whether or not it is recognized as such, it has deep consequences for students as well as for their disciplines.

The third key insight from genre theory that is important for our purposes here is the notion that genres have considerable normalizing force. Because of their rootedness in community tradition and routine—their evolution through constant repetition over time, genres become part of the tacit realm of automatic, ritualized practice, appearing as universal or "common sense" to long-time participants in a genre (Paré, 2002, 2005). This normalizing force has a number of consequences for knowledge production and, in particular, for the participation of newcomers in collective knowledge-making practices, harboring what we have elsewhere described as a paradox (Starke-Meyerring, 2011) that proves highly consequential for students as well as for supervisors (Paré, 2011): On the one hand, as they sink into "common sense," genres provide some degree of stability for efficient interaction for those who have been socialized as participants in these genres. On the other hand, their existence in the tacit realm makes genres less accessible to critical examination and questioning; rather, they become "just the way things are done." And importantly, because long-time participants are immersed in them, genres appear universal, shrouding their historical evolution and specificity to the community in which they evolved. Importantly, for newcomers, what appears as universal to long-time members represents new territory with established, normalized ways of interacting that shape expectations of a genre long before newcomers enter the scene. As Horne (this volume) shows, this dilemma is a considerable source of intimidation, anxiety, and feelings of vulnerability for newcomers. And for doctoral students, this dilemma presents difficult challenges as students aim to participate in a community's normalized knowledge-making practices (Starke-Meyerring, 2011). As we show here, this dilemma also presents challenges for supervisors who must explain the knowledge-making practices of their research communities—practices they can perform but not necessarily articulate.

DOCTORAL SUPERVISION: LOCATING STUDENTS, SHAPING ACADEMIC SUBJECTS

To study the ways in which supervision sessions work to locate students in the ongoing knowledge-making practices of their research communities, we draw on audio-recorded supervisory sessions between faculty members and their PhD students as well as on interviews with students and supervisors about these sessions. All sessions were focused on discussing dissertation proposals or chapter drafts; the topics addressed in these sessions ranged across the sub-disciplines of Education. Our analysis of these supervision sessions and interviews yielded five themes that shed light on the process of locating students in disciplinary knowledge-making practices.

Theme 1: Competing institutional and disciplinary locations

One of the first things to notice about supervision and doctoral writing is their location at the intersection of multiple communities and activities, a location that prompted Green (2005) to observe the "ecosocial" nature of supervision. Similarly, others have referred to this complex setting as the site of "competing activity systems" (Lundell & Beach, 2003) or as "laminations of activity" (Prior, 1998;

Prior & Min, 2008). Both supervisors and students participate in many other collectives, both within and beyond the university. But we wish to draw attention to the ways in which the supervisory dyad functions as the intersection of two workplaces in particular—the local world of the university department and the dispersed world of the academic discipline. As Golde and Walker (2006) note, the academic department is "the nexus of the discipline and the institution" (p. 8). For the individual scholar, the department is home base for participation in a highly diffuse and distributed disciplinary community; thus, the student and supervisor might well be the only members of their particular community in the department—digital literacy researchers, for example, in a department of curriculum and instruction. At the same time, academic departments and faculties have their own history, traditions, and practices. In both the local and far-flung communities, the individual joins collective activities that make, market, and competitively value knowledge in a variety of goods and services: from courses and programs of study to proposals, grant applications, and journal articles. PhD students are learning to participate simultaneously in these dual, articulated communities. They must learn to act with and within the rules and regulations, divisions of labour, and mediational means of two communities of practice.

Our data allowed us to identify exchanges that pertain to the regulatory practices of the local community, the deadlines, procedures, relevant personnel, and rituals of the department: when comprehensive exams are written, what forms must accompany them, when progress reporting forms must be submitted with whose signature, and so on. Examples are not necessary; they are the administrative trivia of our university lives.

However, many of the institutional regulations and practices intersect in significant ways with student opportunities for exploring and developing disciplinary identities; they have deep implications for student's knowledge and identity work, specifically for how students are locating themselves and being located in disciplinary landscapes. When departments require a quantitative research methods course, extra-departmental representation on doctoral committees, or timed comprehensive examinations, for example, they are creating the conditions for the student's intellectual work and identity development. Perhaps one of the most prominent sites of intersection between institutional and disciplinary locations is that of the supervisory committee. As the committee must draw on a limited number of department members for at least some of its composition, it may well bring together not only members from different disciplines, but also members from the same discipline with diverging or even incommensurable epistemological, ideological, or ontological commitments. Such intersections between institutional and disciplinary locations in supervisory committees can lead to considerable tension for students as each committee member seeks to orient the student from a particular disciplinary location, as this student's comment on working with a committee member illustrates (St = Student; Su = Supervisor):

> St: So she [committee member] – at first, she wanted me to scrap my chapter on activists, and I was kind of upset and I really didn't know what to say. I didn't want to just disregard her comments. I said that her comments were very different from the other ones I had received [from other committee members], and I was wondering if we could meet the committee and kind of decide where I would go and she said that she was not open to [deal?] with that.

The student here is encountering competing accounts of disciplinary narratives—of what should and should not be included, and it seems that for the committee members these expectations are normalized, as genre theory would lead us to expect. As we have noted elsewhere (Paré, Starke-Meyerring, & McAlpine, 2009), in some cases, the dissertation proposal and the dissertation itself may well be the most complex documents that researchers ever write, as they negotiate their committee's competing and perhaps conflicting or incommensurable genre worlds, with all the implicit epistemological alignments and expectations of such worlds. While researchers may eventually circumvent those negotiations simply by publishing in journals that are compatible with their own disciplinary values and assumptions, the doctoral committee may place students right in the middle of conflicting normalized disciplinary expectations.

How then do supervision sessions work to help students negotiate competing institutional and disciplinary locations? From our data, one strategy seems to be to provide evidence of the appropriateness of the students' disciplinary locations through publication, that is, through peer-reviewed verification of the student's disciplinary alignment, assumptions, and values. In the following excerpt, a supervisor offers such a strategy, advising the student to indicate that she already has community support for her argument:

> Su: I think maybe what you should say is – have a footnote to say in that chapter – that some of this work has already been published in an international journal, or whatever, because that's gone through a peer review process, it's been published and [that] tells people that you've already got the seal of approval from your academic peers in an international journal.

As this excerpt shows, the more integration into the disciplinary community the new researcher can demonstrate—for example, through previous publications—the more credible her PhD thesis will appear to her departmental committee. However, these sessions also reflect the dilemma of newcomer encounters with normalized discourse practices. Although students encounter the "politics" of conflicting disciplinary locations, they are left to wonder if such politics are simply a matter of idiosyncratic quirks among department members. Without conscious attention to these questions, the deeply rhetorical nature of knowledge making may remain shrouded to them.

Theme 2: Locations on the disciplinary map

A similar theme emerges in the consideration of external examiners of a thesis, although here the act of locating the student may be less constrained by the composition of the department. However, the act is no less rhetorical: just as in the consideration of departmental committee members, the act of location here has consequences for whether knowledge produced by students is accepted or rejected, whether they become members or not. Consider the excerpt below, in which a supervisor explains to a student why it is important to think carefully about the names of external examiners for her nearly-finished dissertation (according to university rules, three are listed, and one is randomly chosen by the graduate school to evaluate the completed dissertation):

> Su: The thing is, with PhD theses, you've got to be careful about who you choose to be external examiners. Someone like [Prof. X], for example, might fail this [dissertation] because, you know, I mean, there's a bunch of people, of which [Prof. X] is part, and I think that she'd have huge problems with this, okay? There are other people who wouldn't, and who would read it the same way that [supervisor and another committee member] would read it, you know. And I think that's who we'll send it to. We'll put them down as the examiners. There's, if you like, a politics to it, right? And I've seen students, a few students every so often – very, very smart, bright students – and they've got very low evaluations simply because their position in the thesis doesn't correspond with that of the examiner, and they pasted them on it.... I saw in one case where the examiner basically wrote a page of comments on the fact that the student hadn't used her work.

By describing a potential examiner as a member of an opposing group, the supervisor is helping the student locate herself in the discipline's "system of social and power relationships" (Sullivan, 1996, p. 229). The excerpt is a prime example of a supervisor trying to alert the student to the disciplinary map, the contradictions, and deeply held conflicting values and disciplinary knowledges the student will need to navigate. As the supervisor notes, while some researchers "would have huge problems" with a set of assumptions or methodological choices, "there are other people who would not, and who would read it the same way [as the supervisor would]." Since the student cannot possibly be expected to align with the underlying assumptions, conceptual, and hierarchical narratives of conflicting disciplinary factions, the supervisor attempts to help the student choose an external examiner whose ways of conceptualizing disciplinary narratives and hierarchies align with those of the student's work.

As Sullivan (1996) notes, rewriting or questioning underlying disciplinary narratives or hierarchical maps is a risky undertaking for any scholar, let alone a new researcher, who will likely be less aware of the conceptual narratives, methodological assumptions, or hierarchical maps specific disciplinary factions may consider appropriate. What is unclear from this example, however, is to what extent the student realizes that what the supervisor is talking about is not simply the individual idiosyncrasy of a particular professor or even of a particular group of people, but the tacit calls of disciplinary groups for allegiance to particular conceptualizations of disciplinary knowledges and perspectives. Other than the word "politics," the conversation does not contain any shared language or terminology with which student and supervisor could explore the dynamics of disciplinarity and the politics of disciplinary subject formation in the genre of the PhD dissertation. As a result, conflicting disciplinary ways of knowing may sometimes be glossed over, sometimes avoided, and sometimes, perhaps, simply suffered. Without direct attention to the rhetorical nature of knowledge making, alignment, and subject formation, students may find it difficult to learn how to make decisions about where and how to locate themselves, where to place what arguments, or when and how to engage in discussions of competing theories.

In guiding students to locations on the disciplinary map, supervisors also explicitly attend to the current narratives of those maps and help students understand whose theories have currency, who should be placed where in the hierarchy, with how much attention, and why. So, for instance, in discussing a dissertation's literature review, a supervisor says the following:

> Su: A lot of adult education theory goes back to them [Gramsci and Freire]. So I think what you should do is figure out, when you read this again, just make sure that you've genuflected enough to them.

Similarly, in the next example, from a session focused on a dissertation proposal, the student is wondering how to draw the disciplinary "map" in her thesis, whom to include, and whom to leave out. The supervisor directs the student to a start based on the student's research question and evokes a "we" or "somebody" audience that needs to understand this map:

> St: I also don't know how much I need to report on previous research in institutional theory in my Conceptual Framework [section].
>
> Su: Well, enough so that we understand what you're using and what you're adding. So, I would say you don't have to be too verbose, but enough so that somebody can understand the pieces that you're putting together.

Although the comment sounds straightforward, chances are that once the map is starting to take shape, the student will learn that the "we" or "somebody" will likely have more expectations of how the current lay of the disciplinary land is to be rendered, such as who will be on the map, next to whom, with how much territory, and more.

Theme 3: The logics of disciplinary locations

Much of the time in the sessions we recorded was taken up with talking through sections of the draft texts, sometimes to determine if problems identified in earlier sessions had been addressed, and sometimes to uncover new problems. During these parts of the conversation, supervisors offered advice in their role as critical readers: clarify a term, expand a definition, provide a transition, reach a conclusion, cite a source. Again, in many cases, the supervisor appears to be discussing a universal reader—someone concerned with things like sentence-level logic (cohesion), repetition, or topical progression:

> Su: Here you sort of rapidly converge on something, and I don't have enough justification for what led you there. And then you need some sort of conclusion here: So, what does this tell us? Research in this field is fragmented? Underdeveloped? Can they [strands of research] be integrated? Or is [fragmentation] a choice? So, you want to give a kind of sum-up. "Here's where things stand. Here's where I see the strengths and weaknesses of each."

There seems the possibility here of explicit instruction in disciplinary rhetoric—that is, the situated ways of knowing in the discipline, including the range of arguments that are available, called for, or possible in advancing a claim; how much justification is needed for certain kinds of claims; why such justification is needed; what kind of evidence is considered persuasive and why; what kinds of conclusions are to be drawn from a given discussion; or in Sullivan's (1996) words, how the logic of a conceptual narrative is to be developed in a given research community. But we saw few examples of such overt attention to a community's knowledge-making practices. Even where readers were more explicitly evoked, they were characterized as generic readers, as anyone who happened to be reading:

> Su: One thing that you need to show in this thesis is what I would call a guiding thread – a sort of conceptual, theoretical backbone that threads through the whole thesis, and that's learning in your case.... [Later in the transcript:] Again, you need ... that guiding thread, the backbone of the thesis. Like a sentence or a short paragraph here and there to pull the reader back into the thesis and to make it clear to them that this is not just a series of essays you've slung together.... When you're writing a thesis, one of the things you need are road signs to guide the readers through the thesis prepare them intellectually to expect what's coming. And, if you don't do that, then they get lost, they get confused, and they get pissed off. So, what you've got to do is continually remind people what you're about.

As Hyland (2004, this volume) shows, however, such "road signs" or metadiscourse are likewise highly situated; that is, they are specific to research communities, serving their particular epistemic needs. A logical connection between ideas that may need to be articulated to an outsider, for example, may well be the only logical connection imaginable to insiders and thus mark a writer who foregrounds that connection as an outsider. Disciplinarity in these examples, then, remains largely implicit, unarticulated. In referring to the conclusion, the supervisor makes tactical statements—concrete questions—that provide a procedure for the student to follow, now and in future academic writing, presumably regardless of disciplinary location. Although the conclusion is largely about engaging in the ongoing research conversation, about what the discussion so far means for the research conversation and for the student's argument, little attention is paid to the rhetorical act of engaging in an ongoing conversation or why such arguments are necessary, what role they play in the collective knowledge-making endeavor or in shaping the specific contribution of the student's work, and so on.

Theme 4: Locations beyond academe

To a large extent, the dissertation is a learning genre—one that is mostly concerned with disciplinary subject formation. As such, dissertations are read mostly by committee members; rarely do practitioners or the public, for example, seek out dissertations to inform their work or other decisions. In qualitative research, however, particularly work employing action or participatory action methodologies, dissertations may well present students with unique complexities of locations beyond academe in that their dissertation may well have an important effect on the participants who have likely built a relationship of trust with the doctoral student researcher. In the next excerpt, a student expresses anxiety about the effect of her action research at the college which is her research site:

> St: I'm feeling more pressure than I thought I would because it's not just my mom who's going to be reading this, and you. [The administration at the research site] is very interested in this work.... So, here I was, I was speaking to four deans and a vice-dean, and everyone kept saying to me, "really looking forward to reading," and I was sitting there thinking, "why are my hands breaking out in a sweat?" ... And it's not that I think that my work won't be of the highest quality, but I feel now the pressure of doing it in a very efficient timeline so that the results are relevant and that I hold up my end of the bargain.

The "bargain" this student must fulfill is the dissertation research she promised to share with her participants in exchange for access to the college. After an academic career in which the sole response to academic texts was a grade and a few notes scribbled by a professor (or TA), the doctoral student is suddenly faced with an authentic rhetorical task, as her supervisor's response confirms:

> Su: It's good that you're thinking about your audience—it's really good that you're thinking of your audience—because ultimately if you want this PhD to do something, at the end of the day, you've got to think about who that audience is going to be and how is it going to be of use to them. And it seems to me that's where you want to position yourself.

We don't believe these types of comments would be made at the Master's or undergraduate levels. The research dissertation is often the first academic text that presents the student with such an authentic rhetorical task beyond academe, and in these comments there is a concern with a "real" audience—that is, one beyond the department and the committee. One of the expectations of belonging to a community is the willingness and ability to communicate beyond its borders. Thus, a key part of learning for doctoral students is shifting their gaze, or extending their locations, to the broader communities—academic and non-academic—that might value their research. This expectation is increasingly being made explicit in the doctoral education literature. For instance, Richardson (2003) sets as a key outcome of Education PhDs that students learn to view research as socially situated and develop sensitivity to different discourses in different settings and with different audiences. And the European Community has developed a common expectation of PhDs that they can effectively interact not just with peers, but with the larger scholarly community, and society in general (Joint Quality Initiative, 2004).

However, the deeply rhetorical nature of such knowledge work across academic and public, community or practitioner locations, remains unaddressed, although it has serious consequences for how disciplinary knowledge may affect communities outside academe. For example, research produced in particular academic locations, with the particular epistemological, ontological, and ideological subject positions they inscribe, may well co-opt, deny, or suppress local knowledges; or it may reproduce dominant class and power structures, facilitate the colonization of people, and reproduce social marginalization (e.g., Canagarajah, 2002; Giltrow, 2002).

Theme 5: War stories, or normalizing the newcomer's encounters with new locations

The final theme we would like to consider reflects a common task for doctoral supervisors: allaying the doubts or rising panic students experience from time to time.

> St: I was a little scared at first [that a published paper was too close to her own work].
>
> Su: No, no, you see that's a common thing. I suffered from that when I was doing my doctorate. I thought that you had to do something that was so innovative, so completely new. And yet, it doesn't work that way. It needs to be founded on [others'] work, but it will never be exactly the same.

**

> St: I still don't know [what I'm looking for].
>
> Su: It's normal it's still fuzzy at this point, but you are at the point where you can start writing out what specific questions you would ask.
>
> **
>
> St: It's hard. I know when I was doing my thesis, you're just so close to it. You can't see the forest anymore, you're looking at the bark.

As the excerpts suggest, the supervisors identify with the students, recalling their own struggles and encouraging the student to feel like a colleague. They make clear that this aspect of the journey is normal for those entering the community. Here we see strong elements of support, affirming the difficulties and attendant emotions that are part of the work of the dissertation. Since isolation is so prevalent as a doctoral experience (Golde, 2005), and attrition particularly frequent during the dissertation process, this type of support may, in fact, be a critical but overlooked feature of these conversations.

To be sure, normalizing the dilemma of entering new landscapes that seem so "common sense" to those inhabiting them may well soothe the sense of anxiety and vulnerability students experience over this process of location and subject formation. And yet, here again, we see an opportunity for supervisors, students, and their research communities to make the established genres that regularize their discipline's ways of knowing subject to critical exploration: dissertation writing is a project of rhetorical subject formation that reproduces world views, epistemologies, ideologies, and ontologies that sustain disciplinary knowledge-making practices. We see thoughtful attention to the rhetorical nature of disciplinary knowledge making and subject formation as vital to doctoral education.

At the very least, critical engagement in the rhetorical nature of subject formation can help free students from a position where they are the object of subject formation—being located by someone for whom the disciplinary landscape has become normalized. Rather, by attending to what we might call "the rhetoric of subject formation," students may not only be able to transcend the anxiety and vulnerability that accompanies the dilemma of entering normalized landscapes, but they may also develop some sense of empowerment over how to make decisions about their locations on disciplinary maps and their participation in disciplinary knowledge-making practices. Indeed, becoming stewards of their disciplines, in Golde and Walker's (2006) terms, may require nothing less than a robust rhetorical awareness of and participation in disciplinary knowledge and identity work.

CONCLUSION

Joining the disciplinary research discussion is a challenging task for new researchers—one that involves a complex process of knowledge and identity work. Understanding this work through the lens of workplace learning allowed us to direct our attention to the writing-intensive nature of the academic workplace and to the role that supervision of doctoral student writing plays in this work. As we illustrated, during discussions of the dissertation, supervisors help students locate themselves on complex disciplinary maps. These rhetorical locations constitute sites of tension between competing epistemologies, ideologies, and ontologies; they inscribe specific disciplinary logics; and they interact in complex ways with locations beyond academe. Thus supervisors are deeply implicated in the shaping of rhetorical subjects.

However, this process of subject formation—if conducted uncritically—reproduces and normalizes "common" sense disciplinary ways of knowing and renders them universal. If the rhetorical nature of the process of subject formation is shrouded in common sense, students are given few opportunities to reflect on who they are becoming, how they are aligning themselves, or whether they wish to reproduce certain disciplinary logics and values. Therefore, as we have argued here, a robust rhetorical awareness of and participation in disciplinary knowledge and identity work is vital to advancing not only knowledge production within and across disciplines themselves, but also to increasing student agency in the production of the subject positions that produce that knowledge.

REFERENCES

Artemeva, N., & Freedman, A. (Eds.). (2006). *Rhetorical genre studies and beyond*. Winnipeg: Inkshed Publications.

Bawarshi, A. S., & Reiff, M. J. (2010). *Genre: An introduction to history, theory, research, and pedagogy.* Reference Guides to Rhetoric and Composition. West Lafayette, IN, and Fort Collins, CO: Parlor Press & The WAC Clearinghouse. Available at http://wac.colostate.edu/books/.

Bazerman, C. (1988). *Shaping written knowledge: The genre and activity of the experimental article in science.* Madison: University of Wisconsin Press.

Bazerman, C. (2002). Genre and identity: Citizenship in the age of the Internet and of global capitalism. In R. Coe, L. Lingard, & T. Teslenko (Eds.), *The rhetoric and ideology of genre* (pp. 13-37). Cresskill, NJ: Hampton.

Bazerman, C., Bonini, A., & Figueiredo, D. (Eds.). (2009). *Genre in a changing world.* Perspectives on Writing. Fort Collins, CO and West Lafayette, IN: The WAC Clearinghouse & Parlor Press. Available at http://wac.colostate.edu/books./

Bazerman, C., & Paradis, J. G. (Eds.). (1991). *Textual dynamics of the professions: Historical and contemporary studies of writing in professional communities.* Madison, WI: University of Wisconsin Press.

Bazerman, C., & Prior, P. (2005). Genre, disciplinarity, interdisciplinarity. In J. Green, R. Beach, M. Kamil, & T. Shanahan (Eds.), *Multidisciplinary Perspectives on Literacy Research* (2nd ed.) (133-178). Cresskill, NJ: Hampton Press. Retrieved from http://www.education.ucsb.edu/%7Ebazerman/chapters/34.genrewithprior.html

Campbell, K. K., & Jamieson, K. H. (Eds.). (1978). *Form and genre: Shaping rhetorical action.* Falls Church, VA: Speech Communication Association.

Canadian Association for Graduate Studies. (2005). Doctoral education in Canada [Electronic Version]. Ottawa: CAGS. Retrieved from http://www.cags.ca/Portals/34/pdf/doctoral_education_canada_1900-2005.pdf

Canagarajah, A. S. (2002). *A geopolitics of academic writing.* Pittsburgh, PA: University of Pittsburgh Press.

Coe, R., Lingard, L., & Teslenko, T. (Eds.) (2002). *The rhetoric and ideology of genre.* Cresskill, NJ: Hampton Press.

Council of Graduate Schools. (2007). Graduate education: The backbone of American competitiveness and innovation: A report from the Council of Graduate Schools Advisory Committee on Graduate Education and American Competitiveness [Electronic Version]. Washington: CGS. Retrieved from http://www.cgsnet.org/portals/0/pdf/GR_GradEdAmComp_0407.pdf

Devitt, A. J. (2004). *Writing genres.* Carbondale, IL: Southern Illinois University Press.

Dias, P., Freedman, A., Medway, P. & Paré, A. (1999). *Worlds apart: Acting and writing in academic and workplace contexts.* Mahwah, NJ: Lawrence Erlbaum.

Dias, P., & Paré, A. (Eds.). (2000). T*ransitions: Writing in academic and workplace settings.* Cresskill, NJ: Hampton Press.

Engeström, Y., & Middleton, D. (Eds.). (1998). *Cognition and communication at work.* Cambridge: Cambridge University Press.

European University Association. (2007). Doctoral programs in Europe's universities: Achievements and challenges [Electronic Version]. Brussels: EUA. Retrieved from http://www.eua.be/fileadmin/user_upload/files/Publications/Doctoral_Programmes_in_Europe_s_Universities.pdf

Freedman, A., & Medway, P. (Eds.). (1994). *Genre and the new rhetoric*. London: Taylor & Francis.

Giltrow, J. (2002). *Academic writing: Writing and reading in the disciplines*. Peterborough, ON: Broadview Press.

Golde, C. (2005). The role of the department and discipline in doctoral student attrition: Lessons from four departments. *The Journal of Higher Education, 76*(6), 669-700.

Golde, C. M., & Walker, G. E. (Eds.). (2006). *Envisioning the future of doctoral education: Preparing stewards of the discipline*. San Francisco: Jossey-Bass.

Green, B. (2005). Unfinished business: Subjectivity and supervision. *Higher Education Research and Development, 24*(2), 151-163.

Hyland, K. (2004). *Disciplinary discourses: Social interactions in academic writing*. Ann Arbor, MI: University of Michigan Press.

Joint Quality Initiative. (2004). Shared 'Dublin' descriptors for short cycle, first cycle, second cycle and third cycle awards: A report from a Joint Quality Initiative informal group. Retrieved from http://www.jointquality.nl

Kamler, B., & Thomson, P. (2006). *Helping doctoral students write: Pedagogies for supervision*. London: Routledge.

Lave, J., & Wenger, E. (1991). *Situated learning: Legitimate peripheral participation*. Cambridge: Cambridge University Press.

Lee, A., & Boud, D. (2008). Framing doctoral education as practice. In D. Boud & Al Lee (Eds.), *Changing practices of doctoral education* (pp. 10-25). London & New York: Routledge.

Lundell. D. B., & Beach, R. (2003). Dissertation writers' negotiations with competing activity systems. In C. Bazerman & D. Russell (Eds.), *Writing selves/writing societies: Research from activity perspectives* (pp. 483-514). Fort Collins, Colorado: The WAC Clearinghouse and Mind, Culture, and Activity. Available at http://wac.colostate.edu/books/selves_societies/).

Miller, C. (1984). Genre as social action. *Quarterly Journal of Speech, 70*, 151-167.

Odell, L., & Goswami, D. (1982). Writing in a non-academic setting. *Research in the Teaching of English, 16*, 201-223.

Odell, L., & Goswami, D. (Eds.). (1985). *Writing in nonacademic settings*. New York: Guilford Press.

Paré, A. (2002). Genre and identity: Individuals, institutions, and ideology. In R. Coe, L. Lingard, & T. Teslenko (Eds.), *The rhetoric and ideology of genre* (pp. 57-71). Cresskill, NJ: Hampton.

Paré, A. (2005). Texts and power: Toward a critical theory of language. In L. Davies & P. Leonard (Eds.), *Social Work in a corporate era: Practices of power and resistance*. Aldershot, UK: Ashgate Publishing.

Paré, A. (2011). Speaking of writing: Supervisory feedback and the dissertation. In L. McAlpine & C. Amundson (Eds.), *Supporting the doctoral process: Research-based strategies* (pp. 59-74). New York: Springer.

Paré, A., & Le Maistre, C. (2006a). Distributed mentoring in communities of practice. In P. Tynjälä, J. Välimaa, & G. Boulton-Lewis (Eds.), *Higher education and working life: Collaborations, confrontations and challenges* (pp. 129-141). Amsterdam: Elsevier.

Paré. A., & Le Maistre, C. (2006b). Active learning in the workplace: Transforming individuals and institutions. *Journal of Education and Work, 19* (4): 363-381.

Paré, A., Starke-Meyerring, D., & McAlpine, L. (2009). The dissertation as multi-genre: Many readers, many readings. In C. Bazerman, D. Figueiredo, & A. Bonini (Eds.), *Genre in a changing world* (pp. 179-193). Fort Collins, CO, and West Lafayette, IN: The WAC Clearinghouse & Parlor Press Available at http://wac.colostate.edu/books/.

Prior, P. (1998). Writing/disciplinarity: A sociohistoric account of literate activity in the academy. Mahwah, NJ: Lawrence Erlbaum Associates.

Prior, P., & Min, Y.-K. (2008). The lived experience of graduate work and writing: From chronotopic laminations to everyday lamentations. In C. P. Casanave &X. Li (Eds.), *Learning the literate practices of graduate school: Insiders' reflections on academic enculturation* (pp. 230-246). Ann Arbor: University of Michigan Press.

Richardson, V. (2003). *The PhD in education, Carnegie essays on the doctorate.* The Carnegie Foundation for the Advancement of Teaching. (www.carnegiefoundation.org/cid.)

Schryer, C. F. (1993). Records as genre. *Written Communication, 10,* 200-234.

Spilka, R. (Ed.). (1993). *Writing in the workplace: New research perspectives,* Carbondale, IL: Southern Illinois University Press.

Starke-Meyerring, D. (2011). The paradox of writing in doctoral education: Student experiences. In L. McAlpine & C. Amundson (Eds.), *Supporting the doctoral process: Research-based strategies* (pp. 75-95). New York: Springer.

Sullivan, D. L. (1996). Displaying disciplinarity. *Written Communication, 13,* 221-250.

Tardy, C. (2009). *Building genre knowledge.* West Lafayette, IN: Parlor Press.

Wenger, E. (1998). *Communities of practice: Learning, meaning, and identity.* Cambridge: Cambridge University Press.

Winsor, D. (1996). *Writing like an engineer.* Mahwah, NJ: Erlbaum.

12 WRITING INTO THE KNOWLEDGE SOCIETY: A CASE STUDY OF VULNERABILITY IN INKSHEDDING

Miriam Horne

Burke (1973) described the way that knowledge is created by likening communities of like-minded peers to a parlour gathering. He wrote,

> Imagine that you enter a parlor. You come late. When you arrive, others have long preceded you, and they are engaged in a heated discussion, a discussion too heated for them to pause and tell you exactly what it is about. In fact, the discussion had already begun long before any of them got there, so that no one present is qualified to retrace for you all the steps that had gone before. You listen for a while, until you decide that you have caught the tenor of the argument; then you put in your oar. Someone answers; you answer him; another comes to your defense; another aligns himself against you, to either the embarrassment or gratification of your opponent, depending upon the quality of your ally's assistance. However, the discussion is interminable. The hour grows late, you must depart. And you do depart, with the discussion still vigorously in progress. (pp. 110-111)

Applied to academia, Burke's description calls to mind a group of scholars, confident and self-assured, intent on participating in the conversation and anxiously engaged in knowledge making. What this perception of knowledge creation, as well as other research that more closely links writing practices with socially situated knowledge practices (Bazerman, 1988; Freedman & Medway, 1994; Paré, 2002; Schryer, 1994), fails to account for, however, is the human experience of joining those disciplinary conversations or disciplinary writing practices and the way that the human experience impacts discourse practices.

Imagine, for example, the feelings of a graduate student or other newcomer entering the established discourse of a community for the first time. She may feel awed by the presence of legendary participants, unsure of the appropriate language to use, unsure of how to join in the conversation, and unsure of how she will be received. In this chapter, I examine the feelings of vulnerability that accompany many newcomers entering the parlour of their disciplinary conversation. Drawing from a broader program of research in which I explore the ways that learning social writing practices of a community facilitates (and occasionally frustrates) community membership (Horne, in press), I explore the intense feelings of insecurity that many newcomers experience, reasons underlying these feelings, and the impacts that these feelings have on the process of membership. Thus, this research seeks to understand the human experience in the link between writing and knowledge by exploring the ways that academic communities "constrain, enable, or otherwise shape writing as a knowledge making practice" (Starke-Meyerring & Paré, this volume). It is valuable in the ways that it acknowledges and gives voice to those who struggle in their efforts to join academe and participate in knowledge practices be it new students, new scholars, or others.

Although I have limited this discussion to my study of a specific academic setting—the annual conference for the Canadian Association for the Study of Language and Learning (CASLL), also known as Inkshed, much of what I describe here resonates with other experiences of initiation and apprenticeship in a variety of academic communities. I have chosen to locate my research in the Inkshed community because of its explicit concern with writing as knowledge practice. This is demonstrated through a collective writing process called inkshedding (from whence the community takes its name) that takes place during the three-day annual conference. Even though the express purpose of this writing activity is to collectively generate knowledge as in a Burkean parlour, my data suggest that feelings of anxiety and vulnerability may hinder newcomer participation in inkshedding and therefore in knowledge creation in the community. In order to gain full membership in Inkshed, newcomers must recognize their anxieties, trust in the support of others who feel the same way, and inkshed. Through inkshedding, they become participants in knowledge construction and the knowledge society.

INKSHEDDING

Inkshedding is a collaborative freewriting activity invented in the early 1980s by St. Thomas University professors Russ Hunt and Jim Reither. Hunt and Reither wanted to make classroom writing assignments rhetorically meaningful for students and dialogically transactional. At the same time that they were introducing inkshedding to their classes, Hunt and Reither were co-founding what is now known as CASLL. They took inkshedding to the first annual conference and it has become a hallmark of the community.

Briefly, at the conference, the inkshedding writing process follows four basic steps. First, participants respond in writing to a common prompt—for example, a conference presentation such as, "What is literacy in the information age," or "Resisting the teaching subtext in composition books" (presentation titles from the 2005 conference) to name two. The writing activity follows one or several presentations on a theme and is similar to a freewriting experience. (Freewriting is a term coined by Elbow, 1973, who describes a writing process, often used for generating ideas, in which participants write for around ten minutes without stopping. There is no concern for grammar, or punctuation, or format, but instead, for getting ideas out of the head and onto paper.) The writing produced is often messy and unorganized, but many Inkshedders (a title taken on by people who attend Inkshed conferences, participate on the listserv, inkshed, and otherwise mutually engage in socially situated and dialogic written interactions) argue that it affords everyone—not just the highly articulate and verbal or the most aggressive community members—equal opportunity to express whatever thoughts the presentations may have inspired. Second, after writing for a few moments, participants pool their writing in the center of the table (there are usually about eight people per table and about eight tables in the conference room). Everyone then takes a text other than her/his own and begins to read. As participants read, if anything stands out to them as significant or meaningful in any way, they draw a line beside it in the margin, underline it, or otherwise highlight it to show other readers that they found the particular section meaningful. Some people will even add a few words reflecting their response. Participants are encouraged to read and respond to as many texts as they can during the allotted time period. Third, the marked up texts are taken to an editorial committee (usually made up of volunteer conference participants) who look at the sections that have been most marked up. These sections are excerpted and typed up. Finally, the typed-up sections are copied and circulated to all participants in order to facilitate and encourage further discussion.

Since the introduction of inkshedding at the first conference in 1984, the annual conference has continued to grow around the philosophy of dialogism that inspired inkshedding. To this end, there are no concurrent conference sessions. Everyone attends the same sessions so that everyone is able to respond to the same prompt. In addition to this, however, the conferences are often held in remote locations where there are few distractions to draw participants away from conference sessions. Participants are lodged under the same roof and share meals and evening entertainment together. In fact, one of the highlights of the conference is a talent night held on the last evening of the conference in which everyone is given the opportunity to participate (the term "talent" is very loosely interpreted). In these ways, people get to know each other and interact more than they might at a larger more traditional kind of conference. As much as possible, conference organizers facilitate social interaction and dialogue in order to generate knowledge. The conference center becomes a Burkean parlour where all who enter, newcomer and old-timer alike, are invited to participate in an on-going conversation. While this invitation to participate comes in the opportunity to present research, participate in talent night, and otherwise engage in socializing, the primary and central means for participation in the Inkshed conversation at conferences is through inkshedding. Thus, those who successfully learn how to join in inkshedding join in the practice of knowledge making in an academic society. Those who do not learn to participate effectively remain peripheral to knowledge creation. In this chapter, I examine the feelings that accompany entry to the Inkshed parlour and address the ways that feelings of vulnerability impact participation in inkshedding and therefore participation in the Inkshed community and knowledge practices.

THEORETICAL FRAMEWORK

My larger program of research, of which the focus on vulnerability is part, examines the ways in which learning to participate in collective writing processes facilitates (and sometimes frustrates) membership in communities. In using the term collective writing processes, I draw on the work of social rhetoricians (Bizzell, 1983; Dias, Freedman, Medway, & Paré, 1999; Faigley, 1986) who argue that writing is not an isolated act. It is not, as Dias and colleagues (1999) explained, "a discrete clearly definable skill learned once and for all" (p. 9). Instead,

> writing is seldom the product of isolated individuals, but rather and seldom obviously, the outcome of continuing collaboration, of interactions that involve other people and other texts. Writing practices are closely linked to their sociocultural con-

texts, and writing strategies vary with individual and situation. (Dias et al., 1999, p. 10)

As a way of understanding this link between writing practices and social contexts, many scholars have turned to genre theory (Bazerman, 1988; Devitt, 2004; Freedman & Medway, 1994; Miller, 1984; Paré, 2002;). As Miller (1984) explained, the purpose of using genre theory to understand texts is that "it seeks to explicate the knowledge that practice creates" (p. 27). It provides a way to understand the social context that drives the creation of a text. It also shows how the text is a response to the situation in which it occurs. In short, genre theory is a way of understanding "dynamic rhetorical forms that are developed from actors' responses to recurrent situations and that serve to stabilize experience and give it coherence and meaning" (Berkenkotter & Huckin, 1995, p. 4). Thus, genre theory informs this examination of inkshedding in the Inkshed community by seeking to understand the relationship between the community and the texts produced within the community.

Many researchers who embrace genre theory also draw on the theory of communities of practice (CoPs) to explain the social context for the documents they study. Understanding a group or organization as a community of practice is a way of understanding shared values, practices, and learning within a community. By studying the writing practices of Inkshed, I have examined the values and practices of the community. These practices bring people together into what Lave and Wenger (1991) described as CoPs. Wenger (1998) explained that

> Collective learning results in practices that reflect both the pursuit of our enterprises and the attendant social relations. These practices are thus the property of a kind of community created over time by the sustained pursuit of shared enterprise. It makes sense, therefore, to call these kinds of communities, *communities of practice*. (p. 45)

Many of the knowledge societies described in this book can be described as CoPs as they engage in shared practices of knowledge making.

The usefulness of the theory of CoPs to my research lies in the ways in which it describes social interactions and dynamics. It helps to expose the ways that individuals learn to participate in various collectives, and what that participation means. In particular, through the notion of legitimate peripheral participation (LPP), theories of CoPs describe how newcomers learn to participate by taking on first small but meaningful tasks, which gradually increase in responsibility. This leads to increased membership in the community. Theories of CoPs combine logically with genre theory as ideas of genre help to focus the practices Wenger (1998) refers to, specifically, on writing practices. It is the experience of learning these writing practices within an academic community that I address.

Through several years of conference attendance, and following a participant observer methodology (Denzin, 1997) through which I was able to participate in a variety of ways, I was able to gain a rich set of data with which to work. These included journals (Lincoln & Guba, 1985), fieldnotes (Clandinin & Connelly, 2000; Maykut and Morehouse, 1994), in-depth individual and focus group interviews (Seidman, 1991), a variety of documents (inkshedding texts, newsletters, the listserv) (Denzin, 1978), and interim writing (Clandinin & Connelly, 2000). I draw from these data for this chapter and note that when names have been used, they have been used with permission. Some data appear without a participant's name. This is in accordance with ethics of privacy.

MULTIPLE PERSPECTIVES

As social constructionists argue, knowledge is not discreet content (Geertz, 1973; Kuhn, 1970; Rorty, 1979). Rather, knowledge is active practice. This research supports notions of writing as situated practice (Dias et al., 1999) and writing as active knowledge building (Bakhtin, 1986; Emig, 1971). As my data suggest, however, feelings of vulnerability can impede that knowledge.

I have chosen to share this theme in two different ways. First, in the following section, I look at the feelings associated with learning to Inkshed; I look at where feelings of vulnerability come from when writing in a community; and I examine the consequences of these feelings to membership in the collective. I use examples from the data to discuss and explain my findings. The second way that I portray the data, however, is somewhat less traditional. I present an audio clip (available because of the medium of this book) that intertwines a variety of data in order to recreate an inkshedding experience. I do this by creating fictional Inkshedders and using their voices to articulate the data. Although the account I present is fictionalized, I have used the exact words of those who participated in my study as much as possible. I have done this in an effort to help readers understand the inkshedding experience. The audio text was performed by amateur actors and no actual recordings of Inkshedders from my data are part of this performance.

I have created this audio clip in an effort to help readers understand the lived inkshedding experience. I have recreated an inkshedding experience in the spirit of bricolage as described by Denzin and Lincoln (2003). They explained, "The interpretive bricoleur produces a *bricolage*—that is, a pieced-together set of representations that are fitted to the specifics of a complex situation" (p. 5). Thus,

I have pieced together a representation of what it may feel like to participate in inkshedding, but many listeners will find that the thoughts expressed here resonate with other experiences of community entrance. In addition, performance ethnography, or the sharing of ethnographic results through means of a performance, is becoming increasingly valued as a way of sharing narratives (Becker, McCall, & Morris, 1989; McCall, 2003; Pollock, 1990). It affords a perspective not otherwise attainable. As Denzin and Lincoln (2003) explained, performance texts are "Dialogical texts. They presume an active audience. They create spaces for give-and-take between reader and writer. They do more than turn the other into the object of the social science gaze" (p. 7). Thus, I have created a performance of an inkshedding experience in order to share the tensions and fears associated with writing within the context that it occurs (the audio text can be found at this link: http://www.MiriamHorne.net/InkshedPlay.mp3).

VULNERABILITY

Although my data deal specifically with the Inkshed community, feelings of vulnerability are not unique to this community. From graduate students entering their disciplinary community to undergraduate students entering academia to professionals entering an unfamiliar work environment, entering a Burkean parlour can be intimidating. Consider the following vignette created from journals and field notes in which I describe my first inkshedding experience:

> We are told to write. I break into a cold sweat. A knot of fear grips my stomach. Write? Here? What if I don't write the right thing! "Respond to what you read," we are told. But people can see me writing. I have to write something significant. How can I protect myself? People will know I'm just a grad student and don't really belong. "Now, pass your paper two people to the right and mark anything that stands out to you with a line in the margin." Panic rises. Too hard! I can't! Can I walk out? No, too many people would see me. I have no choice. I pass it on but notice that others at my table look equally uncomfortable. I read, I respond, I read, I respond. I find myself searching for value in my colleague's writing so that she can feel more comfortable. Momentarily I lose track of my own text. Then it's back in my hands. Lines highlight certain phrases I have written. Sometimes two or three lines for one comment. No one has corrected me. No one has told me I don't belong.

This vignette describes discomfort and insecurity in the inkshedding activity. I was not sure, however, if these feelings were a result of my own personal demons, or if others shared my experience. After reflecting on my own discomfort, I asked Inkshedders to share their feelings and experiences on learning to inkshed. The language of their responses made it clear that inkshedding touched on emotions and feelings far deeper than Burke's utopian parlour accounts for. Inkshedders described their initial participation in the Inkshed conversation in some of the following ways (the emphasis is mine in order to highlight the power of the language used):

> I reacted with *fear* and *trepidation,* assuming critical eyes would fall on my writing. I seriously *doubted* my ability to write anything significant, anything of value to those I was sharing my writing with. (Inkshedding text)

> I was out there, *vulnerable, naked* ... (Inkshedding text)

> I felt very *nervous*—the notion of "publication" and the making public of my "writing" created real *anxiety.* (Inkshedding text)

> I didn't like it—I felt *pressure* to say something intelligent. (Inkshedding text)

> There is something *intimidating* about the first time being asked to Inkshed, not because we don't have responses to share, but because of our *feelings of inadequacy* when it comes to our own writing. (Inkshedding text)

> *Discomfort. Fear* that I had nothing to say that anyone would want to hear. (Inkshedding text)

> As a newcomer to the Inkshed community I also *worried* about my ability to respond intelligently to the issues being presented. (Inkshedding text)

> I felt *uncomfortable* (kind of *exposed* without any desire to do so). (Inkshedding text)

> For many writing is exposure, vulnerability, danger. (Inkshedding text)

Danger, fear, vulnerability, anxiety, exposure—these words express the intense feelings associated with inkshedding—with learning the writing practices of a CoP and learning how to engage with the collective. As the following sections describe, some of these feelings stem from a lack of familiarity with the social context in which the writing takes place, and by extension, lack of familiarity with functions of the inkshedding activity.

SOCIAL CONTEXT

Wenger (1998) pointed out that for a newcomer to become a full participant in a CoP, she must mutually engage with other community members. That is, she must negotiate and create meaning through shared interests and shared practices—in this case, she must continue to build on the shared values of dialogism in the community by participating in inkshedding and her inkshedding must contribute to the ongoing creation of Inkshed knowledge. As a newcomer, however, these values and practices are unknown. Without a full understanding of the community, it is a challenge to engage with it.

Many of the writers who expressed discomfort with inkshedding related their feelings to their relationship with the collective. They explained that part of their discomfort was a result of not really knowing the community. In fact, many newcomers to Inkshed quickly learn that Inkshed is a unique culture; it is a set of values, beliefs and practices that are intricately intertwined, but understanding these is not always easy. Entering the community is like entering an unknown culture. One Inkshedder reflected that his first time at an Inkshed conference was like carrying on a conversation with someone whose background he did not know. He explained,

> I guess my first experience inkshedding was that it resembled other written conversations I had been engaged in, mostly personal, sometimes professional. The only difference is that it was a hybrid of personal/private writing, and writing for a small society whose members and ethos and values I did not yet know. (Inkshedding text)

This excerpt shows that the newcomer recognized a unique set of traits within the community. He made sense of the experience by drawing on other background experiences, but acknowledged that he needed to learn more.

Another participant linked the challenge of entering and understanding the community as similar to learning a new genre. She wrote,

> First experience of inkshedding occurred for me at Inkshed last year. As is usual in using a new genre, I did not have much idea of what an "inkshed" would look like, nor did I really know why the inkshedding process worked. As a newcomer to the Inkshed community, I also worried about my ability to respond intelligently to the issues being presented. (Inkshedding text)

Part of this excerpt describes how not knowing the genre of inkshedding (i.e., the collective values and practices that have led to the relative stability of this writing activity at conferences) contributed to an anxiety about identifying with the community. In other words, learning a new genre requires learning a new set of values and beliefs and how to incorporate those in writing. Lack of familiarity with the Inkshed context led to insecurity in the writing task.

The experience of learning to inkshed can be frustrated if the writer does not know the audience for whom s/he is writing. This awareness of not knowing exactly who the audience is, or what the audience values, permeates many anxiety-filled experiences. It impacts the way participants feel about inkshedding and therefore their participation in the inkshedding activity

Consider again some of the excerpts I used earlier to illustrate the sense of vulnerability that newcomers to Inkshed feel. They illustrate writers' awareness of the community around them and the attempt to write in appropriate ways for the community. Each of the writers in these excerpts qualifies how s/he feels about his/her inkshedding by drawing connections to the audience, i.e., the community. One writer describes the first time inkshedding in the following way: "Discomfort. Fear that I had nothing to say that anyone would want to hear" (Inkshedding text). In this example, the writer expressed a fear not that she might be mute or might lack the ability to express herself, but that no one would want to listen to her ideas. The fear for newcomers is not that there is nothing to say, but rather, whether or not it is worth paying attention to in this particular setting; whether or not it will engage the collective. Similarly, other writers explained,

> I reacted with fear and trepidation, assuming critical eyes would fall on my writing. I seriously doubted my ability to write anything significant, anything of value to those I was sharing my writing with. (Inkshedding text)

> And I was aware, in some ways of trying to please my readers, to write something significant or meaningful, something that

would pique the interest (laughter, philosophical pondering, etc.) of my readers. (Inkshedding text)

The first of these two excerpts echoed the feeling of vulnerability described previously, and, driven by anxiety, anticipated a negative reception by the community. Interestingly, the writers in both of these excerpts went on to question their own abilities, but did so in relation to the community. The language reflects this. The sentences do not end with "significant" or "meaningful." Instead, both writers qualified what they meant by the word "significant." They redefined it for this context to mean something valuable or worthwhile to the audience. Thus, the writers were not concerned with having an idea to write about, but rather, how that idea would engage the collective.

One final example illustrates the same awareness of the relationship of the writer with the community: "I felt a desire to write something impressive that would confirm my ability to function within this academic community that was new to me" (Inkshedding text). Instead of using the word "significant" like the previous two examples, this writer explained the desire to write something "impressive." The writer followed the same pattern as the previous two examples by redefining "impressive" to reflect how the writer negotiates engagement. The writer wanted to write something that would help him belong in the community.

As these data illustrate, the fear and vulnerability that some individuals experience in inkshedding is not a result of a complete mental blank or inability to express oneself. Instead, it reflects a writer's concern with audience—in this case, the Inkshed community—and whether or not the writing will resonate and mutually engage the audience. Without engagement, knowledge and the society generating it remain static.

A long-time Inkshedder helped to illustrate the importance of knowing the audience for whom you write in inkshedding. He explained that, for him, although he does not particularly enjoy the inkshedding activity, he is able to do it because he knows his audience. He explained,

> Part of the problem that I've gotten better at, is that I now have a sense of audience that I never had before. And that sense of audience is the other people around this table in many ways. They're not the initiates there.

The experience that this Inkshedder described represents what many have come to learn. Knowing the Inkshed community facilitates the inkshedding process. However, it is not always easy to know the audience. Sometimes, learning what the community values must come through trial and error in the inkshedding practice and other interactions with the community.

FUNCTIONS OF INKSHEDDING

While one reason for feelings of vulnerability result from a desire to fit into the community by pleasing the reader with clever and intelligent comments in order to mutually engage with the collective, another reason inkshedding may cause anxiety also reflects a desire to please the community, but this time by "doing it right." In other words, newcomers struggle to understand the function or role of inkshedding within Inkshed. While the newcomers seem to be aware that, despite instructions given to the contrary, there is a "right way" to inkshed, they are unclear of the relationship between the writing process and the collective. Unwritten rules hover in the background and writers only learn them when they break them.

Genre theorists explain that responses and actions within social situations are based on the values of the community in which they occur (Devitt, 2004; Paré, 2002). As standardized forms of responses recur, they reinforce the knowledge and values of the community in which they take place (Miller, 1984). Thus, longtime Inkshedders who know the values of the community do not share the same struggles as a newcomer who must learn the values of the community which they must uncover in the unspoken rules of inkshedding.

Even though instructions on "how to inkshed" never suggest that there is a right or wrong way to write, there are unwritten and unstated rules about what works in inkshedding, so those who agonize about doing it right are not without justification. In an interview with an original member of the Inkshed community (i.e., a member who has participated in the community since the first conference in 1984), I learned that rule-bound expectations exist, even if they are not explicitly stated. The Inkshedder explained that

> There's a sense of, not so much that there's a right way to do it, as there are wrong ways to do it, that there are things that people might do to make it not work. (Focus group interview)

This shows that the community does have certain expectations. Unfortunately, the newcomer only learns by doing it "the wrong way" if she has inadvertently broken the rules.

Russ Hunt (co-inventor of the inkshedding activity, and co-founder of the Inkshed community) gave an example of the kinds of things people do to make the inkshedding activity not work. He explained that some people might turn inkshedding into a personal letter to the presenter. They might write something like, "Dear Dorothy, I really enjoyed your presentation." First, by addressing only the presenter, the writer limits the conversation to only one person so that the other people reading the text are not invited to respond. Second, the writer is unable to further any kind of dialogic discussion. "I liked your presentation" ends discussion rather than encourages the deepening of ideas.

Hunt described this phenomenon and the problems with it by saying,

> They will address the speaker directly. They will think of what they're writing as feedback to the speaker ... It always makes me uncomfortable because it really misconstrues what this is about. What it's about is about the conversation ... that kind of discourse is conversation ending. (Focus group interview)

At each Inkshed conference, guidelines are given (sometimes with more and sometimes with less instruction as to "how to") for the inkshedding process. However, not until one actually participates in inkshedding is it really clear how the process works or the importance of the activity to the community. One person explained to me that he held back from the inkshedding experience during the first few rounds of writing because he was not entirely sure how the process worked and what the expectations were. In his words, he preferred to "remain on the periphery" until he knew the rules, or the "right way to do it" (Field notes). Even after this wait, however, it may take several tries to understand the process. It was only after studying the activity in the context of doctoral research (searching to understand how the activity worked) that I was able to write with complete confidence and understand the demands of the unwritten rules constituted by the values of the community.

IMPACTS OF VULNERABILITY ON COMMUNITY MEMBERSHIP

As I stated at the beginning of the discussion of my data, feelings of anxiety and vulnerability may impede both individual and community knowledge by causing individuals to hold back from participating in knowledge generating activities. This section looks more closely at the impacts of vulnerability on community membership and knowledge building.

My data suggest a variety of ways that people cope with feeling vulnerable, all of which impact the writing experience and the ways individuals engage with the collective. First, for some who are completely frightened, the writing experience can be paralyzing so that the writer simply does not participate in the writing activity. One woman described her experience inkshedding for the first time in a writing course. She explained, "I didn't want my classmates to read my writing. So while I did inkshed, I didn't tape my paper on the wall" (Inkshedding text). This example describes a slightly different style of inkshedding, but no less intimidating. Rather than circulating the inkshedding texts in small groups, texts are taped to the walls of the classroom and everyone walks around to read them. (This was done in the early years of inkshedding before the conference became too large to manage the inkshedding in this way). The woman explained that she circulated in the room reading everyone else's writing and pretending that hers was on the wall also. She explained that she was simply too uncomfortable to have her classmates read her writing, so she surreptitiously folded her writing up and put it in her pocket (Field notes). By doing this, although she participated in reading, she did not experience the full writing activity. She did not have the experience of having a reader respond to what she wrote, nor did the collective benefit from her contribution. I have also observed others who decline to participate in the activity and sit and talk quietly while others write, or slip out of the room for an early break. This kind of discomfort is not unique to inkshedding. One of my students recently shared a similar discomfort with me. She admitted that in a previous class, every time she was supposed to participate in a peer review activity with her classmates, during which they read and critiqued each others' writing, she would skip class. She felt too insecure about her spelling and felt like she would be judged harshly because of it. Like the Inkshedder who did not share her writing, this student lost out on the chance to learn and participate because of her vulnerability.

Second, some people participate out of a sense of duty—not because they feel they get anything out of it. One participant explained this by writing

> I didn't—and still don't find the act of inkshedding especially powerful either way. I recognize its value and do it dutifully .... But the published inksheds seem stale by the time I see them, and I find the whole exercise takes away time that I personally would rather use for discussion. But it's an important symbolic ritual, an outward sign of a commitment to shared text that is more important than the actual words shared. (Inkshedding text)

Another person explained how, although he dutifully participates in inkshedding, he is resentful and does not enjoy the experience. The language used to describe the feelings about inkshedding is startling: "comply with this experience that is forced on me, but it is certainly uncomfortable"(Inkshedding text). Ordinarily, language like "comply" or "force" might be used to describe life in a totalitarian state. The implication here is that the writer has no control over the experience and therefore resists participating. Someone who is compliant may be less likely to open up and risk writing anything that may push ideas in the inkshedding and therefore, like the previous example, will not have the benefit of having ideas responded to. In other words, a forced response is likely to be cold and uninviting and therefore not part of the engagement. In the same way that the individual misses out on engaging with the collective, the collective misses out on the contribution of the individual.

The phenomenon of participating out of a sense of duty or compliance is not limited to Inkshed. My experience as a teacher and student shows that students often approach writing assignments in the same way. They often write because they feel forced to, not because it enhances their learning experience. They are unable to see their role as participants in a larger conversation. They protect themselves from the vulnerability of the red pen by writing essays that may be structurally precise, but that lack insight or original thinking.

A third way that some people have dealt with their vulnerability is, unfortunately, through abuse. In the five years I attended conferences and collected data, I did not see any abuse through the inkshedding activity. That is, no one used it to criticize or attack a presenter or another inkshedding text. However, in the early years of Inkshed, as the community identity was forming, "trashing" (as old-timers in the community call it) occasionally happened. There are a variety of explanations as to why this occurred. Some suggest that it happened (and may still happen) when people are not required to sign their inkshedding texts. (Writers are given the choice whether or not to sign their inkshedding—a topic of much debate amongst long time Inkshedders.) Others suggest that it is a result of a miscommunication or misunderstanding—often because the Inkshed community traditionally pushes boundaries, thus opening the possibility of misinterpretation of new ideas. One woman, an original Inkshedder, linked it to the sense of vulnerability that the inkshedding activity seems to engender. She explained,

> One of the things that I think happens in [this] community is that what people have in common is caring strongly about what they do. Strongly enough to be vulnerable in this kind of interchange. And when they're vulnerable, they can be threatened, and that's when the trashing comes in. (Focus group interview)

This interpretation explains that people feel vulnerable because they are exposing some of the ideas that they care most deeply about, and, as a result, they become defensive by lashing out before others have the chance to hurt them.

Thus far, all of the impacts of vulnerability that I have described reflect negative outcomes. Based on these examples, it seems that feelings of vulnerability do not encourage or facilitate writing processes, nor do they facilitate meaningful engagement with the collective in knowledge building practices. However, there are others who have come to the Inkshed community and had an entirely different experience. The feelings of vulnerability still exist, but there seems to be a different attitude about these feelings. In a conversation with a fellow Inkshedder, I asked why she had not included a discussion of vulnerability in her writing on Inkshed. She smiled and explained that it was that feeling of vulnerability that gave inkshedding its edge; that, for her, made it fun (Field notes).

This kind of change in perspective that can open up to and embrace the inherent vulnerability of inkshedding is echoed by Inkshedder Brock MacDonald. Brock, now a well-established member of the Inkshed community, shared his experience in the following way:

> First time inkshedding—the horror! The horror! I was not keen, to put it mildly. I was used to the conventional conference paper aftermath, i.e. the situation in which one has the option of speaking up and posing a question or raising an issue, and one also has the option of remaining silent. Writing my responses on the spot and sharing them made me feel naked, essentially defenseless, vulnerable. (Inkshedding text)

In this description of his introduction to inkshedding, Brock echoed the common feelings of insecurity described earlier in this chapter. He even went so far as to describe this vulnerability as feeling naked—an extreme kind of exposure. What is critical to Brock's feelings of vulnerability, however, is how he interpreted them. He went on in describing his experience to show how this sense of nakedness, or vulnerability, is actually important to being part of the community, part of the action. When describing his enculturation into the community in the same writing, he articulated the connection of feeling vulnerable to feeling part of the collective. He wrote,

> "... hmm—everyone else is in the same boat—it's ok!" Feeling of horror gave way rapidly to a feeling of liberation. The metaphor of nakedness is actually important here—on say, Wreck Beach in Vancouver, one quickly finds that same sense of lib-

eration. Everybody's naked—big deal. Everyone's writing—big deal. (Inkshedding text)

What Brock managed to describe is an experience that is shared by many individuals in the Inkshed collective who manage to return and become part of the community. In order to participate in the writing activity and the community, individuals must live with the inherent discomfort and fear that accompanies inkshedding. They do so with the understanding that others also feel anxious and uncomfortable. Because they are not alone in their fears and self-exposure, they have support in their anxiety and it becomes possible to participate. The shared danger helps individuals to negotiate the path between individuality and becoming part of the collective. As a result, they participate in collective practices which lead to membership in the collective.

The way that Inkshed has allowed people to feel safe, even when doing something "dangerous" like writing in public, has led to a strong sense of community. In reflecting on the way the community has changed and developed over the years, Russ Hunt commented:

> Originally I thought of it [Inkshed] as primarily a way to give people a rhetorical context which would stretch and transform their tacit assumptions about what writing is .... But ... it's clear that that has become secondary .... Now it's about creating and maintaining community, supporting each other, etc. (Inkshedding text)

Thus, as Hunt explained, members of the Inkshed community who continue to come to conferences and write year after year have come to understand collective values and appropriate ways to respond and engage through writing practices to form a CoP. Those who call themselves Inkshedders identify themselves as part of a larger collective that encourages risks (as in the inkshedding activity), but also provides a buffer of support for those who are willing to jump in and expose themselves.

BEYOND THE INKSHED CONVERSATION

One of the aims of this book is to explore the relationship between writing and knowledge. This chapter has shown that participating in writing practices of established communities can be challenging and intimidating. It stands to reason that this also impacts the way knowledge is generated and understood within communities. While it is important to explore the link between writing and knowledge, this research brings a unique perspective by examining the challenge inherent in participating in writing activities. It is not enough to acknowledge a link. Attention must also be paid to the challenges of being able to participate, for without participation there can be no creation.

Acknowledging some of the challenges associated with entering academic discourse provides important insights into students' writing experiences as well as experiences of graduate students or new scholars entering their disciplinary conversations.

These findings resonate beyond the confines of Inkshed conference walls. Like many people who attend Inkshed conferences for the first time, students walking into university classrooms for the first time may feel scared and intimidated by what teachers ask them to write. Compulsory writing tasks, where the rules are hidden or unstated, help to generate students' fears. They enter the writing process often unaware of the generic conventions that typify academic writing, and learn, only when they have broken a rule, what the rules might be. In addition, through writing assignments like literature reviews and research papers, teachers ask students to jump into an academic conversation where a power differential asks them, as novices, to report on the experts who are distant and untouchable. It seems almost impossible that the novice would be able to write something significant enough to truly engage the reader. It is no wonder that feelings of fear, anxiety, and vulnerability surface in academic classrooms.

Graduate students and new scholars face similar challenges. While some may confidently jump into their disciplinary conversations, others may feel uncomfortable, unsure of their voice, wondering about the unwritten rules for speaking up. Ideally, a supervisor will help mentor the graduate student into a place of belonging in the community and perhaps even facilitate the transition to new scholar. But as Paré, Starke-Meyerring, and McAlpine have illustrated elsewhere in this book, those relationships come fraught with their own challenges.

In short, for many writers entering an academic discourse, it is not always easy to follow and learn the conventions of the community. Newcomers may be intimidated and feel nervous and anxious and those feelings may impact the way that the newcomer learns to participate in the community. Some will be able to work through their insecurities and find a place of belonging in the discourse community so that they can take part in knowledge making practices. Others, however, will not. The institutional context that does not acknowledge these insecurities is sure to constrain the potential knowledge of its collective, for the link between writing and knowledge is not only theoretical, but also human.

REFERENCES

Bakhtin, M. (1986). The problem of speech genres. In C. Emerson & M. Holquist (Eds.), *Bakhtin: Speech genres and other late essays* (V. McGee, Trans.). Austin, TX: University of Texas Press.

Bazerman, C. (1988). *Shaping written knowledge: The genre and activity of the experimental article in science.* Madison, WI: University of Wisconsin Press.

Becker, H., McCall, M., & Morris, L. (1989). Theatres and communities: Three scenes. *Social Problems, 36,* 93-116.

Berkenkotter, C., & Huckin, T. (1995). *Genre knowledge in disciplinary communication: Cognition/culture/power.* Hillsdale, NJ: Erlbaum.

Bizzell, P. (1983). Cognition, convention, and certainty: What we need to know about writing. *PRE/TEXT, 7,* 37-56.

Bruffee, K. (1986). Social construction, language, and the authority of knowledge: A bibliographical essay. *College English, 48*(7), 773-789.

Burke, K. (1973). *The philosophy of literary form: Studies in symbolic action.* Berkeley, CA: University of California Press.

Clandinin, D., & Connelly, F. (2000). *Narrative inquiry: Experience and story in qualitative research.* San Francisco: Jossey-Bass.

Denzin, N. (1978). *The research act: A theoretical introduction to sociological methods* (2nd ed.). New York: McGraw Hill.

Denzin, N. (1997). *Interpretive ethnography: Ethnographic practices for the 21st century.* Thousand Oaks, CA: Sage.

Denzin, N. (2006). *Qualitative inquiry and the conservative challenge.* Walnut Creek, CA: Troika.

Denzin, N., & Lincoln, Y. (2003). Introduction: The discipline and practice of qualitative research. In N. Denzin & Y. Lincoln (Eds.), *Strategies of qualitative inquiry* (2nd ed.). Thousand Oaks, CA: Sage.

Devitt, A. (2004). *Writing genres.* Carbondale: Southern Illinois University Press.

Dias, P., Freedman, A., Medway, P., & Paré, A. (1999). *Worlds apart: Acting and writing in academic and workplace contexts* Mahwah, NJ: Lawrence Erlbaum Associates.

Elbow, P. (1973). *Writing without teachers.* New York: Oxford University Press.

Emig, J. (1971). *The composing process of twelfth graders.* Research report No. 13. Urbana, IL: NCTE.

Faigley, L. (1986). Competing theories of process: A critique and a proposal. *College English, 48,* 527-542.

Freedman, A., & Medway, P. (1994). Locating genre studies: Antecedents and prospects. In A. Freedman & P. Medway (Eds.), *Genre and the new rhetoric.* Bristol, PA: Taylor and Francis Ltd.

Geertz, C. (1973). *The interpretation of cultures.* New York: Basic Books.

Horne, M. (in press). *Writing in a community of practice: Composing membership in the Inkshed community.* Winnipeg, Manitoba: Inkshed Publications.

Kuhn, T. (1970). *The structure of scientific revolutions.* Chicago: University of Chicago Press.

Lave, J., & Wenger, E. (1991). *Situated learning: Legitimate peripheral participation.* Cambridge: Cambridge University Press.

Lincoln, Y., & Guba, E. (1985). *Naturalistic inquiry.* Beverly Hills, CA: Sage.

Maykut, P., &Morehouse, R. (1994). *Beginning qualitative research: A philosophical and practical guide.* London: Falmer Press.

McCall, M. (2003). Performance ethnography. In N. Denzin & Y. Lincoln (Eds.), *Strategies of qualitative inquiry* (2nd ed.). Thousand Oaks, CA: Sage.

Miller, C. (1984). Genre as social action. *Quarterly Journal of Speech, 70,* 151-67.

Paré, A. (2002). Genre and identity: Individuals, institutions, and ideology. In R. Coe, L. Lingard, & T. Teslenko (Eds.), *The rhetoric and ideology of genre.* Cresskill, NJ: Hampton Press.

Patton, M. (2002). *Qualitative research and evaluation methods.* Thousand Oaks, CA: Sage.

Pollock, D. (1990). Telling the told: Performing like a family. *Oral History Review, 18,* 1-36.

Rorty, R. (1979). *Philosophy and the mirror of nature.* Princeton, NJ: Princeton University Press.

Schryer, C. (1994). The lab vs. the clinic: Sites of competing genres. In A. Freedman & P. Medway (Eds.), *Genre and the new rhetoric* (pp. 105-124). Bristol, PA: Taylor and Francis Ltd.

Seidman, I. (1991). *Interviewing as qualitative research.* New York: Teacher's College Press.

Wenger, E. (1998). *Communities of practice: Leaning, meaning and identity.* Cambridge: Cambridge University Press.

THE TEACHING OF WRITING AS AN EPISTEMIC PRACTICE IN HIGHER EDUCATION

13 WRITING AND KNOWLEDGE MAKING: INSIGHTS FROM AN HISTORICAL PERSPECTIVE

Paul M. Rogers and Olivia Walling

In recent years, academics, business people, and the media have come to refer to our economy as information based and knowledge driven; we laborers in this enterprise identify ourselves as knowledge workers. One only has to look at the greater number and diversity of technologies by which we communicate and the emphasis on research and development by governments, industries, and universities to see that the accumulation, dissemination, and use of knowledge is a major activity of workers today. In today's economies, particularly in developed countries, texts contribute in measurable ways to the exchange and value of goods and services, while globalization, specialization, and new technologies have increased the need for workers to have mastery of higher order literate skills, such as expertise in science and engineering.

Anxious about how the process of formal education might help prepare students for this new world, researchers, educators, employers, and workers are paying closer attention to the role of workplace writing practices with an eye toward understanding the relationship of writing with productivity and competitive advantage. Implicit in these concerns is the notion that while higher education has successfully prepared graduates for a heavily industrialized society, it must adapt if it is to be useful in the dynamic (and even revolutionary) environment of contemporary globalization. In this chapter, through a synthesis of historical, sociological, and philosophical material, we endeavour to redefine writing and how it contributes to knowledge production in the context of the knowledge society and writing pedagogy in higher education.

While educators perceive a need to respond to the demands of "the knowledge society," scholarship in writing practices in the disciplines of sociology, history, and rhetoric has recognized that writing practices and products are intimately linked with what information consumers consider knowledge. Despite this recognition, we have yet to explore fully the ways that this research might inform writing pedagogy. The historical perspective that we use in this chapter reveals that writing is an active participant in the creation of knowledge. It is not enough to recognize simply that written texts contain things we call "knowledge." While this may be true, taken as an end in itself, it leads to the illogical conclusion that since we now have more texts, we "know" more than past peoples. Of course, however useful our knowledge may seem today, it would not help a contemporary time traveler understand or participate in cultural endeavors in ancient Sumeria, for example. Knowledge is not merely a currency accumulated and traded in texts and other media. Instead, it is created by texts. For example, patents create knowledge by defining the ways that ideas can affect the world because of their form and their legitimacy as legal documents.

In North American universities the common understanding of learning to write as instantiated in classroom pedagogies has changed a great deal in the past three hundred years, but has yet to account for the complex role texts play in the construction of knowledge. In the early days of American universities, practice in composing was supported by the study of rhetoric during all four years of undergraduate instruction. Harvard, for example, began its composition courses in 1642, six years after its founding in 1636. The rhetorical emphasis remained until the mid-nineteenth century, when classical rhetoric was supplanted by the study and recitation of treatises. Then, in the early twentieth century many universities employed works of literature as models of style, and these texts ostensibly replaced instruction in rhetoric. Thus, the rhetorical orientation of writing instruction was altered to maintain a new, subjective and class-based attitude toward English studies and writing in particular (Crowley, 1998). In other words, the answer to the question "what is the purpose of writing instruction?" was being answered with a sort of trickle-down theory of composition that emphasized literature and the development of taste. With the notable exception of a new emphasis on communication skills, writing pedagogy underwent very little theoretical development between 1900 and 1970; in the 1950s and 1960s, introductory composition was still being taught according to this "current traditional" pedagogy based on the 19th century model. However, during the 1970s, writing teachers began embracing process pedagogy, cognitive approaches to writing instruction, and writing across the curriculum. These new emphases have remained strong in writing education, fuelled by research and theory related to writing in the disciplines and professions (Bazerman, 1984; Goodman, 1976; Latour, 1987).

In spite of this increased attention, many administrators and faculty members continue to see writing as a general skill effective in any context, and continue to associate writing primarily with literary forms; a high school graduate is considered to possess all of the right machinery, so to speak, to produce texts in a variety of environments. In college, the student then obtains "knowledge." This knowledge ideally can then be channelled into the writing of all kinds of effective texts. However, this process presupposes a system of knowledge representation that is too narrow and simplistic, for it fails to recognize that for students to pass from merely consuming knowledge to producing knowledge, an effective pedagogical system must account for genres that extend beyond academic and literary forms, as well as the situated and social nature of knowledge-making practices.

In fact, the representation of knowledge, whether in a text or any other medium that uses a visual display, arises from the social engagement of actors who must display novel information in forms that are well recognized and meet the expectations of their peers. Because of the need to meet audience expectations, representations of knowledge must employ and adapt existing conventional representations for new tasks. These tasks become even more slippery when one realizes that representational systems do not unambiguously refer to entities in the world, whether they are concrete or conceptual. Furthermore, in many knowledge-making ventures, knowledge representations are achieved through the interaction of multiple genres or genre systems, which "instantiate the participation of all the parties involved within a knowledge making activity system" (Bazerman, 1994). When these four features of knowledge representation and production are taken into account, it becomes apparent that the traditional model of writing education is insufficient to prepare students to write effectively in any field. However, before we can address the necessity of this consequence in depth, we must first consider why the representation of knowledge in texts is the product of social encounters, constrained by convention, necessarily ambiguous, and involves multiple interrelated genres.

SOCIAL ENCOUNTERS

Researchers working in social studies of science in the last 20 years have amply demonstrated that statements in science can constitute facts about nature only to the extent that their authors are able to enlist the support of their scientific peers (Bud & Cozzens, 1992; Doel, 1996; Latour, 1987; Rossiter, 1982, 1995; Shapin, 1994; Traweek, 1988). In order to have their novel observations and problem solutions accepted as scientific facts, Latour points out that scientists must persuade others to take up their ideas and incorporate them into their own articles, books, and other texts. In other words, members of the scientific community determine facts as a result of their assent and acceptance of statements made in reports of research. In Latour's view, fact determination is social not only because it depends on persuasion and assent but also because scientific actors obtain persuasive power through institutions to which they gain access based on social criteria. Only those who have a laboratory may speak authoritatively about nature, and laboratories are communities that, like towns and corporate boards, act based on selfish interests and communally determined standards of right action.

In his *Science in Action,* Latour (1987) demonstrates the collective nature of science by revealing how scientists use laboratories to order information about the world and, thus, control it. Latour (1987) argues that the success of cartography came from its ability to separate information about a place from the local experience of it. During the age of maritime discovery, ship captains regularly recorded and brought back to Europe latitude and longitude for features of interest like land and shoals. One person's report when compared with another's might have only resulted in an incommensurable collection of shapes, but these pilots used the same diverse and expensive array of instruments like sextants, quadrants, and log books so that their data could be recorded in a way that would make it both mobile and combinable with data collected by other captains. These instruments themselves required the concerted effort of tool makers, pilots, and engineers in order to come into being. We might even extend this recursive study of the means and manpower behind cartographic information by pointing out that the ships used in these adventures were also technological marvels and, indeed, instruments that required the concerted effort of pilots, master carpenters, craftsmen, and engineers. The mobile and combinable data collected with these instruments was then returned to the center, usually the national capital, where it could be manipulated and made meaningful by other groups of investigators cooperating in order to create atlases and maps that record what then constituted "knowledge" about the foreign land (Latour, 1987, pp. 223-224).

Latour further emphasizes how these social networks ultimately create knowledge that then may be used by the central authority (whether a state or another institution) to control and dominate nature and human societies and institutions. His is a story of how scientific knowledge itself is power that may be adapted for political, military, and social ends (Rouse, 1987). For our purposes, it is important to recognize that Latour demonstrates that knowledge is not a subject or topic that is contained in a written form. Instead, knowledge is a human creation that requires the combined efforts of people doing different things.

One ship captain's idiosyncratic report of the coastline constitutes experience rather than knowledge. To obtain knowledge, there must be people who write instructions about how to collect specimens, people who are able to navigate in the open ocean, people who prepare star charts, people who record experiences on the expedition, and people who write scientific articles that report what has been learned. Knowledge is a social accomplishment and does not come merely as a result of discovery or empirical observation.

CONSTRAINTS RESULTING FROM CONVENTIONS

People who create knowledge confront a thorny problem since they must represent, in texts, novel information using well-recognized conventions that will be familiar enough to their audiences to allow communication to take place at all. In his study of spectroscopic articles appearing in *Review of Modern Physics* over a period of 100 years, Bazerman (1984) examines how scientists used the journal article to convey information obtained from spectroscopic investigations. In seeking to persuade readers that results were correct and meaningful, authors had to meet audience expectations "of what appropriate writing in the field is" (Bazerman, 1984, p. 165). Since such expectations will always include the proper form for the presentation of argument, they open up possibilities that the writer might not have considered and also impose constraints on what the writer may say (p. 165). In this way, "writing conventions help define the very thing called 'knowledge'" (p. 166).

While writing conventions partly determine the product of scientific investigation, that is, knowledge, Bazerman's (1984) study also reveals that discourse partly determines epistemology, how we know what we know. For example, he notes that, when writers began to use modeling in the 1930s, physicists' beliefs in what might be known shifted. Unlike a report of an observation, a model makes more limited claims about nature. Rather than asserting the existence of a confirmable fact, a model is authoritative to the extent that it accounts for data better than competing models. Thus, by the 1930s, scientific knowledge no longer could consist of true statements about some entity called "nature." Instead, it constituted a theoretical construct situated with respect to approximations based on phenomena observed in the laboratory. In the early spectroscopic articles, it would have been impossible for the writers to represent their research through a model, a discourse convention that was unavailable when writers were expected to make statements that could be judged true or false according to observations. As Bazerman's study reveals, writing conventions may both demonstrate what counts as a valid statement about nature at a given historical moment as well as shape what a scientist may say about the world.

The historian of science, Hentschel (2002), recently completed a comprehensive study of the visual techniques used to represent spectra of the sun and laboratory samples of elements and molecules, and his work similarly establishes that representations have a life of their own that exists apart from the phenomena under study. Klaus's investigation is particularly enlightening in this regard since the particular representation that he studied is one that many might assume would not allow for artificial manipulation by the scientist-author. One might easily assume that a visual representation of a spectrum is simply the fingerprint of an electromagnetic wavelength recorded on some permanent medium. Hentschel's study shows, however, that different "visual subcultures" employed different kinds of representations that both depended on the visual tradition of the group as well as the purpose for which spectra were studied (p. 60). For example, Isaac Newton's method of representing the spectrum of the sun as a series of circles of different colors persisted despite significant changes in the theoretical understanding that formed the basis of that image (Hentschel, 2002). Johann Jakob Balmer is famous for being the first to represent the relationship between some of the spectral lines of the hydrogen atom using a simple mathematical formula. Hentschel shows that Balmer's ability to see the pattern that gave rise to the mathematical relation of wavelengths resulted from his training as a geometrician who taught perspectival drawing. Thus, Balmer's ability to predict mathematically the location of lines in the hydrogen spectrum arose not out of a fundamental understanding of the structure and behavior of the atom he studied but as a result of the conventions with which he was familiar for representing three-dimensional space.

In the example from Bazerman's (1984) study, we see writing conventions operating to limit what may be known about the world. In the example from Hentschel's (2002) book, we see the novel use of conventions of representation expanding what could be known about the natural phenomena under study. Historical studies by many other researchers have confirmed the importance of conventions, including the genres in which knowledge is represented, as constitutive of what might be known (Edney, 1993a, 1993b; Gilbert, 1976; Gooding, 1986; James, 1985; Kaiser, 2000; Latour & Woolgar, 1979; Simons, 1990). The use of genres and conventions allows for mutual understanding of what might be known and can be highly consequential for the development of knowledge in a particular field (Fleck, 1981). This perspective is highly congruent with work in rhetorical genre studies which shows that genres constrain and enable actions that are available to us, that is, "what motives ... and ends we are able to have" (Miller, 1984, p. 165).

THE AMBIGUITY OF SYSTEMS OF REPRESENTATION

We can recognize that the act of recording information in writing is a creative endeavor when we observe the relationship that systems of representation (like textual statements) bear to their referents. As we point out, as a matter of social practice and as a result of the constraints imposed by existing writing conventions, writers who seek to record or communicate information do not translate the objective experience of reality into symbolic statements. What's more, they cannot. When we represent an idea or tangible entity, our representations—whether textual, visual, or auditory—do not allow us to free the representation from its time, place, and means of production (Goodman, 1976). In order to function as a symbol scheme for faithfully recording what is out there, the symbol scheme would have to operate as a mobile copy of what it represents. This is precisely the model of knowledge that much writing pedagogy presupposes, although most probably unknowingly, since it envisions a representation system that has an existence independent of its knowledge content.

As Nelson Goodman (1976) demonstrates, our representations of knowledge are almost always incomprehensible without an understanding of the time, place, and means of production. Similarity is insufficient to make a symbol function as a representation. As Goodman notes, "A Constable painting of Marlborough Castle is more like any other picture than it is like the Castle, yet it represents the Castle and not another picture—not even its closest copy" (p. 5). While most will agree that painting as a means of representing rests on what we might vaguely describe as "style," we are less willing to recognize that the very nature of representation that prevents a painting from being an unambiguous representation also prevents other forms of representation from speaking unambiguously. Representation is an achievement. With the exception of musical notation, the symbol schemes available for the representation of knowledge do not allow for unambiguous speech.

For a system to be unambiguous, there can be no symbols that intersect semantically (Goodman, 1976). For example, the existence in ordinary English discourse of the symbols "woman" and "doctor" do not permit unambiguous identification of the referent. In addition, the vast majority of symbol systems available to us for representing knowledge do not allow us to determine that a given character is syntactically equivalent to another (Goodman, 1976). In other words, if we exchange one character for another in a statement, sometimes we cannot tell if we have substituted a replica or a new character. We can understand the power and contingency of symbolic substitution if we look at the analogous symbol system of mathematics. In representing conceptual and concrete entities, most generally assume that mathematics, unlike textual representation, is free of ambiguity, but even mathematical knowledge is historically contingent and ambiguous. For example, in mathematics we may represent numbers on a number line in a sequence from smallest to largest. Any high school student can testify to the ease of using the number line to state inequalities like 1 < 5. Similarly, when we extend the number line in both directions, we discover that negative numbers are less than positive numbers: -1 < 5. The novice can also tell us that when we take a big number and divide it by a small number, we can predict that the result will always be a big number

$$\frac{5}{1} = 5.$$

However, if we take the character "– 1" from our inequality and move it to the denominator of our fraction, we observe an anomaly.

$$\frac{5}{-1} = -5.$$

When we divide a big number by a very small number, sometimes we get a very small number. This statement shows us that our character, "-1," may not be a replica of the inscription, "-1." So, even in mathematics, we observe that sometimes an inscription may represent one character and sometimes another.

A little digging reveals that this anomaly results from the historical development of mathematics through texts. Negative numbers entered the field as they became useful to people doing arithmetic in ledger books for commercial transactions (Martinez, 2006). Although useful, they created many difficulties for eighteenth century mathematicians in particular. Previously, numbers had been intuitively and practically associated with quantities and were, therefore, understood to be representative. This association broke down once mathematicians considered using negative numbers for other purposes. After all, what could these expressions mean: $\sqrt{-1}$, -2×-2, or $\log(-1)$? Newton and Leibniz were troubled; Descartes ignored three quarters of the Cartesian plane. What mathematical expressions might mean is contingent because it is the result of an historical process that depended on things external to the expressions themselves, including texts, accounting practices, and contemporary problems in mathematics (Martinez, 2006).

We can see from this historical episode that mathematical use of written symbols depended on social encounters and that the adaptation of the accountants' conventions for the use of negative expressions expanded and complicated mathematical knowledge. It is also important to recognize that the innovative use of symbols to create new knowledge in mathematics actually results (in part) from its inherent ambiguity. Writers would find it terribly difficult to be original if they had to use a symbol set in which the members had unique, real-world referents. It would be harder to suggest new ways of seeing. We do not argue that innovation is impossible using undifferentiated symbols. Instead, we point out that the kinds of innovations that emerge in text intensive communities (like science) appear to thrive on the imperfection of the reference system.

SYSTEMS OF GENRE AND FRENCH EXPLOSIVES DEVELOPMENT IN THE 18TH CENTURY

Finally, we can see how writings contribute to stabilizing facts about the world from the episode referenced in Bazerman and Rogers (2008) concerning the work of French chemists who developed explosives for the government beginning in 1793. This example is extremely illuminating because during this early collaboration of government, industry, and university scientists, (Gillispie, 1992), multiple genres of writing produced by scientists, researchers, government committees, bureaucratic offices, and military officials figured prominently in virtually every aspect of this knowledge-dependent venture. This mobilization of national resources brought academic, scientific, bureaucratic, and other forms of writing to bear on government policy and through texts made scientists accountable to government authorities. Initial scientific papers and communications with the government about the military potential of explosives helped initiate the project, and many scientific papers and patents also resulted in the creation of mobile information about the world. Documents were also produced by researchers that introduced the codification of new scientific procedures, outlined methods, and provided directions, instructions, models, and procedures for activities such as firing, loading, and using bombs and shells. An example of such documents is the specifications for the fuse assembly of incendiary shells. These texts contributed to unique forms of social organization, to the system of knowledge, and to the further mobilization of people, resources, and technology.

Texts recording the results of tests—such as the systematic tests of particular compositions of incendiary howitzer shells, reports, diagrams, and descriptions of accomplishments all flowed from the researchers to the bureaucracy. Table data from the performing of these tests created a different kind of knowledge, wherein scientists could observe that a regularity was occurring; these effects were later controlled, and without such control the same kind of knowledge could not be made. Also, knowledge from experiments dealing with non-military applications of chemical processes, such as the operations and actions of various fabrics and hundreds of coloring agents used in dyeing, were published, creating new possibilities of action; these activities played a role in the continued development of the science of chemistry and chemical technology.

In France, the Academy of Science long held sway over what counted as knowledge about the natural world. Thus, bureaucratic texts of many genres played a role in organizing the resources, the scientific side of the research process, and the public dissemination of knowledge through broader publishing activities, including peer reviewed scientific reports. The bureaucracy became a nexus for the manipulation and control of scientific facts, as government and bureaucratic documentary systems intersected with the work of the researchers and scientists by authorizing, funding, and providing accountability for the project. Government documents authorized the initial allocation of resources for facilities and materials, granted permission for scientists to go forward, and transformed the gunpowder administration from what was originally a privately funded operation into an agency of the Ministry of Finance. Routine administrative writing, such as the recording of minutes of meetings, also played a role.

However, while knowledge-making activities can be characterized as bringing more access to knowledge—through the publishing of scientific articles, for example—in this collaboration with government much of the crucial information was kept secret. Thus, while written texts allowed for the emergence of new categories of knowledge, they also excluded participants; that is, this knowledge only existed within the social systems that understood and had access to these writing conventions.

From the military arose a further series of documents which included detailed accounts of the transfer of weapons, plans for the building of arsenals, and strategic and tactical plans for employing weapons, including novel methods of naval combat to defeat the English Navy. In this way, systems of organizing data about the world were exported to systems for organizing people and things in the world.

Personal correspondence, notes, and letters within the government, between ministers and ministries, and with scientists were crucial in the development, administration, and monitoring of the project: secret letters were also written which directed resources and plans for the development of incendiary cannonballs, and which described their composition; specific orders and responses were also included in letters confirming dates and details of delivery methods. Memoirs and autobiographies, which required government approval, were also published.

Bureaucratic texts authorized, centralized, and coordinated the massive undertaking, assisted in the management of materials and people, controlled the secrecy of the work, and facilitated communication among scientists, researchers, military personnel, government ministers, committees, and field personnel.

Together these participants, through the publishing of research findings and other texts across and within a variety of social networks contributed to the foundations of scientific disciplines and future research activities.

IMPLICATIONS FOR PEDAGOGY

The consideration of the link between texts and knowledge from an historical perspective suggests a new understanding of the functions of texts. In this section of our chapter, we propose three foundational understandings of texts and then explore what they may entail for writing pedagogy. In doing so, we recognize that our conclusions are not entirely novel. Other researchers have noted that interrelated texts act within the world as systems of power and control, and others have suggested that we abandon the idea that generic "good writing" practices can be taught. However, we suggest that the synthesis of historical, sociological, and philosophical material that we include here reinforces those conclusions and offers a framework for continuing our research of writing and its relationship to knowledge.

First, we see that texts actively create and manipulate knowledge by making it nth-dimensional. In other words, the character of textual dimensions like indexicality and reference make possible the creation of systems of knowledge. For example, the precise recording and reporting of experimental results, that is, the creation of portable knowledge, led to recommendations by the French Academy of Science to further advance the project of explosives development. Second, writing is a technology that exists as part of a system by which knowledge is deployed in the world. Text and technology do not lie at opposite ends of a continuum of cultural endeavors that might be aligned with the often opposed categories, science (technology) and the arts (texts). Instead, texts are intimately linked with other knowledge-making technologies. Finally, texts naturalize culture, which then makes it manipulable through technologies including other texts. Thus, texts change our perception of the world.

When we consider these conclusions, we recognize that texts do not contain intangible entities called "knowledge." We can find no latitude and longitude in nature; there is no entity, "-1" that can consistently be instantiated in diverse documents and statements (even within the same knowledge field). Knowledge, as in the case of the development of explosives in France, is created by multiple genres (e.g., texts, diagrams, graphs, reports, personal correspondence). Constructing and communicating knowledge about any subject, whether it is art or science, requires the knowledge worker to read, transform, and manipulate symbols.

While our examination of these few historical examples cannot provide definitive recommendations for pedagogy, it does allow us to articulate some expectations that could be explored in future research. The creation of texts makes demands on writers for which a general approach to writing instruction cannot prepare students. This model presupposes that writing is a container for knowledge rather than a tool for knowledge generation. Instead, we expect that students will master writing abilities better if they learn in social encounters in which they develop and reformulate texts with others who are pursuing similar goals. We expect that there is a place in writing instruction for the use of schemas and rubrics if they are discipline-specific, but we anticipate that the use of rubrics will only be beneficial to the extent that students are required to adapt them to confront novel situations. The strict adherence to rubrics could reinforce the notion that texts are containers for knowledge. We also expect that successful writing instruction will occur when text generation and reformulation exist as part of the student's knowledge-making development. In other words, good writing cannot be taught as something separate from subject matter. This does not mean that there is no place for introductory writing instruction. Rather, it suggests that introductory courses that expose students to writing within specific knowledge domains, including case methods of teaching and assigning genres that invite students to experiment with professional roles they will face in the future (perhaps in the instructor's area of expertise) will be most successful. Further, students should be exposed to an expansive range of inter-related professional genres of writing rather than merely isolated instances of academic and literary forms. Finally, we suggest that theoretical knowledge about writing can be incorporated into writing instruction in meaningful ways. Understanding how texts are produced and function can help expose students to writing's many possibilities. Without knowledge of the ways that writing can be used to shape the world and our understanding of it, we anticipate that students will see writing as an obstacle that stands between them and their goals rather than a powerful instrument for participating in the world.

IMPLICATIONS FOR RESEARCH

This synthesis of literature and case study concerning the contexts, conventions, and representative systems of writing practices strongly suggests that writing pedagogy can benefit from being informed by knowledge of how writing has developed in text-intensive communities. At the same time, we hope that this study will encourage other researchers to use historical methods to expand our understanding of writing as a tool for the creation and dissemination of knowledge. Latour's and others' studies of writing as a laboratory practice have been extremely important in establishing the importance of social aspects of writing practices in knowledge driven societies (Bazerman, 1999; Latour & Woolgar, 1979; Pickering, 1984). Bazerman, Hentschel, Miller, and others have revealed the extent to which the use of conventions and writing genres have constructively shaped knowledge, especially in communities of experts. Historians and philosophers have shown us how our symbol systems serve important epistemological roles as well as challenge writers who seek to communicate novel information (Gooding, 1986; Goodman, 1976; Hacking, 1983). Finally, historians with many different areas of expertise have noted how writing practices reflect and influence our conception of information and systems of knowledge. For example, Long (2001) shows that the emergence of texts on the mechanical arts transformed these activities into discursive and learned subjects: "When authors transformed craft know-how into forms of discursive knowledge, they prepared it for integration into philosophical methodologies pertaining to investigation of the natural world" (p. 249). Her study, as well as others, suggests that much additional scholarship remains to be done that will reveal how intimately writing practices are associated with other cultural endeavors. While historians have performed a good deal of research in this area, "only 2.1% of writing research related articles published between 1994 and 2004 were historical in nature" (Juzwik et al., 2006, p. 467); even fewer were conducted with the aim of reaching a greater understanding of writing as a tool of knowledge making.

REFERENCES

Bazerman, C. (1984). Modern evolution of the experimental report in physics: Spectroscopic articles in *Physical review,* 1893-1980. *Social Studies of Science, 14,* 163-196.

Bazerman, C. (1994). Systems of genre and the enactment of social intentions. In A. Freedman & P. Medway. *Genre and the new rhetoric.* London: Taylor and Francis.

Bazerman, C. (1999). *The languages of Edison's light.* Cambridge, MA: MIT Press.

Bazerman, C., & Rogers, P. (2008). Writing and secular knowledge outside modern European institutions. In C. Bazerman (Ed.), *Handbook of research on writing.* New York, NY: Erlbaum.

Bud, R., & Cozzens, S. E. (Eds.). (1992). *Invisible connections: Instruments, institutions, and science.* Bellingham, WA: SPIE Optical Engineering Press.

Crowley, S. (1998). *Composition in the university.* Pittsburgh, PA: Pittsburgh University Press.

Doel, R. E. (1996). *Solar system astronomy in America: Communities, patronage, and interdisciplinary research, 1920-1960.* New York: Cambridge University Press.

Edney, M. H. (1993a). Cartography without "progress": Reinterpreting the nature and historical development of mapmaking. *Cartographica, 30*(1), 61-67.

Edney, M. H. (1993b). The patronage of science and the creation of imperial space: The British mapping of India, 1799-1843. *Cartographica, 30*(2/3), 54-68.

Fleck, L. (1981). *Genesis and development of a scientific fact* (F. Bradley & T. J. Trenn, Trans.). Chicago: University of Chicago Press (Original work published in 1935).

Gilbert, G. N. (1976). The transformation of research findings into scientific knowledge. *Social Studies of Science, 6,* 281-306.

Gillispie, C. C. (1992). Science and secret weapons development in revolutionary France, 1792-1804. *Historical studies and the physical and biological sciences, 23,* 35-152.

Gooding, D. (1986). How do scientists reach agreement about novel observations? *Studies in the History and Philosophy of Science, 17,* 205-230.

Goodman, N. (1976). *Languages of art: An approach to the theory of symbols.* Indianapolis: Hackett Publishing.

Hacking, I. (1983). *Representing and intervening: Introductory topics in the philosophy of science.* New York: Cambridge University Press.

Hentschel, K. (2002). *Mapping the spectrum: Techniques of visual representation in research and teaching.* New York: Oxford University Press.

James, F. A. J. L. (1985). The discovery of line spectra. *Ambix, 32,* 53-70.

Juzwik, M., Curcic, S., Wolbers, K., Moxley, K., Dimling, L., & Shankland, R. (2006). Writing into the 21st century: An overview of research on writing, 1999 to 2004. *Written Communication, 23*(4), 451-476.

Kaiser, D. (2000). Stick-figure realism: Conventions, reification, and the persistence of Feynman diagrams, 1948-1964. *Representations, 70,* 49-86.

Latour, B. (1987). *Science in action: How to follow scientists and engineers through society.* Cambridge, MA: Harvard University Press.

Latour, B., & Woolgar, S. (1979). *Laboratory life: The social construction of scientific facts.* Beverley Hills, CA: Sage.

Long, P. O. (2001). *Openness, secrecy, authorship: Technical arts and the culture of knowledge from antiquity to the Renaissance.* Baltimore: Johns Hopkins University Press.

Martinez, A. A. (2006). *Negative math: How mathematical rules can be positively bent.* Princeton: Princeton University Press.

Miller, C. R. (1984). Genre as social action. *Quarterly Journal of Speech, 70,* 151-167.

Pickering, A. (1984). *Constructing quarks: A sociological history of particle physics.* Edinburgh: Edinburgh University Press.

Rossiter, M. W. (1982). *Women scientists in America: Struggles and strategies to 1940.* Baltimore: Johns Hopkins Press.

Rossiter, M. W. (1995). *Women scientists in America before affirmative action, 1940-1972.* Baltimore: Johns Hopkins Press.

Rouse, J. (1987). *Knowledge and power: Toward a political philosophy of science.* Ithaca: Cornell University Press.

Shapin, S. (1994). *A social history of truth: Civility and science in seventeenth-century England.* Chicago: University of Chicago Press.

Simons, H. W. (1990). The rhetoric of inquiry as an intellectual movement. In H. W. Simons (Ed.), *The rhetorical turn: Invention and persuasion in the conduct of inquiry* (pp. 1-31). Chicago: University of Chicago Press.

Traweek, S. (1988). *Beamtimes and lifetimes: The world of high energy physicists.* Cambridge, MA: Harvard University Press.

14 REINVENTING WAC (AGAIN): THE FIRST-YEAR SEMINAR AND ACADEMIC LITERACY [1]

Doug Brent

In "The Future of WAC," Walvoord (1996) argues persuasively that the WAC movement "cannot survive as Switzerland" (p. 69): that is, in order to maintain its forward momentum and avoid schism, isolation or atrophy, WAC must align itself with other educational movements that have national stature and staying power. She mentions a number of movements with which WAC has natural affinities: critical thinking, ethical thinking, assessment, and educational reform in general. McLeod, Miraglia, Soven and Thaiss' (2001) recent edited collection *WAC for the New Millenium,* adds further weight to this argument with essays that detail WAC's relationship to related movements such as service learning, learning communities, electronic communication, and writing-intensive courses.

In this paper I wish to argue that WAC also has affinities with another broad national movement: the First Year Experience, and its flagship vehicle, the First Year Seminar. At a number of institutions, these affinities are already being translated into programmatic convergence.

The interests of WAC reach far beyond the first year, of course. But the First Year Seminar, especially in its more recent stages of evolution, can offer an excellent platform for the broad cross-institutional goals and the interactive pedagogy that it shares with WAC and with first year composition. I will describe how First Year Seminars have been steadily evolving in the direction of WAC, and illustrate the convergence through a case study of the First Year Seminar program at the University of Calgary. Through interviews with faculty members and students, I will show how the pedagogy of these seminars integrates writing into inquiry-based research and engages students in writing as a process.

THE FIRST YEAR SEMINAR

The First Year Seminar is a curricular form in the midst of profound changes. It first appeared in the seventies and eighties as part of a broad spectrum of strategies adopted in many American universities to deal with unacceptably high attrition rates, not just among at-risk students but among students at large. Along with learning communities, intensified academic advising, residence life programs and other strategies to help students in transition, First Year Seminars originally appeared in the form of "University 101" or "Extended Orientation" courses. These courses, usually but not always given for credit and compulsory, cover topics ranging from library and study skills to adjusting to university life, dealing with sex, drugs and alcohol, personal values, and career advising.

These U101 seminars still represent over sixty percent of first year seminars offered in the United States (*2000 National Survey*, 2000). But throughout the history of the First Year Seminar movement, a substantially different type of seminar has quietly existed in the background: the "academic content" seminar. Murphy (1989), who published one of the most influential taxonomies of First Year Seminars in the first issue of the *Journal of the Freshman Year Experience*, defines the academic content seminar thus:

> This model differs [from the U101 seminar] primarily because of the emphasis given intellectual content. The great books of literature or current social issues are often the medium of course content. Objectives generally center around the improvement of communications skills, especially the development of critical thinking. (p. 96)

In the years since Murphy published this founding taxonomy, the academic content seminar based on a special theme has become more clearly differentiated from the seminar with common content across sections. The theme-based seminar allows each instructor to develop a seminar formed around his or her particular research interests rather than a more general "great books" or "social issues" theme. This model allows for a more concentrated engagement with the process of drilling down into a specific subject, and encourages the students to become, in Lave and Wenger's (1991) term, "legitimate peripheral participants" in the research community to which the researcher belongs.

Most frequently (but not exclusively) found at research-intensive institutions, academic content seminars concentrate on the intellectual rather than the social transition from high school to university culture. They are designed to counter the typical first-year student's experience of sitting in a large lecture theatre taking notes on the results of research rather than engaging with the process of doing research. By the time students get to third and fourth year and begin to encounter smaller classes, more experienced professors and the opportunity to pursue research on a topic of interest, it may be too late. Whether or not they have dropped out or foundered, they may be convinced that university is all about knowledge uptake, not knowledge creation, and be unable to re-engage with the university as a discourse community.

However, this model continues to be virtually invisible in the First Year Experience literature, most centrally represented by its flagship journal, the *Journal of the First Year Experience and Students in Transition*. A very small number of research studies mention that their sample is an academic content seminar program (see for instance Maisto & Tammi, 1991; Hyers & Joslin, 1998), but the academic nature of the seminars' content is treated as incidental. None of these studies gives examples of the academic content, and the seminars are assessed according to exactly the same standards as U101 seminars. Retention is foregrounded as the most important outcome, with academic skills, grade point average, and general adjustment following behind. In particular, the pedagogy of academic content seminars is rarely theorized.

Despite this relative neglect in the literature, seminars featuring academic content continue to grow in proportion to U101 seminars. In 1991, academic content seminars of both types comprised 17.1% of first year seminars surveyed by the National Resource Center for The First-Year Experience and Students in Transition (Andersen, Gardener, Laufgraben, & Swing, 2003). By 2000, they had grown to 29.5% (*2000 National Survey,* 2000). Moreover, studies of First Year Seminars are beginning to take more of an interest in what goes on in such seminars. The Policy Center on the First Year of College reports that, according to student surveys, academic theme seminars were ranked as more effective than U101 or "transition" seminars on two measures: improving academic/cognitive skills and improving critical thinking skills (Swing, 2002).

The gradual emergence of academic content seminars into the sunlight coincides with a renewed and often highly vocal movement to re-integrate research and teaching, particularly in large research institutions in which research and teaching have threatened to become almost totally disengaged from one another. The Boyer Commission on Educating Undergraduates in the Research University (1998), one of the most high profile studies to engage this problem, laments,

> Recruitment materials display proudly the world-famous professors, the splendid facilities and the ground-breaking research that goes on within them, but thousands of students graduate without ever seeing the world-famous professors or tasting

genuine research.

The Boyer Commission proposes far-reaching remedies for this problem, chief among them being the First Year Seminar used expressly as a tool for fostering intellectual engagement, not just bodily retention:

> The focal point of the first year should be a small seminar taught by experienced faculty. The seminar should deal with topics that will stimulate and open intellectual horizons and allow opportunities for learning by inquiry in a collaborative environment. Working in small groups will give students not only direct intellectual contact with faculty and with one another but also give those new to their situations opportunities to find friends and to learn how to be students. Most of all, it should enable a professor to imbue new students with a sense of the excitement of discovery and the opportunities for intellectual growth inherent in the university experience.

The Boyer Commission thus sets a new agenda for First Year Seminars in which engagement with the research culture is a more important goal than retention for its own sake.

STUDENT RESEARCH AND STUDENT WRITING

This increasing focus on engaging students with the university "research culture" brings the First Year Seminar closer to the orbit of Composition Studies, particularly Writing Across the Curriculum. Although in some ways an orphan or at least peripheral genre in much of the Composition Studies literature, the writing of "the research paper" has long been of interest in the field. In 1982, Larson argued persuasively that "the research paper" is too broad a designation to be useful in defining a genre, and that almost any type of paper could legitimately be called a "research" paper. Yet, like the proverbial bumblebee that is supposed to have been scientifically proven to be unable to fly, the research paper continues to fly anyway. A number of early studies such as those of Schwegler and Shamoon (1982) and Nelson and Hayes (1988) suggest that, pacé Larson, there is indeed a particular and special set of skills, and more important, a special set of tacit assumptions and a special mindset, required when students are asked to write from sources. The stresses of building an essay that incorporates the ideas of others, Nelson and Hayes (1988) argue, can easily drive students to an efficient but intellectually sterile "content-driven" strategy:

> If your goal is to assemble and reproduce what others have written on a topic, then search strategies that allow you to locate sources with easily-plundered pockets of information are especially appropriate. In contrast, if your aim is to "argue for a position" or "find a new approach" to a topic, then you'll need research strategies that allow you to zero in on issues and evaluate the relevance and validity of possible sources. (pp. 5-6)

Literature aimed at the subset of academic librarianship known as "Bibliographic Instruction" follows a remarkably parallel path, though the two bodies of literature rarely cite each other or otherwise connect. Important studies such as those of Fister (1992) and Leckie (1996) reveal a wide gulf between the research processes of professional scholars—which those scholars tacitly expect of their students—and those which most students practice. Like Nelson and Hayes (1988), Fister (1992) and Leckie (1996) note that many students use an efficient but low-investment strategy of scooping up as many citations as they feel they need to fill a certain number of blank pages rather than letting an issue drive a gradually widening and deepening research process.

If we want to encourage students to choose high-investment strategies of research and writing, Nelson and Hayes (1988) argue, the structure of the course is all-important. For good academic discourse to flourish, the classroom environment should offer immediate feedback on drafts, talks and journals, a focus on high-level goals, and sufficient time, in staged assignments, to develop an argument rather than turning to highly efficient but low-investment strategies based on retelling information.

Again, the Bibliographic Instruction literature makes similar points. Article after article registers frustration with the typical fifty minute "library orientation" in which library staff must try to distil what students need to know about finding information into a decontextualized talk of which students will remember almost nothing. Leckie (1996) argues for a more integrated strategy that she calls "stratified methodology," essentially a strategy of presenting an assignment in several phases from proposal to draft to completed assignment, with plenty of time for development and feedback at all stages. She also argues that "using the library" cannot be taught as an atomistic skill but instead should be closely integrated with course content. Her recommendations for librarians could be lifted directly from an introductory handbook for WAC program directors:

> In the stratified methodology, the responsibility for at least introductory bibliographic instruction in a discipline is deliberately shifted to the faculty member, who is then able to put it into the context of the course content. The librarian can be supportive, by providing examples, suggestions, outlines of what needs to be discussed, and/or coming into class for certain parts of the process (e.g., a talk about Readers' Guide). In a way, academic librarians then would become bibliographic instruction mentors, assisting and encouraging faculty with respect to integrating information literacy into their courses.... Furthermore, academic librarians should be visible participants in annual teaching workshops which many universities offer for faculty. (p. 207)

Throughout both bodies of literature on undergraduate research or "academic literacy" (Lea's, 1998, term), the call is loud and clear: the road to academic literacy involves pedagogies of integration, extended process, and grounding in genuine inquiry.

THE FIRST YEAR SEMINAR AS A VEHICLE FOR ACADEMIC LITERACY

Typically, this search for meaningful contexts for research-based reading and writing has felt expression in the WAC movement, most notably in the Writing in the Disciplines variant in which Writing Intensive (WI) courses provide disciplinary context. In its most strongly argued form, this movement represents a sharp turn away from general-purpose first year composition courses—dubbed General Writing Skills Instruction or GWSI courses by Petraglia (1995) and others—toward courses located firmly in established academic disciplines. Russell (1995), for instance, argues strongly that only such contexts can provide the activity systems that constitute specific genres of writing. Outside such activity systems—for instance, in Composition 101—writing inevitably collapses into a set of skills so generalized as to be meaningless. The location of writing-intensive courses within disciplines answers the need to immerse students in the discourse of specific academic disciplines rather than in the grey all-purpose academic discourse which can come to characterize "the research paper" as taught in many composition courses—what Russell disparagingly calls "Universal Educated Discourse" and claims is a myth.

In "Rethinking Genre in School and Society," a later and more theoretical article, Russell extends this analysis by explicitly linking activity theory and genre theory to create a complex model of written genres as activity systems with intricate boundary problems, power relations, and (most important for this discussion) profound implications for the actors who would enter such systems via the set of activity systems represented by school genres. Russell draws a clear distinction between the written genres of full-fledged disciplinary activity systems that make up the professional world and the "abstracted, commodified" genres with which students typically work:

> These abstract, commodified tools are offered as discrete facts, often to be memorized—facts whose immediate use may be viewed by students in terms of a grade ... but also, potentially, as tools for some unspecified further interaction with some social practice outside school. However, because students have not sufficiently specialized—appropriating the motive of a professional activity system—those potential uses remain vague. (p. 540)

Even in a disciplinary course such as introductory biology, Russell suggests, students do not yet have a sufficiently deep history of involvement with the discipline to make sense of the more professional forms of its genres. Somewhat depressingly for those of us who would like to introduce students to at least a taste of the university's research-based activity systems in first year composition or in interdisciplinary seminars, Russell's analysis can be taken to suggest that there is very little point. Only in fairly advanced disciplinary settings, Russell seems to say, can students have enough background that such an introduction can make a difference.

There has, of course, been considerable reaction to such assaults on first year composition. To begin with, it is important to set aside the purely political. Although WAC can, and often does, co-exist in a complementary relationship to a first-year composition program, the relationship between WAC and FYC can be soured by arguments over whether academics in content areas, with little or no training in composition, are qualified to teach writing. Blair (1988) and Smith (1988) presented both sides of this argument in a classic pair of articles in *College English,* and the argument is more recently continued in Chapman's (1998) article, "WAC and the First-Year Writing Course: Selling Ourselves Short." At its worst, this argument can degenerate into a power struggle between the English department and the rest of the institution. When decorum is maintained, the argument proceeds along the more substantive lines articulated by Bazerman (1995). Despite being a pioneer in the study of discipline-situated discourse, Bazerman also argues that there is a place for a less discipline-specific type of writing course. He argues that undergraduate education should

> make real and visible over the period of a student's education a variety of discourses, so that the students can reorient to and evaluate new discourses as they become visible and relevant. A course that spans boundaries and sits precisely at a juncture in the discursive lives of students, as the first-year course does, is a place that can effectively make that point. (p. 257)

The intricate struggles between FYC and WAC programs, and the concomitant blurring of programmatic genres, make much too long a story to tell here. Each institution will need to make its own choices in the context of its own local politics, local histories, local funding and local prejudices. It may suffice simply to point out that the choice is not necessarily either/or, and many institutions with sufficient resources to do so have been able to work out a vast range of strategies for allowing FYC and WAC to co-exist in amicable and often mutually supportive relationships. The purpose of this article is simply to point out that the emergence of research-oriented First Year Seminars offers an alternative, or additional, site for explicit or tacit teaching of academic discourse, or as Bazerman would prefer, a variety of academic discourses.

While not as highly situated as a discipline-specific WI course, the First Year Seminar can be far more situated than the typical first year composition course. By introducing freshman students to the research community in the context of an interdisciplinary theme, generally coupled more or less tightly to the instructor's own area of research, the First Year Seminar can be highly effective in reaching an audience of students who may not yet be themselves situated in a discipline without pretending to offer an introduction to such a thing as Universal Educated Discourse.

In many ways, the thematic First Year Seminar is better positioned to introduce students to the academic research community than are many first year "Introduction to X" courses that function as gateways to disciplines. In the survey mentioned earlier, Swing (2002) compares the interdisciplinary seminar on a special theme with discipline-specific seminars, defined as "an introduction to a major or academic department." Discipline-specific seminars come in dead last on all measures of transitional adjustment, including those in which thematic seminars are particularly strong: improving critical thinking and academic/cognitive skills. It should surprise no-one that discipline-specific seminars score poorly on measures that have little to do with the purpose of such seminars: none of the measures used by the National Policy Center comes anywhere close to measuring the degree to which these seminars are successful in introducing students to the basic concepts of the discipline. But this is exactly my point: when academic discourse is introduced in the context of a discipline, attention to more general outcomes such as academic literacy is apt to be overshadowed by a strongly felt need to "cover the material." In the case study that ends this article, I will show this effect in more detail.

The National Policy Center's findings mirror the experience of many WAC programs in which WI courses slowly become more and more oriented to transmitting the information considered crucial to the discipline and less oriented toward making explicit the processes of academic literacy. However, in a thematic rather than a discipline-specific First Year Seminar, the active engagement of students in research culture and academic discourse is foregrounded, and the course content is treated as a vehicle rather than the *raison d'etre* of the course. Thus faculty members are liberated from the "anxiety of coverage" that can sabotage many a well-intentioned WI program.

Another major advantage of embedding WAC in a First Year Seminar program, rather than a WI program, is strategic. Particularly at institutions without a strong writing culture, funding, in many cases, is easier to find for programs with this more respectable (Boyer-certified) agenda, as there is little incentive to see the problem as one that "should have been fixed at high school." If the word "writing" is left out of the course title, senior faculty members (and students) from across the institution are less likely to equate these programs with current-traditional spelling and grammar, less likely to protest that they do not have the time or training to engage in them, and less likely to feel that such courses are somehow or other "remedial." Even if the word "writing" is left in the title of the course, or at least of the program, the focus on research allows considerable baggage to be left behind. Hjortshoj (2003) shows us this phenomenon in his description of Cornell's Writing in the Majors program, which he directs.

> Because writing assignments and other features are included in course descriptions and syllabi, students who enroll in these courses know what they are getting into, but they are often unaware that a course is affiliated with Writing in the Majors. As much as possible, we have tried to put work with language into solution with learning, so that writing becomes, as Martha Haynes noted in her syllabus for Astronomy 201, "a natural consequence of trying to understand *any* subject." (Hjortshoj, 2003, p. 45)

Further examples stud the literature, although they tend to be scattered and seldom thematized in most WAC discussions. In "Ending Composition as We Knew It," Runciman (1998) describes how Linfield College has replaced first year composition with a series of seminars "taught by any teacher on any topic that lends itself to inquiry, provided the course adopts certain pedagogical practices and encourages in students a self-conscious awareness of the intellectual habits of minds associated with those practices" (pp. 44-45). The First Year Seminar, argues Runciman (1998), is the ideal vehicle for cherished WAC goals such as context-specific writing and broad cross-institutional responsibility for instruction. Moon (2003) tells similar success stories from Gustavus Adolphus College and Willamette University. Her stories foreground the importance of faculty workshops on innovative pedagogy and the degree to which they are able to shift faculty notions regarding what constitutes "writing" and "research." The First Year Seminar taught by faculty from across the disciplines provides a pedagogical focus that encourages discussion of issues related to pedagogy, writing and general education. In effect, it creates an environment in which more general educational outcomes are problematized and therefore made foci for discussion in ways that are less likely to occur in the safe confines of faculty members' traditional disciplinary homes.

Runciman (1998) admits that the experience of Linfield College is highly local and not necessarily generalizable. In a response, Daniell (1998) picks up on this issue of local context and argues that, while discourse-intensive First Year Seminars may be possible in a small teaching-intensive college, they are unlikely to work in large research universities in which the undergraduate teaching agenda takes a back seat to graduate teaching and research. Moon (2003) expresses similar concerns about First Year Seminars in environments other than the small liberal arts college.

I think that they are selling the model short. Although the First Year Seminar doubtless works differently in a large research university, the Boyer Commission underscores a strong connection between the content-oriented First Year Seminar and the research agenda of such institutions. The model was pioneered by large research-based universities in the United States. Cornell, for instance, replaced its writing program centered in the English department with a far-reaching and well-funded program of first year writing seminars—in companion with the more senior Writing in the Majors program mentioned above—in a long process of development that started in 1966 (Monroe, 2003). Princeton, working in some ways from the opposite direction, has recently replaced its program of disciplinary writing-intensive courses with explicitly labelled Writing Seminars, in parallel with "Freshman Seminars" but fulfilling different requirements (Walk, Jurecic, & Musial-Manners, n.d.). In a survey that explicitly targets Doctoral/Research Extensive universities, the Policy Center on the First Year of College lists 70 universities that have some form of First Year Experience program, of which at least 18 feature content-based First Year Seminars similar to those I have been describing (Cutright, 2002). In the Canadian context, the model has been emulated by two of the biggest and most research-intensive universities in the country, the University of Toronto and McMaster University. The research-based First Year Seminar, then, is not only feasible in larger institutions, it is arguably an excellent vehicle for introducing students to academic discourse in a research-intensive context.

THE FIRST YEAR SEMINAR AT THE UNIVERSITY OF CALGARY

This brings me to my own experience of leading the development of a First Year Seminar program that incorporates the lofty ideals of the Boyer Commission with the trench warfare of Writing Across the Curriculum. The University of Calgary is a mid-sized (29,000 students) research/doctoral university with a strong and rapidly growing research agenda. Its recently adopted Academic Plan emphasises the engagement of undergraduate students with "the foundation of scholarship, on which all our activities rest, [and which] distinguishes us from other post-secondary institutions" (University of Calgary, 2002). It is therefore a fertile ground for research-oriented First Year Seminars.

On the other hand, the University of Calgary has been an extremely difficult nut for WAC to crack. There is no clearly articulated composition program beyond a writing program that has, by close association with an entrance test, become intractably bundled in faculty members' minds with remediation. The English Department does not teach composition at all. In 1992, a high-level committee to investigate the possibility of a WI program returned with the information that it would be too costly and that faculty would not like it. A wide-ranging curriculum review process in 1996 simply ignored WAC in favour of other goals, despite the protests of a few people associated with the writing program (such as myself). In short, the University of Calgary is an excellent place to test the theory that First Year Seminars can accomplish WAC-related goals even in a WAC resistant environment.

In most Canadian universities, departments are grouped into faculties such as Humanities, Social Sciences and Science—higher-level groupings that fulfill the function often filled by colleges or schools in American institutions. At the University of Calgary, local politics dictate that first year programs operate at the faculty level. In other universities, particularly smaller institutions, they typically operate across the entire institution. This distinction is not particularly important for the purposes of this article, although any one considering setting up such a program would be well advised to select a level (department, faculty, or institution) at which political support and funding are the most secure.

The First Year Seminar program at present exists as such only in one faculty, the Faculty of Communication and Culture, although other faculties are attempting related experiments in somewhat different forms. Communication and Culture is a small, non-departmentalized faculty with a specific mandate to offer general education and interdisciplinary programs, including Communication Studies, Women's Studies, Canadian Studies, and other programs that fall between the cracks of more conventional disciplines. It is therefore a natural home for interdisciplinary thematic seminars designed to introduce students, not to a discipline as such, but to the process of making knowledge through interdisciplinary inquiry. From a pilot of two sections in 1999, the program has grown to 14 sections—still insufficient to accommodate all the students in the faculty, let alone the university, but substantial enough to introduce a significant number of students to the research environment.

After the expiry of initial start-up funding, the seminars have been sustained by diverting staffing from other courses. In Communication and Culture, this is made easier by the fact that the faculty has no departments with individual budgets. The program is not big enough to have its own dedicated director, but the seminars are in the portfolio of the Associate Dean (Academic)—myself—who has considerable responsibility for the sharing of resources across all programs. I can decide to mount, say, two fewer sections of Canadian Studies courses and three fewer sections of Women's Studies courses, and ask the faculty members who would otherwise have taught them to mount first year seminars instead. At other institutions with a less centralized structure, the same results are secured by "taxing" the departments—that is, requiring each department to supply a certain number of first year seminars to the institution. Clearly there are tradeoffs to be made in balancing the numbers of first year seminars against the need to provide sufficient sections of discipline-specific courses. In the absence of special funding such as Cornell's enviable Knight Institute for Writing in the Disciplines (see Monroe, 2003), keeping a first year seminar program alive and healthy requires considerable institutional commitment and political leadership willing to make these tradeoffs and convince both upper administration and individual faculty members of their value. I credit the success of my own nascent program to a great deal of direct support both from my own Dean and, more abstractly, from the senior administration, which has made various forms of inquiry-based learning an institutional priority.

Sections are limited to 25 students—more than the 16 to 18 typical of first year seminars elsewhere, but a huge stride from the typical introductory course that is limited in size only by the fire marshal. Full-time faculty members are recruited to teach sections, tempted by the relatively small class size and the opportunity to design a course around their own research interests. Pedagogy varies from one section to another, but by a combination of teaching workshops (funded by the faculty) and moral suasion (administered chiefly by the Associate Dean Academic, in whose portfolio the seminars reside), a number of important features have become standard. Each section takes students through a cumulative process of small assignments leading by degrees to a major research project. Faculty members mentor students through multiple drafts of assignments, and schedule at least one (usually more) individual conference with each student as the drafts develop. Library staff are deeply embedded in the process, mentoring students through stages of an ongoing research assignment rather than being limited to hit and run workshops. Finally, although the seminars are not labelled "writing" seminars, students find themselves doing writing, writing and more writing.

THE EXPERIENCE OF RESEARCH IN A FIRST YEAR SEMINAR

We have a variety of survey results that suggest the seminars are "working," according to various definitions of "working." Students generally report that they like the seminars, pointing in particular to small class sizes and interaction with faculty members. They report that the seminars are most effective in helping them find material, followed by developing their writing and reading skills. Other surveys, designed to measure changes in attitude rather than simply satisfaction levels, suggest that students who have taken the seminars are more positive about approaching faculty members for assistance, using the library, and generating knowledge collaboratively with other students. These surveys also suggest that the seminars increase students' confidence in their ability to function effectively at university.

To give more depth to this quantitative data, I interviewed four of the six faculty members who taught the course in Fall 2003, and 19 of the approximately 100 students taking the course from those faculty members. I was especially interested in how the faculty members saw their role as teachers of the course, and how their students experienced their first exposure to university research both in the First Year Seminar and in other courses they were taking simultaneously.

The Faculty Members

The four faculty members interviewed are all tenured or tenure-track professors. Only one is a rhetoric specialist, specializing in historical rhetoric rather than composition studies. Another teaches Canadian Studies from the perspective of a historian; the other two teach Museum and Heritage Studies.

The impression that leaps out of the interviews with faculty members is one of passionate intensity. All four declare an interest in helping students learn the nuts and bolts of university work—using the library, writing research papers, making sense of complex and sometimes difficult material—but in all cases this toolbox approach is subordinate to a larger mission of helping students share at least a small part of the faculty member's love of research:

> And the thing about research is, it's a passion. You won't succeed in writing great papers or doing great research unless it really consumes you. I mean you can write competent papers but the stuff that really goes, you have to really care about it .... And the thing is that if you do get the bug it's fun, it's enjoyable and I was hoping that at least some of the students would learn to enjoy research as much as I do.

This passion for the craft typically translates into a pedagogy that foregrounds personal mentoring. The faculty members I spoke to are very positive about the practice of scheduling one-on-one appointments to discuss students' drafts—something they tend not to do in other courses, even when enrollment is low enough to make it feasible. In addition, this focus on mentoring translates into classroom practice that I can only describe as "intimate":

> I move around them a lot and I sit with them, I bring them out. Like I want you to talk about the Plus 15 in Calgary [a system of overhead walkways], bad or good. How people are going to hate it or love it. Discuss it. Give you ten minutes. In the meantime, Jocelyn, come sit beside me, tell me where you're at, give me your term paper, what's happening in your young life.

> When eight or 10 are done, then I just stop it and we discuss the Plus 15. A lot of interaction, bringing forth, back and forth, back and forth. And all the time paternal yet non threatening, enthusiastic, yet demanding. That's the crucial balance I've got here of paternal yet welcoming and friendly.

Three of the four faculty members explicitly use the image of a paternal or maternal relationship with their students as they guide them through the wilderness of university practices. It seems as though, by offering faculty members the opportunity not just to talk about their favourite topics, but to mentor students in their favourite *activity* (researching), the seminars bring out a pedagogical style that emphasizes building relationships with students above transmitting information to them.

The faculty members also note freedom from the "anxiety of coverage" as a key to their pedagogical style. When I asked them whether they would teach other courses in the same way, especially if they could be guaranteed a similar class size, most at first declared that they would. But when I probed a bit more for exactly how they would teach a disciplinary course in their content area, they began to talk of subtle but important differences:

> I don't see it as my job to teach students how to write papers in Museum and Heritage Studies 201. It may be incidental in that I might put comments on people's papers like "you're repeating yourself," or maybe "you should start out with an outline." But I'm not there to teach them how to use the library or those things. I am there to give them an overview of the field of Museum and Heritage Studies and that's what I do. I take the Handbook of Museum Management and I identify the topics that are important and I make up my course outline because I know that if I can cover the main points of the Handbook of Museum Management you can't go wrong because it covers everything that is important and that's what I do. But in this course I'm teaching them about research ultimately and what makes university different.

By releasing faculty members from the felt need to keep plowing through topic after topic to make sure that they have not missed anything that the students really need to know, the seminar gives them license to concentrate on *process* in ways that only composition teachers (and sometimes not even them) are typically licensed to do.

I do not want to suggest that this is magic. Developing this interest in process pedagogy requires ongoing conversations on the purpose of the seminars and recipe swapping sessions among the faculty members who teach them. It also requires constant vigilance over course outlines to make sure that they do not creep into being introductory surveys rather than interdisciplinary explorations of a topic in some depth. But I cannot emphasize enough the importance of creating a space free of "coverage," a space in which process pedagogy has room to happen.

The Students

When I spoke to students, I did not, of course, find that all share their professors' passion for research. More often than not, they had taken the course because the handbook recommended it, with little advance appreciation of what the seminar would do for them. Most chose sections that fit their timetables with little reference to the specific topic. But the students' descriptions of what happened in the seminars, compared to what happened in other courses that they identified as having a "research paper" component, is highly instructive.

When asked to describe research experiences outside the First Year Seminar, most report experiences that I can only describe as "meagre." For instance, this student describes doing a "research paper" on *Oedipus Rex* in a Greek and Roman Studies class:

> We just took the textbook and had to go to the library and find other texts so it was like a literary research. Um, and just found points and other information that supported my thesis.

When I pressed her on this a bit, she elaborated on how she had developed her thesis that Oedipus had caused his own downfall:

> I had come to that conclusion before I found my sources. Then when I went through the sources I found points that supported what I had already thought was true.

This student is reporting what Nelson and Hayes (1988) describe as a "low investment" strategy, marked by the assumption (perfectly reasonable, but not the one we would wish students to adopt) that the purpose of research is to find support for a more or less preconceived point of view.

Aspects of this attitude also appear when students describe their research experiences in the First Year Seminar. In particular, they report using the question, "Does this source support my point of view?" as a major device for sorting through the deluge of material available. But they also frequently report a much difference *pace* that allows them to become personally engaged with the topic at a much deeper level:

> I went into the library like five weeks basically before it was due and really wanted to get into it. I found straight off so much you know? I had aboriginal narrators that I wanted to do and

> Hollywood narrators to find out what is different in film stories compared to novels. I just bounced around quite a bit until I came to something that we actually read in the text book. There was one little line in our text book that said that gossip was the foundation of narrative. So I went into it and started reading it a little more. I took out probably six or seven books out of the library and just sat there and went through them and underlined things and just wrote it all out and it was very broad. Then I handed in an outline to my professor and she handed it back and said that it wasn't very good. So I basically re-wrote it in about a week period.

I know from speaking to the professor that there was a lot more to this conversation than simply saying "it wasn't very good." But what I most want to note is the fact that the student reports digging into material in pursuit of questions rather than simply looking for support for a preconceived answer. She also plays with her topic until, based on a small reference in the course material, she finds a line of inquiry that she wants to follow. This is much more like the "high investment" research process that Nelson and Hayes (1988) describe.

Some students found themselves far more personally engaged than they expected or even wanted to be. One student whose grandparents survived the Ukrainian Famine in the thirties researched it exhaustively, interviewing family members and trying (unsuccessfully) to access the archive of the Institute of Ukrainian Studies in Toronto.

> I had a lot of personal emotion issues though because what I was dealing with was really horrendous. I really don't deal well with atrocities. But when I got my grandmother's accounts there were so many things I didn't know, and when it happened to someone you know I had a lot of personal issues. I'd start working at it, and I couldn't work on it because I was just too angry. I did not expect that at all. In the end while I had learned a lot and for me as a person it was important, I don't think I would do this topic again. You know, it's just university. I mean you read something and you can't sleep for two nights, I don't have that much invested in research.

Although this extreme level of engagement is rare in the interviews, a repeated theme is the way the pace of the course and its emphasis on spiralling deeper and deeper into a topic of interest sparks a level of engagement rarely seen when students describe their experience of research in other courses.

I also heard a number of students showing some understanding of how knowledge is built as a shared social act. The following is a response to a question about what helped the student feel comfortable seeking answers to complex questions:

> Not just the professor but the other people in my class as well because we kind of all worked together. So if one person couldn't find the book or didn't know where to look they would you know, we would ask and we would all go in a big group together to the library and all kind of help each other find stuff. And so it was a very good class that way, the professor helped you a lot and told you which floor to go to and stuff but if you couldn't figure it out you all helped each other.

In fact, this instructor divided the students into two groups and told one group to come only on Tuesdays and the other to come only on Thursdays. This gave the students an unparalleled opportunity to work together in a commonly assigned time that had already been booked off their timetables:

> We had all assumed at the beginning that we were going to have all that time for class, right? So all of a sudden we all had this chunk of free time. You'd get an assignment on Tuesday, you'd go the library on Thursday, get most of it done and then you would have the next Tuesday and Thursday to polish it. So we all went together on Thursdays.

The collaborative aspect of the course also works itself out in the form of oral work-in-progress reports. Oral presentations of results are common in many seminar courses. However, they typically tend to be presentations of completed or almost completed work. In the First Year Seminar, however, the focus on research as an unfolding process leads most faculty members to schedule oral presentations relatively early in the process and to use them as an additional mechanism for students to develop their research collaboratively from the get-go:

> We also each of us stood in front of the class and talked about what our initial findings were or what direction we would like to go in. And then we ended up actually having a class discussion. And I was able to gain more that way too, because some

people had suggested stuff that I hadn't considered, or the way they had worded it, and I kind of put my thoughts to words. So that was helpful.

I don't want to paint too rosy a picture of how well students in their first year picked up on the finer points of being part of a research community. Although all students I spoke to had been shown how to use journals, and most had used them to at least a certain extent, not a single one was able to tell me clearly how the material got into the journals or for what purpose. This effect was magnified when we discussed articles in online journals which provide even fewer reference points for context. But even students who had put their hands on bound print journals had little conception of the conversations that occur in them.

Moreover, of the nineteen students I spoke to, only one reported following up a reference in another piece of reading. More typically, they research by combing the plethora of bibliographic tools they have been given, turning up sources individually and treating each as if it were unique, picked out of space, rather than as a part of a vast web of discourse.

In turn, this lack of a sense of a web of discourse is related to a highly instrumental sense of citation. The students were all highly aware of the use of citation as a means of avoiding accusations of plagiarism. It seems that we have taught this lesson very well. However, none of the students demonstrated a sense that they were leaving tracks for a reader who could conceivably be interested in where their ideas came from or want to track them down:

> Interviewer - Do you feel that the main purpose of those footnotes was just to protect yourself against plagiarism or ... ?
>
> Respondent - Very much so. When I write it's a stream of consciousness, I never even think about anything else. There's no other reason for it.
>
> Interviewer - So, if you were writing now purely for your own benefit?
>
> Respondent - There would definitely be no footnotes, no. They have no purpose for me. I'm sure everything I've ever written someone else has at some point before me written, so, no, the whole idea of original thought – because you can never keep track of who did what first.

This is gratifyingly post-modern thinking on the one hand, but on the other hand it shows no awareness of the ways researchers depend on references to lead them back through the ongoing conversation about their subject. As Hunt (2002) puts it:

> Scholars—writers generally—use citations for many things: they establish their own *bona fides* and currency, they advertise their alliances, they bring work to the attention of their reader, they assert ties of collegiality, they exemplify contending positions or define nuances of difference among competing theories or ideas. They do not use them to defend themselves against potential allegations of plagiarism.

This mirrors the research of academic librarians such as Leckie (1996), who reports gloomily,

> It is safe to say that most undergraduates do not possess a vision of a scholarly network, and they do not have a sense of a significant mass of research findings appearing in certain journals over time, nor how to tap into this research.

This finding is disappointing, since developing this awareness of academic culture is one of the express goals of the course. But a First Year Seminar cannot do everything all at once. In particular it cannot undo at once the effects of long exposure to school-based "research" written from readily available sources in a school library and addressed only to the teacher, who presumably knows it all already and has no interest in the students' references beyond checking to make sure they have not plagiarized. Moreover, it is arguable (by Leckie (1996) among others) that only long-term immersion in the discourse of a discipline can provide a strong "felt sense" of how that discourse hangs together as a conversation. Expecting a first year seminar, particularly an interdisciplinary seminar, to provide students with a deep awareness of how an academic community operates would certainly be immensely over-ambitious. But perhaps it is not too much to ask that such a seminar at least introduce students to the fact that they can use references as a trail of breadcrumbs leading back to other material that may be useful to them. In future iterations of the course I hope to design activities that will encourage students to do exactly that. By doing so I hope to at least crack the door a little on the world of interconnected texts and thereby help students start the long journey toward understanding how academic knowledge actually works.

CONCLUSIONS AND IMPLICATIONS

My conversations with students in this one course are clearly not sufficient to allow much generalization. But the course can stand as an illuminating case study of a marriage between the goals and ideals of WAC and those of the academic First Year Seminar. In particular, it illustrates a case of WAC goals being realized in an institution that has not made a substantive institutional commitment to WAC. The First Year Seminar is a powerful teaching genre, often more readily accepted by both faculty members and administrations than WAC "in the raw," and much less likely to be stigmatized as "remedial." If it can achieve the results I have observed at an institution with a record of low-grade hostility to WAC, think what it can accomplish at institutions where WAC is already respected and positioned to make a strategic alliance with First Year Seminars across the disciplines.

However, I want to use this case to illustrate more than a way to sneak WAC in the back door. It also illustrates the degree to which the shape of the container can liberate pedagogy. The faculty members teaching the University of Calgary's First Year Seminar understood their mission to be "teaching research" as a complex process. It did not take them long to discover that in order to do so effectively, they needed to allow time for students to explore the unfamiliar alleys and back roads of the process, to mentor students individually, to send work back with revision-promoting rather than editorial comments, and, above all, to empower them to make mistakes. When we remove the anxiety of coverage and give faculty members the opportunity to work with students on subjects that they really care about—and most important, foreground the *activity* of research rather than just the transmission of results—we create an environment conducive to process pedagogy.

It is not yet clear whether the convergence of WAC and the First Year Seminar is a major movement or just a few straws in the wind. Certainly we must never forget the advice of WAC literature that initiatives such as WAC are profoundly local in their structure, history and administrative shape. I do not expect First Year Seminars to swallow up either first year composition or Writing Across the Curriculum at more than a few institutions such as the ones described by Moon (2003) and Runciman (1998). But what is clear is that the First Year Seminar movement represents an excellent opportunity for strategic alliances with writing programs. Translating the parallel goals of FYS and WAC into shared strengths can only be to the advantage of students.

NOTE

1. Copyright 2005 by the National Council of Teachers of English. Used with permission.

REFERENCES

Andersen, C., Gardener, J. N., Laufgraben, J. L., & Swing, R. L. (2003). *Moving toward excellence: Assessing and institutionalizing first-year seminars* [Teleconference resource packet]. Columbia, SC: National Resource Center for The First-Year Experience and Students in Transition.

Bazerman, C. (1995). Response: Curricular responsibilities and professional definition. In J. Petraglia (Ed.), *Reconceiving writing, rethinking writing instruction* (pp. 249-259). Mahwah, NJ: Erlbaum.

Blair, C. P.. (1988). Only one of the voices: Dialogic Writing Across the Curriculum. *College English, 50,* 383-89.

The Boyer Commission on Educating Undergraduates in the Research University. (1998). *Reinventing undergraduate education: A blueprint for America's research universities.* Stony Brook: State University of New York at Stony Brook.

Chapman, D. W. (1998). WAC and the first-year writing course: Selling ourselves short. *Language and Learning Across the Disciplines, 2,* 54-60.

Cutright, M. (2002). *Research universities and first-year students: Now for the good news.* Brevard, NC: The National Policy Center on the First Year of College. Retrieved from http://www.brevard.edu/fyc/ruproject/essay.htm

Daniell, B. (1998). F-y comp, f-y seminars, and WAC: A response. *Language and Learning Across the Disciplines, 2,* 69-74.

Fister, B. (1992). The research processes of undergraduate students. *Journal of Academic Librarianship, 18,* 163-69.

Hjortshoj, K. (2003). Writing without friction. In J. Monroe (Ed.), *Local knowledge, local practices: Writing in the disciplines at Cornell* (pp. 41-61). Pittsburgh: University of Pittsburg Press.

Hunt, Russ. (2002, December). Four reasons to be happy about Internet plagiarism. *Teaching Perspectives, 5,* 1-5. Retrieved from http://www.stthomasu.ca/~hunt/4reasons.htm

Hyers, A. D., & Joslin, M. N. (1998). The first year seminar as a predictor of achievement and persistence. *Journal of the First-Year Experience and Students in Transition, 10,* 7-29.

Larson, R. L. (1982). The "research paper" in the writing course: A non form of writing. *College English, 44,* 811 16.

Lave, J., &Wenger, E. (1991). *Situated learning: Legitimate peripheral participation.* Cambridge: Cambridge University Press.

Lea, M. (1998). Academic literacies and learning in higher education: Constructing knowledge through texts and experience. *Studies in the Education of Adults, 30,* 156-71.

Leckie, G. J. (1996). Desperately seeking citations: Uncovering faculty assumptions about undergraduate research. *Journal of Academic Librarianship, 22,* 201-208. Retrieved from Academic Search Premier.

Maisto, A. A., &Tammi, M. W. (1991). The effect of a content-based freshman seminar on academic and social integration. *Journal of the Freshman Year Experience, 3,* 29-47.

McLeod, S. H., Miraglia, E., Soven, M., &Thaiss, C. (2001). *WAC for the new millenium: Strategies for continuing Writing-Across-the-Curriculum programs.* Urbana, IL: National Council of Teachers of English.

Monroe, J. (2003). Local knowledge, local practices: An introduction. In J. Monroe (Ed.), *Local knowledge, local practices: Writing in the disciplines at Cornell* (pp. 3-21). Pittsburgh: University of Pittsburg Press.

Moon, G. F. (2003). First-year writing in first-year seminars: Writing Across the Curriculum from the start. *Writing Program Administration, 28,* 105-118.

Murphy, R. O. (1989). Freshman year enhancement in American higher education. *Journal of the First Year Experience, 1,* 93-102.

Nelson, J., &Hayes, J. R. (1988). *How the writing context shapes college students' strategies for writing from sources.* Center for the Study of Writing Technical Report No. 16. Berkeley: University of California. ERIC Document ED297374.

Petraglia, J. (1995). Introduction: General writing skills instruction and its discontents. In J. Petraglia (Ed.), *Reconceiving writing, rethinking writing instruction* (pp. xi-xvii). Mahwah: Erlbaum.

Runciman, L. (1998). Ending composition as we knew it. *Language and Learning Across the Disciplines, 2,* 44-53.

Russell, D. (1995). Activity theory and its implications for writing instruction. In J. Petraglia (Ed.), *Reconceiving writing, rethinking writing instruction* (pp. 51-77). Mahwah: Erlbaum.

Schwegler, R. A., &Shamoon, L. K. (1982). The aims and processes of the research paper. *College English, 44,* 817 24.

Smith, L. Z. (1988). Why english departments should "house" Writing Across the Curriculum. *College English, 50,* 390-95.

Swing, R. L. (2002). *The impact of engaging pedagogy on first-year seminars.* Brevard, NC: The National Policy Center on the First Year of College. Retrieved from http://www.brevard.edu/fyc/fyi/essays/essay2.pdf

The 2000 National Survey of First-Year Seminar Programs: Continuing innovations in the collegiate curriculum. (2000). Columbia, SC: National Resource Center for The First-Year Experience and Students in Transition.

University of Calgary. (2002). *Raising our sights: An academic plan for the University of Calgary 2002-2006.* Retrieved from
http://www.ucalgary.ca/UofC/events/unicomm/raising/AcademicPlan.pdf

Walk, K., Jurecic, A., & Musial-Manners, D. (n.d.). *Princeton writing program.* Retrieved from http://web.princeton.edu/writing/pwp.pdf

Walvoord, B. E. (1996). The future of WAC. *College English, 58,* 58-79.

15 A CODE OF ETHICS AS A COLLABORATIVE LEARNING TOOL: COMPARING A FACE-TO-FACE ENGINEERING TEAM AND MULTIDISCIPLINARY ONLINE TEAMS

Anne Parker and Amanda Goldrick-Jones

Elsewhere in this book, Bazerman proposes that both students and teachers of technical communication face a dual challenge. On the one hand, we must negotiate new forms of communication that transform work, citizenship and personal relations. On the other hand, we must continually re-orient ourselves to what Bazerman calls the "changing locations of encounter" that shape, and are shaped by, an evolving knowledge society. In this chapter, we examine a small spectrum of "changing locations" for collaborative writing: the discipline-specific and classroom-based location, and the multidisciplinary, online location.

While integrating collaborative projects into the classroom is now commonplace in technical communication courses as well as in engineering courses, what motivates and engages students to write together effectively and ethically, whether face-to-face or online? Collaborative writing alone, though integrating an important social dynamic into writing, provides no guarantee of student engagement—as every teacher who has integrated teamwork into a traditional or online writing course knows all too well. A fundamental part of the problem with engagement lies in assigning so-called workplace genres in a technical communication class; collaborative or not, such genres are dissociated from the social contexts that have shaped them in the first place. But if, as Artemeva (2004) points out, "it is only logical for us to agree that teaching genre conventions of workplace genres is useless at best" (p. 25), the question then becomes: what acts of writing in a technical communication classroom are indeed useful, and for what purposes?

One obvious use of team writing assignments is their educational value. Tonso (2006) argues that "teamwork improves learning, whether using discipline-specific, or interdisciplinary teams, in face-to-face settings or in virtual climates" (p. 26). In this paper, we further suggest that technical communication students benefit most from collaborative writing when it is not simply a means to teach workplace genres. Rather, the value comes about when such assignments enter the realm of the social: engaging students in the dynamics and challenges of teamwork and inviting critical reflection about the role of writing in the formation and governance of viable professional communities.

Consequently, an example of what we would consider a "useful" collaborative technical writing assignment rests on the following principles. First of all, the assignment must engage students and, secondly, it must promote responsibility and accountability. Finally, and most of all, the assignment must provide students with a glimpse, at least, of what it is like to be part of an ethical "community of practice"; that is, a group of people who both perform a function and learn together—thus understanding, to some extent, what it means to participate in a knowledge society. Students also learn both the requisite social skills (such as interpersonal skills) and the intellectual ones (such as learning about writing and genres). Collaborative assignments grounded on these principles and outcomes can be personally enriching as well as eminently practical, in that they encourage students to construct their identity not only as writers but also as members of a cooperative professional community.

In this chapter, we look at how one particular collaborative assignment—a written code of ethics governing team conduct, created and endorsed by team members—can help technical communication students, both face-to-face and online, gain useful insights into the social dynamics and challenges of participating in a professional community. We further suggest that such an assignment opens up another "location of encounter" created by a contemporary need to bring multiple knowledges together to solve increasingly complex problems, including the social and ethical concerns we outline here.

COLLABORATIVE WRITING AND THE ETHICS OF COMMUNITY BUILDING

Well-designed collaborative assignments play a key role in preparing students for future membership in professional communities. Through collaboration with peers, students learn to converse in ways that are valued within an intellectual community at the same time as they become engaged in thought and reflection within a dynamic social context—what Bruffee (1984) calls "a community of status equals" (p. 642). Collaborative learning challenges the notion that knowledge originates from designated experts; rather, "to learn is to work collaboratively to establish and maintain knowledge among a community of knowledgeable peers" (Bruffee, 1984, p. 646). Bruffee highlights how peer learning reflects professional (and particularly scientific) practices by defining and creating knowledge as a social construct, as a process of negotiating community values.

Arising out of these principles are a number of practices fostering cooperative and engaged learning, practices that increase the chances that a collaborative writing assignment will be "useful." Cooperative learning involves group-based activities and depends on successfully realized interrelationships and communication among group members. A cooperative learning and writing environment needs an appropriate balance between facilitating/coaching (such as encouraging, rather than imposing, appropriate strategies for social interactions and behaviour) and supporting/directing group work (such as providing a rich array of materials and manipulating the environment to make group work easier) (Tinzmann et al., n.d.). Not surprisingly, cooperative-learning strategies can strongly influence student engagement. Students can begin to have a sense of actively participating in such a learning environment, of having a personal stake in the community building that happens within—and, at times, beyond—the classroom.

Increasingly, however, collaborative writing takes place in online environments where face-to-face interactions may not be possible (Lind, 1999; Reilly & L'Eplattenier, 1996), and, if this kind of immediacy is not possible, the question becomes whether collaborative learning can still occur. While the promotion of engaged and cooperative learning is not so new from the standpoint of teaching collaborative writing, this "social element" of participating in a community cannot be taken for granted in an online environment. Some critics, likeFranklin (1999), argue that electronically mediated environments do not promote the kind of community building essential for collaboration. In her view, community building depends on physical locale and reciprocity, the latter term meaning "some manner of interactive give and take, a genuine communication among interacting parties" (Franklin, 1999, p. 42). Rheingold (1993), however, would challenge this view that community depends on locale and face-to-face forms of reciprocity. Though often criticized for his view of electronic technology, he nonetheless believes that it can help us form new kinds of communities. For wholly online teamwork, then, we can take some inspiration from Rheingold's position that interactivity can flourish in communities "not of common location, but of common interest" (Rheingold, 1993, p. 24). Specifically, from the standpoint of forming professional communities, Turns, Wagner, and Shuyler (2005) describe how students who use a computer-supported or online learning environment to fashion a shared repository of knowledge create a knowledge-building community in which knowledge production processes become visible to others.

However, such knowledge production processes are often inseparable from interpersonal interactions. Bazerman points out in his chapter in this book that while online connections "may seem to be pale shadows of those in embodied lives, seeking the easiest simulacra of gratification," people are nonetheless "drawn to these in a hunger for connection, a connection that will focus and activate our complex neural systems of meanings and emotions." Thus, a collaborative writing assignment—particularly one used in an online environment—ignores the interpersonal and the emotional to the peril of both students and instructors.

Since online course environments compel participants both to create a written product and also, in essence, to document all other processes, instructors can see this as an opportunity for documenting and reflecting on interpersonal and community building processes as well. In the online, multidisciplinary technical communication course profiled below, this reliance on writing remains, even when online student teams go offline to do some of their project planning (such as meeting face-to-face or talking on the phone). For, in the interests of record-keeping, accessibility, and accountability, online student teams are still required to post summaries of offline planning decisions in their team discussion thread. Another reason is that face-to-face team processes are usually tacit, inscribed by and through oral discourse, and therefore not always visible. Thus, one important difference between face-to-face and online teams lies in the degree to which the teams rely on writing as a planning and community-building tool. Though the face-to-face team discussed here also created a computer-supported repository of knowledge and shared it with each other, many of these important planning and community-building discussions took place while they were face-to-face in the classroom.

We must consider one final element in designing a written code of ethics assignment for a wide variety of student teams: assessing team effectiveness, or how well the team functions as a team. Indeed, team effectiveness "has emerged as central to understanding the use of teams in classrooms" (Tonso, 2006, p. 26) and, we would add, certainly in an online environment. In large part, the success of the project and the collaboration as a whole will depend on how effectively the teams are able to interact, either face-to-face or online. So, two fundamental principles govern how we look at teams and how we measure team effectiveness. These are responsibility and accountability, the two lynchpins of collaboration and, coincidentally, of the engineering profession. On the one hand, responsibility relates to the project functions or the task needs; that is, the jobs or tasks to be done: "Responsibilities are *obligations*," such as "*role* responsibilities, acquired when we take on special roles such as parents, employees, or professionals" (Martin & Schinzinger, 2005, p. 14). Each member of a team will assume a "communication role" that will help to "facilitate knowledge sharing and exploration and task coordination" (Dong, 2005, p. 447). Setting group rather than personal goals, sharing information, summarizing information, balancing the workloads and the contributions, knowing what the tasks are and who is "doing what and how," and setting project standards (such as the number and quality of the drafts) are other examples of the task functions (Dong, 2005, p. 446).

Accountability, on the other hand, "refers to the general disposition of being willing to submit one's actions to moral scrutiny and be open and responsive to the assessment of others" (Martin & Schinzinger, 2005, p. 99). As such, accountability relates to the process functions; that is, the social and emotional needs of the team as well as the team's interactions. For example, process functions would include such things as off-task interactions that occur when a team behaves as people rather than as members of a team; it will also include providing encouragement, compromising and managing conflict, demonstrating a willingness to have one's actions and ideas scrutinized by others in the group, encouraging participation, respecting the expertise of other team members and setting team standards, such as a code of ethics. As a team member, one accepts responsibility and, in doing so, holds oneself accountable to others on the team.

ENGINEERING TEAMS: ETHICS AND "THE NEW PARADIGM"

Because a knowledge-sharing community exists already for the engineering students, one would think the engineering team would be in a better position than the multidisciplinary team to achieve a productive "ethic of collaboration"— a set of "principles and values" grounded in a sense of "stewardship" (Haskins, Liedtka & Rosenblum, 1998, p. 34). Engineering students, for example, already share certain community norms, thus arguably laying a solid groundwork for cooperative learning and writing. As Davis (1998) states in *Thinking Like an Engineer*, "To claim to be an engineer is not simply to claim to know what engineers know; it is to claim to act as engineers act" (p. 115); that is, ethically.

For the past several years, however, engineering education has been changing, so much so that it "has been moving toward a new paradigm" (Donath et al., 2005, p. 403), one that has meant "substantial revision" of conventional practices, such as the traditional lecture, and one that demands that engineering educators recognize that learning is a social activity (Tonso, 2006, p. 25). Hence, the new paradigm includes teamwork and active learning, and there is now an increased emphasis on "a variety of non-technical competencies," such as good communication and interpersonal skills (Loui, 2005, p. 385). This new paradigm is also important precisely because it promotes "scientific literacy" and "science learning" (Tonso, 2006, p. 26); within the context of engineering, it facilitates knowledge gained through "hands-on" activities. In an increasingly complex and technological world, this kind of knowledge is even more important to engineering education and, indeed, signals the profession's ability to adapt to a world where the "locations of encounter" are constantly shifting, both locally and globally.

This new emphasis has significant implications for a technical writing course, which can effectively promote this new paradigm by developing team-based projects that give students the chance for this kind of "hands-on" learning. Fairly recent work on the subject of collaboration has supported the notion that collaborative writing projects help students learn the values and protocols and language of the engineering profession (Ingram & Parker, 2002; Lay, 1992). Put another way, "the construction of knowledge occurs through conversations about a subject matter, which serve to make knowledge explicit" (Dong, 2005, p. 447). Thus, the process of communication in which a team engages will help them gain and share their knowledge about a topic at the same time as it "instills the social element so critical to the success of the team's interactions" (Parker, 2009, p. 209). For example, when students participate in group projects and team-based learning, they catch a glimpse of the professional world they hope to some day enter, a professional world that is increasingly team-based (Reimer, 2002; Sageev & Romanowski, 2001; Vest, Long, Thomas, & Palmquist, 1995). A code of ethics is an integral part of this professional world, and the course can adapt a common engineering practice by introducing students to the need for a code of ethics within the collaborative setting.

It is this need for a code of ethics that points to the changes occurring in what we have called the "knowledge society," where technology has changed how and where we communicate. The ethics involved in working in this knowledge environment—and especially in a collaborative environment—are nowhere more pronounced than in the world of the engineer. Students are now becoming acutely aware that engineers must solve problems correctly because "they are personally responsible for the social consequences of their technical decisions" (Loui, 2005, p. 386). Aware of "how engineers daily cooperate in a risky enterprise in which they exercise their personal expertise toward goals they are especially qualified to attain," engineers likewise become aware of their accountability (Martin & Schinzinger, 2005, p. 100). For students, this awareness of social actions and social consequences becomes integral to their view of themselves as professionals who are governed by rigorous standards of behaviour; that is, by a code of ethics. Hence, by writing their own code of ethics, students gain an insight into their very own ethical community of practice. According to Davis (1998), a group can achieve "full status as a distinct profession" if and when "they adopt their own code of ethics" (p. 115). At least in part, the reason that a code of ethics is so important to a profession is the confidence it helps to instill in the public—confidence in the profession itself and in the proficiency of its members (Sidnell, 2005). In part, too, codes are important because they "state the moral responsibilities of engineers as seen by the profession and as represented by a professional society" (Martin & Schinzinger, 2005, p. 44).

This designation of a profession rests on the view that its practitioners are responsible and accountable both to the public and to the profession itself. For example, most professional engineering societies consider their mandate to be devising a code of ethics that will contain standards of conduct related to the practice of professional engineering within a social, public setting; indeed, the code of ethics "is designed for the protection of the public" (The Engineering and Geoscientific Professions Act, 2004, p. 70). It is this commitment to the public—and their declaration of this commitment in a code of ethics—that links the profession to the community at large. Additionally, this commitment depends entirely on the specialized knowledge that engineers use to serve that wider community. For this reason, the code will demand a commitment to the continued pursuit of knowledge. Usually, too, the code will also outline that, in addition to "uphold[ing] and enhanc[ing] the honour, integrity and dignity" of the engineering profession, engineers must support their colleagues as well (Association of Professional Engineers and Geoscientists of the Province of Manitoba, n.d., Canons 3.2, 4 and 5).

Thus, it is because of the jobs they do and the responsibilities they fulfill that the code of ethics becomes so central to any definition of an engineering professional. A code of ethics "emphasizes professional responsibility," especially as it relates to safety (Loui, 2005, p. 385), and "functions as a commitment by the profession as a whole that engineers will serve the public health, safety, and welfare" (Martin & Schinzinger, 2005, p. 44). In fact, Loui (2005) concludes that professional responsibility can be understood both "as a liability for blame" and "in a capacious sense as stewardship for society" (p. 383). In fact, in Canada, an engineer's iron ring serves as a constant reminder of an early engineering disaster and is thereby a symbol of this stewardship.

In sum, a code of ethics for engineers typically will serve the following functions: "serving and protecting the public, providing guidance, offering inspiration, establishing shared standards, supporting responsible professionals, contributing to education, deterring wrong-doing, and strengthening a profession's image" (Martin & Schinzinger, 2005, p. 44). In the classroom, of course, the code will reflect only some of these different functions since we are not directly affiliated with industry or the public (although co-op programs and capstone courses are to some extent). Nevertheless, the code of ethics that each student group in the technical communication class creates and adopts becomes an important link between the team and the profession's commitment to integrity and stewardship within a highly complex and ever-changing knowledge society.

ONLINE MULTIDISCIPLINARY TEAMS: A CODE OF ETHICS AS SELF-GOVERNANCE

In technical communication classes that are open to students from a range of disciplines, it is obviously difficult to model team assignments or expectations of self-governance on distinct sets of professional practices. Add to this the challenge of communicating effectively and ethically in a wholly online environment. In this ever-shifting "location," the code of ethics assignment plays a different role: not as a link between a student team and an established set of professional commitments, as it is for the engineering students, but as a means of engaging first-hand with the challenges of creating a viable self-governed knowledge community in a CMC environment. In contrast to the face-to-face teams who are moving toward an established professional community, the online multidisciplinary teams define (based on instructor resources and other forms of scaffolding) standards of conduct, process, and accountability that they themselves consider "professional."

To understand both the challenges and the "usefulness" of a collaborative code of ethics assignment in the multidisciplinary online course under discussion here, some background is needed. The University of Winnipeg's "Strategies for Technical and Professional Communication (Online)" is open to students in second-year or higher, and there is no assumption of previous technical or professional experience. The only official pre-requisite is to have received a passing mark in the university's first-year writing course, or to have been exempted from the first-year course by other means.

The goals of "Tech&Pro Comm" are reflected in the instructor's statement of outcomes:

By the end of this course, you should be able to:

- appreciate some of the rhetorical and ethical challenges of technical/professional writing in general, and computer-mediated communication in particular

- define and describe specialized concepts in ways appropriate for your primary audience

- research, organize, and design professional looking electronic documents

- revise and edit your documents so they meet basic professional standards

- appreciate and incorporate basic visual and design elements

- manage a team online project and collaborate effectively with colleagues in a CMC environment.

The course has two distinct assignment streams: (1) completing a number of small documents (value 50%) designed to be folded into a final individual proposal addressing a "real life" problem, and (2) working on a team to create an informational web site not related to the larger proposal. As well as meeting basic expectations for expression, formatting, and content development, the team web project must also show some evidence of rhetorical and genre competence (though obviously a professional level of development in design and content lies beyond the scope of the assignment). However, the criteria for evaluating assignments are embedded as much as possible within real-world social expectations, encouraging students' engagement with meaningful issues. Also, to serve that end, assessment rests to a large extent on students' written evidence of cooperation, engagement, and team effectiveness (responsibility/ accountability), making their knowledge production "visible" to others (Turns et al., 2005, p. 53). To gain insights into the team and its effectiveness, the instructor relies on the team's code of ethics, the postings in each team's discussion forum, and a final individual report on team processes, seen and approved by the other team members.

Teamwork begins with self-selection (another precept of engaged learning) when students begin discussion-clusters around topics of interest to them. Thus, students are conditionally united by common interest, but this alone is not enough ground on which to build a viable knowledge-sharing community with colleagues whom they may never meet face-to-face. One reason is that self-selection on the basis of interest can disadvantage students who, for various reasons, do not participate actively in discussion clusters and who end up on a team by default. The worst-case scenario here is that such teams become dumping grounds for unengaged students, which militates heavily against a good outcome. While cooperatively writing a code of ethics does not guarantee success (as the two profiles below illustrate), the assignment nonetheless improves students' chances of creating an engaged, effective ethic that will ground both process and product in a computer-mediated environment.

Four female students comprised the first team from 2005 profiled here, "Group Home." These students self-selected early and quickly reached consensus on their topic: how to find rental accommodation in Winnipeg (a city notorious for its low vacancy rate). The second team, "Life Without TV," included two females and one male, who joined late, having not participated in the discussion clusters. The two females had reached a tentative agreement to create a web site about how to live without TV, and the male endorsed that topic once he joined the group.

All teams are required to begin by first collaborating on a one-page code of ethics (worth 5%) that they agree will govern their social interactions and collaborative process. To prepare for this, students must complete required readings about leadership and teamwork (both face-to-face and online) as well as examine and discuss models or sample standards, some provided by former students. As evidenced by the two excerpts below, teams end up creating not only a set of expectations for completing the project but also a social contract governing their interactions. The "Group Home" code of ethics included the following:

- All group members will visit our private discussion group every second day.

- All group members will respect [other] team member's ideas and promote a positive working attitude.

- If a disagreement should arise, all group members will address the problem in a prompt manner via further email discussion or by phone.

- All group members will respect group and project deadlines.

- All group members will work individually on their Web

pages, but collaborate to edit each other's work.

- All group members will be open to editing suggestions and advice.

- All group members will contribute to the creation of the home page.

The "Life Without TV" code of ethics included the following:

- The team will be in contact frequently through email or on the team's private discussion thread, a minimum of twice per week.

- Each team member will be assigned specific duties that he/she feels comfortable with and commits to completing in advance of any due dates for peer review by fellow team members.

- If a team member has difficulty doing his/her share of the project, other team members must be advised so they can help.

- Each team member will be available for discussion or if help is needed by others.

- Each team member will share information in a mutually respectful manner.

- The team will collectively negotiate expectations to keep the team and the project moving.

- Conflicts will be resolved in a respectful manner giving each team member an opportunity to voice [his/her] opinion.

Using their codes of ethics as a basis, teams make more specific group decisions about the topic, the division of labor, rhetorical considerations such as audience and purpose, and content and design. As evidenced by their team forum postings and an interim progress report, all "Group Home" team members contributed points to the code of ethics. Furthermore, as the project progressed, it became clear that "Group Home" was effectively basing social interactions and task decisions on this code. However, "Life Without TV" began losing cohesion when one member took most of the responsibility for drafting the code of ethics, with the second team member playing a supporting role and the third mainly unengaged. This trend continued, particularly evidenced in the two teams' postings throughout the project. In the "Group Home" forum, postings were frequent, thread-specific, substantive (task- and content-oriented), as well as personally supportive; however, postings in "Life Without TV" were more sporadic and often re-used the same subject/thread heading. They were also often one-sided; the same team member tended to initiate and the others to respond.

As mentioned earlier, when teams complete their project, students must summarize their own individual contributions to the team project and have all members of their team "sign off" on that summary. They also send a separate, private message to the instructor, and there they may add information they may not be comfortable sharing with the team. As might be expected, the final reports from "Group Home" were extremely positive, with two members agreeing this online collaboration was one of the most rewarding team experiences they ever had. There were no contradictory opinions in the private e-mails.

One might have expected more negative reports from the "Life Without TV" team, but all were supportive in tone, with the least engaged team member expressing great admiration for the hard work of the other two. In this case, however, the desire to cooperate outweighed truth. While this team's code of ethics spoke both to conduct and accountability, its promise was undermined by conflicting interests, differing levels of engagement and a common problem with teamwork: one well-meaning member taking control of the process in the interests of efficiency. Indeed, the "Life Without TV" team exemplifies—in miniature—Bazerman's caution about the "distances and obstacles" that online interactions pose for engendering "an ethos of care and trust" that goes beyond lip-service. In many ways, then, their online team experience underscores some of the challenges of creating and sustaining a knowledge society in this new "location of encounter."

THE FACE-TO-FACE COLLABORATIVE WRITING ENVIRONMENT: THE STUDENT ENGINEERING TEAM

Because engineers—as problem solvers—are expected to communicate their solutions to others and to serve the public interest (Mathes & Stevenson, 1976, p. 31), all engineering students must complete the technical communication course before they are allowed to graduate and become members of the profession. The learning outcomes for the course grow out of the engineer's need to communicate effectively: students must demonstrate an ability to manage a group project, to collaborate effectively within a face-to-face team environment, and to present their work in both written and oral genres. To facilitate these learning outcomes, the course provides formal instruction in the "engineering method" used in other technical courses (like the design courses) and in the practice of engineering (Parker, 1989, 1990), and then links this method to the requisite rhetorical principles, a connection other writing scholars have also discussed (for example, Dunkle & Pahnos, 1981; Flower, 1981; Maki & Schilling, 1987; Moran, 1982). For example, students learn about problem definition and criteria development, as well as about how to cogently express their analysis in writing, including how to formulate their report purpose and determine their audience.

Students begin by first choosing a broad topic area of interest, normally within their engineering discipline. They then research their particular approach to the topic, which will entail learning what the technical problems are and then developing criteria by which to evaluate any solution. Over the course of the term, they work on drafting and revising the various documents the project demands, such as the final written report. Along the way, they also prepare oral briefings, such as project updates. During this process, teams will brainstorm possible directions for the project, or prepare any upcoming assignments. More importantly, teams will engage in substantive discussions on the project and share their knowledge with each other; they must also help and support each other. Without these kinds of interactions, reflecting as they do a professional code of ethics, students are not gaining personal knowledge about the topic or about themselves. It is only "by writing and working as a team and by generating a product" that students will become more competent as communicators and thereby "more ready to assume their professional status" (Parker, in press).

Throughout the course, scaffolding is possible through the tutorials, where the instructor begins with a brief overview of the material, including any relevant theory, and the teams then engage in hands-on activities, such as reading and commenting (both verbally and in writing) on each other's work, or discussing various issues as a team. Thus, teams are first given the broad guidelines they will need for a particular task. Once they begin the task, there are various instructional materials available (such as sample reports) that they can consult as needed, or they can take advantage of the opportunity for many different interactions during a class. Indeed, one of the ways that we track a team's evolution and monitor their progress is by observing their in-class interactions. Individual students interact with the team in the first instance, but they might choose to interact with the instructor should they need any help. Teams often confer with other teams as well. Students also have access to a campus-wide portal that allows them to communicate online with each other, to consult with the instructors or other members of the class, and even to store any of their documents. Finally, throughout this process, the tutorials and the assignments are interconnected so that the current one will build on the last and anticipate the next. Students thereby see the communication process in action.

The student team to be discussed here, the ME-2 team, will illustrate this process. This was one of two teams who chose "Mechanical Engineering" as their broad topic area for their final report; hence their name. The team was comprised of four students, most of whom were at different stages in their Mechanical Engineering program. One student, in particular, was a senior co-op student who, presumably, had some experience with team projects within a workplace environment. At the beginning of the project, however, he was disengaged and did not seem to share any such knowledge with his colleagues. In fact, all of the individual team members tended to come and go during group work in class; sometimes one or more of them would be absent altogether. Because of this initial reluctance to engage in the class itself or even in their own collaborative process, the team progressed very, very slowly.

This kind of cavalier attitude extended to their conversations in class, where they had the opportunity to share their knowledge of the topic. As noted earlier, Dong (2005) contends that the "construction of knowledge occurs through conversations about a subject matter," and it is these conversations that "serve to make knowledge explicit" (p. 447). Instead, often the entire team would sit looking at each other rather than discussing their project and sharing ideas. Nor did they seem to have the types of conversations (when they did have them) that would lead to shared knowledge. At first, for example, the team's conversations seemed fairly low-key, often with little animation displayed during their discussions and usually with just two of their members engaged in talking or in interacting with each other at all. In other words, conversations, and hence knowledge-building, were limited. Taken together, these signs of the team's cavalier approach to the project impacted how well they were able to construct and communicate their already acquired knowledge about the field of Mechanical Engineering in general.

After a couple of weeks of observation, coupled with a series of classroom oral briefings and in-class consultations, it became apparent that the team was struggling with choosing and focusing on a topic. When they began, for example, the ME-2 team announced that "anything automotive" was to be the focus of their paper; then it was "turbochargers" toward the end of the first month of classes. To their credit, the team did research the area of mechanical power generation more thoroughly than they had previously done and, together with the instructor's help and the help of a graduate student who had completed a thesis in the area, the team finally settled on their topic: the feasibility of micro-hydro as an alternative to diesel generation in a remote northern community (micro-hydro, as its name suggests, is a smaller version of the typically large hydro dams that most power grids require and, as such, micro-hydro can feasibly supply the power to remote communities, such as the one eventually chosen by the team). It was after this decision was finally made that they noticeably "picked up the pace"; they began working harder in class and were less inclined to leave before the class had ended. More importantly, their conversations became more animated and more frequent as they began the task of constructing and sharing their knowledge of micro-hydro with each other.

The written, confidential documents that the team handed in clearly illustrate the students' increasing willingness to reflect on the team and the project as well as their growing sense of reciprocity. These documents represent another form of scaffolding that has worked especially well in this class. Not surprisingly, all ME-2 team members expressed the view that the "team could have been more organized" for half the course, as one of them remarked in his individual project log. Another commented that the team was often "scrambling" or "last-minute" in getting their work done. All agreed that the team needed to follow their own internal deadlines more closely, as they had been too lax as a group in honoring deadlines. But in their individual confidential reviews of the team's progress, two of them remarked that they would try and make the meetings—and the team—more effective. Although they were not too specific as to how to accomplish that, the in-class meetings subsequently seemed to be livelier than they had been and most of the team would be involved in the discussions. Clearly, there was some reciprocity beginning to develop.

Similarly, the team's project file—the record of the team's project work and its work as a team—showed that over the course of the semester they did begin to develop some "team building" mechanisms that would allow them to function more effectively. For example, in their meeting agendas and minutes, they started to introduce verbal "status checks" (as they called them) into their meetings. Here, they would provide progress reports on their individual work as well as updates on their project responsibilities and their team files. They also provided a detailed revision history of the final document to show how the drafts for the final report evolved over time. Detailed project standards were also included, and these showed they had indeed paid attention to the requirements for such things as visuals and report mechanics. In addition to these task-related functions, however, there was also a revised code of ethics that clearly reflected some of these changes to the way they worked.

Although student teams are expected to submit both an earlier version of the team's code of ethics and a later one, usually there are few, if any, differences between the two. As well, the versions that most teams submit typically speak of very general expectations, such as "all team members will attend all meetings" or "all team members will work hard." ME-2, however, did rework their code of ethics, and these revisions reflect some of the precepts contained in the profession's code. For example, they set out "shared standards," such as defined project standards for the report; supporting each other as responsible members of the team; "contributing to education" by sharing information and knowledge; "deterring wrong-doing" by including specific details that would govern members' behaviour and interactions more exactly (Martin & Schinzinger, 2005, p. 44). In other words, they tried to outline issues of accountability and responsibility, both key to effective collaboration, in their code of ethics.

For example, they demanded that, if a team member could not attend a scheduled meeting, then that member must "notify the entire team by email at least 12 hours prior to the meeting and send regrets to the team"; likewise, they limited the number of times a team member could be late or absent either for in-class or out-of-class meetings. Most teams were not this exacting, even though issues of attendance are critical to many teams because attendance affects both the workload and the decision-making. But, at least toward the end of term, the ME-2 team did acknowledge the importance of attendance. They saw the impact that attendance issues could have and incorporated clear guidelines that would ensure that the task functions could be handled responsibly. So, too, with the process functions. This team's expectations of behaviour and interactions reflect their growing awareness of the need for respect, compromise and participation; this awareness likewise mirrors the local professional society's canon that professional engineers must support their colleagues. Even more important, perhaps, is their growing recognition that there is a need for "status checks." It is this guideline that the team added to their earlier version of the code, and it illustrates their growing commitment to reciprocity.

ASSESSING THE EFFECTIVENESS (AND EFFECTS) OF COLLABORATIVE CODE-OF-ETHICS ASSIGNMENTS

While at first the ME-2 team was certainly not an ideal team from the point of view of work ethic or even in-class behaviour, they did come to understand the value of the two lynchpins of collaboration and the underlying impetus for a code of ethics—accountability and responsibility. Without these, an ethic of collaboration cannot flourish, nor will the inherent richness of face-to-face communication be possible. In the workplace, as Vest and colleagues (1995) found, this kind of interaction is highly valued because it promotes knowledge sharing and enhances the sense of a professional community. At the same time, it promotes the reciprocity that Franklin (1999) speaks of, that "give and take" that represents a "genuine communication among interacting parties" (p. 42).

This is clearly seen in their code of ethics. Timely resolutions of any conflicts; finishing pre-assigned work and meeting all the team's deadlines, even detailing the consequences should a team member fail to do so; committed and full participation; respect for others and for orderly exchanges of information; integrating status checks into the team's routine tasks—all of these provisos in the team's code of ethics demonstrate that the team has finally acknowledged the importance of their community and their commitment to it. So, at least for this student engineering team in the technical communication class, participating in a collaborative project has given them a taste of this community while showing them the importance of reciprocity.

A high degree of reciprocity also underlies the code of ethics written by "Group Home," the first multidisciplinary online team, and is sustained by subsequent textual interactions among members of that team. It is interesting to consider whether the code of ethics set the tone for this team, or whether the members' initial willingness to create a truly collaborative set of standards set the tone for the code of ethics: allowing the team to adhere to its code and rely on it as a means to achieve success. The code of ethics for the "Life Without TV" team also sets high standards—at times perhaps too high. Unrealistic expectations can quickly undermine team process and morale. However, perhaps a more influential factor for "Life Without TV" is the fact that the code of ethics was mainly the creation of one member. Arguably, this set the tone for subsequent problems; namely, low reciprocity in this team's interactions and a final product that did not achieve its initial promise. The team could not create or sustain a sense of shared engagement that would have enabled them to trust each other's abilities and cooperate in decision-making, forming a dynamic and productive learning community. Either way, how a team handles the code of ethics assignment can provide the instructor with some early insights into, and means to diagnose and support, team effectiveness.

Another problem for "Life Without TV" is that the available scaffolding, which included support for the code of ethics assignment, may have been insufficient. This result reminds instructors that requiring and conscientiously supporting a code of ethics cannot guarantee a successful team outcome in any environment, let alone one that combines the challenges of online (often asynchronous) communication with a multidisciplinary, heterogeneous student population: conditions increasingly shaping the nature of technical and professional instruction or training.

What does seem clear is that building an ethic of collaboration in the "new location" created by a multidisciplinary CMC environment requires instructors to provide a considerable infrastructure for support. But, as Bazerman (this volume) points out, this new location demands, in effect, that there be new ways to monitor and even shape both the new community that develops as well as the "virtual space" from which it emerges. These techniques and supports include:

- A forum for expressing, discussing and consolidating common interests

- Definitions and examples of accountability

- Models of helpful and unhelpful "codes of ethics"

- Sufficient scaffolding before, during, and after the "code of ethics" assignment

- Monitoring of team effectiveness

- Regular but not heavy-handed monitoring of discussions within forums

However, these strategies are designed to compensate for a mainly textual interface. Improvements in Web 2.0 technologies will likely allow teachers, students and professionals to incorporate more real-time, interactive (voice and visual) tools into online teaching and teamwork processes, which will arguably make it easier to create reciprocity and build viable learning communities.

TOWARD AN ETHICS OF COLLABORATION FOR TECHNICAL COMMUNICATION CLASSES

Even if the interactions of these disparate student teams—face-to-face and discipline-specific on one end of the spectrum, and distant, asynchronous and multi-disciplinary on the other end—were not entirely successful, they nonetheless opened the way toward conceiving and writing an ethic of community building within the knowledge society. Both types of teams must create, own, and hold themselves accountable to ethical codes governing not only the task but also the team process. For the engineering students, the lynchpins of responsibility and accountability help facilitate a richer collaborative experience. This emphasis on collegiality and professional commitment might well define engineers as a kind of "community," at least in the terms Matei (2005) uses: that is, they "display community characteristics—group sanctioned identities, jargons, norms, strong personal relationships" (p. 346).

For online, multidisciplinary, technical communication teams, faced with creating and sustaining a learning community where none existed before, it is essential to lay the groundwork for cooperative decision-making through cooperative and engaged learning activities: in particular, "ground-up" ethical standards governing conduct and process. A written code of ethics can play a central role in compensating for the lack of interpersonal checks and balances that enrich face-to-face interactions—again, what Franklin (1999) considers essential for reciprocity. Writing a code of ethics can even play an important role in promoting respect and support, and enhancing engagement with the collaborative project.

While a team's code of ethics may only provide general guidelines for behaviour, it can nonetheless provide "helpful guidance concerning the main obligations" of the team members along with a shared sense of commitment (Martin & Schinzinger, 2005, p. 45). In this way, teams begin to take responsibility for their own learning at the same time as they nurture a sense of reciprocity that is so essential to both face-to-face and online student teams as a foundation for ethical community building. The outcome is not to master yet another decontextualized genre but, rather, to gain the experience of becoming meaningfully and ethically engaged; collaboratively writing a code of ethics can be seen as an effective analytic and learning tool as well, one that can be valuable in either learning environment. As such, writing together becomes a form of proto-professional engagement as well as "useful" exposure to the challenges of knowledge sharing in a variety of learning "locations of encounter."

In the final analysis, while encouraging and facilitating these ethical collaborative practices cannot guarantee either a positive team process or a successful product, we would argue that these ethical practices do encourage students to view teamwork as a professional activity that is "principle driven, valuing the people, engaging the culture and productive energies, and working as a collaborative workplace" (Marshall, 1995, p. 14). In this way, disparate individuals—both face-to-face and online—can come to think of themselves as a group of professionals who do indeed "share common interests, activities, and initiatives; who communicate regularly; and who derive benefit from their association" (Redish, 2004, p. 1; Quesenbery, 2005, p. 25). More broadly, integrating student teamwork within an ethic of community building helps foster the formation of a shared set of values and meanings (Artemeva & Freedman, 2001), all of which are essential to forming communities of practice that are both productive and sustainable within the knowledge society.

REFERENCES

Artemeva, N. (2004). Key concepts in rhetorical genre studies: An overview. *Technostyle, 20*(1), 3-38.

Artemeva, N., & Freedman, A. (2001). "Just the boys playing on computers": An activity theory analysis of differences in the cultures of two engineering firms. *Journal of Business and Technical Communication, 15*(2), 164-194.

Association of Professional Engineers and Geoscientists of the Province of Manitoba. (n.d.). *Code of ethics for the practice of professional engineering & professional geoscience* [Pamphlet].

Bruffee, K. A. (1984). Collaborative learning and the "conversation of mankind." *College English, 46* (7), 635-652. Retrieved fromhttp://www.jstor.org/view/00100994/ap020352/02a00010/0

Davis, M. (1998). *Thinking like an engineer: Studies in the ethics of a profession.* New York, NY: Oxford Press.

Donath, L., Spray, R., Thompson, N. S., Alford, E. M., Craig, N., & Matthews, M. A. (2005). Characterizing discourse among undergraduate researchers in an inquiry-based community of practice. *Journal of Engineering Education, 94*(4), 403-417.

Dong, A. (2005). The latent semantic approach to studying design team communication. *Design Studies, 26,* 445-461.

Dunkle, S. B., & Pahnos, D. M. (1981). Decision-making and problem solving: An holistic writing assignment. In D. W. Stevenson (Ed.), *Courses, components, and exercises in technical communication* (pp. 205-209). Urbana, IL: National Council of Teachers of English.

Flower, L. (1981). *Problem-solving strategies for writing.* San Diego, CA: Harcourt Brace Jovanovich, Publishers.

Franklin, U. (1999). *The real world of technology.* Toronto, Ont.: House of Anansi Press.

Haskins, M. E., Liedtka, J., & Rosenblum, J. (1998). Beyond teams: Toward an ethic of collaboration. *Organizational Dynamics, 26*(4), 34-50.

Ingram, S., & Parker, A. (2002). The influence of gender on collaborative projects in an engineering classroom. *IEEE Transactions on Professional Communication, 45* (1), 7-20.

Lay, M. (1992). The androgynous collaborator: The impact of gender studies on collaboration. In J. Forman (Ed.), *New visions of collaborative writing* (pp. 82-104). Portsmouth, NH: Boynton/Cook Publishers.

Lind, R. (1999). The gender impact of temporary virtual work groups. *IEEE Transactions in Professional Communication, 42*(4), 276-285.

Loui, M. C. (2005). Ethics and the development of professional identities of engineering students. *Journal of Engineering Education, 94*(4), 383-390.

Maki, P., & Schilling, C. (1987). *Writing in organizations: Purposes, strategies, and processes.* New York, NY: McGraw-Hill Book Company.

Marshall, E. M. (1995). The collaborative workplace. *Management Review, 84*(6), 13-17.

Martin, M. W., & Schinzinger, R. (2005). *Ethics in engineering* (4th ed.). Boston, MA: McGraw Hill.

Matei, S. A. (2005). A sounding board for the self: Virtual community ideology. *Journal of Technical Writing and Communication, 35*(4), 345-365.

Mathes, J. C., & Stevenson, D. W. (1976). *Designing technical reports: Writing for audiences in organizations.* Indianapolis, IN: Bobbs-Merrill Educational Publishing.

Moran, M. G. (1982). A problem-solving heuristic. *Technical Communication, 29*(3), 38.

Parker, A. (1989). A case study workshop and a problem-solving approach to technical communication. *Technostyle, 8*(1/2), 38-51.

Parker, A. (1990). Problem solving applied to teaching technical writing. *The Technical Writing Teacher, 17*(2), 95-103.

Parker, A. (2010). Introducing a course in technical communication into the curriculum of a Canadian school of engineering. In D. Franke & A. Reid (Eds.), *Design discourse: Composing and revising the professional and technical writing program.* Perspectives on Writing. Fort Collins, CO, and West Lafayette, IN: The WAC Clearinghouse & Parlor Press. Available at http://wac.colostate.edu/books/.

Quesenbery, W. (2005, January). Virtual communities: Weaving the human web. *Intercom,* 26-29.

Redish, G. (2004). STC transformation project: Focus on communities. *Devil Mountain Views:* Newsletter of the East Bay Chapter of STC, May/June, 1-4. Retrieved from: http://www.ebstc.org/newsletter/0504/mountford.htm

Reilly, C. A., & L'Eplattenier, B. L. (1996). Redefining collaboration through the creation of World Wide Web sites. *IEEE Transactions on Professional Communication, 39* (4), 215-223.

Reimer, M. J. (2002). English and communication skills for the global engineer. *Global Journal of Engineering Education, 6*(1), 91-100.

Rheingold, H. (1993). *The virtual community: Homesteading on the electronic frontier.* Reading, MA: Addison-Wesley. Retrieved from http://www.rheingold.com/vc/book/intro.html

Sageev, P., & Romanowski, C. J. (2001). A message from recent engineering graduates in the workplace: Results of a survey on technical communication skills. *Journal of Engineering Education, 90*(4), 685-693.

Sidnell, J. E. (2005, October/November). The code of ethics: What weight does it carry in the courts? *Canadian Consulting Engineers: Engineers and the Law.* Retrieved from www.canadianconsultingengineer.com

The Engineering and Geoscientific Professions Act, (2004). *2004.* Winnipeg, MB: Association of Professional Engineers and Geoscientists of the Province of Manitoba.

Tinzmann, M. B., Jones, B. F., Fennimore, T. F., Bakker, J., Fine, C., & Pierce, J. (n.d.). *What is the collaborative classroom?* Retrieved from http://www.ncrel.org/sdrs/areas/rpl_esys/collab/htm

Tonso, K. (2006). Teams that work: Campus culture, engineer identity, and social interactions. *Journal of Engineering Education, 95*(1), 25-37.

Turns, J., Wagner, T., & Shuyler, K. (2005). Moving toward knowledge-building communities in informational web site design. *Technical Communication, 52*(1), 52-63.

Vest, D., Long, M., Thomas, L., & Palmquist, M. E. (1995). Relating communication training to workplace requirements: The requirements of new engineers. *IEEE Transactions on Professional Communication, 38* (2), 11-17.

16 "AN ENGRAINED PART OF MY CAREER": THE FORMATION OF A KNOWLEDGE WORKER IN THE DUAL SPACE OF ENGINEERING KNOWLEDGE AND RHETORICAL PROCESS

Natasha Artemeva

> I'm involved in a field where your career is essentially based upon the writing you can produce.
>
> -- Novice Engineer, Interview, 26/07/2003

INTRODUCTION

The growing role of professional communication in the knowledge society has attracted researchers' attention for the past 20 years, starting from the 1985 publication of Odell and Goswami's *Writing in Nonacademic Settings*. The learning and knowledge of professional genres in school and workplace have been examined by such researchers as Devitt (2004), Dias, Freedman, Medway, and Paré (1999), Freedman and Medway (1994a, 1994b), and others. These scholars studied the learning and knowledge of rhetorical strategies used in various professions, for example, in architecture, economics, engineering, law, medicine, and social work (e.g., Bazerman & Paradis, 1991; Dias & Paré, 2000). The findings of some of these studies (e.g., Dias & Paré, 2000; Dias et al., 1999) indicated that communications that the students experience at university and in the workplace are often "worlds apart." After having observed and compared traditional classroom-based professional communication instruction and workplace communication, the researchers reached the conclusions that such instruction often fails to prepare students for the world of work. These observations led the researchers to raise a question of the portability of rhetorical strategies from one context to another. While some authors (e.g., Dias et al., 1999) doubted that such portability was possible, others (e.g., Artemeva, 2005, 2008; Tuomi-Gröhn & Engeström, 2003) observed that some transfer of learning and knowledge was possible across the contexts.

As Geisler (1994) noted, for novice professionals to become experts—and, I would add, expert communicators—they need to develop expertise within the dual space of the domain-content knowledge and rhetorical process. In other words, to become a successful communicator in the knowledge society, individuals must be in possession of the professional knowledge that they need to communicate ("the what" of their profession) and the appropriate rhetorical strategies that allow them to deploy this information within their professional community or beyond it ("the how"). A theoretical notion that allows us to explore the dynamics of the dual space of professional expertise is the notion of genre. Rhetorical Genre Studies (RGS) (also known as North American genre theory or New Rhetorical genre theory) (e.g., Coe, Lingard, & Teslenko, 2002; Devitt, 2004; Dias et al., 1999; Dias & Paré, 2000; Freedman & Medway, 1994a, 1994b; Miller, 1984/1994a) provides a useful theoretical framework for research into genre learning by moving the study of genre to the analysis of the social contexts that give rise to and shape genres (Miller, 1984/1994a). However, as Freedman (2006) explains, while theories both help us understand the data and shape further studies, "sometimes the data force researchers to reconsider the theory" (p. 98), modify, and/or complement it with other theoretical perspectives. This is why Freedman (2006) argues that empirical research has proved essential for RGS. Following the empirical data and in order to better flesh out relationships between the individual and the social (cf. Berger & Luckmann, 1967), and between agency and structure (cf. Giddens, 1984; Schryer, 2000, 2002; Wegner, this volume), some researchers have successfully complemented RGS with such social theories as Bourdieu's (1972) theory of practice (e.g., Schryer, 2000; Winsor, 2003), activity theory (AT) (e.g., Le Maistre & Paré, 2004; Russell, 1997, 2005; Schryer, this volume), and theories of situated learning (e.g., Artemeva, 2008; Freedman & Adam, 2000a, 2000b).

In an attempt to understand what constitutes professional genre knowledge and how novice professionals learn to operate within the dual problem space of the domain content knowledge and rhetorical process, I conducted a large longitudinal study of novices learning genres of engineering (Artemeva, 2005,

2008, 2009). The case study presented in this chapter is part of that research project that assumed a unified theoretical framework based on RGS, thus allowing me to focus on the study of a novice's learning of engineering genres, as her perceptions of these genres and ability to use them change over time. In this chapter I briefly discuss the methodology of the longitudinal study, present a case study of the novice engineer, Rebecca (the name is fictitious), entering the world of the engineering profession, and then briefly review the main notions of the theoretical framework that I developed for the study. I then present a theoretical interpretation of Rebecca's story, discuss the implications of the case study for the research into professional genre learning, and speculate about further applications of the unified theoretical framework.

METHODOLOGY OF THE STUDY

As mentioned above, the case discussed in this chapter is part of a longitudinal study of novices learning genres of engineering (Artemeva, 2005, 2008, in press). In the study, I followed a group of ten former engineering students who took an engineering communication course (ECC) that I developed and taught in 1997-1999. The data collection continued over a period of eight years, starting with the term when the students were enrolled in the communication course. The data for the study were collected through questionnaires that students completed while they were enrolled in the course, student postings to the course electronic discussion group during the course, electronic questionnaires administered annually after the course completion, follow-up e-mail exchanges that served to clarify and/or complement responses to annual questionnaires provided by the study participants, face-to-face interviews, field notes taken during interviews and other encounters with participants, and multiple informal e-mail exchanges. The last stage of the study included collection of member checks from the participants, as a triangulation strategy (cf. Maykut & Morehouse, 1994). To analyze and triangulate the data, I used multimethod, multicase qualitative methodology.

On the basis of the participants' responses to in-class questionnaires, I designed a series of asynchronous electronic interviews that I e-mailed participants. I continued to e-mail electronic questionnaires on a regular basis over the time span of the study, regularly repeating—sometimes verbatim and sometimes in a rephrased form—important questions to trace changes in the participants' responses over time and including new questions developed on the basis of the analysis of responses received to the previous ones. In Rebecca's case, all transcribed data constituted 74 pages of single-spaced text. I analyzed the responses immediately upon receipt and sent follow-up e-mails to the participants for clarification, if needed. All responses received from participants were analyzed qualitatively, with particular themes emerging from the analysis. As a form of representation, I adapted Individual Case Synopsis (ICS) (Fischer & Wertz, 1979) to present an individual participant's learning trajectory in her learning of engineering communication strategies, with a focus on change through time. In my study, the modified ICS produced in the process of data analysis reflected the historical—in Vygotsky's (1978) terms—development of the individual participant's learning trajectory. In this chapter, I present and discuss in sufficient detail one such individual case synopsis, that of Rebecca.

REBECCA'S INDIVIDUAL CASE SYNOPSIS

Rebecca grew up on a small farm in Central Canada. She "always knew" that she would have to leave the farm eventually and decided to choose a career that would allow her to travel and see other parts of the country. When she lived on the farm, Rebecca thought that "an engineer was a mechanic" and was not aware of what the profession involved until she started university (EM, 12/09/2003) (please note abbreviations used in this chapter: EM = e-mail; I = Interview).

In the first year of university, Rebecca felt confused and could not understand practical applications of the courses she was taking. The result of this confusion was low marks in several first-year courses. Rebecca took the engineering communication course in the fall term of her second year, as she was repeating some of the first year courses in an attempt to improve her grades. At the beginning of the term, she noted in the in-class questionnaire that she considered creativity her main strength and grammar, her weakness; she expected that the communication course would improve her "ability to write and speak in regards to ... engineering courses, as well as ... humanities courses" (09/1997). At the end of the term, her reaction to the ECC was strongly negative: in response to the end-of-term questionnaire's question "Have you learned any useful communication strategies in [the ECC]?" Rebecca wrote "No" and added, "I didn't find that my grammar and language approved [sic] at all during the course" (12/1997).

A term later, Rebecca expressed a changed perception of the effects of the course. When answering a question from an electronic questionnaire about whether the ECC had helped her with her studies and other engineering-related work, she wrote,

> Yes, actually it has. Many second year subjects require the writing of formal and semi-formal reports. [The ECC] ... provided

a basis of knowledge for these reports since they are not based on what was learned on writing reports in the first year courses. These lab write-ups include an extensive amount of documentation and written work.... Most of the concepts presented in the course _are_ quite useful. It will eventually pay off to do the work. (EM, 25/03/1998)

In the summer that followed, Rebecca worked full time for a small engineering company and then continued to work part-time at another small engineering company during the school year. When a full year passed since her strongly negative reaction to the Engineering Communication course (see the first response), she received another electronic questionnaire from me. This time, her response to the question "Did [the ECC] help you in your engineering course work?" was

There was theoretical value in ... [the ECC] ... such as organization of long projects .... The great thing that I found quite worthwhile was the final report, and the orals/abstracts/proposals that went along with it. I found it quite a good idea to concentrate on one big subject for a course such as [the ECC] then to try and ... throw a whole lot of little things in as well. (EM, 30/10/1998)

A comparison of the three responses above suggests that at the end of the ECC Rebecca did not feel that she had learned anything useful in the course. Even though she had chosen to work on an engineering communication project based on both the Calculus course she was repeating at the time and her future engineering specialization, her negative response indicated annoyance and frustration with the course, and perhaps with the whole Engineering Program (later in an interview she said, "I was so disappointed in the first year by what engineering was and what engineering writing was" [18/03/2002]).

At the time of her graduation, four and a half years after the first response, Rebecca reflected on her original negative reaction in the following e-mail message, "I do remember thinking that [a lot] of the exercises performed in the original [ECC] lacked a 'point' or a foreseeable goal, and perhaps that was what the 'No' meant" (21/04/2002). Reflecting on her more positive second response four years later, Rebecca, who by that time had already had significant engineering workplace experience, noted in an e-mail, "Communication had very little effect on my [courses] 1st through 3rd years. I found that the professors provided 'cookie cutters' that work had to match and there was little deviation from this rule" (21/04/2002). Nevertheless, she claimed, "After the year I believe I found ways to apply [what was taught in the ECC] ... to other course work" (21/04/2002). This claim reinforces her second response in which she speaks about her ability to use what has been learned in ECC in her other engineering courses and work.

It appears that the first year's confusion about the engineering program had a lingering effect on Rebecca. While in her second and third years, Rebecca was still going through some difficulties, including being on probation for a year. In the third year, one of the professors suggested that she should contact the University centre for students who require special academic accommodation. This suggestion proved very helpful, and, with the help that the centre offered her, Rebecca was finally able to overcome her problems and successfully complete the third year of the program (I, 18/03/2002). Nevertheless, in her final year at university she was still unhappy about her early academic experiences and indicated that only by the third year did she begin to understand purposes of and connections between courses in the engineering program.

The fourth year of the engineering program brought a dramatic change to the amount and importance of communication. According to one of Rebecca's e-mails, in the fourth year she was writing more than ever before in her life: "The amount of writing that I did was quadrupled at the very least. Term papers, essays, reports, design meetings, project meetings etc, consumed most of my days" (21/04/2002). In an interview, she noted that the following communication strategies that had been introduced in the ECC were particularly useful for the fourth year project: the group work strategies and "having to evaluate" her classmates' written drafts and oral presentations (18/03/02). However, she kept lamenting that she had not been able to apply these and other communication strategies taught in the ECC until the fourth year, by which time she claimed to have forgotten how to apply them. For example, when commenting in an interview on the understanding of the principles of technical oral presentations she had gained in the communication course ("Because without that course, we wouldn't know what to look for when a person was presenting"), Rebecca added, "But it wasn't useful in the 4th year project presentation because it was so long ago" (I, 18/03/02). In the fourth year, presentations became an important part of the final project that all students in Rebecca's program were required to complete in order to graduate, and again, Rebecca commented on insufficient experience she had had with presentations prior to the fourth year project:

> Other than [in the ECC], we never did anything [like oral presentations], and that was a long time. And we did nothing like that, absolutely. No presentations for three years .... We did

a small tiny presentation, four minutes, four people: you just present one slide—it was negligible. It was a real challenge, the 4th year presentation. (I, 18/03/2002)

Based on this experience, Rebecca made a suggestion:

> I think [the ECC] would be a great 3rd year course. That's when you start writing all your [assignments], and doing your presentations. And 3rd year students would have more experience.... And your first year physics labs are so different from your advanced labs [in the third year] and you finally have an idea of what you learn and what you want to learn, and you finally start paying attention. (I, 18/03/2002)

The data provide evidence that Rebecca's view of the ECC became more positive from year to year: she started seeing the purpose of the course activities and claimed that, though she had "forgotten much of what was taught in the course," she felt that it was "necessary to have such a course" (EM, 21/04/2002). But even though she would repeat that the course was important, Rebecca did not seem to see it as integral to the Engineering Program, and she would not explain why the course was important for future engineers.

Only after Rebecca had worked in the field as a junior engineer, rather than a student, did her view of the role of communication in her engineering work become better defined:

> I'm involved in a field where your career is essentially based upon the writing you can produce. It would be very difficult for me to pick out one situation where I didn't use writing. Whether it is writing to my supervisor on email, or writing a final report on my projects, or presenting data to a group of people, I use writing skills every single day, all day ... I find communication an engrained part of my career, both when I was a student, and now that I am working in the engineering field. (EM, 26/07/2003)

Even though Rebecca claims in this e-mail message that she has considered communication "an engrained part" of her career as a student, never before did she articulate why it was so.

Rebecca worked in several small engineering companies and government departments throughout all the years of her university studies. In the fourth year of the Engineering Program, she was hired by a department that later offered her a job upon graduation. As Rebecca was moving into the engineering practice as a new practitioner, she commented in an e-mail on the differences between school and workplace:

> I find University very structured, and very creatively limiting. In the workforce, I'm given free rein to try new ideas, new methods and different implementations. This I find is almost expected practice. At school, the formulas must be followed, the due dates met, and all margins must be exactly 1" around. This is the largest problem I found with moving from being an engineering student, to an employed young engineer--you have to refind [sic] creativity. (21/04/2002)

In this message the theme of creativity appears again, for the second time after it had appeared in Rebecca's response to the very first ECC in-class questionnaire ("My strengths are my creativity" [09/1997]). Never did she refer to creativity in the course of her studies at university; only after having accumulated some work experience did she return to her idea of creativity in engineering work. This may indicate either her limited view of the engineering program at the time when she was attending university or the somewhat creatively limited and over-regulated engineering program she was enrolled in. She reported that she felt confused even in the fourth year and even after having worked in engineering companies part-time for a few years. She did state repeatedly that her experience working on the fourth year project with 22 other students had been "very unique" (I, 18/03/2002) in that it made her part of a group that worked together on the same engineering task, but continued to express her frustration:

> I found it very tough at school to have your voice heard. In the 4th year project you have to go through several people [students working on different parts of the same project], and it's difficult to get the information and understand what they've done. It's hard to find the correct channel at school because there are so many people. (I, 18/03/2002)

At work, perhaps because she always worked in small organizations or departments, she started feeling part of the community of practice (CoP) faster and more easily: "Even people I speak [to] on the phone, I speak to the same people all the time" (I, 18/03/2002). In an interview, Rebecca contrasted her communication experiences at university and at work:

> They [at work] had to make sure I had access to reports and information and knew who to ask questions .... As a student [at university] there are a lot more barriers: [at work] you can always ask a question, or knock on a door, or ask a question at a meeting—a lot of opportunities to talk to people. As a student, the doors are not always open, it's really difficult to get to professors. Some profs don't make office hours because they don't have time. At work everyone is doing their job, while at school, many people are not there to be a teacher. In school, it's very difficult to relate to people from different cultures and when you can't understand their accent. At work, it's individual and you can ask them to speak more slowly ... It might be surprising, but I find at work it's a lot more informal. You get to know each other really well. (18/03/2002)

After only a few years in the new workplace, she seemed to have a strong sense of being part of a CoP that included not only her immediate co-workers in the department but also engineers from all over the country. This identification appears to be much stronger than her identification with the academic community or with engineering students ever was. In an interview, she reflected on her work as being part of a large national network of engineering experts:

> I write [reports] for the use by ... engineers and I write them for the use by senior engineers who are trying to deal with the whole system (the whole [engineering object of her investigations]) ..., for the departments, not for somebody in particular. (18/03/2002)

At the end of the study in 2004, Rebecca's responsibilities as an Engineering Analyst involved much written and oral communication. She estimated that she was spending approximately 55% of her time at work communicating, out of which up to 90% was spent writing, because "most of the requirements of the job are satisfied by producing reports from ... engineering work" (EM, 06/03/2004). She produced reports on engineering investigation findings, internal procedure documents, formal engineering reports, memos, and letters to industry. Rebecca estimated that she was spending about 10% of her formal "communication" time communicating orally (internal briefings or external promotional formal presentations) (EM, 15/09/2003).

THEORETICAL FRAMEWORK

To help me interpret the broad range of data collected in the study, I have applied a unified social theory of genre learning (Artemeva, 2008, in press), which integrates RGS with AT (Engeström, 1987; Leont'ev, 1981) and situated learning (Lave & Wenger, 1991; Wenger, 1998), and which I have complemented with selected notions from Bourdieu's (1972) social theory of practice. Such an integration of these complementary yet distinct theoretical perspectives has allowed me to explore the interplay between the individual and the social in the novice's trajectory in her learning to communicate engineering knowledge (Artemeva, 2005, 2008, 2009).

Within the RGS framework, genre is defined as social action in response to our construal of recurrent situations (Miller, 1984/1994a) and, at the same time, as constructing rhetorical situations (Paré & Smart, 1994). While recognizing that genres can be characterized by regularities in textual form and substance, current RGS thinking perceives these regularities as reflections of an underlying regularity in social situations (Miller, 1984/1994a). This regularity is characterized by its temporal and spatial dimensions, which can be productively explored (cf. Schryer, 2002) through Bakhtin's (1981) notion of the chronotope. For Bakhtin, time is inseparable from space; that is, temporal and spatial relationships are intrinsically connected. Schryer (1999, 2002) further extended Bakhtin's discussion of the chronotope by observing that the notion of the chronotope expresses the connectedness not only of place and time but also of human values and current social beliefs and that our knowledge of genres is inseparable from our understanding of the chronotope. The notions of chronos and kairos, borrowed from classical Greek rhetoric, complement this view of time-space by reflecting different qualities of time and proportion (Artemeva, 2005). Kairos, the qualitative aspect of time, was defined as the right moment, the opportune, the due/right measure or a proportional response; in other words, as a unity of its temporal and spatial aspects. Chronos, a quantitative, measurable, aspect of time, designated the continuous flux of time (Kinneavy, 2002; Miller, 1992, 2002), and, according to Miller (1994b), "genre becomes a determinant of rhetorical kairos—a means by which we define a situation in space-time and understand the opportunities it holds" (p. 71). The notions of kairos and chronos became important to my research as they provided a perspective that allowed me to explore and interpret the timing and sequencing of engineering genres in a university engineering communication course and to uncover how individuals responded to different forms of time in different social contexts. The view of genre that includes the understanding of its chronotopic or, in other words, its temporal and proportional qualities, highlights its dynamic nature that is both constraining and enabling for a rhetor.

Schryer (1993, 1994, 2002) developed an argument about the temporary stability of genres by proposing to use "genre" as a verb: we genre our way through social interactions, choosing the correct form in response to each communicative situation we encounter—and we are doing it with varying degrees of mastery. At the same time "we are genred" (Schryer, 2002, p. 95), that is, we are socialized into particular situations through genres. Building upon the notion of constellation introduced by Campbell and Jamieson in 1979 and drawing on Bourdieu's (1972) social theory of practice, Schryer (2000) redefined genres as "constellations of regulated, improvisational strategies triggered by the interaction between individual socialization ... and an organization" (p. 450). This view of genre as stabilized only for now, allowing for change, and forming the rhetor's behaviour within the organizational context not only provides insights into Rebecca's learning trajectory but also illuminates how she is "genred" into the rhetorical situations she encounters in various settings.

As powerful as RGS has proved to be in the study of workplace genres, used alone it does not seem to allow for a productive analysis of the role of individual agents involved in the process of learning genres of their discipline and profession, and particularly, of the role of the agent's background. Some selected notions of Bourdieu's (1972) social theory of practice provide necessary tools for such an analysis (e.g., Artemeva, 2005). One such notion is the notion of capital. Bourdieu's capital may take both material and nonmaterial forms that can be converted into each other (for example, monetary capital may be used to pay for, or be converted into, education). Among other forms of capital, Bourdieu introduces social capital (for example, hierarchical positions within an organization) and cultural capital, which refers to particular cultural knowledge (e.g., engineering knowledge) or competency (e.g., professional engineering competency) (Winsor, 2003). Cultural capital is defined as "a form of values associated with culturally authorized tastes, consumption patterns, attributes, skills and awards" (Webb, Schirato, & Danaher, 2002, p. x) and thus, for example, includes the ways people communicate within particular situations or, in other words, use certain genres (e.g., engineering genres). The appropriation of this type of capital by an individual depends on the sum of cultural capital that her family possesses, the appropriateness of this capital in a particular socio-historical formation, and the forms and time of its implicit transition from the family to the individual. In this study of Rebecca's trajectory in learning engineering genres it is particularly important to remember that cultural capital can be converted into social capital:

for example, one's education and background in a particular discipline can lead to, or be converted into, a position within an organization.

Although RGS recognizes and celebrates dynamism, the unpacking of the precise mechanisms through which genre learning and execution occur requires additional compatible theoretical perspectives, as has been demonstrated in a number of studies (e.g., Bazerman & Russell, 2002; Dias et al., 1999; Russell, 1997). Theories of activity and situated learning have successfully expanded and complemented the RGS framework (e.g., Artemeva, 2008, in press; Le Maistre & Paré, 2004; Russell, 2005; Winsor, 2001). Elsewhere (Artemeva & Freedman, 2001), we have argued that, when compared to RGS, AT provides a higher level of theorization to account for change as well as resistance and conflict and offers a complementary perspective on "social motive, and on the action aspect of genre" (Dias et al., 1999, p. 23). AT (Engeström, 1987, 1999a, 1999b; Leont'ev, 1981; Wertsch, 1981, 1985, 1991) and theories of situated learning and communities of practice (Lave & Wenger, 1991; Rogoff, 1990; Wenger, 1998) share common origins in the cultural-historical theory of the development of human psychological functions proposed by Vygotsky in the 1920s-1930s (Engeström & Miettinen, 1999; Vygotsky, 1978). The important aspects of Vygotsky's theory that served as the starting points for the development of AT and theories of situated learning are the concepts of the mediating role of tools, signs, and symbols in human development and Vygotsky's understanding of "the mechanism of individual developmental change [as] rooted in society and culture" (Cole & Scribner, 1978, p. 7). These concepts are equally important for both AT and situated learning. One of the important concepts proposed by Vygotsky (1935/2003) was the concept of the zone of proximal development (ZPD) based on the notions of the actual and potential levels of child development. Vygotsky suggested that instead of using the actual developmental level as a determinant of a child's mental development, one should use the potential level, determined by the difficulty of the tasks that the child can solve in collaboration with an adult or a more capable peer. From this perspective, individual cognitive change is seen as effected by the social. One of the developmental outcomes of learning leading development in the ZPD is that the learner becomes able to engage in developmental activity with conscious awareness rather than merely spontaneously.

Both theories of activity and situated learning consider the social context in which human activity takes place as an integral part of human activity rather than just the surrounding environment. Activity and situated learning theorists agree that "every cognitive act must be viewed as a specific response to a specific set of circumstances. Only by understanding the circumstances and the participants' construal of the situation can a valid interpretation of the cognitive activity be made" (Resnick, 1991, p. 4). This view of human activity is close to the current

RGS perspective on the reciprocal relationship between genre and its social context (Bawarshi, 2000; Paré & Smart, 1994).

Leont'ev (1981) developed his theory of human activity from Vygotsky's idea of mediated human action. Leont'ev saw work as mediated by tools and performed in conditions of collective activity. The three-level model of activity proposed by Leont'ev provides distinction between collective activity, individual action, and operation. The uppermost level of collective activity is driven by an object-related motive; the middle level of individual (or group) action is driven by a conscious goal, and the bottom level of automatic operations is driven by the conditions and available tools (Leont'ev, 1981; Wertsch, 1981). I would like to speculate that the three-level model of human activity with the radical changes occurring at the points of change from operation to action to activity is, in fact, rooted in the "Hegelian nodal line of measure relations—in which quantitative change suddenly passes at certain points into qualitative transformation" (Engels, 1877/1947, para. 29). To illustrate this phenomenon, Engels uses Hegel's example of the aggregate state change of water from the liquid into solid state at 0°C and from the liquid into the gaseous state at 100°C, under normal atmospheric pressure, thus demonstrating "that at both these turning-points the merely quantitative change of temperature brings about a qualitative change in the condition of the water" (para. 29). In other words, in the Hegelian nodal line of measure relations, the accumulation (not necessarily in the numerical meaning of the word) of one factor leads to a sharp qualitative change in another. Similarly, in the three-level activity model, repeated performance of actions at the conscious level leads to their transition to the subconscious level; that is, to the level of operations. In other words, a qualitative change in the nature of the activity component occurs, following the accumulation of experience at the action level. These concepts have proved to be revealing in the study of changes that occur in novices as they accumulate engineering knowledge and learn genres of their profession.

A number of researchers (e.g., Engeström, 1999a; Witte, 1992, 1999) criticized Leont'ev's version of the theory for a major contradiction that lies at its heart: the use of object-oriented activity both as an explanatory principle of the psychological theory and the object of the study. In an attempt to resolve the ambiguities of the three-level model, Bracewell and Witte (2003) proposed an alternative interpretation. They suggested that Leont'ev's construct of activity—and the motive associated with it—"should be regarded as having the status of a general explanatory principle (in Vygotsky's terminology), and the constructs of action/goal and operation/condition should be regarded as having the status of objects of study" (Bracewell & Witte, 2003, p. 526). In this context, Bracewell and Witte introduced the construct of task, "the set of goals and actions that implement these goals, which are developed in order to achieve a solution to a complex problem within a specific work context" (p. 528). Another attempt to overcome the ambiguities of Leont'ev's three-level model was made to some extent in the so-called second generation of AT (University of Helsinki, n.d.) with the introduction of a new unit of analysis, "the concept of object-oriented, collective, and culturally mediated human activity, or activity system" (Minnis & John-Steiner, n.d.). Engeström (1987) proposed to expand Leont'ev's basic mediational triangle, subject-tool-object, to represent an activity system. He suggested that the triadic structure of the basic mediational triangle should be extended to account for the socially distributed and interactive nature of human activity, that is, for rules, community, and division of labour. As I have noted elsewhere (2006), the expanded view of AT may be interpreted as an attempt to overcome the dualism of collective and individual units of analysis. Presenting human activity as a systemic function is one way to overcome this dualism.

Sharing its origins with AT, the view of learning as situated in the social is based on the Vygotskian understanding of higher mental functions in the individual as being derived from social life (Wertsch, 1991) and on his recognition of the social as primary. Theorists of situated learning see "knowledge, and not just learning, [as] situated" (Brown, Collins, & Duguid, 1989, p. 37). Central to the literature on situated learning are the notions that learning and knowing are context-specific; that learning is active and accomplished through coparticipation; and that cognition is socially shared (Freedman & Adam, 1996, 2000a, 2000b). Vygotsky developed his theories on the premise that individual intellectual development of higher mental processes cannot be understood without reference to the social milieu in which the individual is embedded and without consideration of the social roots of both the tools for thinking that novices are learning to use and the social interactions that guide their use of these tools (Rogoff, 1990). The unit of analysis in Lave and Wenger's (1991) version of the theory of situated learning is a community of practice and its central analytical viewpoint on learning is legitimate peripheral participation (LPP) (Lave, 1991; Lave & Wenger, 1991; Wenger, 1998). Wenger (2005) defined CoP as a group of people who work on something together—not necessarily at the same location—and interact regularly to learn how to do it better. For CoPs, "learning is not a separate activity. It is not something we do when we do nothing else or stop doing when we do something else" (Wenger, 1998, p. 8). Each CoP is constituted by distinct intellectual and social conventions, and the development of one's ability to engage in situated learning occurs through participation in a CoP. As situated learning theorists (e.g., Lave, 1996a, 1996b; Lave & Wenger, 1991; Wenger, 1998) note, a primary, and most effective form of the development of one's increasing engagement in situated learning is apprenticeship (see Russell, 1998 for the discussion of limitations of the apprenticeship model in writing studies). By apprenticeship they understand a process in which newcomers to a CoP learn the expert practices used in that community by being actively engaged in these expert practices and by taking "an active part in authentic but ancillary community tasks, under the guidance of more experienced 'oldtimers' and with only limited responsibility for the outcome" (Smart & Brown, 2002, p. 119). The notion of apprenticeship includes so called cognitive apprenticeship (Brown, Collins, & Duguid, 1989), a way of novices' enculturation into authentic practices of knowledge work through a process similar to craft apprenticeship. The concept of CoP as a unit of analysis acknowledges the importance of mediational means as does the concept of activity system in AT.

Lave and Wenger (1991) introduced the concept of LPP as an analytical perspective on, or a descriptor of, situated learning that focuses on the action itself and on its social outcome. LPP describes a range of social practices that situated-learning theorists refer to as apprenticeships. LPP views learning—a characteristic of all communities of practice—as taking place in the process of creation or action and as accomplished through coparticipation (Lave & Wenger, 1991; Rogoff, 1990). Newcomers and oldtimers in a community of practice learn during their cooperative activities, which they both want to finish successfully. The LPP model describes the situation of newcomers trained by oldtimers in the process of cooperative activity. Peripheral participation in this view gradually leads to full participation and full membership in a community of practice. Under the condition of LPP, apprentices are initiated into the communities of practice by participating in authentic tasks that are not invented as opportunities for getting them to learn (Freedman & Adam, 2000b; Hanks, 1991). Lave and Wenger's theory of situated learning often contrasts learning that occurs as a process of social participation in communities of practice and the classroom, or curriculum, learning that is expected to occur as a result of teaching. Learning in the framework of Lave and Wenger's theory is viewed as gradually increasing participation in a community of practice. Through their engagement in practice, peripheral participants (newcomers) can develop a view of what the whole enterprise is about, and what there is to be learned. Learning is, therefore, seen as an improvised practice. The proposed key mechanism of learning within communities of practice is a gradual movement of a newcomer from peripheral to full participation (Lave, 1991; Lave & Wenger, 1991; Wenger, 1998). Moving from peripheral toward full participation in practice requires from a newcomer a deeper involvement in the life of community, increased commitment of time, gradually intensified efforts "but, more significantly, an increasing sense of identity as a master practitioner" (Lave & Wenger, 1991, p. 111). As Lave and Wenger noted, the process of becoming a full practitioner, a master—or an expert, to use Geisler's (1994) term—in a CoP involves concurrent production of continuity within the CoP. In addition, Lave (1996b) claimed that part of what it means to be engaged in a practical learning activity "is extending what one knows beyond the immediate situation" (p. 12).

Building upon Vygotsky's (1978) understanding of learning through internalization and externalization, Engeström (1987, 1992, 1999a) introduced the concept of expansive cycles that describes the process of a novice's acculturation into an activity system. Expansion is Engeström's metaphor for transformative processes and outcomes (Minnis & John-Steiner, n.d.) and an "expansive cycle is a developmental process that contains both internalization and externalization" (Engeström, 1999a, p. 33). The concept of expansive cycles is remarkably similar to the process of the movement from peripheral to full participation in a CoP as described by Lave and Wenger, and, thus, provides a link between the activity theory perspective, the situated view, and the RGS view that includes both constraining and enabling features of genres.

In my study of students' trajectories in accumulating engineering knowledge and becoming professional communicators, I have closely investigated the origins, theoretical grounding, and methodologies of the perspectives reviewed above—RGS, AT, and situated learning—and developed a unified theoretical framework for the study of professional genre learning (see Artemeva, 2008, for a more detailed discussion). This unified framework allows one to explore genre learning in a professional activity system as a component of the novice's movement from peripheral to full participation, accomplished under the mentorship of oldtimers. Having presented the overview of the theoretical framework, I proceed to the theoretical interpretation of Rebecca's story.

INTERPRETATION OF REBECCA'S STORY

Selected notions from Bourdieu's social theory of practice complement the unified theory of genre learning in this analysis of Rebecca's journey through school to workplace. At the centre of my inquiry is Rebecca's learning trajectory as she was developing into a full-fledged communicator within the dual space of engineering content knowledge and rhetorical process. While RGS has provided a perspective that situates professional genre learning within authentic and timely activities, the three-level model of human activity and the relationships between subject, mediational artifact, and object within an activity system has helped me trace causes of Rebecca's changing perceptions of the role and place of communication in engineering and her developing sense of her professional identity as an engineer and engineering communicator. The situated learning perspective has helped me illuminate Rebecca's integration into the engineering workplace CoP and her realization of herself as an engineer and engineering communicator, while the discussion of the ZPD has allowed me to better understand Rebecca's positive experiences learning to communicate with her colleagues and superiors in the workplace. The combination of RGS with AT and situated learning within a unified framework has been particularly helpful in the analysis of Rebecca's case as this combination has aided me in unpacking a learning trajectory of an engineering student as she gradually becomes a professional engineering communicator.

The three-level model of activity is one of the theoretical tools that allows me to explore changes in Rebecca's perceptions of the ECC usefulness for her engineering studies and work. For example, when she reacts negatively to the whole course and says that a lot of activities seem to have lacked "a 'point' or a foreseeable goal" (EM, 21/04/2002), Rebecca is providing us with a fairly common novice's perception of an academic course in an unfamiliar discipline (such responses were often given by students at the end of the ECC). Rebecca's cultural capital did not appear to include the expectations of the engineering profession and she had not been exposed to the field before taking the ECC; she took the communication course at the beginning of her engineering studies when her domain content knowledge was practically non-existent. All these factors made it unfair and unrealistic to expect that she would gain the understanding of the integral role of communication in engineering from an introductory communication course.

Generally, the ECC instructors comment that they perceive the course as part of the activity of introducing students to the foundations of engineering communication and, hence, of preparing students for the engineering profession. These instructors are aware of the course's connections to other courses, the engineering curriculum as a whole, and industry expectations. Instructors design specific course tasks to provide input to students' learning of engineering genres and perceive these tasks as connected and forming a coherent series of pedagogical tools. As the three-level model of human activity suggests, inexperienced students do not and cannot engage with each exercise at the operation level because every "exercise" for them has its own goal and becomes an action that requires full conscious attention. That is, what for the instructor is a mediational artifact, for a student is an object. In other words, as Dias et al. (1999) put it, "The two activities, teaching and studenting, seemingly complementary and operating in parallel, represent different perspectives and generate actions whose goals are often at odds with one another" (p. 67).

Students entering the ECC often approach every course task as a separate action in itself, while for the instructor, separate course tasks are operations that contribute to the action of completing the course project, which in turn contributes to the activity of introducing students to engineering communications and teaching them how to communicate in response to particular rhetorical situations in the context of an engineering program. One may speculate that later, as the students become more and more immersed in the context of the engineering discipline and/or engineering practice, these separate tasks of performing in particular genres (such as writing a cover letter, writing a progress report, or preparing and delivering an oral presentation of completion report) in a sense drop down to the level of operations, and the students start seeing a "larger picture" of the professional communication and its role in the engineering profession. That is, the action becomes completion of a project, rather than writing a report. On the other hand, one may argue that acts of writing are never routinized so that they become Leont'ev's operations (cf. Dias, 2000). In this case, Bracewell and Witte's (2003) construct of task, introduced earlier in this chapter, becomes helpful: for the course instructor the course is a task (i.e., "the set of goals and actions that implement these goals" [p. 528]), but for a student, each goal and corresponding action represent a task in itself. Eventually, for some students, depending on the time that passed, experience in the course, prior experiences, and so on, these tasks become goals and the students become able to see a "larger picture." Some routinization occurs at this stage, but what actually becomes an operation is a matter for further research (Bracewell, personal communication, November 18, 2005).

Only with time and after having experienced situations that require the use of strategies learned in the course for other purposes, i.e., other courses and/or at work, some students start realizing that discrete exercises were not as randomly discrete as it appeared while students were enrolled in the course (as Rebecca demonstrated in the third response). It is significant that, as the time passes and as Rebecca becomes more involved in the context of engineering—both as an academic discipline and as a profession—her view of the effects of the ECC change from the abrupt "No" in her first response, to the recognition of the usefulness of particular course activities in the second response (e.g., writing formal and semi-formal technical reports, lab write-ups, and so on) to the view of the course as a whole ("one big subject") in which all discrete activities find their place, as reflected in her third response. In other words, to learn a genre, one needs to use it "to get things done" in an authentic setting for a particular purpose (Dias et al., 1999). Or, to return to the parallel I drew above between the three-level activity model and Hegel's nodal line of measure relations (1812/1969), the accumulation of experience of a genuine activity that consists of numerous actions leads to a sharp qualitative change in the student's perception of the whole activity, in this case, learning and using genres of engineering.

Rebecca's changing responses to the ECC and her growing understanding of the engineering profession as rooted in the inseparable unity of engineering knowledge ("the what") and engineering communication ("the how") reflect both the importance of time (chronos) and timing (kairos) in students' perceptions of communication in engineering and the importance of the domain content knowledge in the process of becoming an expert (cf. Geisler, 1994). It also reflects Rebecca's "movement" through Engeström's (1987) expansive cycle from the time she was internalizing the knowledge of the discipline to the time she started to externalize it through engineering genres. Her growing understanding of the engineering program chronotope (Bakhtin, 1981) and the importance of timing and preparedness in terms of students' engineering content knowledge is reflected in Rebecca's insistence that the communication course should be offered at the third year level because only by the third year can the majority of students start understanding "what's happening" and have a real need to apply the communication strategies that they experienced in the communication course. Rebecca provided this suggestion at the end of her last year at university, by the time things had fallen into place and she had become able to see connections between courses in the program. At this point in time, the real need becomes a clear driving force for the learning of engineering genres; in other words, it is a clear kairotic moment in the engineering program. This is the time when Rebecca starts looking at the curriculum critically and says that it would be more beneficial for students to have such a communication course later in their academic careers.

Genres of engineering communication that Rebecca was trying to master while in the ECC (the objects of the learning activity in the course) became mediational means during her fourth year project and at work, just like lab reports and log books that serve as objects in engineering laboratory courses become mediational artifacts in the fourth-year project and in the workplace. For example, Rebecca named progress reviews and the project completion report as most important and memorable components of the ECC: "The progress reviews ... were probably the best things to learn" (I, 18/03/2002) simply because these genres were necessary for her to communicate the progress and results of her engineering work. While she was enrolled in the communication course, these genres constituted the object of the learning activity; later, in the fourth year of university and at work, Rebecca had to use them again and again as a mediational means when working on different projects (for example, the object of Rebecca's activity in the fourth year project was to find a solution to a real engineering problem that a group of 22 students was given by their engineering professors). From her various comments, it follows that Rebecca did not find the university chronotope comfortable and did not adapt to it even by the end of her studies: she never felt like a full member of the engineering student community at university.

However, her development as a knowledge worker and integration into the workplace chronotope appeared to have been much smoother, and she seemed to be in control of her integration into the workplace CoP. In an interview, she described strategies that she had developed to ease her transition into this workplace CoP: a) At the beginning, she heavily relied on her boss's advice, as she wrote in an e-mail, "to make sure that the work I do ... is correct for the situation" (18/09/2003). In this e-mail she referred to the situation as the context to which her written work must respond, which reflects a developing rhetorical genre perspective on engineering communication, from types of documents to the contexts to which such documents respond. b) Because Rebecca was not a licensed Professional Engineer (P. Eng.) yet, she told me that she would give all her reports to her boss, who had a P. Eng. designation,

> because I ... can't sign them. He reviews them and then I fix ... them up and they go up the chain.... Now [I receive] a lot less feedback than before. At the beginning, [I had to do] a lot of editing; [I] had to rearrange my whole style. (EM, 18/03/2002)

c) Not only did she have to rely on her boss's evaluation of her written work while working in her ZPD with him, she had to change her writing to ensure that the boss would feel comfortable signing it. That is, the style she had developed at school and at her other engineering jobs had to be adapted to the context of the new workplace (cf. Anson & Forsberg, 1990/2003; Dias et al., 1999). d) Rebecca seemed to have become a skillful reader of the local CoP's chronotope. Since she had been a student, she developed a strategy to let her co-workers know that she was a newcomer to the CoP, signalling to them that she might need more information than an oldtimer:

> In the past, I would say I'm a student so they knew who I was and not get wrong impressions.... [I am] a bit more comfortable now, but I still make sure they know I'm a student.... [Now that I am an employee] I'll make sure they know that I'm a junior engineer. (EM, 18/03/2002)

These strategies were apparently considered legitimate in Rebecca's workplace CoP as they helped Rebecca both to learn more about her job, get her job done, and become accepted as the CoP member. Thus, while being socialized into an organization, Rebecca was able to adapt workplace genres so that they served her purposes and remained accepted by the oldtimers (cf. Artemeva, 2005).

In an interview, she said that she had learned much in the workplace, and this gave her confidence and allowed her to gain co-workers' respect (I, 18/03/02). This observation and her ability to devise effective communication strategies reflect the development of Rebecca's professional identity as a knowledge worker and a legitimate member of her CoP. Rebecca also seems quite successful in using at work the knowledge and communication practices she learned elsewhere. In an e-mail, she once noted,

> I'm lucky that I get to do the same work [in the workplace] as what I took in University--I'm using the vast majority of my education to help me with my job.... All the skills I've learned on the job have been practical applications of what I learned at school. (EM, 18/09/2003)

This quote appears to indicate that much of what Rebecca draws on at work, including genres, was, in fact, taught outside of the local workplace context, and later transferred by Rebecca to other, more complex, contexts (cf. Artemeva, 2005).

In addition, Rebecca's self-evaluation of her strengths and weaknesses as an engineering communicator has changed from a vague one provided at the beginning of the ECC ("my strengths are my creativity ... my weaknesses are my grammar" [Q, 09/1997]) to a very specific one provided a year after graduation ("I know that I am a good report writer, but a poor public speaker" [EM, 14/09/2003]). In 2003, six years after having taken the ECC, she was not only able to identify her strong and weak points as a mature communicator but also capable of identifying ways of using the strengths to her advantage and dealing with her weaknesses: "I tend to choose tasks that display my strengths. I also believe, however, in trying to improve areas in [communications] where I have demonstrated that I am relatively weak" (EM, 14/09/2003). This self-evaluation reflects a level of maturity and professional confidence and a good grasp of what is important to be a functioning member of her CoP.

REBECCA'S MEMBER CHECKS

At the end of my longitudinal study, I asked all study participants to read my reports on their individual cases and send me their member checks (cf. Winsor, 1996). These member checks provided additional validation of my interpretation of the data collected over the years. In an e-mail, Rebecca reflected on her case based on 74 single-spaced pages of questionnaire responses, e-mail messages, and interviews,

> I never kept track of my responses to your questions/interviews over the years, and I find it incredible how I've changed, and

how my responses have changed. 74 pages! I didn't even realize it. The study is very interesting. (EM, 13/09/2004)

I've had a chance to thoroughly review the document and I can find no errors. In fact, I quite enjoyed reading your analysis of my case. As I mentioned in my previous email, I did not keep track of my own responses to your questionnaires, but all the quotes sound exactly as what I would have said over the years. Thank you again for the opportunity to review my case. (EM, 1/10/2004)

CONCLUSIONS AND IMPLICATIONS

The study of written and oral professional communication allows us to better understand the workings of a contemporary knowledge society. The development of professional expertise (or, as Geisler, 1994, defines it, a dual problem space of the domain content knowledge and rhetorical process), as reflected in genre knowledge is one of the key issues of the current research into the formation of professional identities of knowledge workers. In this chapter, I presented a case of a young engineer's trajectory in her development as a professional and a professional communicator. I introduced and discussed a theoretical framework that allowed me to closely analyze the development of her professional identity as a member of an engineering CoP. The unified social theory of genre learning based on the integration of RGS with AT and situated learning theories, coupled with selected concepts from Bourdieu's social theory of practice, has proved effective in the analysis of Rebecca's trajectory in learning engineering genres, as the trajectory unfolded in time and space.

I applied the unified social theory of genre learning to the analysis of her learning and use of engineering genres in various contexts in an attempt to understand what constitutes professional genre knowledge and how novice knowledge workers learn to operate within the dual problem space of the domain content knowledge and rhetorical process. From the analyses that I presented in this chapter and elsewhere (Artemeva, 2005, 2008, 2009), it follows that genre knowledge consists of multiple ingredients (Artemeva, 2005, 2008), which go far beyond audience awareness and knowledge of the textual features of genres. The study has shown that novices can learn particular ingredients of genre knowledge both in the classroom and in the workplace; they can later modify and adapt these ingredients to more complex communication contexts. Hence, the question of the portability of rhetorical genre knowledge may now be viewed in a different way. For example, on the basis of recent findings, researchers (e.g., Tuomi-Gröhn & Engeström, 2003) do not necessarily interpret the portability of knowledge in traditional terms, that is, as the effect of a prior task on the subsequent task of the same level of complexity. They, rather, see it as a continual learning from one changing situation to another, a more complex one. In the latter case the portability of knowledge and learning plays an important role in one's successful performance in more and more complex tasks. Rebecca's ability to successfully cross boundaries (Wenger, 1998) between different activity systems, i.e., school and various workplaces, reflects her ability to carry learning and professional knowledge—in particular, genre knowledge—from one social situation to another.

Säljö (2003) suggested that cooperation with other activity systems and the provision for rich boundary-crossing between them should be encouraged, and that novices should have an opportunity to analyze, contribute to, and modify daily practices as a means to develop knowledge. In other words, learners should act as agents of change, rather than copy the knowledge and skills of expert members. As Rebecca's Individual Case Synopsis has shown, she developed her own strategies to comfortably deal with the workplace situations, rather than attempting to copy what she referred to as "cookie-cutter" strategies that had been offered in many of her university courses. In other words, she was able to creatively apply her knowledge of engineering genres learned at university and use it in workplace situations.

The use of the unified social theory of genre learning allowed me to uncover complex processes in Rebecca's learning trajectory. Thus, the integration of RGS and the three-level model of human activity permitted me to analyze teaching and learning in the communication classroom as two independent activities. Rebecca's case provides additional evidence that activities of teaching and studenting (Dias, 2000) are radically different and that Bracewell and Witte's (2003) notion of task allows us to unpack these differences: While the course instructor sees the whole course as a task, for a student, each goal and corresponding action represent a task in itself.

One of the questions that arise then is how a student can assess the quality of teaching while still being enrolled in a professional communication course. As Rebecca's case and other cases investigated in the longitudinal study (Artemeva, 2005, 2008, 2009) demonstrate, the ability to see the course as a whole comes to students only much later, once the course experience becomes contextualized within the university and/or workplace activity systems. This observation raises a concern about the timing of traditional teacher evaluations in professional courses that usually come at the end of the course. Another related question, which I have already raised elsewhere (Artemeva, 2005), is the question of the assessment of students' professional genre knowledge. Rebecca's case supplies additional evidence that such an assessment may provide accurate information only much later, after the course has been completed and the professional identity has been formed. Detailed answers to these questions require further research.

Rebecca's case indicates that there are important connections between genre knowledge and the novice's ability to develop into a successful professional and professional communicator in the contemporary knowledge society. This genre knowledge is necessary for a smooth integration of novices into workplace CoPs. In Rebecca's case, genre knowledge was accumulated later in her academic and professional career (unlike in the cases of two other students in my longitudinal study who had accumulated their cultural capital from their families [see Artemeva, 2005, 2008]) and included her academic experiences in engineering classes, the ECC, and workplaces. Rebecca's case provides evidence that the engineering communication course had supplied her with a foundation in professional generic practices that she was able to draw and build upon throughout her subsequent academic and professional experiences. It is notable that, contrary to the findings presented in Anson and Forsberg (1990/2003), Dias et al. (1999), Dias and Paré (2000), and MacKinnon (1993/2003), Rebecca had no difficulties drawing on genres learned in one context when applying them in another (cf. Artemeva, 2005, 2008). This observation allows me to speculate that the knowledge of genre ingredients, which she had possessed by the time she needed to draw on genre flexibility and adapt genres learned in one context to another (cf. Schryer, 1993), provided her with the confidence and ability to do so. It also appears that by that time, for Rebecca, the genres of engineering no longer were the objects of the engineering activity—they had long turned into mediational artifacts (cf. Le Maistre & Paré, 2004).

Rebecca's case indicates that if a student has not yet accumulated the necessary ingredients of genre knowledge, it may be futile to expect her to learn even the basic domain-specific communication strategies in a single communication course. Comments provided by other longitudinal study participants (Artemeva, 2005, 2008) and Rebecca's movement through activity levels, in particular, suggest that offering a domain-specific communication course in the first or second year may not be optimal for those students who have not accumulated "the critical mass" of domain content, genre knowledge, and relevant cultural capital, which may allow them to perceive a communication course as a coherent whole rather than a mosaic of discrete actions. It appears that for such students, the third year of the engineering program serves as the kairotic moment in their accumulation of domain content expertise and other genre ingredients necessary to focus their view on the communication course and see connection between knowledge, genres, and practice of engineering.

The case study discussed in this chapter sheds light on one of the important processes involved in the education of knowledge workers, i.e., the formation of their professional identities as they learn to occupy the dual space of domain-content knowledge and rhetorical process. As we have seen, this education goes beyond the years spent in a university program. Further studies of this process are needed to locate new evidence of the portability of rhetorical strategies between the education and workplace contexts and to identify conditions that make such portability possible.

REFERENCES

Anson, C. M., & Forsberg, L. (2003). Moving beyond the academic community: Transitional stages in professional writing. In T. Peeples (Ed.), *Professional writing and rhetoric: Readings from the field* (pp. 388-410). New York, NY: Longman. (Reprinted from Written Communication, 7, 1990, pp. 200-231).

Artemeva, N. (2005). A time to speak, a time to act: A rhetorical genre analysis of the calculated risk-taking by a novice engineer. *Journal of Business and Technical Communication, 19*(4), 389-421.

Artemeva, N. (2006). Approaches to learning genres: A bibliographical essay. In N. Artemeva, & A. Freedman, (Eds.). *Rhetorical Genre Studies and beyond* (pp. 1-90). Winnipeg, MB: Inkshed Publications.

Artemeva, N. (2008). Toward a unified theory of genre learning. *Journal of Business and Technical Communication, 22* (2), 160-185. doi: 10.1177/1050651907311925

Artemeva, N. (2009). Stories of becoming: A study of novice engineers learning genres of their profession. In C. Bazerman, A. Bonini, & D. Figueiredo (Eds.), *Genre in a changing world* (pp. 158-178). Fort Collins, CO, and West Lafayette, IN: The WAC Clearinghouse & Parlor Press Available at http://wac.colostate.edu/books/

Artemeva, N., & Freedman, A. (2001). 'Just the boys playing on computers': An activity theory analysis of differences in the cultures of two engineering firms. *Journal of Business and Technical Communication, 15*(2), 164-194.

Bakhtin, M. M. (1981). Forms of time and of the chronotope in the novel: Notes towards a historical poetics. In M. Holquist (Ed.), *The dialogic imagination: Four essays by M. M. Bakhtin* (C. Emerson & M. Holquist, Trans.) (pp. 84-258). Austin: University of Texas Press.

Bakhtin, M. M. (1986). The problem of speech genres. In C. Emerson & M. Holquist (Eds.), *Speech genres and other late essays* (V. W. McGee, Trans.) (pp. 60-102). Austin, TX: University of Texas Press.

Bawarshi, A. (2000). The genre function. *College English, 62* (3), 335-360.

Bazerman, C., & Paradis, J. (1991). *Textual dynamics of the professions: Historical and contemporary studies of writing in professional communities.* Madison, WI: University of Wisconsin Press.

Bazerman, C., & Russell, D. (Eds.). (2002). *Writing selves/writing societies: Research from activity perspectives.* Perspectives on Writing. Fort Collins, CO: The WAC Clearinghouse and Mind, Culture, and Activity. Retrieved from http://wac.colostate.edu/books/selves_societies/

Berger, P. L., & Luckmann, T. (1967). *The social construction of reality: A treatise in the sociology of knowledge.* Garden City, NY: Anchor Books.

Bourdieu, P. (1972). *Outline of a theory of practice* (R. Nice, Trans.). Cambridge: Cambridge University Press

Bracewell, R. J., & Witte, S. P. (2003). Tasks, ensembles, and activity: Linkage between text production and situation of use in the workplace. *Written Communication, 20* (4), 511-559.

Brown, J. S., Collins, A., & Duguid, P. (1989). Situated cognition and the culture of learning. *Educational Researcher, 18*(1), 32-42.

Campbell, K. K., & Jamieson, K. H. (1979). Form and genre in rhetorical criticism: An introduction. In K. K. Campbell & K. H. Jamieson (Eds.), *Form and genre: Shaping rhetorical action* (pp. 9-32). Falls Church, VA: Speech Communication Association.

Coe, R., Lingard, L., & Teslenko, T. (Eds.). (2002). *The rhetoric and ideology of genre.* Cresskill, NJ: Hampton Press.

Cole, M., & Scribner, S. (1978). Introduction. In L. S. Vygotsky, *Mind in society: The development of higher psychological processes* (pp. 1-16). Cambridge: Harvard University Press.

Devitt, A. J. (2004). *Writing genres.* Carbondale, IL: Southern Illinois University Press.

Dias, P. (2000). Writing classrooms as activity systems. In P. Dias & A. Paré (Eds.), *Transitions: Writing in academic and workplace settings.* Cresskill, NJ: Hampton.

Dias, P., Freedman, A., Medway, P. & Paré, A. (1999). *Worlds apart: Acting and writing in academic and workplace contexts.* Mahwah, NJ: Lawrence Erlbaum Associates.

Dias, P., & Paré, A. (Eds.). (2000). *Transitions: Writing in academic and workplace settings.* Cresskill, NJ: Hampton.

Engels, F. (1947). *Anti-Dühring. Herr Eugen Dühring's revolution in science.* Moscow: Progress Publishers. Retrieved from http://www.marxists.org/archive/marx/works/1877/anti-duhring/ch10.htm (Original work published in 1877)

Engeström, Y. (1987). *Learning by expanding: An activity-theoretical approach to developmental research.* Helsinki, Finland: Orienta-Konsultit Oy.

Engeström, Y. (1992). Interactive expertise: Studies in distributed working intelligence. *Research Bulletin, 83.* Helsinki: University of Helsinki, Department of Education.

Engeström, Y. (1999a). Activity theory and individual and social transformation. In Y. Engeström, R. Miettinen, & R.-L. Punamäki (Eds.), *Perspectives on activity theory* (pp. 19-38). Cambridge: Cambridge University Press.

Engeström, Y. (1999b). *Learning by expanding: Ten years later.* Introduction to the German edition of In Lernen durch Expansion. Marburg: BdWi-Verlag. Retrieved from http://communication.ucsd.edu/MCA/Paper/Engestrom/expanding/intro.htm

Engeström, Y., & Miettinen, R. (1999). Introduction. In Y. Engeström, R. Miettinen, & R.-L. Punamäki (Eds.), *Perspectives on Activity Theory* (pp. 1-16). Cambridge: Cambridge University Press.

Fischer, C. T., & Wertz, F. J. (1979). Empirical phenomenological analyses of being criminally victimized. In A. Giorgi & D. Smith (Eds.), *Duquesne studies in phenomenological psychology: Vol. 3* (pp. 135-153). Pittsburgh, PA: Duquesne University Press.

Freedman, A. (2006). Interactions between theory and research: RGS and a study of students and professionals working "in computers." In N. Artemeva & A. Freedman (Eds.), *Rhetorical Genre Studies and beyond.* Winnipeg, MB: Inkshed Publications.

Freedman, A., & Adam, C. (1996). Learning to write professionally: "Situated learning" and the transition from university to professional discourse. *Journal of Business and Technical Communication, 10*(4), 395-427.

Freedman, A., & Adam, C. (2000a). Bridging the gap: University-based writing that is more than simulation. In P. Dias & A. Paré (Eds.), *Transitions: Writing in academic and workplace settings* (pp. 129-144). Cresskills, NJ: Hampton.

Freedman, A., & Adam, C. (2000b). Write where you are: Situating learning to write in university and workplace settings. In P. Dias & A. Paré (Eds.), *Transitions: Writing in academic and workplace settings* (pp. 31-60). Cresskills, NJ: Hampton.

Freedman, A., & Medway, P. (Eds.). (1994a). *Genre and the new rhetoric.* London: Taylor & Francis.

Freedman, A., & Medway, P. (Eds.). (1994b). *Learning and teaching genre.* Portsmouth, NH: Boynton/Cook.

Geisler, C. (1994). *Academic literacy and the nature of expertise: Reading, writing, and knowing in academic philosophy.* Hillsdale, NJ: Laurence Erlbaum.

Giddens, A. (1984). *The constitution of society: Outline of the theory of structuration.* Berkeley, CA: University of California Press.

Hanks, W. (1991). Foreword. In J. Lave & E. Wenger, *Situated learning: Legitimate peripheral participation* (pp. 11-21). Cambridge: Cambridge University Press.

Hegel, G. W. F. (1969). *Hegel's Science of Logic* (A. V. Miller, Trans.). London, England: Allen & Unwin. Retrieved from http://www.marxists.org/reference/archive/hegel/works/hl/hlbeing.htm#HL1_370 (Original work published in 1812-1816)

Kinneavy, J. L. (2002). Kairos in classical and modern rhetorical theory. In P. Sipiora & J. S. Baumlin (Eds.), *Rhetoric and Kairos: Essays in history, theory and praxis* (pp. 58-76). New York, NY: State University of New York Press.

Lave, J. (1991). Situating learning in communities of practice. In L. B. Resnick, J. M. Levine, & S. D. Teasley (Eds.), *Perspectives on socially shared cognition* (pp. 63-82). Washington, DC: APA.

Lave, J. (1996a). Teaching, as learning, in practice. *Mind, Culture, and Activity, 3*(3), 149-164.

Lave, J. (1996b). The practice of learning. In S. Chaiklin & J. Lave (Eds.), *Understanding practice: Perspectives on activity and context* (pp. 3-32). Cambridge: Cambridge University Press.

Lave, J., & Wenger, E. (1991). *Situated learning: Legitimate peripheral participation*. Cambridge: Cambridge University Press.

Le Maistre, C., & Paré, A. (2004). Learning in two communities: The challenges for universities and workplaces. *Journal of Workplace Learning, 16*(1/2), 44-52.

Leont'ev, A. N. (1981). The problem of activity in psychology. In J. V. Wertsch (Ed.), *The concept of activity in Soviet psychology* (pp. 37-71). Armonk, NY: Sharpe.

MacKinnon, J. (2003). Becoming a rhetor: Developing writing ability in a mature, writing-intensive organization. In T. Peeples (Ed.), *Professional writing and rhetoric: Readings from the field* (pp. 411-422). New York, NY: Longman. (Reprinted from R. Spilka [Ed.]. [1993]. Writing in the workplace: New research perspectives [pp. 41-55]. Carbondale: Southern Illinois University Press).

Maykut, P., & Morehouse, R. (1994). *Beginning qualitative research: A philosophic and practical guide*. London: The Falmer Press.

Miller, C. (1992). Kairos in the rhetoric of science. In S. P. Witte, N. Nakadate, & R. D. Cherry (Eds.), *A rhetoric of doing: Essays on written discourse in honor of James L. Kinneavy* (pp. 310-327). Carbondale: Southern Illinois University Press.

Miller, C. (1994a). Genre as social action. In A. Freedman & P. Medway (Eds.), *Genre and the new rhetoric* (pp. 23-42). London: Taylor & Francis. (Original work published in 1984).

Miller, C. (1994b). Rhetorical community: The cultural basis of genre. In A. Freedman & P. Medway (Eds.), *Genre and the new rhetoric* (pp. 67-78). London: Taylor & Francis.

Miller, C. (2002). Foreword. In P. Sipiora & J. S. Baumlin (Eds.), *Rhetoric and kairos: Essays in history, theory and praxis* (pp. xi-xiii). New York: State University of New York Press.

Minnis, M., & John-Steiner, V. P. (n.d.). *Are we ready for a single, integrated theory?* [Essay review of Engeström, Y., Miettinen, R., & Punamäki, R.-L. (Eds.).

(1999). Perspectives on Activity Theory. New York, NY: Cambridge University Press]. Retrieved from http://lchc.ucsd.edu/MCA/Paper/00_01/AT_Vera.htm

Odell, L., & Goswami, D. (1985). *Writing in non-academic settings.* New York, NY: Guilford Press.

Paré, A., & Smart, G. (1994). Observing genres in action: Towards a research methodology. In A. Freedman & P. Medway (Eds.), *Genre in the new rhetoric* (pp. 146-154). London: Taylor and Francis.

Resnick, L. B. (1991). Shared cognition: Thinking as social practice. In L. B. Resnick, J. M. Levine, & S. D. Teasley (Eds.), *Perspectives on socially shared cognition* (pp. 1-20). Washington, DC: APA.

Rogoff, B. (1990). *Apprenticeship in thinking: Cognitive development in social context.* New York: Oxford University Press.

Russell, D. R. (1997). Rethinking genre in school and society: An activity theory analysis. *Written Communication, 14*(4), 504-554.

Russell, D. R. (1998). *The limits of the apprenticeship models in WAC/WID research,* Paper presented at the Conference on College Composition and Communication, Retrieved from http://www.public.iastate.edu/~drrussel/russell4c98.html

Russell, D. (2005). *Texts in contexts: Theorising learning by looking at literacies.* Paper produced for ESRC TLRP Thematic Seminar Series: Contexts, communities, network: Mobilising learners' resources and relationships in different domains, June 2005, Lancaster University.

Säljö, R. (2003). Epilogue: From transfer to boundary-crossing. In T. Tuomi-Gröhn & Y. Engeström (Eds.), *Between school and work: New perspectives on transfer and boundary-crossing.* Amsterdam: Pergamon.

Schryer, C. (1993). Records as genre. *Written Communication, 10*(2), 200-234.

Schryer, C. F. (1994). The lab vs. the clinic: Sites of competing genres. In A. Freedman & P. Medway (Eds.), *Genre and the new rhetoric* (pp. 105-124). London: Taylor & Fancis.

Schryer, C. (1999). Genre time/space: Chronotopic strategies in the experimental article. *Journal of Advance Composition, 19*(1), 81-89.

Schryer, C. F. (2000). Walking a fine line: Writing negative letters in an insurance company. *Journal of Business and Technical Communication, 14*(4), 445-497.

Schryer, C. F. (2002). Genre and power: A chronotopic analysis. In R. Coe, L. Lingard, & T. Teslenko (Eds.), *The rhetoric and ideology of genre* (pp. 73-102). Cresskill, NJ: Hampton Press.

Smart, G., & Brown, N. (2002). Learning transfer or transforming learning? Student interns reinventing expert writing practices in the workplace. *Technostyle, 18*(1), 117-141.

Tuomi-Gröhn, T., & Engeström, Y. (Eds.). (2003). *Between school and work: New perspectives on transfer and boundary-crossing.* Amsterdam: Pergamon.

University of Helsinki, Finland, Center for Activity Theory and Developmental Work Research (n.d.). *Cultural-Historical Activity Theory.* Retrieved from http://www.edu.helsinki.fi/activity/pages/chatanddwr/chat/

Vygotsky, L. S. (1978). *Mind in society: The development of higher psychological processes* (M. Cole, V. John-Steiner, S. Scribner, & E. Souberman, Eds.). Cambridge: Harvard University Press.

Vygotsky, L. S. (2003). Umstvennoe razvitie detey v procese obuchenia [Mental development of children during education]. In L. S. Vygotsky, *Psikhologia razvitia rebenka* [Psychological development of a child] (pp. 327-505). Moscow: EKSMO. (Original work published in 1935).

Webb, J., Schirato, T., & Danaher, G. (2002). *Understanding Bourdieu.* Ten Thousand Oaks: Sage Publications.

Wenger, E. (1998). *Communities of practice: Learning, meaning, and identity.* Cambridge: Cambridge University Press.

Wenger, E. (2005). *Communities of practice: A brief introduction.* Retrieved from http://www.ewenger.com/theory/index.htm

Wertsch, J. V. (Ed.). (1981). *The concept of activity in Soviet psychology.* Armonk, NY: M. E. Sharpe.

Wertsch, J. V. (1985). *Vygotsky and the social formation of mind.* Cambridge, MA: Harvard University Press.

Wertsch, J. V. (1991). *Voices of the mind: A sociocultural approach to mediated action.* Cambridge, MA: Harvard University Press.

Winsor, D. (1996). *Writing like an engineer: A rhetorical education.* Mahwah, NJ: Lawrence Erlbaum.

Winsor, D. (2001). Learning to do knowledge work in systems of distributed cognition. *Journal of Business and Technical Communication, 15*(1), 5-28.

Winsor, D. (2003). *Writing power: Communication in an engineering center.* Albany, NY: SUNY Press.

Witte, S. P. (1992). Context, text, intertext: Toward a constructivist semiotics of writing. *Written communication, 9*(2), 237-308.

Witte, S. (1999, May). *Tools, technologies, artifacts of speedbumps.* Paper presented at the Carleton University Seminar in Applied Language Studies, Ottawa, ON, Canada.

17 INTERNATIONAL STUDENTS AND IDENTITY: RESISTING DOMINANT WAYS OF WRITING AND KNOWING IN ACADEME

Heekyeong Lee and Mary H. Maguire

> Whenever I tried to write [something] – even my diary, I couldn't write my feelings, opinion and information on my paper. Everything I had huge writing materials in my brain, something that is like a strong guardian seemed to protect the exit gate where my writing material could go out from my brain to on the paper. So this situation made me throw my pencile to the wall strongly or snap it into two. (Excerpt from Seong-jin's free-write logs, ESL student, December 10, 2001)

> It was very difficult and time consuming to write three papers which was about 30 pages long per paper. In Korea, a person who can be good at actual translation is more appreciated, rather than the one who is knowledgeable in theory. They focus more on practice than on theory. That's why it was particularly difficult for me to include some theories in my paper. (Interview with Sang-eun, a graduate student in Translation and Interpretation, January 16, 2002)

These excerpts from two South Korean students reflect some of the challenges they encounter in their socialization into North American academic discourses and second language (L2) literacy practices in a new country. Seong-jin, a twenty-three-year old undergraduate political science student from a South Korean university, enrolled in an intensive English as a Second Language (ESL) program at a Canadian university to improve his English. In the above excerpt from one of his free-write logs, he presents a vivid image of his frustrations with not being able to write when he refers to his symbolic action of throwing the traditional writing tool, his "pencil to the wall strongly." Sang-eun is a twenty-nine year old graduate student studying for her PhD in Translation Studies at a Canadian university. Before coming to Canada, she had obtained her M.A. degree in Interpretation and Translation in Korean and Spanish from a South Korean university. From her interview excerpt, we infer that her difficulty in writing academic papers, frequently 30-page papers focusing on theory, is influenced by the different discursive emphases in her field of translation studies in both countries.

In this chapter, we draw on case studies of these South Korean students in order to illustrate the challenges international students can face in negotiating new contact zones (Bakhtin, 1981) of competing textualities—zones of contact where they "struggle against various kinds and degrees of authority" (p. 345). These challenges raise questions about writing and knowledge making in academic settings (Canagarajah, 2006a; Hull & Katz, 2006; Matsuda, 2006). Drawing on the late Witte's (1992) intriguing question about what it means to be able to write in society, we ask what writing can be, especially for international students, who are often discursively labelled as ESL writers or "non-native" writers. As teachers of writing, what are our ethical and professional responsibilities to students like Seong-jin and Sang-eun, who experience conflicting discursive practices for making knowledge? How can we ensure that they are able to write with authority and develop their own writing identities and authorial selves?

To address these questions, we first situate the cases within a brief discussion of international students on Canadian university campuses. We then review prevailing discourses of academic writing for international students, showing how international students have been perceived in the literature in the past. We draw on Bakhtin's (1981) concepts of authorial activity, and authoritative and internally persuasive discourse to argue for a view of writing as a situated cultural activity that is responsive to the experiences of diverse student populations inhabiting our academic institutions. We conclude that traditional institutionally constructed and attributed labels, such as native/non-native writers or ESL writers need to be challenged for their assumed cultural and linguistic homogeneity of international students and cultural groups. We argue for the reconceptualization of L2 writers and international students within a discourse of possibility (Canagarajah, 2006a; Holland, Lachicotte, Skinner & Cain, 1998; Hull & Katz, 2006) rather than painting portraits of their struggles as deficits and problems.

INTERNATIONAL STUDENTS ON CANADIAN UNIVERSITY CAMPUSES

The growing presence of international students from countries where English is not the dominant language raises academic, linguistic, and political questions within North American hosting institutions. Although institutions readily affirm diversity as a desirable and indispensable element of academic excellence, the enrollment of international students is often also seen as a source of revenue for colleges and universities trying to compete in the global marketplace. International students bring foreign capital, increase visible ethnic diversity, and enhance the international reputation of the hosting institutions (Matsuda, 2006). However, international students on Canadian campuses face numerous challenges, which include adapting not only to the country, but also to new educational systems, social relationships, and discursive academic literacy practices. In their socialization into academic discourses, international students are positioned between different cultures and languages. Their perceptions of the academic literacy practices they are expected to appropriate and emulate may differ from those of their North American professors (Hull & Katz, 2006).

Prevailing Discourses of Understanding L2 Academic Writers' Challenges

Over the forty years of L2 composition study, much attention has been given to identifying difficulties encountered by L2 student writers that are attributed to their limited proficiency of the target language (Hamp-Lyons, 1991; Johns, 1990). Some researchers (Jenkins, Jordan, & Weiland, 1993) attribute novice academic writers' difficulties with organization to their lack of clear and logical thinking. Other researchers (Dong, 1998; Smith, 1999) have claimed that students from a Confucian educational background experience difficulties with developing arguments and critical evaluation of theories in the literature since they have presumably been trained not to challenge the ideas and thoughts of their academic superiors. The implication of these studies is that writing instructors should initiate L2 students into the literacy practices of the target cultures, often in English, a language with huge hegemonic power.

However, we view the notion of explicit pedagogy as promoting a one-size-fits-all model for L2 students based on the assumption that international students from similar cultural backgrounds share similar knowledge, beliefs, and values or needs. This over-simplified understanding of socio-cultural influences on L2 writing, stereotypes L2 students as academic writers and neglects the socio-cultural dimensions of their diverse identities. As Kubota (1999) argues, studies in contrastive rhetoric, for example, tend to dichotomize Western and Eastern cultures and draw rigid cultural boundaries between them. According to Kubota, these studies have given "labels such as individualism, self-expression, critical and analytical thinking and extending knowledge to Western cultures on one hand and collectivism, harmony, indirection, memorization, and conserving knowledge to Asian cultures in general on the other" (p. 14). This reductionistic line of thinking ignores the complexities of L2 students' diverse identities and knowledge-making processes.

We join with scholars who challenge prevailing assumptions about "English learners" and the cultural and linguistic homogeneity of L2 writers (Canagarajah, 2006a; Gutièrrez & Orellana, 2006; Hull & Katz, 2006; Matsuda & Silva, 1999). Accordingly, we see the terms "ESL writers" and "non-native writers" as institutionally constructed and attributed labels. Current theories of difference and deficit cannot explain the difficulties Seong-jin and Sang-eun encountered. L2 researchers therefore need to explore the socio-cultural dimensions of writers and their personal aspirations in academic writing more deeply from the students' perspectives. We need to reconceptualize how we represent L2 writers without painting portraits of their challenges as deficits. Rather, we need to understand these challenges as struggles with dominant academic discourses.

UNDERSTANDING THE IDENTITIES OF INTERNATIONAL STUDENTS: BETWEEN AUTHORITATIVE AND INTERNALLY PERSUASIVE DISCOURSE

We look to identity theorists from different disciplines that are confronting issues of identity in authoring selves and others. Silverstein (2003) refers to this millennium as the "Era of Anxieties of Identities":

> We hear constantly of crises of identity, of the workings of identity politics, of identity work that needs to be done and so forth. By identity, we can understand a subjective intuition that one belongs to a particular social category of people with certain potentials and consequences of this belonging. This participation suggests participation in ritual occasions and socializing in certain ways in variously institutionalised forms to make our identity clear to ourselves and to others on a continuing basis. This already suggests a kind of temporality to the way identity is and as it were practiced and understood. (pp. 1-2)

Similarly, adopting a hermeneutical conception of identity as a recursive process of self-interpretation, Taylor (1994) links identity to a complex politics of recognition that refers to something like a person's understanding of who they are, of their fundamental defining characteristics as a human being. To appreciate the complexities of L2 students' challenges and identities in academic literacy practices, we appropriate the discursive construction of identity as an interpretive tool for understanding South Korean international students' challenges. As Ivanič (1998) notes, writing is "an act of identity in which people align themselves with socioculturally shaped possibilities of selfhood, playing their part in reproducing or challenging dominant practices and discourses, and the values, beliefs and interests which they embody" (p. 31).

To examine this alignment in ways that are respectful of the experiences of diverse student populations in academic settings, we draw on Bakhtin's (1981) theory of dialogism and authoritative and persuasive discourses. Bakhtin's sense of dialogism assumes that the production of utterances always involves the speaker's appropriating, invoking, or ventriloquating through the voices of others, thereby involving the speaker in a dialogic encounter with them. According to Bakhtin, language lies on "the borderline between oneself and another. The word in language is half someone else's. It becomes 'one's own' when the speaker populates it with his own intention, his own accent, when he appropriates the word, adapting it to his own semantic and expressive intention" (p. 293). For international student writers studying in a North American context, this usually means appropriating the norms of academic writing in English. Individual students may engage in multiple discourses as a consequence of participating in a variety of literacy events and practices (Ivanič, 1998). Thus, appropriation of particular discourse patterns becomes an expression of personal, social, and cultural identities. Students draw on existing macro level discourse structures and resources to create their own locally relevant positionings of self and others (Maguire & Graves, 2001).

Recognizing the dynamism of all texts and the situatedness of all speakers/writers within cultural, historical, and institutional settings, Bakhtin (1981) sees two competing discourses: authoritative discourse and internally persuasive discourse. Authoritative discourse refers to privileged languages and official discourses, such as official government policy and legislation, the discourse of tradition, generally acknowledged beliefs and authority that cannot be disrupted. Internally persuasive discourse refers to everyday discourse that constantly changes in social interactions. It is the discourse of personal beliefs, values, and ideas that influence our responses to the world and others and allows for negotiation. The two discourses can co-exist and create socio-political tensions between languages and power, texts and power, self and others. When international student writers are engaged in learning authoritative discourses in North American academic contexts, they may experience conflicts derived from the power relationships between the new authoritative discourse of others and their internally persuasive discourses as authoring selves. Regardless of a teacher's explicit instruction about cultural knowledge of a target discourse, some students may choose not to appropriate that knowledge because it conflicts with their preferred internally persuasive discourses (Lee, 2005). Some students might accommodate themselves rather easily to the conventions and expectations in a particular academic discourse community. Others might not be willing to compromise how they position themselves in order to become a member of the authoritative discourse communities.

To understand this phenomenon of writer alignment, we present Seong-jin and Sang-un as case examples of what international students may be trying to accomplish as they negotiate academic literacy practices in two Canadian universities.

METHODOLOGY AND METHODS

In this interpretive, qualitative inquiry, we examine two South Korean students' experiences of their academic literacy practices in Canadian universities, focusing in particular on their negotiation processes with complex social relations inside and outside their school settings. We do not intend to produce any generalizations about international students in Canadian universities. The two cases serve as entry points into the conversation about discursive identity, positioning, and knowledge making embedded in the L2 literacy practices of international students. An interpretive methodology assumes an epistemological stance that human beings are self interpretive beings and agents in various social contexts.

The primary source of data is the students' personal narratives that emerged from open-ended interviews. The face-to-face, open-ended interviews were conducted in Korean from November 2001 until April 2002 and audiotaped. Interviews were transcribed in both Korean and English, but Korean excerpts are not included in this chapter due to the lack of space. Various sets of data that are relevant to the participants' narratives were also collected, such as writing samples of course work, personal notes and e-mails, administrative documents, research journals, and observation notes of various social activities.

Situating the Participants

Seong-jin and Sang-eun, born in South Korea and raised in Korean families, have experienced the South Korean national education systems up to post-secondary school. Seong-jin came to Canada by himself in September 2001 when he was twenty-three years old; this was his first time abroad. He postponed his studies in political science in a Korean B.A. degree program in order to enroll in an intensive ESL program offered at an English-speaking Canadian university. According to the ESL program's web site, the official goal of the intensive course was to help students develop English language skills for academic or professional purposes. Seong-jin received financial support from his parents in Korea to cover tuition fees and accommodation. He was very conscious about how much money he spent on his ESL studies since the main source of income for his family was his father's salary as a civil servant. Seong-jin was living with a Canadian homestay family and two other roommates.

Sang-eun came to Canada in 1999 with her husband to pursue her PhD degree in the Department of Translation and Interpretation at a Canadian university. She had obtained her Bachelor's and Master's degree in Translation, majoring in Korean and Spanish, from a Korean university with a reputation as a very prestigious school in her field in Korea. After finishing the M.A. program, she worked for a short while as a professional translator. She then decided to pursue her PhD degree in the translation field. Her Canadian university offered her an admission scholarship covering tuition for four years.

In the next section, we analyze the challenges Seong-jin's and Sang-eun face as "newcomers" to academic literacy practices at Canadian universities.

SEONG-JIN'S CHALLENGES: DEVELOPING A NEW IDENTITY AS AN ACADEMIC WRITER

Seong-jin's case illustrates his challenges negotiating the authoritative discourse, the normative ways of academic essay writing, and his internally persuasive discourse that emerged from his free-writes in his early ESL class. The intensive ESL program in which Seong-jin was enrolled in a Canadian university placed students in five different levels of language skills: low- and high-beginner, low- and high-intermediate, and advanced. During the period of interviews from November 2001 until April 2002, he took three semesters of the intensive ESL program. In the 2001 fall term, he was placed in the high-beginner level of English. He then moved to the high-intermediate level in the 2002 winter term and to the advanced level in the 2002 spring term. At the beginner and intermediate levels, Seong-jin engaged in many free-writing tasks in his classes, which led him to regard writing as an important part of his identity and to explore his internally persuasive discourse.

From the beginning of the interviews with Seong-jin, it was evident that he was studying English extremely hard and doing so mostly through reading

Harry Potter. He spent about five hours a day studying English, reading and memorizing vocabulary from the book. His approach to learning English is reflected in this excerpt from his free-writing on the word "strong," a prompt provided by his ESL teacher:

> "Strong?" What does this word – "strong" mean? What is that "strong". These questions have preyed on my mind for long time, specially after 'the accident in the elementary school'. I was just at the age of 12 or 13 years old. I got to be sprawled out on the floor, having mouth and nose bleeding, and lots of bruises all over my body after many classmates pummelled me because I was a new student to their class from another school ... Then I asked myself about "strong" and decided to be strong ... so to become strong man, I was extremely interested in the fighting skills—the boxing, Takwon-do, judo etc.... but I just learned only one kind of fighting skill – boxing and a little.... Oneday I knew the strength on my mind is more important and just physical power is a part of various aspects that the real strong man must have ... I hope that oneday I stood confidently and powerfully in front of millions of people and lead them. Then maybe I will not aspire to be the strong man any more.

The title 'Strong' can be traced to a childhood incident in elementary school in which he was "pummelled by his classmates." He vividly produces an image of his being "sprawled on the floor, having mouth and nose bleeding and lots of bruises all over [his] body." In response to the experience, he aspires to become a strong man and to be "self confident and powerful in front of millions of people" by strengthening his physical power as well as his mind.

We find it intriguing that Seong-jin has the desire to have the "strength on my mind" in addition to building physical strength. The next interview excerpt reflects how he links "the strength on my mind" specifically to writing:

> I think ... there are many people who speak well but not many who write well. I believe that a person who writes well is the one who thinks deeply. In my view, if you want to be a better person and a deeper thinking person, it is important to write well. (Seong-jin, interview, February 1, 2002)

Seong-jin portrays himself as an individual who highly values the linguistic capital of writing as a key to being a "better person and a deeper thinking

International Students and Identity

person." In the next excerpt, he even emphasizes writing as the most important thing he learned in Canada:

> Everyone have been in foreign countries said to me, I would feel value of country and value of family. If I felt values like that, there would be the most important thing I've learned in Canada so far. But unfortunately I have not had that feelings ... Most important thing is for me in [this] class, specially in writing class. Maybe because of shame, timid ... I could not read my writing. But it's truth. I didn't like writing. Never! Despite I wanted to write novel, opinion and a letter very well, always something prevented my brain from moving actively.... I know writing is very hard, long journey. To write well need to read many books and practice much time. But It's not problem for me ... I keep going to read and write writings. Someday I will make popular novel like 'Harry Potter' composed by Joanne Rowling and nice report about my major. I believe. I dream a dream like Martin Luther King.

Seong-jin's autobiographical self continues to emerge as he reiterates how he values good writing skills and aspires to be a good writer for his ESL class and in his future pursuits. Interestingly, this free-write excerpt reveals that he is passionate about producing creative writing and what he perceives as good writing is a novel such as Harry Potter. This writing disposition is not one we would have likely predicted from the first projected image of this "studying hard student," which he presented in his first interview.

The next excerpt entitled "Music" strongly reflects his potential as a creative writer—an image that is affirmed by his teacher's response to this log.

> I am extremely thirsty. Eagerly diving into cold, blue, infinite sea [...] I can drink all water till the bottom [...] I need not sea. Just I can be satisfied with a bottle of coke [...] What is this thirst to me? Why do I feel fever on my chest [...] I am just standing, seeing absent-mindedly, stretching arms without strength. I am wearing good suit. I have aspiration. I hope someone is being next to me. I can recline my head against someone's shoulders, and someone can recline head against my shoulders. I don't know someone is my friend or my lover. But if we stood on the street between people, we would not feel alone [...] What will I do? [...] For what and who will I live? [

> ...] Let me believe myself. Let me love my family. Let me help wretched people. Let my people think me valuable. Let me soar to the sky. Let me have brightness of sun. Let me fly away to sun. Let me see opposite side of moon.

Here is the teacher's comment

> This is wonderful—like a poem. Maybe you should write it that way (in the form of a poem). I can see that you really know how to put your imagination, your mind on paper. Sometimes, we call free writing "mind writing". You do a really good job of that. You've done a great job describing the freedom of a wondering mind. Sometimes we also call this "stream of consciousness" writing.

However, in the following semester, Seong-jin advanced to the high-intermediate level class. In this class, he struggled with two conflicting discourses—the authoritative discourse of normative ways of writing an academic essay required in his ESL class and his internally persuasive discourse that had emerged in his previous ESL class.

According to Seong-jin, since the high-intermediate class was a more advanced level class, the focus of the instruction was more geared toward English for academic purposes. During this semester he occasionally talked about his difficulty in participating in the class. Unlike the free-writes he had enjoyed in the previous course, he found it very difficult to write an essay in a formal academic style, such as a reading response or an argumentative essay. His identity and aspirations to be a creative writer often contradicted the expectations of the formal writing conventions he was expected to appropriate in this ESL class.

The next excerpts from a reading response Seong-jin wrote in this ESL class and his teacher's comment illustrate the tensions between his internally persuasive discourse and the authoritative discourse norms of the ESL class.

> Willam Cowan! I can easily guess what your job is. Surely your job is professional, maybe mathematician. If my guess is wrong, anyway you're very thorough person because anyone doesn't think carefully why we're not using metric measuring in only time measurement [...] It is great! Especially, your suggestion that a day begin at sunrise, 0:00 o'clock and a year begins at the time when the day begins longer or shorter, are fabulously ingenious. I can't find proper way to praise your peculiar

thought, efforts to form a theory and result, "This hour has 100 minutes." But to complete your theory not just interesting article but a practical provocative power, you had to give audiences the reasons why we must change present time structure into new [...] I don't understand metric time measuring is natural? I don't think so because metric measurement was also invented by human being [...] Have you ever thought why metric time measuring is revolutionary comfortable even though enormous cost to change? [...] I will give some examples against yours. Have you ever heard about salary man's Monday disease? [...] Monday disease is about tiredness and laziness that salary man suffers from usually after holidays. Let's guess to adopt you're a three-day work period with two days off. Salary man would be supposed to suffer from twice Monday disease a week and this would affect the economy seriously. [...] If I had read your theory in those, I would have thanked you to expand my thinking. But I was sorry that I read yours in the class and had to respond my opinion for or against yours [...] Before finishing my writing, I will give you fantastic idea to make your theory more superior. Make your theory easier and clearer, then issue it in the scientic book or magazine ofr teenagers .... (Seong-jin, reading response, Janurary 28, 2002)

Here is the teacher's comment

> Leo (Seong-jin's nick name in the ESL class), this article is only a proposal. When you write your critique, you should not address the writer. You have to keep it more neutral, you have to write about the article and about the author and about his theory...
>
> ...Tone down your sarcasm. This paper looks more like a political satire than a reading response. A reading response is an academic paper, where a sound argument is valued more than an emotional outburst.

This exchange shows Seong-jin's struggles balancing the 'authoritative discourse' of this ESL class and the 'internally persuasive discourse' of his free writes. He feels forced to appropriate the authoritative discourse and to engage in the formal academic writing practices as instructed by his ESL teacher. He is told to tone down his sarcasm, not to dialogue with the writer, to keep his tone neutral and just to write about the article and the author and his theory. The values of this authoritative discourse are explicit in the teacher's response to his response paper: "A reading response paper is an academic paper where a sound argument is valued more than an emotional outburst."

The next excerpt reveals that Seong-jin was aware of the institutional norms for what constitutes a good writing sample of an argumentative essay in this ESL class:

> Seong-jin: I like writing based on my intuition. I don't like writing based on logic and by adding references. There always has to be a fixed structure. You have to write "a positive argument with example sentences" first, and then "a negative argument with example sentences." At the end, then, you have to come up with "solution" stating what is the best argument. This is sort of what they consider as a good writing sample.
>
> Heekyeong: So, you know then what they expect from your writing.
>
> Seong-jin: Yeah, but I don't like to do that. It [my writing] becomes then the same as all the other students'. I don't like to follow the same form as others ....(Interview with Seong-jin, February 15, 2002)

Seong-jin's awareness of the norms may have been reinforced by his identity as a hard-working ESL student who wanted to achieve high marks from the course. Before he experienced the free-writes in his previous ESL writing class, this may indeed have worked for him. However, he now valued the internally persuasive discourse of his free-writes, which may have been influenced by his aspirations to become a creative writer and his former writing teacher's affirmation of his authorial self. He believed that writing should be produced intuitively rather than by focusing on form and structure. Struggling to find his own identity as a writer, he did not want to implement the rules for writing an argumentative essay that he was certainly aware of because he felt his writing would be "the same as all the other students" work. He resisted becoming a writing clone and did not like writing based on "logic and by adding references." This belief seemed to be so strong that it prevented Seong-jin from producing an argumentative essay for his ESL class. Understandably, it took much time for him to finish one essay for his homework. Furthermore, he started to skip class frequently, particularly when he did not complete the homework assignment:

> I feel I have become a dummy. I can't make points in an academic writing ... The unfinished homework is piling up. I know I tend to write based on my feelings ... but I can't write if I don't come up with any feeling. (Seong-jin, interview, February 1, 2002)

> So, one day, I tried to write an essay in the free writing style. I was of course able to quickly write one and a half pages. But, even to me it did not look coherent at all. I tried to write it again a few days later, but decided to give up. After that, I did not go to the class and studied in the library by myself instead. (Seong-jin, interview, February 15, 2002)

As this interview excerpt indicates, Seong-jin's sense of self had shifted from that of a self-confident writer with aspiration to be a creative writer to that of someone who felt like a "dummy" and inarticulate in academic writing.

Seong-jin's dilemma provides a good example of the salience of the dialectical tensions between authoritative and internally persuasive discourses in understanding a student's frustration as a novice academic writer. As Canagarajah (2006b) argues, "not every instance of non-standard usage by a student is an unwitting error: sometimes it is an active choice motivated by important cultural and ideological considerations" (p. 609). In Seong-jin's case, two contradictory discourses are both equally dominant and one suppresses the other. This internal conflict appeared to paralyse and prevent him from completing his homework assignment. Since he viewed "writing well" as an important means to become a "good," "wise," and "strong" person, he became traumatized by the fact that he was not able to write. Writing in an academic context, then, may be a site of struggle for students to meet the demands of teacher's instructions at the local classroom level.

SANG-EUN'S CHALLENGES: STRUGGLES BETWEEN INSTITUTIONAL POLICY AND PERSONAL VISION

Sang-eun's challenge involves a very pragmatic issue many graduate students face: choosing a dissertation topic and an appropriate supervisor. Her struggles between her personal vision of a dissertation topic and the institutional policy of finding a dissertation supervisor in the department point to more institutional systemic tensions.

Sang-eun had obtained her Bachelor's and Master's degrees in Korean and Spanish Translation in South Korea. The Canadian university where she had chosen to pursue her PhD studies in Translation and Interpretation is an official English/French bilingual academic institution. As a bilingual academic institution, this university requires students to have proficiency in at least one of the two official languages and some knowledge of the other. Students are allowed to produce their work and answer examination questions either in English or in French—in whichever language they feel most comfortable. Since her language proficiency in French was not very strong, Sang-eun chose English as her main language in which to carry out her academic tasks, such as completing her course work and writing her dissertation proposal.

Upon her arrival, Sang-eun had received an admission scholarship covering a four-year tuition fee. As she became more familiar with the program, however, she was confronted with different expectations than she had anticipated. As reflected in the interview excerpt below, she became aware that the academic discourse of her Canadian PhD program was different from that of her MA program in Korea:

> It was very difficult and time consuming to write three papers which was about 30 pages long per paper. In Korea, a person who can be good at actual translation is more appreciated, rather than the one who is knowledgeable in theory. They focus more on practice than on theory. That's why it was particularly difficult for me to include some theories in my paper. (Interview with Sang-eun, January 16, 2002)

Sang-eun's difficulty was to include a theoretical analysis in her course papers and to balance theoretical arguments with her own. This difficulty may have been influenced by the academic literacy practices in her MA program in Korea as she thought that theory would not be very useful when she would look for a job in Korea in the future. Noticing the difference between her PhD programs' emphasis on theory and her need for a more practical approach, Sang-eun became frustrated about choosing her dissertation topic and writing her proposal authoritatively from her subject position.

Additionally, because of the nature of the field of translation studies, Sang-eun had to find a supervisor with a good knowledge of the target languages she was interested in. Unfortunately, no professor in her program had expertise in Korean, which made her choice of a dissertation topic more difficult. As revealed in the following interview excerpt, she was aware of the pros and cons as well as of the political consequences of different choices:

> Sang-eun: It's because there is no one who can be my supervi-

sor since my mother tongue is Korean. There is no one who can supervise for Korean language. Nevertheless, I can still do my research on the context of Korean language, under the condition that either I find a Korean supervisor by myself or they do not have to find a Korean supervisor for me.

Heekyeong: So, your PhD thesis would be ...

Sang-eun: Yeah, I can do in Korean and English or English and Spanish. However, due to my mother tongue, I will probably be doing in Korean and English.

Heekyeong: I see ... Do you feel more confident with English than Spanish?

Sang-eun: No, that's not why. There is no market for Korean and Spanish [in this field].

Heekyeong: Oh, is that right?

Sang-eun: Yeah, so if you want to do research, the result of research should be something useful in the field, so, I believe that the work on English and Korean is more useful in Korea [than the one on English and Spanish]. Also, it is not meaningful for me to do research on Korean and Spanish ... (Interview with Sang-eun, November 7, 2001)

In February of 2002, at the end of the second year of her PhD studies, Sang-eun became more frustrated because she had not yet come up with a clear idea for her dissertation. She could not find a supervisor who had the linguistic expertise to work with Korean texts. It became increasingly clear to her that it would neither be good nor feasible for her to have a Korean context in her thesis. She felt that her department did not seem welcoming to her case, nor could they support her financially if she chose to work with Korean. The next interview excerpt reflects tension in Sang-eun's struggle between her personal vision of her dissertation topic, the institutional policy, and the availability of professors in the department.

Sang-eun: The other day I spoke to the director of the program about my thesis topic. She suggested I should work on English,

> French or Spanish contexts so that they can support me.
>
> Heekyeong: Why don't you then work on English or Spanish contexts?
>
> Sang-eun: Then, my uniqueness will disappear and thus, it will be difficult for me to get some funding ... I thought about writing my thesis related to 'Terminology' field, but terminology itself is not considered as a specialized field in Korea, unlikely here. (Interview with Sang-eun, February 27, 2002)

Due to the difficulties in finding a supervisor for her PhD thesis, Sang-eun even thought of transferring to an MA program since many of her colleagues seemed to continue what they had done in their MA program. However, she decided to discard the idea because she would lose her scholarship if she changed her program.

Furthermore, Sang-eun felt marginalized as the "only Asian in the department." This led her to reflect further on her dilemma and her sense of self:

> In my case, I am the only Asian in the department. There is one Arabic student and she says to me that she is proud of being Arabic. I don't mean that I am not proud of being Korean. I mean because of the fact (being Korean) there are many disadvantages for me ... So, I feel that this is not a right school for me, it's not a place I should stay. I don't mean that they [people in the department] did something wrong to me. What can they do, this is a bilingual school, which is funded by the government of which English and French are the main languages ... I think I should go somewhere what I can do can be appreciated. (Sang-eun, interview, April 24, 2002)

This excerpt reveals that Sang-eun considered another academic institution to pursue her doctoral studies: "I should go somewhere what I can do can be appreciated." This need to find an alternative space for her work seems to have emerged when she realized that she could not negotiate any further with her current academic institution. Embarking on PhD studies presents students with many challenges, most importantly making life choices about what research communities they aspire to embrace and with whom they want to align themselves. In this institutional context, we can infer that there are no textual possibilities for Sang-eun to realize her vision of her dissertation.

REFLECTIVE UNDERSTANDINGS OF TEXTUAL POSSIBILITIES AND INTERNATIONAL STUDENTS

We return to the questions posed at the beginning of this chapter: What are our ethical and professional responsibilities as educators in responding to the needs, goals, and expectations of international students? What should authorial activity look like in post secondary academic institutions as our student populations become increasingly diverse? What kinds of textual possibilities can institutions envision for international students? We reflect on some implications from the cases of these two South Korean international students' challenges and negotiations between their internally persuasive discourses and those of their Canadian institutions.

What we draw from these two cases is the need to challenge the frequently ascribed labels, such as "non-native" writers, and to understand how the identities of international students can be better appreciated, recognized, and respected. We believe that writers' texts offer glimpses into how they are positioning themselves and establishing their points of reference as they appropriate or resist prevailing discourses. As engaging in multiple discourses, these students construct their identities and negotiate how to make others' words their own (Bakhtin, 1981). The re-accenting and re-voicing involved in this negotiation does not mean that teachers reformulate their utterances with a correct linguistic construction in the right language—usually English. We do not envision this re-accenting and re-voicing process in classrooms as exercises in reformulating, repeating, and memorizing the well formed utterances of others. Rather, engaging in L2 writing activities and processes offers textual possibilities for enacting a self. Seong-jin's and Sang-eun's narratives about writing within the academy illustrate that, during the processes of appropriating the authoritative discourses of their North American academic institutions, these students were constantly organizing and reorganizing their sense of being and how they were relating to their social worlds. They were experiencing what Bakhtin (1981) calls the process of "ideologically becoming," which refers to the process of "distinguishing between one's own and another's discourse, between one's own and another's thought" (p. 345).

The appropriation of a new discourse is not simply a matter of picking up new information or new discursive practices as new ways of knowledge-making. For some international students in their study-abroad contexts, this can mean appropriating new ontological and epistemological assumptions that can be very different from those they have previously held in their home schools and communities (Lee, 2005). Accordingly, they may need to create new positionings and dialectical relationships between their performances and their wider socio-political and economic contexts (Lee, 2007).

Bakhtin (1981) acknowledges that experiencing the power struggles among different discourses is an uneasy process: "Our ideological development is just such an intense struggle within us for hegemony among various available verbal and ideological points of view, approaches, directions and values" (p. 345). Seong-jin struggled with the process of appropriating authoritative discourses introduced by his ESL teacher. Sang-eun experienced tensions between the conflicting demands of her academic institution and professors and her project of selfhood. Both students felt that they might lose the internally persuasive discourses with which they felt comfortable and believed to be good for their textual performance. However, new authoritative discourses forced them to cross the borders between authoritative and internally persuasive discourses and to position themselves in ways that may exclude them from participating in knowledge-making practices. So, who is responsible for these tensions? What are the responsibilities of teachers when such tensions arise? Certainly, teaching international students to write solely a North American normative text is not the answer.

Rather, these two cases call for a re-examination of hegemonic approaches that have become normative ways of framing, representing, and describing "English Learners" and their learning challenges from a deficit view. Considerations of explicit pedagogy or mimetic teaching approaches for L2 students seem to operate from the assumption that international students from similar cultural backgrounds share similar knowledge, beliefs, morals, and values. As Kubota (2001) argues, such assumptions lead to the 'othering' of ESL students by stereotyping their cultures and languages, and they presume the existence of the unproblematic 'Self' of European/ Western images of power relations that engender feelings of superiority or inferiority. Framing "English Learners" as a distinct group of students who are somehow different from an invisible and mostly unspecified but assumed mainstream norm by using ethnic labels, pan-ethnic labels (Asian), or national-origin labels (e.g., Korean) results in reifying essentialized uni-dimensional categorical concepts of identity (Gutierriz & Orellana, 2006).

Many educators and policy makers may erroneously assume that international students are struggling because they do not know or do not understand the expectations of academic discourse in North American academic institutions. This may lead teachers to feel it is their duty to explicitly teach a particular set of textual expectations. In her 2004 Richard Braddock Award article, Lu (2004) stresses that we, as educators, need to delay our assessment of what novice writers need and how they need to use English until we have studied their understanding of ways of writing. This understanding includes the interpretive process involved in one's efforts to map the actual discursive resources of individual students. Seong-jin's and Sang-eun's narratives show that they had developed the meta-cognitive awareness and self-reflexivity that enabled them to understand implicit expectations of academic discourse for their success in their academic programs. While they were struggling, they were in fact very aware of what was required in their course work to receive a good grade. However, what was required conflicted with their internally persuasive discourses. Their struggling has more to do with the influence of oppressive normative expectations and systemic influences on their writing rather than with not knowing those expectations.

Seong-jin and Sang-eun's challenges reflect international students' options for making choices for their future life trajectories when crossing borders. Unfortunately, both students' academic institutions did not respond to their needs, expectations and aspirations. A commitment to diversity and multiculturalism, which is one of the primary principles of Canadian higher education, is much more than simply having an adequate representation of international students among the student body. Rather, as Paré (2005) notes, "a critical reflection on language holds the possibility of enormous and fundamental change" (p. 88). This commitment inevitably means openness to change and requires systemic strategies and transformative programs that help everyone adopt a critical approach to texts and power (Paré, 2005) that offers new possibilities for addressing the questions raised in this chapter: What kinds of selves, writers, people are we asking international students to become when they inhabit our academic institutions and engage in authorial activities? In classrooms? In communities? In society? How can international students write with authority?

REFERENCES

Bakhtin, M. M. (1981). *The dialogic imagination: Four essays* (C. Emerson & M. Holquist, Trans., M Holquist, Ed.). Austin, TX: University of Texas Press.

Canagarajah, A. S. (2006a). Toward a writing pedagogy of shuttling between languages: Learning from multilingual writers. *College English, 68*(6), 589-604.

Canagarajah, A. S. (2006b). The place of world English in composition: Pluralization continued. *College Composition and Communication, 57*(4), 586-620.

Dong, Y. (1998). Non-native graduate students' thesis/dissertation writing in science: Self-reports by students and their advisors from two US institutions. *English for Specific Purposes, 17,* 369-390.

Gutièrrez, K. D., & Orellana, M. F. (2006). At last: The "problem" of English learners: Constructing genres of difference. *Research in the Teaching of English, 40*(4), 502-507.

Hamp-Lyons, L. (1991). *Assessing second language writing in academic contexts.* Norwood, NJ: Ablex Publishing.

Holland, D., Lachicotte, W., Skinner, D., & Cain, C. (1998). *Agency and identity in cultural worlds.* Cambridge, MA: Harvard University Press.

Hull, G. A., & Katz, M. (2006). Crafting an agentive self: Case studies of digital storytelling. *Research in the Teaching of English, 41*(1), 43-82.

Ivanič, R. (1998). *Writing and identity: Discoursal construction of identity in academic writing.* Philadelphia: John Benjamins.

Jenkins, S., Jordan, M., & Weiland, P. (1993). The role of writing in graduate engineering education: A survey of faculty beliefs and practices. *English for Specific Purposes, 12,* 51-67.

Johns, A. (1990). Coherence as a cultural phenomenon: Employing ethnographic principles in academic milieu. In A. Connor & A. Johns (Eds.), *Coherence in writing: Research and pedagogical perspectives* (pp. 209-226). Alexandria, VA: TESOL.

Kubota, R. (1999). Japanese culture constructed by discourses: Implications for applied linguistics research and ELT. *TESOL Quarterly, 33,* 9-35.

Kubota, R. (2001). Discursive construction of the images of U.S. classrooms. *TESOL Quarterly, 35,* 9-38

Lee, H. (2005). *A socio-cultural-historical analysis of six Korean students' experiences in second language learning contexts: Learner agency and symbolic power* (Unpublished doctoral dissertation). McGill University, Montreal, Canada.

Lee, H. (2007). Korean students' perceptions of identities and cultural capital. *Sociolinguistic Studies, 1*(1), 107-129.

Lu, M. Z. (2004). An essay on the work of composition: Composing English against the order of fast capitalism. *College Composition and Communication, 56,* 16-50.

Maguire, M. H., & Graves, B. (2001). Speaking personalities in primary children's second language writing. *TESOL Quarterly, 35*(4), 561-593.

Matsuda, P. (2006). The myth of linguistic homogeneity in U.S. college composition. *College English, 68*(6), 637-651.

Matsuda, P., & Silva, T. (1999). Cross-cultural composition: Mediated integration of U.S. and international students. *Composition Studies, 27,* 15-30.

Paré, A. (2005). Texts and power: Toward a critical theory of language. In L. Davies & P. Leonard (Eds.), *Social work in a corporate era: Practices of power and resistance.* Aldershot, UK: Ashghor Publishing Limited.

Silverstein, M. (2003). The whens and wheres—as well as hows—of ethnolinguistic recognition. *Public Culture, 15*(3), 531-557.

Smith, D. (1999). Supervising NESB students from Confucian educational cultures. In Y. Ryan & O. Zuber-Skerritt (Eds.), *Supervising postgraduates from non-English speaking backgrounds* (pp. 146-156). Suffolk: Open University Press.

Taylor, C. (1994). *Multiculturalism: Examining the politics of recognition.* Princeton, NJ: Princeton University Press.

Witte, S. P. (1992). Context, text & intertext: Toward a constructivist semiotic of writing. *Written Communication, 9*(2), 237-308.

ARTICULATING AND IMPLEMENTING RHETORIC AND WRITING AS A KNOWLEDGE-MAKING PRACTICE IN HIGHER EDUCATION

18 REPRESENTING WRITING: A RHETORIC FOR CHANGE

Roger Graves

To articulate the central role of writing in the production and sharing of knowledge, we, as Writing Studies scholars, teachers, and program administrators, must acknowledge the importance of universities in this process since they constitute important sites of knowledge creation and dissemination. At the same time, many institutions in Canada have not reflected seriously on the role that writing and communication play in this process of knowledge production and dissemination. In fact, universities act as microcosms of the wider community, especially when instructors of writing and communication prompt their institutions to focus on discursive practices, and are therefore particularly important sites for enacting a "rhetoric for change." The lessons gained in the effort of enacting a "rhetoric for change" within universities can reveal important insights into the challenges that writing studies scholars face in the larger community. Yet, aside from Smith's account of such a rhetoric for community building (this volume) and Procter's diachronic analysis of such efforts in the case of a writing centre (this volume), few accounts exist from writing program administrators at Canadian universities that detail how their programs seek to create space for themselves within their home faculty, within their university, and on the national stage. In this chapter, I present a case study of my work as a writing program administrator at one university and review some of the lessons learned through my efforts to foster a "rhetoric for change" to contribute to the discussions of how writing programs can make their place and value known in a knowledge-based society.

I am using my work as a relatively new (less than three years) director of a writing program as a case study to explore the rhetorical challenges faced by individuals in this type of position at Canadian universities virtually every day. It is not only the directors that face these challenges, but the programs themselves and those who work within them. My own experience and that of my program reveal something important and useful about the challenges involved in helping university colleagues, administrators, students, and others to see and accept writing as central to knowledge-making. I believe others who face similar challenges may find my experience and insights useful as they work to overcome similar challenges at their institutions. I flesh out the case study by analyzing four different documents that I have had to draft over the past three years as I try to develop and strengthen the writing program at my institution.

My goal has been to use writing—the drafting of official institutional documents—as a means of making the value of writing instruction known throughout the campus and beyond. Recently, for example, I worked on a submission to the committee that will select the next dean of our faculty. Over a dozen people on the appointments committee will review this document, starting with the vice-president (academic) and including representatives from across the university, including students. What issues do I highlight for them? How do I present myself and re-present the Writing, Rhetoric, and Professional Communication program to them? What values and conception of writing (as grammar, as epistemic, as practical career training) can I count on them holding? What knowledge about writing should the next dean have? What do I want our program to accomplish in the next five years, and therefore which applicant will best help me to accomplish these goals?

This sort of rhetorical challenge comes my way routinely. While some of these documents must be written, many opportunities to write can be safely ignored or reduced to brief, unsubstantiated, and ineffective missives. And yet, if these documents are not written, we have little hope of changing the circumstances we find ourselves in: part-time labour forces, under-developed curricula, and under-funded research agendas. The short-term costs are often low, but the long-term effects of failing to engage with the broader communities of the university and the society can be severe.

Our engagement with our publics must be primarily rhetorical. Faber (1998) highlights "organizational change as a discursive process, sparked by a rhetorical conflict in an organization's narratives and images" (p. 217). Porter, Sullivan, Blythe, Grabill, and Miles (2000) also maintain that "institutional critique is an unabashedly rhetorical practice" (p. 612) where "sometimes individuals ... can rewrite institutions through rhetorical action"(p. 613). Too often, however, our field has not articulated "effective [rhetorical] strategies for institutional change" (Porter et al., 2000, p. 616). Porter et al. conceptualize "institutions as rhetorical systems of decision making that exercise power though the design of space (both material and discursive)" (p. 621) and that "these processes (rhetorical systems) are the very structure of the institution itself" (p. 625). The authors provide a case study of obtaining a usability lab for the professional writing program to show how administrators can open up rhetorical spaces that garner support for their programs (pp. 629-630). Schneider and Marback (2004) reiterate the role of rhetorical action in initiating institutional change for program development:

> the intellectual work of writing administration is best evaluated not as bureaucratic functionalism (or service), nor as ideal reform discourse (or scholarship), but rather as guided institutional action, as introduction of a critical discourse that makes knowledge in, for, and about a writing program. (p. 9)

The sorts of documents I outline below are situated examples of "locations where rhetorical reinterpretation of the structure of institutions is possible" (Schneider & Marback, 2004, p. 10). But as Jurecic (2004) notes in her description of the changes in the writing program at Princeton, the scope of this reinterpretation often means "learning how to work creatively within constraints to alter structures and practices so that the institution becomes more responsive and humane to those within it" (p. 71).

To reinvent our institutions, we need to focus on rhetorics of change: passion, emotion, language, and narrative and how these are used to convey our practices in the writing, rhetoric, and technical communication programs we inhabit. We need to emphasize "development" over "remediation," strategy over skills, narrative over certification. These are just some of the shared places and premises for argument, what Aristotle called special topoi, that convey our values and commitment. In meetings with other administrators, I emphasize the role of rhetoric and judgment over form and skills, of Aristotle and Toulmin over the Harbrace Handbook and reductive approaches to language use. Ultimately, I hope these arguments will help our publics understand the intellectual, interesting, and useful work performed by our discipline and programs.

RHETORIC FOR CHANGE

What would a rhetoric for change look like? In the 21st century Canadian educational context, administrators (especially those with a quantitative research methodology bias) tend to be drawn toward a rhetoric skewed toward quantitative data. National Survey of Student Engagement (NSSE) data, for example, provide one "benchmark" that can be used to compare performance across university departments and faculties. Each "unit" identifies goals, objectives, and deliverables (Center for Postsecondary Research, 2007). This language, however, creates an entire rhetorical world that most faculty engage only when all other options vanish. An alternative rhetoric for change focuses on constructing a rhetoric that privileges narrative and qualitative data that capture the richness of the intellectual, interesting, and useful work of programs.

The most important challenge of a rhetoric for change is audience. It is telling that, academics expend the vast majority of their words writing to other academics (e.g., see Hyland, H. Graves, Paré et al., this volume). As an administrator, I spend most of my time writing not only to academics, but also to other, non-academic, audiences. Table 1 associates audiences with the genre sets I write:

These last four audiences may include academics, but they are not academics in Writing Studies; the nature of our communications is administrative, not scholarly. Current writing research in genre studies suggests that instead of looking at these audiences as the determining factor, we give primacy to the genre as social action and genre sets. Each text belongs to a set of texts or textual artifacts; some of these are "stable for now" (Schryer, 1993) while others seem stable for longer than I'll be working there (for example, writing calendar copy and proposals to create new courses).

This model of dealing with publics helps keep the focus on social action—what actions do I want to accomplish through the various texts I create day after day? The remainder of this essay explores that question in the context of a series of the texts I have written.

Table 1. Audiences and genres in administrative writing.

Audience	Genre
Students	Brochure Display unit Web site Ads in Gazette (student paper)
Parents	Brochure Display unit
Alumni	Marie Smibert Stewardship Report
Faculty and staff	Western News (university-sponsored weekly paper)
Dean's Office	Budget request Academic plan
Provost's Office	Budget request Academic plan

RHETORIC FOR (AND WITH) STUDENTS

The immediate audience and main participant in the social exchanges of the Writing program are students. They write me frequently—almost always electronically—with questions, requests, complaints, and appeals. In some instances, reproducing what these students write can be the most effective way to communicate with other students:

> I am a Western Computer Science alumnus who took Writing 101 in the spring term of 2004. I just wanted to say that it was the single most important and useful course I took in university, and I use the skills I learned in that course every day at work. (personal communication, September 2005, reproduced on program web site)

I reproduced this e-mail message, sent to me by a former student, for prospective students of our courses because I thought other students would be persuaded by it. In this case, one student speaks, indirectly, to others without having the text re-written in the administrative voice of the program. The claim that the course is "important" relies on the further claim that the writer uses what he learned in the course "every day at work." One warrant for this argument connects the value of study with future employment goals, an argument that I thought students would agree with. Another e-mail reported a similar success story:

> I just got a phone call yesterday from the Ontario _____ News saying that my article will probably be in one of the next two issues (the editor just wasn't sure about space, but she does want to use my article). She also said that she thought my writing was very good and is going to recommend me for a job there writing breeder profiles!

The data here—that the student's article would be published—is used to lead to the consequence: the student will be recommended for a job as a writer for this publication. The warrant behind this good news report assumes that one of the purposes of taking this Writing course (Writing for Publication) is to get published and, if possible, hired as a writer.

When I revised the copy for the Writing program brochure and Web site (Figures 1 and 2 below), I engaged the discursive world that these, and other, students expressed with my own arguments.

Figure 1. Writing to students: the Web site.

In the texts in Figures 1 and 2, I was concerned with several ideas: that the students see their development as writers as ongoing; that they conceptualize writing as a broad range of kinds of writing; and that they understand writing as both academic and career-related. Beyond this initial introductory argument, the brochure and Web site describe the specifics of what the courses cover and what the requirements are for the certificate and diploma. In the design of these documents, we tried to convey professionalism through the production values (more successfully in the brochure, where we had a budget for a graphic designer).

On my office door, a less formal and more transient discursive field prevailed. At one point I posted the syllogism shown in Figure 3.

Ultimately, the appeal to money in Figure 3 falls short. It works with a portion of the student population, but not generally with the arts students. In fact, money and survival are low on Maslow's hierarchy of needs; at the top is self-fulfillment. With that in mind, I created the advertisement shown in Figure 4) and placed it in the student paper.

Representing Writing

Figure 2. Writing to students: the program brochure.

> Good writers get paid more (*Fortune* magazine, December 7, 1998, 244)
>
> Take a Writing course.
>
> Get paid more.

Figure 3. Posting on Writing Program Administrator office door.

> # Want to get published?
> # Improve your grades?
> # Prepare for a career as a writer?
>
> Consider taking Writing courses.
>
> **Certificate/Diploma in Writing Requirements**
> Writing 101
> 2 other Writing courses (Level 1)
> 4 other Writing courses (Level 2)
>
> **Special topics for 06/07**
> 291F: Technical Editing
> 292F: Rhetorical Theory
> 293G: Legal Rhetoric
> 294G: Humour Writing
>
> **200-level courses**
> Writing for Publication
> Creative Writing
> Advanced Exposition,
> Rhetoric,
> And Persuasion
>
> Technical Writing
> Teaching Writing
> Document Design
> Writing for Oral Presentation
> Contemporary Grammar
>
> For more information,
> Visit our website or
> Drop by our offices in
> UC 66
>
>
>
> www.uwo.ca/writing UC 66

Figure 4. Advertisement copy for student newspaper.

In this advertisement, I tried to draw attention to the desire many students have to see their name in print. Getting published, in any forum, validates the author/writer. About 25% of the students in the "Writing for Publication" class do get published, and their e-mails to their instructors convey the emotional satisfaction that they derive from seeing their names in print.

A RHETORIC FOR ALUMNI

As a graduate student at Ohio State in the late 1980s and early 1990s I witnessed firsthand the power of public discourse applied skillfully to promoting Writing Studies programs. Andrea Lunsford, then vice-chair for rhetoric and composition, led a grant writing effort for Writing Studies initiatives in a series of successful grant competitions both within the state and nationally. One competition involved assembling over a dozen binders of documents in support of arguments extolling the virtues of our program and the vision Ohio State had for extending writing instruction to the city of Columbus and beyond. The money raised from these various grants paid for all sorts of initiatives and research that would not have been possible without them.

At the University of Western Ontario, an alumnus—Marie Smibert—created an endowment for the Writing program. As one of my responsibilities I write an annual report of how this money is spent. One report began this way

> It was a pleasure to hear Ms. Smibert speak at the alumni meeting in late October, and wonderful to witness the standing ovation in response to her inspiring address and call for more attention to the development of writing skills in students. We spoke for a minute or two after the awards ceremony, and I appreciate the depth of feeling and commitment that Ms. Smibert has given to the common cause of improving the writing of students at Western.
>
> In the past year since I joined Western in July, 2005 we have begun a series of initiatives to develop the Writing Program, including some things that were only made possible through the Marie Smibert Writing Endowment. Last summer we developed a new brochure ...

Ms. Smibert had given a short speech at an alumni fundraising recognition event that I had attended. The speech, the last of 8 consecutive speeches lasting over an hour, drew an extended, standing ovation from the audience of over 200 people. The "depth of feeling" referred to above is not an exaggeration; this gathering of alumni reacted immediately and forcefully to her call for attention to the improvement of writing. By referring to this event I wanted her to know that I had been at the event and shared her goal of improving the writing of Western students. The rest of the document outlines the specific activities in which I had been engaged, including establishing a series of awards for student writers using money that she had donated to the University.

Since then I have written follow-up documents outlining how the Writing Program would spend further money that she was considering giving to the University. I have also met with, brainstormed, and then written proposals for obtaining funding from other potential sponsors to obtain money to support student internships, guest speakers, and course development. These arguments do not delve into the research literature of writing studies. There are no APA-style reference to (Graves 1994b). Instead, these conversations and the resulting documents focus on outcomes: what can we make happen, and why would that be a good thing? These documents are a product of social interactions—phone calls, e-mail queries, site visits by alumni representatives, drafts of documents outlining how gifts of time and money would change the curriculum—and are themselves part of the larger social system of fundraising and curriculum change within the university. Each document offers an opportunity to enact a rhetoric for change, rewriting, as Porter et al. (2000) emphasize, the space and role of Writing Studies in the institution, and changing how our various publics understand our programs and our discipline as a whole.

ARGUMENTS FOR THE ADMINISTRATION

Perhaps the most important group that writing studies scholars must address consists of university administrators. A third core area of rhetorical action takes place through documents discussed, negotiated, and written for various administrative offices of the university. Perhaps the most important of these are budget documents. Budget documents, contrary to their name, are not about money—at least, not directly. They are used to obtain money, but they do not involve sophisticated formulas and spreadsheets for program directors. The key aspect of a budget document is argument: why should the administration fund the writing program/department?

To illustrate this aspect of the discourse, consider the following argument for a new faculty position for our program:

> To support the development of the technical communication aspect of the Writing Program, we request a probationary ap-

> pointment in the area of technical communication to support the Faculty of Arts and Humanities strategic areas of focus on applied language study and visual culture (new media). This person would enable us to broaden the technical communication curriculum within the Writing Program. This person would also enable us to work effectively with the Faculty of Engineering as it expands its communication curriculum beyond the third-year course they presently offer. For example, this position would enable us to develop a graduate technical communication course that could be offered through the Advanced Design and Manufacturing Institute (ADMI) and at the Sarnia campus. The position would also enable us to run workshops for the graduate students and faculty in Engineering on writing for publication, writing dissertations, and presenting the results of research orally.

This request was not successful for many reasons, not the least of which was competition from within our Faculty. In addition, the link to the study of visual culture, while it made sense to me, was not followed up by conversations and negotiations with the Visual Arts department to get their support for the position. Contrast this request with the following argument that was successful:

> To support the development of the technical communication aspect of the Writing Program in the Faculty of Arts and Humanities, we request a probationary appointment in the area of technical communication. While this person would be located in the Faculty of Arts and Humanities, their work would be interdisciplinary in two ways: first, writing courses draw on communication genres from a wide variety of disciplines: reports, white papers, instructions, letters and memos; and second, these courses teach students from a wide variety of disciplines.
>
> This proposal responds to the Ontario Council of Academic Vice Presidents (OCAV) Guidelines for University Undergraduate Degree Level Expectations, an important outcomes benchmark for evaluating all university undergraduate programs in Ontario. Item 4 on this list is Communication Skills, "The ability to communicate information, arguments, and analyses accurately and reliably, orally and in writing to a range of audiences." This position would also help improve the National

[US] Survey of Student Engagement (NSSE) results because it contains four items that measure communication ability: 1c, 1d, 11c, and 11d. When students write in class, they often do so in groups, yet another measure of student engagement on the NSSE survey. Finally, it is imperative that UWO improve the ability of Western students to write because good writers on average earn three times more than poor writers (*Fortune*, December 7, 1998, 244).

The first proposal focuses on how this position would build the curriculum within the Writing program itself and then goes on to make the case that the position would also help with curriculum development in one other faculty, Engineering. While this made sense to me, it does not foreground the more general, widespread goals of the university as expressed in the budget documents sent out to solicit proposals. Those documents identified graduate education and the University's theme of "the best undergraduate experience at a research-based institution." The second proposal links explicitly to another theme identified in the budget—interdisciplinarity. By explicitly and immediately arguing that the new position would contribute to the university's goal of increasing our interdisciplinary work, the second proposal attracts the attention of senior university administrators.

The second paragraph of the second proposal highlights another important theme from the budget solicitation for proposals: the undergraduate student experience. In Ontario, the Ontario Council of [University] Academic Vice Presidents (OCAV) (2005) developed a set of degree expectations for university graduates in all academic programs. These guidelines identify six areas of competence: breadth and depth of knowledge, knowledge of methodologies, application of knowledge, communication skills, awareness of limits of knowledge, and autonomy and professional capacity. All students in every university program are expected to demonstrate "the ability to communicate, accurately and reliably, orally and in writing to a range of audiences." This requirement, set by the universities themselves to head off benchmarks imposed by the provincial ministry of education, creates an obligation to create and staff academic programs. The senior administrators who ultimately allocate budget lines were on the OCAV committee and presumably found this aspect of the argument persuasive.

Another argument targets "benchmarks" or "outcomes" using the National [US] Survey of Student Engagement (NSSE) . The University had adopted the National NSSE survey and scores as "benchmark" data to use to compare how successful we were in improving student engagement. NSSE data is used extensively in the United States and increasingly in Canadian universities to measure how well a particular university, faculty, and even department achieves its mission. The survey is given to students after their first year at the university and again six months after they graduate. Of the 80 questions on the survey, four questions ask students specifically about how well they have improved their oral and written communication skills. The comment about writing in groups links writing instruction to other questions on the NSSE survey and thus was meant to indicate that offering more writing instruction opportunities would improve the scores on other questions as well.

The last sentence of the successful proposal excerpt for a new position refers to an article in *Fortune* magazine. This brief article refers to a study done for the US Department of Education, but other reports could also have been cited to serve the same purpose (Conference Board of Canada, 2007; National Center for Educational Statistics, 2006; National Commission on Writing, 2003; 2004). Most recently, the TD Bank Financial Group (2007) issued a report called *Literacy Matters: A Call for Action*. The report identifies university graduates as examples of the startling decline in general literacy levels:

> [I]t is a quite shocking fact that many Canadians lack the necessary literacy skills to succeed in today's economy: a situation that is eroding their standard of living. Surveys show that almost four in 10 youths aged 15 have insufficient reading skills; while more than two in 10 university graduates, almost five in 10 Canadian adults and six in 10 immigrants have inadequate literacy. (TD Bank Financial Group, 2007, p. 2)

The report argues that these levels of literacy have both economic and social affects, including high school drop out, long-term unemployment, and crime rates (2). For writing program administrators, the following passage is of particular interest:

> However, one surprising statistic is that 22 per cent of university graduates do not achieve adequate scores in prose literacy. There is an age and immigration effect within these results. Between 11 to 14 per cent of Canadian-born university graduates aged 26 to 55 have inadequate prose literacy. This highlights the weak literacy in Canada's two official languages of older university graduates and immigrant university graduates. It also poses the question whether it is acceptable that roughly one tenth of Canadian-born university graduates do not have adequate prose

literacy. (TD Bank Financial Group, 2007, p. 8)

Because senior administrators interact with the Senate of the university, the Board of Governors, the press, alumni, and the federal and provincial governments, they must attend to documents like *Literacy Matters: A Call for Action*. By citing them in budget documents and linking writing initiatives to them, writing program administrators can attract budgetary resources to their programs. But to do so, we need to continue to share these documents when they become public. We also need to understand what Aristotle might call the "special topoi" of arguments, that is, the specific resources for argument, that appeal to university administrators and budget decision makers. To some extent these topoi vary from institution to institution, but public policy documents and reports can be used to create and support arguments for our work.

WRITING, KNOWLEDGE, ACTION

As the case analysis in this chapter illustrates, advancing programs in Writing Studies requires a robust effort to enact a "rhetoric for change" in our institutions. To build well-funded, research-based, and intellectually stimulating programs in universities, we need to write ourselves into the narratives of our institutions (Faber, 1998), insert ourselves into the rhetorical practices that affect decision-making (Porter et al., 2000), and create plans and documents for guided institutional reform (Schneider & Marback, 2004) within the constraints of our institutions (Jurecic, 2004).

This is done by working within genres or writing sets of documents that attempt to enact change in how writing is conceptualized (for example, as knowledge-making and not correctness in spelling). We need to create an awareness of how writing works to enhance student learning in their courses across the curriculum—writing is a fundamental part of learning in any subject area. As we continue this work, we need to attract research funding to continue the work by contributors to this volume of demonstrating how writing is a fundamental part of knowledge-making in disciplines throughout the university and beyond. For this purpose, we need to write to a variety of audiences using evidence from think-tanks, businesses, government studies, and students themselves. But most importantly, we need to continue to build a rhetoric for change specific to the worlds we work in so that we can apply the knowledge base of writing studies to improving the material circumstances of our programs and our discipline.

REFERENCES

Center for Postsecondary Research, Indiana University School of Education. (2007). National Survey of Student Engagement (NSSE). Retrieved from http://nsse.iub.edu/index.cfm

Conference Board of Canada. (2007). About Workplace Literacy and Basic Skills. Retrieved from http://www.conferenceboard.ca/workplaceliteracy/about-skills.aspFaber, B. (1998). Toward a rhetoric of change. *Journal of Business and Technical Communication, 12*(3), 217-237.

Fisher, A. (1998). The high cost of living and not writing well. *Fortune, 138*(11), 244.

Jurecic, A. (2004). Writing beyond the headline: Building a writing program at Princeton. *Writing Program Administrator, 27*(3), 69-81.

National Center for Educational Statistics, US Department of Education Institute of Education Sciences. (2006). National assessment of adult literacy: A first look at the literacy of America's adults in the 21st Century. NCES 2006-470.

National Commission on Writing. (2003). The neglected "R": The need for a writing revolution. College Entrance Examination Board.

National Commission on Writing (2004). Writing: A ticket to work ... or a ticket out. College Entrance Examination Board.

Ontario Council of Academic Vice Presidents (OCAV). (2005). Guidelines for university undergraduate degree level expectations. Retrieved from http://www.uwo.ca/univsec/handbook/general/OCAV_Guidelines_2005.pdf

Porter, J., Sullivan, P., Blythe, S., Grabill, J., & Miles, L. (2000). Institutional critique: A rhetorical methodology of change. *College Composition and Communication, 51*(4), 610-642.

Schneider, B., & Marback, R. (2004). Judging WPAs by what they say they do: An argument for revising "Evaluating the Intellectual Work of Writing Administration." *Writing Program Administrator, 27*(3), 7-22.

Schryer, C. F. (1993). Records as genre. *Written Communication, 10,* 200-234.

TD Bank Financial Group. (2007). *Literacy matters: A call for action.* Retrieved from http://www.td.com/economics/special/literacy0907.pdf

19 BUILDING ACADEMIC COMMUNITY THROUGH A TOWN HALL FORUM: RHETORICAL THEORIES IN ACTION

Tania Smith

Many faculty members have attempted to forge communities of knowledge and organizational practice in their classrooms that enable students to develop habits of thinking critically and acting like citizens in the wider community and workplace (Guarasci & Cornwell, 1997). Likewise, administrators are more frequently being asked to enhance students' experience of the university as "a community of learners" (Boyer Commission, 1998, p. 33) and to foster "student engagement" not only within classrooms, but also within the academic environment in general (Belcheir, 2003). Students also often wish to engage in experiential learning that integrates their academic knowledge and learning processes with social and organizational learning "both on and off campus," and "students want to be in conversation with college presidents and other administrators" (Long, 2002, pp. 9, 11).

These three constituencies have something in common: they can all benefit from the development of an overarching academic community that models in its organizational practices—and therefore most powerfully teaches and influences—civic engagement and responsibility. Indeed, in the vision of the undergraduate student participants of the Wingspread Summit on Student Civic Engagement in 2001, "students should also be viewed as producers of knowledge, not consumers" (Long, 2002, p. 13), and therefore, in order to model community problem-solving methods,

> Colleges and universities ... should make a commitment to

> finding new ways to foster student voice and incorporate student concerns into discussions and decision-making. If students, faculty, administration, and community partners are able to work together, they will have the potential to successfully address important campus and community issues. (Long, 2002, p. 13)

As Schoem and Hurtado's (2001) edited collection illustrates, various institutions now practice "intergroup dialogue" across academic hierarchies.

However, in many institutions, there are few traditions of collective knowledge-making that transcend the classroom, laboratory, and boardroom within academia—forums that include administrators, teachers and students working together to build and sustain their own community (Tetteh, 2004). The literature on "academic community" rarely considers students as members, and one critical analyst has considered the idea of students belonging to the academic community a conceptual danger (Kogan, 2000). Even publications that promote faculty-student mentorship and inclusion welcome only graduate students (Bennett, 2000, 2003; Hall, 2007). The key question for this chapter, therefore, is how scholarship in rhetoric could aid in the design of an academic community that invites all of its members into reflexive, collective knowledge-making about the values, purposes, and most effective structures and processes of its own organization.

To address this question, this chapter analyzes a town hall forum event initiated by the author in a liberal arts college of a large urban university as a "boundary event" (Wenger, 1998) to allow members of the college—students, faculty, administrators, and staff—to engage in a collaborative process of creating a shared understanding of the challenges facing the college and of engaging in shared knowledge-making about solutions. Drawing on rhetorical theories of exigence, genre, and identification, the chapter begins by situating the town hall analysis in the larger rhetorical exigence for academic community building and then briefly outlines some of the challenges the college faces that gave rise to the town hall event. The chapter then discusses key insights from Wenger's theory of communities of practice, as well as from rhetorical genre theory and from scholarship on town hall events to inform the analysis of the event's planning, the event itself, and the event's outcomes. My purpose here is not to provide a detailed analysis of the issues discussed at the event or even to conduct an in-depth analysis of the discourse that planned and constituted the event. Rather, in line with the purpose of this section of the book, the chapter aims to illustrate how theories of rhetoric and writing can inform the design of collaborative events for shared knowledge making and for facilitating academic community building and change in higher education institutions in ways that reflect their mission of civic engagement.

For this purpose, the chapter is based on Schön's (1995) recommendations for a "scholarship of application" through action research. This form of research involves "the generation of knowledge for, and from, action" by the researchers themselves (Schon, 1995, p. 31). The "practice knowledge—generated in, for, and through a particular situation of action—may be made explicit and put into a form that allows it to be generalized" to similar situations (Schön, 1995, p. 31). Theory can inform practice and help make sense of practice, and writing enables the integration of knowledge gained through cycles of action, reflection, and reflection-in-action. This method proceeds through interpretation and synthesis. It is therefore not subject to common critiques of qualitative methods such as "the plural of anecdote is not data"—such phrases portray the collection of second-hand anecdotes that cannot be verified, as well as claims that individual cases represent larger phenomena. In contrast, this chapter focuses on respected humanistic and social methods. It gathers communally verifiable evidence from direct observation and textual artifacts, and analyzes their features through a method that applies and tests general theories using the particularities of local practice. Informed performance, not universal truth, is the knowledge it aims to produce.

Accordingly, the chapter weaves together ethnographic narratives and thick descriptions of rhetorical practice, theories of written and oral rhetoric, and the analysis of rhetorical artifacts. Knowledge-making methods include rhetorical analysis of organizational documents, auto-ethnographic narratives of events personally experienced by the event organizer, and a macro-level analysis of the written materials produced by the town hall forum. The analysis concludes by discussing the various institutional outcomes of the event.

Far from a heroic tale, the theoretical and analytical elements of this case study provide an assessment of both the strengths and weaknesses of a process in which a deep understanding of written and spoken rhetoric influenced and interpreted a mode of building academic community within a small liberal arts college in a large research university.

RHETORICAL EXIGENCE FOR ACADEMIC COMMUNITY-BUILDING

Challenges for academic community building vary across higher education institution types, sizes, and locations, but in many of today's large research universities, even the most devoted of teachers, staff, and students can find it difficult to overcome the lines of traditional academic hierarchy that separate them. Academic communities can often work fairly well even in the presence of hierarchy, disciplines, and conflicting ideologies, but only when people practice what

Bennett (2000) refers to as genuine "hospitality," which "involves welcoming the other through openness in both sharing and receiving claims of knowledge and insight" (p. 92) can they engage in shared knowledge making.

As theorized by Bennett (2003), academic community is an ideal that is difficult to achieve in practice because of the "insistent individualism," "unilateral one-way power," and even the "simple fatigue" often experienced by all parties in academic contexts (pp. 53, 59). "Insistent individualism" is Bennett's term for a phenomenon in which people take advantage of a university's inherent divisions of labor, status, and knowledge in order to build empires of status, fame and power out of academic programs and individual careers. Bennett believes that "insistent individualism" is fostered in Western society in general, but may be heightened by academic culture because of the structures of reward for individualistic accomplishments. However, it can be overcome by introducing academic events and communication processes that enhance "relationality, hospitality, and conversation" (Bennett, 2003, p. 52).

Such practices of hospitality, collegiality, and collegial governance that soften academic hierarchies must be renewed as reigning ideologies shift regarding what makes a university a successful organization. Universities adopting a business approach focused on markets, efficiency, and division of labor can impose additional divisions between administrators, teachers, staff, and students as they are increasingly viewed (and more often view themselves) as managers, employees, and customers with economically-defined functions and identities (Bogue, 2006; Washburn, 2005). The business model is quite different from the educational model developed by the Boyer Commission (1998), which portrays the university as an "ecosystem" consisting of interdependent members of a multigenerational learning community (p. 9).

The institutional challenges described here, especially when they are brought on by gradual changes, do not necessarily lead to rhetorical action that addresses them. People need to be made aware that challenges create opportunities for beneficial communication. Rhetorical theorists like Bitzer (1968) have taught us that every rhetorical act starts with an "exigence," which is a need or a call from the "rhetorical situation" that makes a certain act of communication necessary or desirable. A communication strategy without an understanding of its exigence is bound to fail because speakers will not understand their rhetorical purposes and opportunities. An exigence, such as a perceived crisis in an academic community, also makes it possible to evaluate whether a rhetorical act has appropriately responded to the exigence and satisfied the needs of the communities and their audiences.

Other theorists provide further insight into how exigence can be crafted, not just discovered, in organizations. Vatz (1973) reversed Bitzer's causal relationship between exigence and act. He argued that rhetoric is not merely a response to an obvious situational exigence, but rhetoric itself creates exigence by giving certain features of a situation rhetorical "salience" or relevance to an act of communication. Because of this recursive and cyclical relationship, rhetorical situations are not objectively measurable and separable from rhetorical acts. Exigencies are also selectively perceived and justified. Therefore, collectively understanding and agreeing upon one's exigence is also a process involving interpretation and persuasion. In situations where a crisis is not obvious because communication has declined gradually over time, it is often necessary to take Vatz's approach and raise awareness of a need to communicate with one another.

However, once a community identifies an exigence for community-building rhetoric, it needs a healthy awareness of the complex nature of communities. Academic and non-academic "communities" are not idealized, homogeneous, harmonious collectives, but rather, the various identities, hierarchies and divisions within their own boundaries make it extremely difficult to engage in the ethical construction of a shared set of beliefs and values. Even the act of articulating a community boundary of who belongs and who does not is an act of persuasion that includes some and painfully excludes others. Faculty and students participating in a community discussion take real personal risks that may result in their own exclusion or loss of reputation, so the dialogue often involves the performance of existing hierarchies as an act of survival.

Rhetoric and writing scholars Ornatowski and Bekins (2004) caution that "community building" writing and speech used by particular people in strategic situations always involves selectively articulating various beliefs and values while excluding others. They demystify the notion that nonacademic non-profit or public communities are by definition any more virtuous, "civic," or harmonious than business and academic communities. As Burke (1970) might have cautioned, community can easily become a "god-term," a totalizing word used to organize all desirable knowledge and to typify all that is virtuous about rhetorical practice, and it can become an expression of an ideal or natural order which followers must obey.

However, whether community is imagined as a static ideal or a democratic process, it is constituted through continual negotiation and reinforcement of its purposes, boundaries, and roles—largely through rhetoric. Burke (1969) has aptly theorized that rhetoric is as much about creating divisions between people as it is about creating identification between people. He explains why and how a process of "division" occurs through communication. "In pure identification there would be no strife," he explains.

> But put identification and division ambiguously together, so that you cannot know for certain just where one ends and the

> other begins, and you have the characteristic invitation to rhetoric.... When two men collaborate in an enterprise to which they contribute different kinds of services and from which they derive different amounts and kinds of profit, who is to say, once and for all, just where 'cooperation' ends and one partner's 'exploitation' of the other begins? (Burke, 1969, p. 25)

In the college, where did students', administrators', and faculty members' "cooperation" begin and end, and what practices defined mere economic or academic "exploitation" of one another? Uncertainty about the borders and ethical practices of a community create an exigence, an "invitation to rhetoric." Identification and division will be shown at work below in the analysis of challenges facing the college.

SPECIFIC CHALLENGES FACING THE COLLEGE

The college that was the site of rhetorical action described in this chapter is veiled in order to emphasize the communication process and to protect the institutions and people involved. At the time of the events described here, the large research university in a major North American city had a student enrollment of over 20,000, 2,000 of which—full and part-time undergraduate and graduate students—were enrolled in a small liberal arts college.

The college's town hall event originated with discussions of what the event organizer and other members of the academic community perceived to be their challenges. Reduced government funding of postsecondary education, resulting budget cuts within the university at large, and the increased pace of the growth of the city and its demand for increased access to postsecondary education, had conspired to increase everyone's workload by increasing the faculty-student ratio. All units in the university were told to generate their own revenue, and liberal arts faculties found this more difficult to do than professional faculties. Fears regarding whose program would be shut down or cease growth in full-time faculty numbers due to insufficient resources weakened academic morale and made it difficult for everyone to practice open, trusting communication across levels of hierarchy. A general sense of cynicism and frustration arose about the academic planning process as individual administrators, students, and faculty were struggling with a high workload, tight budgets, high tuition, social and workplace isolation and competition, all of which weakened the community, making it less capable of dealing effectively with crises and changes.

Liberal arts programs in general, especially in research universities, often struggle to find appropriate rhetorical strategies to articulate their value to students, each other, and the public. Faculty members often regard with ambivalence the relationship between their perceived academic roles on the one hand and marketplace and student demands on the other hand (Axelrod, 2003; Nelsen, 2002; Pocklington & Tupper, 2002). Faculty feel concerned about

> shifting the balance between ... the technologically and professionally-oriented disciplines and the more academically oriented disciplines; undermining the sharing of knowledge, and the responsibility of academic researchers to adopt independent and critical stances; and displacing collegialism in favor of corporate-managerial practices of decision making. (Newson, 2000, p. 188)

Exemplifying this phenomenon, faculty members at this college had developed a culture that resisted consumerist or industry-driven approaches to education. They desired to distinguish their university programs from programs offered at community colleges or technical institutes, and they did so by emphasizing research, theory, and critical skills.

The students in the college, however, had a different concern about their college community. In classroom discussions about the identity and purpose of majors, students reported that their families and friends often asked them what they were studying, and they found it hard to articulate the scope, focus, and market value of their program. Liberal arts students were being ridiculed by peers and employers for their choice of a major that was often perceived as inferior to professional programs in nursing, business, engineering, or social work. The tension was especially acute for communication majors because "communication" had been frequently ridiculed in the media as a worthless degree. In addition to numerous derogatory jokes spread through the Internet, in an episode of *The Simpsons,* for example, a football player is ridiculed for having a communication degree and he confesses it is a "phony major" in which he learned nothing (Mula & Kruse, 1999).

A brief analysis of the communication program's Web site revealed how the faculty's public communication may have exacerbated the division between faculty, student, and society expectations for a communication degree. Under the heading "What is Communication?" their page proclaimed

> Communication is a broad interdisciplinary field that encompasses both social sciences and humanities perspectives on communication. At [university name], a BA degree in communication is a liberal arts degree that gives students the option

of taking a generalist approach, or concentrating in media or rhetoric and discourse.

This opening used the academic language of faculty members to articulate a field and its intellectual breadth. It seemed to be written by and for academics as a marker of disciplinary territory and philosophy. For students and the public, the opening did not attempt to define "interdisciplinarity," describe "social sciences and humanities perspectives on communication," name the studies denoted by the term "liberal arts," or explain the market value of either a "generalist approach" or concentrations named by the undefined terms "rhetoric and discourse."

The next section under the heading "Is this a Professional Degree?" articulated the communication program's resistance to perceived demands from students for practical job training:

> It is not intended to be a professional degree, so you will not receive specialized training in media production broadcasting, journalism, film, etc., nor training beyond an introductory level in public relations or organizational communication. While not specifically a professional program, it will help prepare students for careers in both print and electronic journalism, public relations, as well as in business, politics and other related fields. The courses you will take emphasize a critical perspective on communication as a cultural process.

This Web site explained neither how "a critical perspective on communication as a cultural process" ... "will help prepare students for careers" named, nor why this goal would be important to the college and its students. A later section titled "Help with Finding a Job" vaguely claimed that "the breadth of knowledge that a Communication Studies degree represents may improve your flexibility and long-term career prospects." The Web site stated (now in everyday language, clearly addressing students) that it was the students' job, not the college's, to supplement the program with job skills training through highly skilled volunteer positions, enrolling in the co-op program, or taking additional practical degrees, certificates or workshops. Thus the program distanced itself from students' and society's views of the practicality of a postsecondary degree.

As this necessarily brief sketch of the college's challenges indicates, the situation of the college called for a rhetoric that would overcome the divisions expressed in the communication program's document. The written articulation of this divide made it difficult for scholars, teachers, students, and the general public to understand their common ground and interdependence, an understanding which is essential to a healthy academic community. The college needed to discover, in Burkean (1969) terms, that neither were students merely "exploited" for their tuition, nor were students the marketplace merely "exploiting" academics for certification. This process required learning how to use discourse to identify with each other as a community.

DESIGNING COMMUNITIES OF PRACTICE FOR ACADEMIA

For guidance to the process of analyzing and designing communication that enables academic community building, I turned to Wenger's (1998) theories of "communities of practice" (CoP) and "learning communities" as they can inform how shared communication and engagement constitute communities within academia, and how these communities can be designed in real institutions to structure and enable learning. The town hall forum in the college can be seen as an exploration of the feasibility and relevance of this model of community-building within academic institutions.

Appropriate to the vision of universities, Wenger's (1998) concept of CoPs portrays them as "a locus for the acquisition of knowledge" as well as "for the creation of knowledge" (p. 214). CoPs are valuable for universities because effective knowledge-making abilities and roles for students, teachers, and researchers are acquired most efficiently and deeply when novices and experts are embedded in a real social context that makes their communication meaningful. Learners develop their roles and communication together through apprenticeship and coaching within a mixed community of expert practitioners, marginal and peripheral members who form the community of practice.

However, according to Wenger (1998), an institutional unit such as a classroom (or a college within a university) is not necessarily a community of practice: "It may consist of multiple communities of practice, or it may not have developed enough of a practice of its own" (p. 119). CoPs may also be unrealized: they may be only "potential" among people who share a form of association, or they may be "latent" among people who have had a past association (Wenger, 1998, p. 228). Wenger continually states that CoPs—the realized, active communities that enable organizational action and learning—are defined by three features: 1) a joint enterprise, 2) mutual engagement that increases social bonds, and 3) a shared repertoire of behaviors and communication strategies.

Although Wenger (1998) claims "learning cannot be designed" because learning happens with or without design, he emphasizes that "there are few more urgent tasks than to design social infrastructures that foster learning" (p. 225). Whether pursued consciously or subconsciously, learning is inevitable within a CoP, and designs can help to foster these communities.

The building of a college-wide community that bridges or overlaps several communities of practice, even temporarily, can be facilitated through what Wenger (1998) calls a "boundary encounter," a communication event whereby a "broker," an individual member of multiple communities, enables people to travel across boundaries into each other's communities. One powerful form of a boundary encounter is a "delegation" event, which involves a number of participants from separate but related communities who come together to negotiate meaning. A boundary encounter can be a discrete event, or it can evolve into a "boundary practice":

> If a boundary encounter—especially of the delegation variety—becomes established and provides an ongoing forum for mutual engagement, then a practice is likely to start emerging. Its enterprise is to deal with boundaries and sustain a connection between a number of practices by addressing conflicts, reconciling perspectives, and finding resolutions. The resulting boundary practice becomes a form of collective brokering. (Wenger, 1998, p. 114)

These boundary encounters can eventually lead to the formation of CoPs. The town hall event to be analyzed here can be seen as an attempt at coordinating a "delegation" type of boundary encounter through which a community of practice could emerge.

To create the kind of boundary encounter theorized by Wenger (1998), its design must "create channels of communication among practices" and "coordinate multiple kinds of knowledgeability" (p. 247). A boundary encounter is a new genre of communication, or collection of genres, that mediates and coordinates communities and their multiple forms of knowledge. Theories of genre therefore play an important role in guiding the design of such a boundary event.

RHETORICAL GENRE THEORY FOR ACADEMIC EVENT DESIGN

Rhetorical genre theory explains how genres of communication reflect and constitute a community. Genres of communication, such as "journal article," "faculty meeting," and "town hall" are not defined by their internal linguistic form and structure (such as the headings and style of a scholarly book chapter), but, rather, by the social actions and communal contexts that make them meaningful (Miller, 1984).

As Miller theorized in her seminal 1984 article "Genre as Social Action," a genre is embedded in and constituted by social action. Genres are solidified through repeated use until they gradually become known as a typified response to a rhetorical exigence. When audiences are familiar with genres, they approach them with expectations about the types of communication that will occur in them, and they also tend to take on the identities and roles that writers, speakers or audiences usually play in such genres. Miller and other genre theorists (Artemeva, 2005; Ervin, 2006) acknowledge Vatz' (1973) critique and modification of Bitzer (1968): genres and their rhetoric are not just a product of social action, but rhetors can use existing genres, or construct new hybrid genres, to actively construct or maintain rhetorical situations and exigence.

According to a rhetorical understanding of genre, genres of communication that arise in organizations (such as an academic unit within a research university) accomplish the mutual goals of people in the organization. Rhetorical genre theorists have taught that the systems of activity determine the form and content of a "repertoire" of written and oral genres, and that these genres in turn shape the kinds of activity occurring through them. Orlikowsky and Yates (1994) explain that "A community's genre repertoire indicates its established communicative practices. Hence, the concept of genre repertoire can serve as a useful analytic tool for investigating the structuring of a community's communicative practices over time" (p. 546).

Genre change is linked to organizational change. Communities and genres are intertwined, and as the community changes, so do its genres. As Bazerman (2003) writes, "the emergence of genre is intricately bound with changing professional roles and relations, changing institutions, the emergence of professional norms and professional identities, ideology, epistemology, ontology, and psychology" (p. 7). New genres can enter existing repertoires and alter people's ways of thinking and understanding their identities and communities. New genres are necessary to facilitate new forms of collaborative activity between multiple activity systems or CoPs, such as those of students, administrators, and faculty members. This enables us to see the role of rhetorical action in transforming an institution.

However, genres are also about communication habits and regularities that resist change. When people face a new communication situation, they will tend to look for familiar generic patterns. Genres reify, or make concrete, a community's abstract values, activities, and knowledge. If one wishes to create new communities that bridge existing ones, one cannot simply adjust the content and style of the communication genres currently in use in each. Yet because genres evoke familiar behaviors, a completely unfamiliar genre, or a genre viewed to be inappropriate to social action, may fail to be understood.

In the case of universities, the three primary goals or social actions are teaching, research, and service (to institution and community). However, if these activities and roles within an institution are functionally separated by institutional boundaries with their own leaders, they may each have separate generic repertoires. Thus, some genres may arise around teaching practices, others around research, and others around university or community service. Yet faculty members and administrators need to have the genre knowledge to communicate in all three of these sets of repertoires, and universities' internal cohesion and educational effectiveness will benefit by inviting students to participate productively in each. Social actions need to be coordinated across members of all three domains, and there are few genres that enable this cross-domain interaction.

Community brokers must therefore be very careful in choosing, modifying, and portraying new, boundary-spanning genres of communication, especially in the beginning phases of facilitating communication across institutional boundaries. As research reviewed by Orlikowski and Yates (1994) suggests, "at the formation of a new community, members may import norms from other communities in which they have participated" (p. 548). In this case study, the import was the genre of the town hall.

THE POTENTIAL OF THE TOWN HALL GENRE

Scholars have traced the history of the town hall to the meetings of the colonial-era United States, where deliberations and debates would be held in a town's central hall. The town hall is commonly discussed in the context of a variety of genres that promote "participatory democracy" (Delli Carpini, Cook, & Jacobs, 2004, pp. 315-316). Participatory democracy is "talk-centric" rather than "voting-centric," and "focuses on the communicative processes of opinion and will formation that precede voting" (Chambers, 2003, p. 308). Delli Carpini and colleagues (2004) also note that experimental research "has found that face-to-face communication is the single greatest factor in increasing the likelihood of cooperation" (p. 324). In this way, a town hall could help participants aim for Burkean (1969) rhetorical identification and Bennett's (2000) academic hospitality, especially in light of the Web site communication that had demonstrated division.

The benefits of the town hall's local, inclusive, slow, multi-directional communication over quick, one-way communication are reflected in an 1881 speech given by Whitelaw Reid at a town hall in Xenia, Ohio. He argued that it should be the forum for political discourse "in the community, from the community, and about the immediate concerns of the community. It should stimulate what we may call a real municipal life" (Reid, 1881, pp. 25-26). The slow and difficult exercise of face to face deliberation on local issues such as morality, taxation and education, in contrast with the short-cut to debate in the print newspapers, would help a community achieve the benefits of democracy. The process of the town hall, therefore, had a practical educational value. According to Reid, benefits of the town hall discourse would include not just wiser decisions but "broader views of life and duty; a recognition of the fact that something can often be said on the other side; a wider toleration than is always common in rural communities, of what other people think, and of their right to think it, in politics, education, temperance or religion" (pp. 27-28). In a similar vein, Mendelberg (2002) explains that "if it is appropriately empathetic, egalitarian, open-minded, and reason-centered, deliberation is expected to produce a variety of positive democratic outcomes," such as tolerance for diverse views, the ability to justify one's views, and the tendency to give up adversarial approaches and embrace interdependence (p. 153).

However, the town hall genre has not always lived up to its ideals. Lukensmeyer and Brigham (2002), for example, argue that as they have been recently used in American political culture, town halls have been ineffective.

> Public hearings and typical town hall meetings are not a meaningful way for citizens to engage in governance and to have an impact on decision making. They are speaker-focused, with experts simply delivering information or responding to questions. Little learning occurs, for citizens or decision makers, because airing individual concerns too often devolves into repetitive ax grinding, grandstanding, or even a shouting match between various stakeholders. In the end, decision makers don't know which points of view have the most salience for various groups because there has been no authentic, informed exchange of opinion and no opportunity to build a true consensus. (Lukensmeyer & Brigham, 2002, pp. 351-352)

Surely, then, as an imported genre, the town hall inherited valuable ideals of democratic deliberation from its past, but also required customization to the situation at hand, which was important to address in the planning of the event.

ANALYSIS OF EVENT PLANNING COMMUNICATION

The idea for an event first came about as I, then an untenured communication professor, conversed with a senior professor about the divisions and miscommunication between faculty and students. In a collective e-mail to our college administrators, we both suggested some ideas for increasing constructive dialogue with students. While they resisted the initiation of any additional formal committee or ombudsperson, they approved our suggestion to hold an informal "faculty and student brainstorming session" about how to meet some of the challenges that our college community faced in its academic programs.

Since I was not a member of all three communities, the event needed to be collaboratively planned and executed by a loosely defined planning committee. When the administrator of student affairs offered her assistance and support, I gradually gathered a planning team of about eight students and another faculty member. Communicating about the institutional and program-specific challenges outlined above as the exigence or invitation to a rhetoric of identification, we set about co-constructing a new event through which students, staff, teachers, and administrators could talk constructively about the issues related to the identity and goals of their programs. We went about planning for the event in a cautious, gradual fashion, initiating a planning process six months prior to the event. Given everyone's workload, effective planning required time.

Collaborative writing, revision, and the use of both online and print communication were essential to the process of planning and communicating about the event. To make the planning process open to all who were interested, the university's online course management system facilitated planners' discussions and welcomed others into the dialogue who could not meet with us face-to-face. This is where a written outline of the meeting was distributed to the planning committee, and decisions were made regarding which planners would become event volunteers, panelists, or fill other roles. By the close of the actual event, this online forum had 29 members and 17 messages, and 10 people were active in attending face-to-face planning meetings. The messages functioned less often as a live discussion and more often as a location for posting updated written information about the event. Planning meetings and follow up e-mail among meeting participants were the primary genres of communication. The fact that oral discussion was preferred by planners despite their busy schedules demonstrates the value of physical, oral forums for "mutual engagement" when designing an event for the purpose of facilitating a CoP.

The involvement of administrators also brought legitimacy to our event and reassured both administrators and other participants that it would not be counterproductive. Members of the planning group met face-to-face with our dean and associate dean the month before the event to finalize the meeting's context, purpose, methods, and advertising strategy. In support of the forum, the associate dean arranged for the room and sponsored some light refreshments for the event. The college's main offices were to be closed during the event in order to enable administrative support staff members to participate, reflecting the value we placed on their participation as members of our college community. The dean also spoke as one of several panelists, and even invited to the event a consultant to the senior administration who was conducting a study of the potential restructuring of the liberal arts college. Involvement of all members of our academic community was essential to make this a community-building event.

As Wenger (1998) cautions, vital community engagement is "bounded" by "physiological limits" (p. 175) since we can only be in one place at a time, we can only handle so much complexity, and it takes physical and mental energy for direct, sustained relational engagement with people. As a 1994 report issued by the American Association of University Professors showed, faculty work on average between 48 and 52 hours per week, and college faculty members were indeed very busy (AAUP, 1994). However, full-time faculty were invested in the academic community and had already established relationships of engagement, so that they were more likely to participate than students. In contrast, students normally engaged with only one faculty member at a time within the context of scheduled classes that were already quite demanding of their energy. Outside of class time, most students in the university engaged in paid work to afford tuition and the cost of living in the city. Moreover, according to the university's institution-wide student surveys, approximately 50% of students spent 6-15 hours a week commuting between campus, home, and work because of a lack of affordable student housing on and near campus. Unsurprisingly, students spent little time on campus outside of attending classes: few were involved in extracurricular activities, approximately 50% of students reporting 0-1 hour per week in co-curricular activities and 30% reporting 1-5 hours per week. Attending an extracurricular event such as this, although short, would be costly of time and energy for faculty members, but even more so for students. Communication design had to take account of participants' limited resources for engagement and would have to involve carefully crafted and audience-targeted persuasion.

Early in the planning process, the faculty and student "brainstorming session" was therefore renamed a "town hall." It was hoped that this genre would raise expectations of an event of political weight and seriousness, thereby invoking in participants an identity of responsible citizens who should gather to discuss the issues we faced. I added the term "forum" as well, calling it a "town hall forum" because a "forum" was a more broadly known term in our culture for an open, public discussion and would at least give a hint to those who were unfamiliar with town halls.

However, student participation was challenging because of the failure of a previous "town hall" event on campus. A university-wide town hall to discuss the university's budget, hosted by the Student's Union and delivered by the university's senior administration, was advertised by e-mail to every student at the university. As the student newspaper reported, it was finally cancelled due to "virtually zero attendance."

The town hall genre was quite different from the traditional genres through which student voices were channeled at the college. Student communication was usually both called forth and controlled by the mediation of genres used by administrators or teachers (a course evaluation form, a student satisfaction survey, an assignment, an exam, or an appeal hearing). These are genres through which students are evaluated by those who have more power than they, or in which students are used as research subjects to evaluate their courses and teachers. The teacher-student power relationship within a course context can constrain student communication so that when students freely express a legitimate concern or problem outside of these formal channels, or even offer a helpful suggestion, students know it may easily sound like a threat or a complaint against the instructor, rather than as an opportunity for student and instructor to work together to improve future courses or the program as a whole.

Therefore, educating students about the purpose and potential effectiveness of the forum was crucial. The exigence for this event had to be discerned by its audiences as something more than a reaction to student apathy, a negative appeal that would put students on the defensive and make them more aware of their reasons for non-communication. It had to be worth their time and effort, more than an administrative feel-good talk that would inform us of policies made by others. The event also had to be guarded against devolving into the opposite, such as a corporate pep talk, for instance, a venting session, or a heated argument that would just make divisions worse. It clearly had to hold out an opportunity to break down the negativity and misunderstandings articulated by Bennett (2000) and to enact the forms of academic hospitality that he theorized.

In our event advertisements our planning team tried to articulate the event's purposes so that the community could better understand this unfamiliar genre. The social meaning of the event was needed to justify drawing people into a new way of communicating with each other. Our advertisement for the event began with the statement *"We all know our college is facing serious challenges.* Now let's discuss solutions." This advertisement thus activated the resources of Burkean "identification." It enabled each person to imagine whichever challenges they felt were most important to our faculty, rather than having us articulate those challenges in advance, and it raised curiosity. Through the use of "our" and "we," we hoped to create a sense of identification with the college's interests.

To help provide a little more focus after the vague opening statement, three main questions were posed on the advertisement: "What is our college all about?" "How do we build more value into our work, our courses, research, programs, and degrees?" and "What should we save and protect for the future?" These questions, which we drafted and revised together in our planning meetings, provided a structure, topic, and purpose for the communication that occurred at the meeting, making the event not merely a matter of one-way information dissemination but of the negotiation of meaning and of community boundaries.

In order to ensure that the invitation was well adapted to an audience of faculty and students, the president of the undergraduate communication students' club and I worked together to draft and distribute the e-mail invitations to faculty and to students. The week before the meeting, I finalized and posted our event advertisement posters on walls and sent e-mail reminders to planners and those who said they intended to attend. The personal reminders through the familiar channels of e-mail gave people a sense that their individual contributions were strongly desired and that they would meet with people they already knew personally.

ANALYSIS OF COMMUNICATION DURING THE EVENT

The event had 33 participants of which 18 were students, which means that only a small fraction of all our college's students attended. However, half of the participants were staff and faculty members. Approximately 25% of our full-time faculty and nonacademic staff were present, and this included a significant portion of our administrators, including the dean, two associate deans, a division head, and three program coordinators. The range of participants was reflective of the "delegation" boundary encounter described by Wenger (1998).

The overall plan of the meeting (described more fully below) was to open with a general introduction of purpose and plan, and then to proceed through four stages of structured written and oral discourse activity (several panelist speeches, large group discussion, small group discussion with note-takers, and a collaborative free-writing activity). Each of these stages engaged the participants more actively than the stage before it: first they participated as listeners to the panelists, then as a large group of idea contributors, then as small group problem-solving participants, and then as individual writers and readers of suggestions and thanks.

To open the meeting, I addressed the issue of genre expectations by comparing the town hall to familiar genres and articulating rhetorical purposes: the meeting was not an official decision-making meeting like the bimonthly college council, but it still had important purposes and outcomes: to inform each other of what is going on in different areas of the faculty, to understand each other's unique perspectives, and to generate productive ideas. In accordance with the communication ethics of our community, I informed the participants at the outset that event planners were volunteering to take notes during the event and we were going to compile a report and distribute it to the faculty members and those who provided their e-mail addresses. We then explained the anonymity and confidentiality protections and clarified that participants who did not feel comfortable with our process could choose to avoid participating in ways they did not wish.

After the general introduction, four panelists—the dean, a staff member, an instructor and a student—gave brief speeches about how they perceived the strengths and challenges of our faculty. This representative panel sent the message that people of all levels of status and hierarchy were authorized to have a voice at this meeting.

We then moved to a large-group discussion facilitated by an instructor, during which we wrote on the chalkboard the major issues that participants had noted in the panelists' talks and the participants were able to suggest their own issues. This exercise ensured that we gained an understanding of each other's interpretation of our rhetorical situation and exigency, and that we as the event planners and panelists were not merely imposing our own ideas. The exigencies that people reported were largely those discussed in the opening sections of this article: organizational hierarchy and division, the language used to explain the program, and the perceived and real market value and social value of liberal arts degrees. Students also spoke of the need to learn more about global cultures and issues of globalization.

Then, as the third step, we organized these issues into four general topic areas and broke the participants into four smaller groups to analyze the problems further and brainstorm solutions to the issues. In line with the purpose of the event as a boundary encounter, we ensured each small group had a diverse composition of administrators, teachers, students, and nonacademic staff. Volunteer student note-takers (members of the planning committee and students I knew personally) accompanied each group to record ideas as well as participate. This note-taking practice ensured that students' perspectives and vocabulary were involved in the authoritative act of translating oral to written communication.

After the groups had some time to discuss, we facilitated a collaborative writing and reading activity called "inkshedding" (described below), a practice developed by Reither and Hunt (Hunt, 2004), which involves informal writing in response to an issue or a presentation as well as reading and possibly commenting on the responses of other participants (for a detailed explanation and study of inkshedding, see Horne, this volume). This final activity was chosen because it ensured that each person was given the opportunity to contribute a written, articulated message. Oral discussion is often dominated by the most outspoken or powerful persons, and feasible suggestions and well-reasoned comments are more often a product of written reflection. Inserting written communication in an oral forum would guard against the negative features of town halls noted by Lukensmeyer and Brigham (2002). It would also ensure that undergraduate students also had a written voice as co-producers of institutional knowledge alongside faculty and administrators, as the Wingspread conference participants desired (Long, 2002).

The inkshedding activity engaged the full resources of rhetoric, not only written language: it engaged spatial, aural and physical communion, like a dance without music, orchestrated in respectful communal silence. It created institutional time and space for participants to contribute their written ideas without specific questions or prompts other than those provided by the event itself. When each participant finished their own piece of writing, they left it on the desk, got up and found another piece of paper with someone else's comments. While they read another person's inkshed, they could underline what they thought was important, and they could add comments of their own if they agreed or disagreed. Most participants had never experienced inkshedding before, but when the time came to get up to read and comment on other people's thoughts, they found it quite exciting. Participants could be observed looking for another inkshed they had not read yet, and mild interjections and quiet laughter could be heard from readers. Finally they were able to return to look at their own inkshed and see what others had written on it.

At the end of the meeting, participants submitted their inkshedding papers to the event organizers. These documents helped provide direct, anonymous quotations of participants for the event report.

ANALYSIS OF EVENT OUTCOMES

A few weeks after the event, the event report was distributed to over 50 individuals by e-mail, including to the event participants, as well as to additional people involved in the planning phases and to several people who were unable to attend, but had expressed an interest in the event.

Through the report, the event was able to influence institutional change, not just generate mutual understanding among participants. As a result, the town hall became part of the college's history, open to criticism and praise, and available for quotation in planning documents. It reified the experience of participants and made their shared knowledge and knowledge-making process accessible to others as an institutional object. According to Wenger (1998), reification "shapes our experience .... by focusing our attention in a particular way and enabling new kinds of understanding" (pp. 59-60).

The event was very successful according to the written and oral responses of participants and the outcomes described below. Although the student attendance was small, the success should be measured in light of the challenges facing our initiative. Our event, for example, was able to draw more students than the Student's Union's university-wide town hall forum four months earlier.

By permitting the open discussion of topics of mutual concern, participating students were able to articulate their own vision of liberal education that seemed to respond to the divisions revealed in our communication Web site. Although it was not a theme or topic forced upon the discussion, our town hall enabled our faculty to better understand students' desires for experiential learning opportunities, such as community service learning and co-op learning, so that their desire was no longer imagined as mere careerism opposed to the theoretical and humanistic aims of our educational programs. Participants began to understand that both aims and value sets could overlap and coexist, or at least be communicated by way of respectful contrast as a necessary complement to one another.

By discussing how we as instructors could balance and combine these values, we developed our collective capacity to construct and provide experiential learning opportunities—we came away with practical ideas and now had some idea of how to draw on the creative energy of our students to achieve our common educational goals. This communication enabled the articulation of our common ground and fed the imagination of an academic community that crossed boundaries.

In addition to these more conceptual outcomes, the town hall resulted in some tangible decisions and new structures designed to continue the kinds of boundary practices the town hall forum was meant to encourage.

In a college meeting one week later, faculty members and administrators raised specific recommendations and proposals that they explicitly said were influenced by the town hall dialogue. The program head for communication brought forward a proposal for a new course in experiential learning, which was eventually accepted into the curriculum. An associate dean proposed a revision of the list of courses in the "world areas," citing what students had said about the internationalization of their education.

In addition, the event's focus on experiential learning catalyzed the creation of our college's community service learning (CSL) committee the following summer. Prior to the committee's formation, the college had been unaware that its community-based learning activities were part of the larger CSL movement in North America. Many instructors were happily surprised to discover that their peers in other programs of study were also involved in service-learning.

The following year the CSL committee held a forum among several of the college's community partners, students, faculty and administrators and subsequently circulated an event report to participants. The report was voluntarily compiled by an undergraduate student who was also writing an honors thesis on service-learning experiences of students in the college. The committee's co-chairs and members continued to actively support and promote CSL in the college and university at large through supporting CSL grant-writing and research, mentoring CSL instructors and students, and creating a new CSL course (separate from the experiential learning course mentioned above).

In addition to these new initiatives, the outcomes also included a new position. The dean soon appointed another instructor to a new part-time senior administrative position in the college that was specifically designed to bridge administrative and student communities and enhance co-curricular engagement among students.

In the same community-bridging spirit, the articulation of the divisions between faculty and students enabled the co-design of an innovative program to foster mutual engagement between faculty and students. A new senior-level practicum course on peer mentoring and collaborative learning educated student leaders who collaborated with participating instructors to serve as peer mentors to the students taking their courses. Over the years, this boundary practice developed into a CoP that was institutionalized through curriculum and funding. Teachers' and students' relationships became more like the model of hospitable community outlined by Bennett (2000).

Finally, the event also had implications for my organizational identity as a rhetoric and writing studies scholar, which I felt expanded in unexpected ways. Besides co-chairing a service-learning committee and developing a new boundary practice, I was also invited to participate in a few university-wide task forces and committees. I was also better able to argue for the value of rhetorical studies to the college when it was threatened.

However, much community-building work remained to be done after this experimental "boundary encounter." While it gave birth to curricular and administrative changes and a new community of practice, the town hall itself did not lead to a CoP. The town hall event was not repeated because of the collective time and effort involved and because the rhetorical situation changed.

This set of outcomes, while disappointing in some ways, is consistent with Wenger's (1998) portrayal of the experimental and temporary nature of boundary encounters and the fluidity of CoPs: "They negotiate their own enterprise.... They arise, evolve, and dissolve according to their own learning, though they may do so in response to institutional events.... They shape their own boundaries" (p. 241). The learning that occurred through the town hall strengthened its constituent communities of practice. Community-building knowledge, as well as knowledge of rhetorical practice, developed through the event were not lost: they still resided in the shared history of the participants. Members of "latent" and "potential" communities of practice, as described by Wenger (1998), could once again design appropriate "boundary encounters" to bridge divisions between communities.

CONCLUSION

As the case of the college town hall forum analyzed in this chapter illustrates, the fragmentation of academic communities in universities is a situation that calls for creative rhetorical action. Simply improving the effectiveness of existing communication modes in courses and meetings is unlikely to enable an academic community to function as a whole. Mutual encouragement and instruction between faculty and students—in the increasingly narrow institutional space beyond formally structured engagement in credit courses and business meetings—is sorely needed if faculty aim to teach ethical or democratic communication practices, to collectively demonstrate the value of the liberal arts to the public, to resolve internal institutional divisions, and to meet the external pressures and opportunities facing higher education and society.

In this context of fragmentation, rhetoric and writing studies provide theories and models for the bridging of often divided communities, the facilitation of collaborative knowledge making, the creation of a constructive shared understanding of challenges faced by academic communities, as well as the generation of solutions. Traditionally concerned with facilitating the participation of citizens in democratic deliberation and decision making, rhetorical theories can be put to action in the spirit of the Boyer Commission and the Wingspread Statement on Student Civic Engagement and engage students as co-producers of institutional knowledge for democratic decision making. After all, a complete education not only forms the mind through theory, but also offers opportunities to learn experientially within one's own institutional community. An academic community, despite all its imperfections, can become a working example of how it hopes citizens and their leaders will practice communication in organizational and public contexts.

REFERENCES

AAUP. (1994, January-February). The work of faculty: Expectations, priorities, and rewards. *Academe, 80*(1), 35-48.

Artemeva, N. (2005). A time to speak, a time to act: A rhetorical genre analysis of a novice engineer's calculated risk taking. *Journal of Business and Technical Communication, 19*(4), 389-421.

Axelrod, P. (2003). *Values in conflict: The university, the marketplace, and the trials of liberal education.* Montreal: McGill-Queen's University Press.

Bazerman, C. (2003). Social forms as habitats for action. *Journal of the Interdisciplinary Crossroads, 1*(2), 123-142. Retrieved from http://education.ucsb.edu/bazerman/articles/3.habitats.doc

Belcheir, M. J. (2003, February). *The campus environment as viewed through the lens of the National Survey of Student Engagement.* Research Report 2003-01. Retrieved from http://cpr.iub.edu/uploads/Belcheir,%20M.J.%20(March,%202003).pdf

Bennett, J. B. (2000). Hospitality and collegial community: An essay. *Innovative Higher Education, 25*(2), 85-96.

Bennett, J. B. (2003). Constructing academic community: Power, relationality, hospitality, and conversation. *Interchange, 34*(1), 51-61.

Bitzer, L. (1968). The rhetorical situation. *Philosophy and Rhetoric, 1,* 1-14.

Bogue, E. G. (2006). A breakpoint moment: Leadership visions and values for trustees of collegiate mission. *Innovative Higher Education, 30*(5), 309-326.

Boyer Commission on Educating Undergraduates in the Research University. (1998). *Reinventing undergraduate education: A blueprint for America's research universities.* Retrieved from http://naples.cc.sunysb.edu/Pres/boyer.nsf/

Burke, K. (1969). *A rhetoric of motives.* Berkeley, CA: University of California Press. Retrieved from http://books.google.ca/books?id=bEo8HlSCodcC

Burke, K. (1970). *The rhetoric of religion: Studies in logology.* Berkeley, CA: University of California Press. Retrieved from http://books.google.ca/books?id=sHD-u9uK-AAC

Chambers, S. (2003). Deliberative democratic theory. *Annual Review of Political Sciences, 6,* 307-326.

Delli Carpini, M. X., Cook, F. L., & Jacobs L. R. (2004). Public deliberation, discursive participation, and citizen engagement: A review of the empirical literature. *Annual Review of Political Science, 7,* 315-344.

Ervin, E. (2006). Rhetorical situations and the straits of inappropriateness: Teaching feminist activism. *Rhetoric Review, 25*(3), 316-333.

Guarasci, R., & Cornwell, G. H. (1997). *Democratic education in an age of difference: Redefining citizenship in higher education* (1st ed.). San Francisco: Jossey-Bass Publishers.

Hall, D. E. (2007). *The academic community: A manual for change.* Columbus, OH: Ohio State University Press.

Hunt, R. (2004). *What is inkshedding?* Retrieved from http://www.stthomasu.ca/~hunt/dialogic/whatshed.htm

Kogan, M. (2000). Higher education communities and academic identity. *Higher Education Quarterly, 54*(3), 207-216.

Long, S. E. (2002, August). *The new student politics: The Wingspread statement on student civic engagement* (2nd ed.). Retrieved from http://www.cpn.org/topics/youth/highered/pdfs/New_Student_Politics.pdf

Lukensmeyer, C. J., & Brigham, S. (2002). Taking democracy to sale: Creating a town hall meeting for the twenty-first century. *National Civic Review, 91*(4), 351-366.

Mendelberg, T. (2002). The deliberative citizen: Theory and evidence. In M. X. Delli Carpini, L. Huddy, & R. Shapiro (Eds.), *Research in micropolitics: Political decisionmaking, deliberation and participation* (Vol. 6, pp. 151–193). Greenwich, CT: JAI Press.

Miller, C. R. (1984). Genre as social action. *Quarterly Journal of Speech, 70,* 151-167. Retrieved from http://www4.ncsu.edu/~crmiller/Publications/MillerQJS84.pdf

Mula, F. (Writer), & Kruse, N. (Director). (1999, January 16). Faith off [Television series episode]. In Gracie Films and 20th Century Fox Television, *The Simpsons.* Fox Broadcasting Company.

Nelsen, R. W. (2002). *Schooling as entertainment: Corporate education meets popular culture.* Kingston, ON: Cedarcreek Publications.

Newson, J. (2000). To not intend, or to intend not ... that is the question. In J. L. Turk (Ed.), *The corporate campus: Commercialization and the dangers to Canada's colleges and universities* (pp. 183-194). Toronto, ON: James Lorimer and Company.

Orlikowski, W. J., & Yates, J. (1994). Genre repertoire: The structuring of communicative practices in organizations. *Administrative Science Quarterly, 39*(4), 541-574.

Ornatowski, C. M., & Bekins, L. K. (2004). What's civic about technical communication? Technical communication and the rhetoric of "community". *Technical Communication Quarterly, 13*(3), 251-269.

Pocklington, T. C., & Tupper, A. (2002). *No place to learn: Why universities aren't working.* Vancouver, BC: UBC Press.

Reid, W. (1881). *Town hall suggestions: An address at the opening of a new city hall, Xenia, Ohio, February 16, 1881.* New York: Henry Holt & Company. Retrieved from http://books.google.ca/books?id=kqzW2pTwuK4C

Schoem, D., & Hurtado, S. (Eds.). (2001). *Intergroup dialogue: Deliberative democracy in school, college, community, and workplace.* Ann Arbor: University of Michigan Press.

Schön, D. A. (1995, November/December). Knowing-in-action: The new scholarship requires a new epistemology. *Change, 27*(6), 27-34.

Tetteh, E. N. A. (2004). *Theories of democratic governance in the institutions of higher education.* iUniverse.

Vatz, R. (1973). The myth of the rhetorical situation. *Philosophy and Rhetoric, 6*(3), 154-161.

Washburn, J. (2005). *University Inc.: The corporate corruption of higher education.* New York, NY: Basic Books.

Wenger, E. (1998). *Communities of practice: Learning, meaning and identity.* Cambridge: Cambridge University Press.

20 TALKING THE TALK AND WALKING THE WALK: ESTABLISHING THE ACADEMIC ROLE OF WRITING CENTRES

Margaret Procter

Writing centres fill a distinctive and essential role in the Canadian teaching of writing at the university level, and their role is growing in importance as writing gains recognition within university curricula as an engine for the generation of knowledge and an important component in students' maturation as thinkers. The trend towards recognition of writing centres as drivers of a broader view of writing is suggested by the contrasting titles of Roger Graves' two books on the history of writing instruction in Canada. Graves' seminal 1994 study outlines the historical development of writing courses using the title *Writing Instruction in Canadian Universities* (Graves, 1994). His 2006 collection with Heather Graves (Graves & Graves, 2006) divides its focus among different types of instruction, and its title gives writing centres pride of place: *Writing Centres, Writing Seminars, Writing Culture: Writing Instruction in Anglo-Canadian Universities*. At least four of the 15 chapters concentrate on the work done by specific writing centres, outlining their development into hubs of writing instruction in their universities.

And yet, writing centres are also key examples for Hunt's (2006) assertion in his "Afterword" to the same book that writing instruction in Canada has merely "infiltrated the cracks" in university structures without finding a home in the traditional university departments and administrative structures (p. 376). Published discussions of Canadian writing centres have tended to focus on anxieties about positioning. The seminal study commissioned in the mid-1970s by the Association of Canadian University Teachers of English (Priestley

& Kerpneck, 1976) recognized that the new generation of university students needed "remedial" individual writing instruction, but reiterated emphatically that responsibility for such instruction should not dilute the attention of English Departments to the study and teaching of literature—or, one can infer, influence the allotment of the few English appointments then available in Canadian universities. It remains true that in Canada, with its relative paucity of composition and rhetoric programs, and thus its lack of trainee instructors and of a clear relationship to any one department, writing centres have no standard model of institutional structure or employment. A 1996 survey of Canadian writing centres by Bell and Hubert recorded that half of its 33 respondents still had to "fight for" their funding on a yearly basis; one-third held staff rather than faculty positions. Bell's very useful article about a research method for self-study was titled "Small-Scale Evaluations for Writing Centres in These Times of Trouble" in its Canadian publication (1996), though only "When Hard Questions Are Asked: Evaluating Writing Centers" in its US publication (2000). A recent Master's thesis by Kraglund-Gauthier (2006) concludes that, although the 13 Atlantic Canada writing centres in her study could measure local success in very positive terms, as units within their universities they still had to struggle for identity and frequently received only marginal support. Since its founding in early 2006, the listserv of the new Canadian Writing Centre Association (CWCA-L@ LISTSERV.UOTTAWA.CA) has also circled back obsessively to anxieties about funding, employment status, and reporting structure.

This chapter will argue, nevertheless, that writing centres have helped create a distinctive position for Writing Studies in the Canadian university culture, one that does not necessarily depend on a departmental home. They can raise awareness of writing issues precisely because to sustain themselves as non-departmental units, they need to argue publicly about the nature of writing as an intellectual activity and to show how their writing instruction across the curriculum contributes to the knowledge creation that is the core value of a university. Because writing centres offer individual instruction to students without the structures of class enrollments and grades that bring income and accrediting power to the institution, they have to define the reasons for their existence repeatedly and progressively in the face of curricular and institutional changes. In this competition for self-justification they have the advantage that their contact with students across the curriculum gives them insights into the patterns of learning for which universities purport to stand. Writing centre instructors know from daily engagement with students how the process of writing generates and shapes ideas, rather than simply transmitting or packaging them. Moreover, discussions about the existence of specific writing centres—the crises, arguments, proposals, and reports that have given them a continuing if not always stable footing in their institutions—have often taken place in wide university forums rather than in closed departmental meetings or specialized academic journals, and thus have engaged public attention and open discussion. Though not always reflected in publicly available documents, these discussions have left textual traces in such forms as letters, newspaper articles, internal proposals, and committee and individual reports. These traces offer a way to analyse the prolonged and often messy discussions and an historical perspective on the directions they have taken and the issues they have raised generation by generation.

The public discussions around writing centres at the University of Toronto in the 1990s exemplify the range of challenges, both intellectual and practical, involved in the positioning of writing within a Canadian institution. Because of its size, diversity, and decentralized nature, the University of Toronto has experimented with a range of models for writing centres. This chapter offers some components of its history as a kind of display cabinet for structural and theoretical issues likely to be shared by other writing centres in Canada. My analysis will draw on documents that are part of my files as University of Toronto Coordinator of Writing Support and some that are

Table 1. University of Toronto writing centres: Changes in staffing, September 1991- September 2006.

Employment figures for September 1991	Employment Figures for September 2006
9 Writing Labs (undergraduate colleges)	14 Writing Centres (undergraduate colleges, professional faculties, graduate studies)
36 people in 34 positions 10 faculty appointments 4 full-time, 6 part-time / shared = 7 FTE	76 people in 85 positions 27 faculty appointments 22 full-time, 5 part-time / shared = 25 FTE
usually Tutor (short-term contract) or Senior Tutor (renewable 5-year contracts)	22 full-time faculty, 5 part-time 12 Lecturers (renewable 1-3 year contracts) 10 Senior Lecturers (continuing appointments = tenure)
	36 Sessional Lecturers (short-term contracts, usually part-time, with some security and benefits; CUPE 3902 since 2005)
10 hourly-paid part-timers (no rank)	
15 graduate students (mainly English/Drama)	18 graduate students (10 in / from professional faculties)

publicly available. (The References list gives URLs for those that have been archived online.) I will quote and comment on a selection of these documents in order to identify some of the strengths that a writing-centre perspective can bring to institutional awareness of writing as a knowledge-making practice and, therefore, as central to the university mission. My discussion will also suggest some constraints and frustrations resulting from writing centre instructors' efforts to establish their work on a valid and stable footing in challenging circumstances.

DEFINING WRITING CENTRE WORK: FIRST STEPS, FIRST WORDS

The University of Toronto was among the earliest adopters of the writing-centre model in Canada, and it faced, from the start, the full range of issues in defining and defending that work. In 1964, the year of its founding, Innis College established a teaching operation offering individual instruction to students working on papers in any of their courses (King & Cotter, 1970). Similar "writing laboratories" were in place in several of the other constituent undergraduate colleges by the mid-1970s. Unlike the writing labs also emerging in US universities (Griffin, Keller, Pandey, Pedersen, & Skinner, 2006; Kinkead & Harris, 1993; Murphy, 1996), these teaching units did not arise from Composition or Rhetoric programs. The early instructors were often recent Masters or PhD graduates in English or another humanities discipline. Their students brought work predominantly, but not only, from humanities departments, and predominantly, but not only, from undergraduate Arts and Science courses. Departments in the humanities took a particular interest in this teaching and sometimes supported it, but the interest was often tinged by distrust and anxiety.

It was clear from the start, for instance, that the Department of English would support the remedial function of writing centres and supply underemployed graduates as instructors, but it was no more eager than its members Priestley and Kerpneck in their 1976 report for ACUTE to let any kind of writing instruction become part of the department. In a 1970 article for English Quarterly, the two original Innis College writing-centre instructors King and Cotter note that some faculty members accuse them of "spoon-feeding academic cripples" and assume that their work is a second-class occupation that should be taken on only by "housewives and starving graduate students" (King & Cotter, 1970, p. 56). Priestley and Kerpneck (1976) also use harsh words to downgrade the work of writing centres, by then present in at least four colleges on their own campus. They assert, for instance, that "writing clinics" should be tolerated only as long as they do not "doctor" the work brought to them for "individual diagnosis and treatment" (pp. 32-5). They assume that English professors will supervise graduate students doing the teaching, but do not consider the possibility of faculty appointments focussed on writing, much less writing as a field of inquiry within the department. Those working in the new teaching operations are not expected to discuss their work except to report on students' progress in attaining "acceptable university-level English," and perhaps to supply figures to high schools about how many of their graduates are "languishing in the laboratories" (p. 35). The professors of English will decide what is acceptable as English and how much remedial instruction can be tolerated; writing instructors will uphold the standards and supply the teaching without having a voice of their own.

In practical terms, however, people working in writing centres at the University of Toronto have regularly had to raise their voices to define what they do and to defend the value of their teaching. In the 1990s, one of the must urgent needs was to establish a different basis for their work than the one assumed by the faculty members and administrators who might speak about them in the terms noted above. Their employment in an institution dominated by departmental power and with somewhat fluid categories of faculty appointment (Nelson, 2007), left writing-centre instructors in a particularly vulnerable position. During the 1970s and 1980s, the decentralized nature of the university could generate teaching jobs without requiring a uniform type of contract. But with budget retrenchment in the early 1990s, faculty status became a burning issue for people who did not have "regular" appointments, and it has been closely interwoven since then with other questions about the function and value of writing centres and writing instruction. The success of writing-centre instructors' arguments about their employment status can be seen in the following table comparing data from the period of an employment crisis and the most recently available figures.

The more than doubling of the number of people employed since 1991 tells only part of the story. The rank of "Tutor" and the short-term contracts that accompanied it have been replaced by the term "Lecturer" and the establishment of tenured status for Senior Lecturers. Many of the people in the lower left of the table have become those in the upper right, as part-timers and graduate students won full-time positions. Whereas there were once nine isolated teaching units, each led by a single faculty member (with one spare) in a distinctly ambiguous appointment category, now a set of teaching units constitutes a network of colleagues who hold formally-defined faculty appointments. The 14 or so writing centres are still separate entities reporting to deans and college principals rather than forming a single department or free-standing unit. As described in two chapters of Graves and Graves' recent collection (Irish, 2006; Procter, 2006), University of Toronto writing centres have capitalized on their independent status to develop innovative programs of credit and non-credit courses, collaborative instruction of disciplinary courses, and highly respected methods of instruction. The range of work represented by the right-hand column is much larger than that in the left-hand column. Writing labs were once marginal, but the units now called writing centres are now indeed central to many areas of the university.

DEFINING WRITING CENTRE WORK: CRISIS AND RESPONSE

These changes in size and status did not happen automatically or easily, even though writing centres had the advantage of a relatively well resourced institution (well resourced in parts, at any rate) and a field that very clearly needed cultivating as the university grew in size and began to mirror the multicultural nature of the Greater Toronto Area. The creation story for the current state of writing centres at the University of Toronto took place in 1991 with an employment crisis at one of the suburban colleges. It was an event that turned the spotlight on writing instructors' terms of employment, but also reminded the university community of the need to define the role of writing in relation to university learning.

On August 31, 1991, the Principal of Scarborough College called Adele Fisher, the Senior Tutor who had directed the Scarborough College Writing Lab for fifteen years, to notify her that she should not come to work the next day because she was going to be replaced by five Mac computers equipped with the new grammar-checking software Grammatik. She was told to serve out the final year of her third five-year contract by staying at home and looking for employment elsewhere. The facts of this story have been narrated elsewhere (e.g., Procter, 2006), but its textual traces in the form of unpublished documents and university records are worth examining further. The texts reflecting this story reveal the assumptions about power and about writing that governed the conditions of writing-centre work in this period—assumptions that have changed radically over the last fifteen years because writing instructors and others have challenged them by both words and deeds.

Here is a revealing passage from the first public communication about this administrative attack on the writing centre, now resting in my file as a sheet of mimeographed paper. It consists of a memo on college letterhead that was duplicated and placed in the mailboxes of all Scarborough College faculty members during Reading Week in the spring term of 1991:

18 February 1991

To Members of the College

You are all aware that the College is being required to meet an overall budget reduction by 1995, 5% assigned by the Provost and a further 1.45% to meet faculty renewal commitments. Each budget head has been asked by the Principal to participate in developing a plan for meeting this reduction.

After long consideration and consultation with the Principal and the Administrative Group at the College, I have proposed meeting the reduction in my budget by replacing the present Writing Lab with a Writing Centre, equipped with computers, where students will be able to use various software programmes to analyse and improve their English writing.

This administrator sees writing solely in terms of problems and deficiencies—sometimes in students, sometimes in budgets. The assumption is that students need only mechanical drill in language correctness in order to improve the products of their writing, and that cost concerns are central; thus if machines are cheaper than people in applying the required drill, it is logical to pay for them rather than people. The tone of the memo is impersonal and managerial, relying on passive verbs ("is being required" and "has been asked"), but it uses personal pronouns to confirm power relationships. The "you" group of recipients is reminded in the letter's first words to keep economic considerations primary, and then "I" speaks magisterially only after invoking the other top administrators. Though the decision is called a proposal, this note is clearly an announcement ("students will"), not an invitation to comment.

But those affected did comment, starting with students and faculty members at Scarborough College. Here is a glimpse of the History Department, as a group, writing to the Principal. By addressing the Principal by name, their two-page letter went above the administrator who had written the memo. It also went beyond the Principal by distributing copies to other faculty members. As with other similar letters from members in other departments, the authors signed their names individually but also invoked their academic department.

2 March 1991

Dear [*first name*],

... [*expression of shock and dismay*] ... Much language learning derives from the home environment, which means that many Scarborough students may be consequently disadvantaged in their English communication skills. The Writing Lab is the last chance these young people have of improving their skills before seeking careers in an increasingly competitive workplace. As Harvard University Business School Professor Michael Porter points out, one must achieve lower-order skills before advancing to higher orders. If our students do not learn how to write proper English before they leave the University, they never will, and their future will be severely compromised.

In our capacity as Historians, we expect our students to be able to express themselves clearly. When they cannot, we invariably counsel them to seek assistance from the Writing Lab. It is our experience that some students who do so have been able to raise their marks by as much as two full grades (that is, for example, from a 'C' to an 'A'). Is it fair to deprive them of this possibility?

... [*call for faculty consultation on the decision about the Writing Lab*] We trust that you share our concern and that you will give this subject the attention it deserves.

Respectfully submitted,

[*individual signatures*].

    This letter adopts a different type of rhetoric from the managerial announcement of the Vice-Principal's letter. The signatories address the Principal directly, presenting themselves as his colleagues ("Dear Paul"), and they express indignation at being excluded from the college's decision. Though the letter does not touch on the termination of the writing director, it speaks confidently about the place of writing in the university. The professors base their sweeping categorical statements on presumptions of common knowledge about language learning and "the home environment," and then on a citation from an academic authority (authoritative in being from Harvard, at least, though not from a field one might recognize as related to the issue). The expertise they claim as teachers comes from being Historians representing an established discipline. These professors are clearly happy to leave the transmission of skills to others. Their language displays the same set of assumptions about deficiency ("improving") and gatekeeping ("proper English") as those held by the first administrator, though writing tutors are shown as holding the gate open for students who acknowledge their deficiencies. The goodwill of this and other faculty letters was broad and sincere, and in 1991, the public support for the Writing Lab was timely and welcome. From the present perspective, however, the conception of writing and writing instruction seems sadly limited.

Student journalists involved themselves even more publicly and heatedly in the controversy. They, too, noted that the administrator had made the announcement when people were generally off campus, and they, too, protested the lack of consultation. Students were also much quicker than the professoriate to protest the unsuitable use of technology. A story in one of the downtown student newspapers used a picture of a computer monitor replacing the head of a business-suited male, heading it "Professor IBM"—a picture that was copied and posted in several other places around campus as summing up a general problem of reliance on impersonal teaching methods. Within a week of the administrator's memo, the Scarborough College student paper published an editorial protesting the proposed change:

> 16 February 1991, editorial
>
> Welcome back from Reading Week! Oh, and by the way, while you were gone the Administration has decided to "restructure" the Writing Lab, restructure it right out of existence.
>
> The Writing Lab has offered personal tutoring to students on their writing and grammar at this campus for almost twenty years. As of June 30, 1992, the Writing Lab will no longer exist and in its place will be computers.
>
> Computers may be great, but they can only do so much. They may be able to help with punctuation and other grammatical errors but they are not able to help a student clarify ideas or write an essay which flows properly. Computers fail to offer a personal one-on-one conference, which many students desperately need.

> Scarborough Campus has many foreign students whose first language is not English. Such students may have trouble writing grammatically correct English, or, like many other students, just have trouble expressing their ideas. It is not fair to set them down in front of computers and wish them the best of luck. In fact, it is downright cruel.

Speaking from experience and observation, and drawing on emotional terms rather than intellectual generalizations to express their concerns about equity, the students comment more pointedly on teaching methods than did the professors. In mentioning students' need to clarify ideas and to write essays that "flow properly," the editorial is reaching towards the recognition that writing instruction involves idea-generation and logical organization as well as language correctness. The list of those who need writing support includes both the out-group labelled "foreign students" and also "many other students." The editorial rises to considerable eloquence in expressing a sense of violation and inequity when students are given a technological substitute for personal instruction. It sees writing instruction as part of university learning, not just as remedial activity to be administered on the margins of the institution.

DEVELOPING DISCOURSE ABOUT WRITING AND WRITING CENTRES

The clear threat to their employment brought together the remaining writing-centre instructors across the university and impelled them to join in the public uproar—and eventually to find powerful ways to speak on behalf of writing instruction as a vital part of the academy. Because of the decentralization of the various writing centres, writing instructors at this time barely knew each other and had no official reason to work together. But in September 1991, the University of Toronto Association of Writing Tutors came together and began to act and speak collectively on behalf of their work—a group of more than 30 people who knew how to communicate and could call on the concern and outrage of both students and faculty members.

The following is a retrospective summary of what this group of writing instructors found they needed to say and do, in 1991 and over the next few years, to define a place for writing instruction within the university. Both practical and political themes will be evident. So will the growing ability of writing-centre instructors to speak and write thoughtfully about the nature of writing and writing instruction, and the growing acceptance of their views of writing.

First of all, writing instructors had to speak for themselves, and speak not just as employees but as authorities on learning and teaching writing. They had to speak as faculty members to other faculty members, whether they held that status or not. By mid-September of 2001, a group of a dozen or so people began meeting regularly to think through the nature of the challenge. That involved much discussion and hand-wringing, but it also required informed analysis of what Grammatik actually did and reflective investigation of writing-centre work within the University of Toronto and other universities.

In early 1992, at the initiative of the graduate student Cynthia Messenger, the group wrote to the Provost demanding a seat along with deans and department chairs on a university-wide Steering Group on writing that had been set up to quell the increasingly hysterical protests about betrayal of students and misuse of technology. Gay MacDonald of New College, one of the three remaining full-time writing-centre instructors, filled that seat very effectively over the next four months, speaking confidently from her 15 years of experience teaching writing in the New College Writing Lab. The writing instructors in the new association quickly learned the value of working with her as our spokesperson. Though most of us lacked position titles and job security, we knew how to act like researchers, initiating, for instance, a critical analysis of the chosen software, a step that the university administrators had neglected. We began by reviewing the literature on grammar-checking software; then we tested Grammatik empirically on actual student work and reported on its often absurd results. We analysed other types of instructional technology in terms of the actual range of student needs, and we summarized our findings cogently in written reports that we sent to MacDonald for distribution at meetings of the Steering Group. With our help, MacDonald spoke knowledgeably to the committee on the primitive nature of Grammatik as an editing tool and on its even more limited function as an instructional resource. Her clear and well-grounded explanations faced down the enthusiasm of the computational expert from English who also served on the committee and gradually became accepted as key elements in the committee's discussion. MacDonald also kept insisting that the error-fixing that Grammatik seemed to promise was not the only or main function of writing centres. Starting with her reports on the unsuitable technology, she made the most of her chances to outline the ways that individualized writing-centre instruction helped students develop their ideas and come to terms with larger issues of evidence, reasoning, and authority.

By the time the Steering Group wrote its report to the Provost, MacDonald's points were further supported by an eloquent collection of written statements from other writing instructors about what they actually did in their work. The Writing Tutors' Association's 14-page submission to the Steering Group answered a call for public input and again made the most of the opportunity to speak authoritatively from an informed and reasoned basis. The committee read and discussed this submission in detail and with considerable respect, eventually publishing it in full as an Appendix to its 35-page report. The contributions to this submission displayed different perspectives and voices, but were sent without individual names attached because of concern about retribution by local supervisors. Three representative excerpts suggest the range of topics raised and the level of discussion:

> a. Because we are concerned to make students more aware of the relation between language and thinking, we deal with writing not just as product but also as process: with developing essays from the most preliminary stages of analysis to the editing and polishing of the final draft. While many of us offer basic theoretical instruction in grammar and composition, the main thrust of our approach is practical. Dealing primarily with essays in progress, we show students, often over a number of sessions, how to build on their strengths and how to identify and overcome their characteristic problems. These may involve language errors, and are equally likely to include matters of focus and argumentation.... Our success comes from our unique opportunity to combine basic pedagogic principles: practical focus, interactive work, and a flexible approach that changes with the individual student's development.
>
> b. In the oral exchanges typical of writing lab appointments the student's thinking becomes subject to immediate critical analysis—his own as well as that of the tutor—before it can be returned to the page as writing. This kind of discourse amazes students on their first meetings with us: often they have not previously realized the depth or closeness of attention that goes into critical reading. They emerge, however, with clearer expectations both about how their papers will be read and about how they themselves can exercise this kind of reading and analysis.
>
> c. Our experience with such style-checking software as Grammatik IV, Correct Grammar and Right Writer convinces us that its relevance to teachers of writing is limited. Since we do not offer proofreading services to students, such programmes cannot help us directly in our work. Their method of attempting to comment on every instance of possible stylistic weakness runs counter to the pedagogic principle of concentrating on the most important

problems, seeing them in context, and working on them consultatively. Because of the low reliability of the present generation of programmes (an accuracy rate of well under 50%, according to recent popular and scholarly reviews), we cannot yet recommend their use even outside the writing lab.

These voices make broad assertions about the nature of writing and of student learning, mentioning both experience and pedagogical principle as the basis of their statements. The various authors use personal pronouns confidently ("we" and "us"), asserting a collective identity even if individual names are not displayed.

The Steering Group's report displays a remarkable transformation of the university's discourse about writing. After four months of intense discussion, including the direct and indirect contributions of writing-centre instructors, the report turned away from instant solutions, put the spotlight on the responsibility of administrators and professors for offering appropriate instruction, and began to frame the issues in terms of student needs rather than only budgetary problems. The conclusions of the Steering Group Report of May 1992 show a much more solid and inclusive understanding of the pedagogical and institutional issues underlying academic writing than had been seen in any of the previous discussions. Though the recommendations still refer to academic requirements as self-evident monolithic standards and equate them with the conventions of the disciplines, writing is no longer merely a matter of student deficiency to be dealt with by separately-delivered remediation. The following resolutions (from a list of 13) call on the university as an institution to face up to its responsibilities for teaching students writing:

> 6. That all divisions be required to concern themselves with the quality of student writing and its improvement in meeting their academic requirements.
>
> 7. That divisions be encouraged to provide opportunities in credit courses for all their students to expand their writing skills within the specific conventions of their disciplines.
>
> 8. That divisions and departments review the role of writing in their academic programmes, with particular reference to the types of assignments required, the services needed and available to students within the department, and the expressions in calendars and brochures of the academic unit's interest in effective writing.

The two explicit references to writing labs in the recommendations sum up their liminal position at this point in administrative awareness. Recommendation 11 asks that writing labs work with the college principals to consider "ways to optimize the cost effectiveness of the services provided" (still services, not yet teaching, and still distrusted in terms of their cost). Then recommendation 12 gives writing labs a position on a Writing Board that will assist the divisions in achieving their goals. Even if the value of their teaching needed more consideration, the value of their voices was now clear.

The central Writing Board never did materialize, but writing instructors have more than fulfilled its intended function through their own initiatives. When I took on the new position of University of Toronto Coordinator of Writing Support in 1994, I knew I would have to continue grounding discussion of writing in references to research and explanations of the underlying pedagogical principles—in other words, to act as if I were a faculty member representing a coherent discipline. My first efforts were to produce heavily documented research reports, first on writing software (Procter, 1994), and then on post-admission testing (Procter, 1995), using academic weaponry to ward off the most imminent threats. Other writing-centre directors have continued to do the same, writing thoughtful reports to their deans and principals and offering well-informed comments on divisional curricula and teaching even before they are asked. Similarly, instead of merely following another of the Steering Group's recommendation to compile and disseminate existing departmental wisdom on writing, writing instructors have created their own instructional material for students and professional-development material for faculty. Their work now takes the shape of Web sites used widely as course resources by students and instructors across the curriculum at the University of Toronto and elsewhere, this time with each file displaying its author's name (see the list of topics at http://www.utoronto.ca/writing/advise.html). Several textbooks and handbooks have also been published (e.g., Gilpin & Patchet-Golubev, 2000; Northey & Procter, 1998), with more forthcoming on specific areas of expertise (for instance on proposals from Jane Freeman; on Engineering communication from Rob Irish and Peter Weiss; on writing in the health sciences from Dena Taylor).

SHAPING THE PLACE OF WRITING IN INSTITUTIONAL CULTURES

The 1991 crisis demonstrated unmistakeably to writing-centre instructors that they should engage proactively in institutional planning processes rather than being subject to others' decisions about budget and pedagogy. Such participation is not easy when writing centres lack the departmental status that gives an automatic right to sit on committees and take part in official discussions. Nevertheless, writing-centre instructors have managed to capitalize on their understanding of curriculum and teaching processes in order to help steer university change. Their knowledge and awareness of these topics give them an advantage in institutional discussions, even if they have no more formal training in educational theory or policy analysis than other academics. Again, this is evident in the textual traces of the discussions that founded at least six new writing centres in the 1990s.

The four professional-faculty writing centres, which account for about half of the growth in writing-centre employment shown in Table 1 above, sprang up in the mid-1990s in response to overall curriculum changes and to new administrative awareness that writing centres had a record of achievement. Small-scale pilot initiatives used both actions and words to demonstrate and document ways that professors could teach their subjects more effectively when writing tutors worked alongside them. Typically, writing tutors would first give in-class presentations to get students to do what the course instructors wanted them to, and then take active roles in discussions about teaching methods and eventually in collaborative teaching. Freeman's (1997) account of her work in an Engineering Thermodynamics course encapsulates this development: she started by standing at the back of the room in lab sessions and answering students' questions about spelling and format, but soon began to help the graduate student Teaching Assistants answer more complex questions about sentences and wording that the students brought them, followed up by talking to these TAs after class about their own puzzlements as graduate writers and teachers. Within a few weeks she was giving presentations on precision and logic in scientific writing from the front of the room and eventually offering training sessions for the whole group of course TAs (Freeman, 1997; Irish, 2006). Similar types of work in Engineering and other professional faculties, including that of Andy Payne in Architecture and Dena Taylor in several Health Science faculties, helped shape course assignments and assessment methods, and, eventually, also influenced divisional curriculum reform (see Procter, 2006, for a fuller account).

The university's budget planning cycle of 1995-2000 generated a number of divisional reports that reflected the newly recognized writing experts' views about teaching and learning—sometimes only as distant echoes, but eventually more directly because writing instructors were members of the planning committees and sometimes drafters of the reports. All of the following sentences are excerpted from divisional proposals for funding of new or renewed writing centres from that crucial planning cycle. (These were once public documents within their academic divisions, but only the 1998 University of Toronto at Scarborough report and the

1999 University of Toronto, Faculty of Arts and Science resolution are still recoverable as references, having been archived online for public access.)

> Faculty of Pharmacy (1994). Subcommittee recommendation to Curriculum Committee:
>
> That undergraduate course coordinators be encouraged to require effective writing in their assessment of students. Writing-intensive components of Pharmacy courses should be encouraged. In the senior years of the undergraduate curriculum, attention to student writing should be continued through greater emphasis on writing assignments and the level of proficiency should be taken into account in establishing the final grades.
>
> Pharmacy and Nursing deans (1995). Proposal to Council of Health Science deans:
>
> The ideas in this report build on our self-analysis, suggesting that cooperatively the Health-Science programs can achieve a flexible and practical solution to their acute need for writing support. The writing-lab model, now available only to undergraduate Arts and Science students, can with suitable adaptations provide the specialist help needed to support the kinds of teaching and learning done in the Health Sciences.
>
> Faculty of Applied Science and Engineering (1995). Jane Griesdorf, Language across the curriculum: A proposal:
>
> If the importance of literacy becomes a critical factor for all aspects of the Engineering curriculum, our students will learn to communicate more fluently and have greater confidence to work with others. And with commitment from a range of faculty and with support from specialized instructors, students will come to see that good communication is a practical tool for both academic work and future employment.
>
> University of Toronto at Scarborough (1998). Final report of task force on writing:
>
> [after considering and rejecting post-admission testing] The

Task Force therefore turned its attention to what is often referred to as 'writing across the curriculum': the incorporation of writing—its evaluation and improvement—into all programmes so that students have the opportunity to graduate as competent writers. The major thrust of this report is that we should focus our attention on the improvement of writing as an integral part of the learning experience and develop a College culture of good writing.

Faculty of Arts and Science, General Committee (1999). Resolution on writing:

a) That every major and specialist program in the Faculty of Arts and Science (FAS) integrate writing components into its program requirements.

b) That the FAS assist in the re-design of key first-year courses so that they incorporate writing components.

c) That the FAS develop criteria by which to approve and evaluate existing or proposed writing components in programs.

d) That the above be implemented incrementally during the period 1999-2004.

Faculty of Architecture and Landscape Architecture (2000). "Aims of writing across the curriculum programme," Academic plan:

- To use language as a way of learning Architecture and Landscape Architecture, not as a subsidiary subject or requirement.

- To prepare students for the professional life of architects and landscape architects, especially the need to articulate visual ideas in words.

- To counterbalance the tendency of visually oriented people to neglect their capacity for using language.

- To pay special attention to the needs of students learning English as a second language.

- To maintain high standards of learning, and to monitor our students' progress.

- To support both students and faculty in this enterprise.

The sequence of excerpts here makes evident the shift in perspective since 1991 about writing as a topic in divisional planning. The new Provost, Adel Sedra of Engineering, read the Steering-Group Report of 1992 with respect. At the start of the 1995-2000 planning cycle he made it known that he intended to fund initiatives demonstrating the commitment of professional faculties to curricular change that included writing instruction. The discourse about writing in the documents that responded to his invitation now uses the type of language and approach introduced by writing centres in their discussions of their own work. In their own ways, these documents all affirm the value of writing as part of learning. At first relying on such general terms as "proficiency" and focussing on grading rather than instruction, the statements gradually become more precise about the position of writing as a means of knowledge generation in their own disciplines. The University of Toronto at Scarborough report of 1998 is dramatically different from the 1991 memos quoted earlier in its confident assertion that writing should be part of "all programmes." Influenced no doubt by the Boyer Commission Report (1998) and the currents in US writing instruction that it reflects, Arts and Science and Architecture make sweeping promises about integrating writing instruction across their curricula. All these documents now specifically position writing centres as the key resources for learning and teaching writing, whether in terms of individual instruction or the "writing across the curriculum" method cited in the later documents.

INFLUENCING APPOINTMENT POLICIES

At the same time that they began to participate in divisional planning and its implementation, writing instructors also became active in another aspect of university governance, the University of Toronto Faculty Association (UTFA). The 1991 termination at Scarborough College was again the precipitating event. The non-certified Faculty Association was not able to save Adele Fisher's Senior Tutor job in 1991 (she took up a tenure-stream position in the State University of New York), but it was galvanized into attending to the insecure nature of its other Tutor positions. In 1991 this group encompassed about 150 teaching-specialized faculty across the university, including the three remaining full-time Tutors and the six part-time Tutors in writing centres.

The major advances since that time in faculty appointments at writing centres have been shaped by writing instructors' strong record of speaking up and active engagement in UTFA—the same combination of assertive talk and concerted action that was also winning them their place in the curriculum. As in so many other Canadian universities, writing instructors have played key roles in the Faculty Association Executive. Guy Allen (now director of the Professional Writing and Communication Program at the University of Toronto Mississauga) was chair of the Tutors' Stream Committee in the early 1990s, using his eloquence to inform and persuade other faculty members of the urgency of policy changes for Tutors. I served from 2000 to 2005 as chair of what was by then called the Teaching-Stream Committee, helping implement an arrangement in 2001 that changed a further 100 positions (including those of at least 10 writing-centre instructors) from "casual" part-time jobs into Lecturer positions, mostly full-time. Cynthia Messenger—in 1992 the Teaching Assistant who called for a writing-centre representative on the Steering Group on Writing and now the director of the Innis College program in Writing and Rhetoric—served for two years as the chair of the UTFA Teaching-Stream Committee and is currently the Vice-President of Grievances.

The main policy improvement affecting writing-centre instructors was a revision in 1999 to the Policy and Procedure on Academic Appointments (University of Toronto Governing Council, 1999/2003) that secured continuing status, the equivalent of tenure, for Senior Lecturers. Promotion to that rank comes after a rigorous review procedure parallel to the tenure review. Before 1999, Senior Tutors had to undergo a review every five years in order to obtain another five-year renewal, and even then there was no guarantee that a renewal would result from a successful review. This crucial change came about only after UTFA refused for nine years in a row to implement revisions in any negotiated policy until the university administration agreed to improve the policy for Tutors.

The revised Appointments Policy was phrased carefully to include writing-centre instructors, who by 1999 constituted about 20 of the 150 or so people in the Tutor rank as well as an equal number working part-time without that rank. Its wording recognizes that they contribute to students' earning of degrees whether or not they teach courses. The stiff legal language and the careful choice of "may" rather than "should" conceal the heated discussions within UTFA and between UTFA and the administration that went into this formulation:

> The ranks of Lecturer and Senior Lecturer are to be held by faculty members whose duties normally consist of teaching students who are in degree programs or the Transitional Year Programme, and related professional and administrative activi-

ties. Lecturers may have independent responsibility for designing and teaching courses or significant components of courses within their departmental and divisional curricula.

... Performance will be assessed on teaching effectiveness and pedagogical / professional development related to teaching duties, in accordance with approved divisional guidelines on the assessment of teaching. Administrative service will be considered, where such service is related to teaching duties or to curricular and professional development.

Though this new policy provides the security and protections for academic freedom of a faculty position, not to mention entitlement to sabbaticals and recognition for good work in terms of merit pay, it is far from perfect in that it still divides faculty members specializing in teaching from those specializing in research. In stating the criteria for promotion and merit pay, the odd collocation "pedagogical / professional development related to teaching duties," substitutes for references to scholarship in the tenure-stream section of the document. The narrow interpretation of that language in some departments has been the subject of a group grievance by the Faculty Association, still unresolved in some details. Research work is not excluded from Lecturers' activities, but it is not always mentioned in job descriptions even as an option, and some contradictory language remains in the reporting documents used to award merit pay and grant sabbatical leaves.

Despite such ambiguities, the new procedures have given writing instructors more chances to demonstrate within the university what they do and how well they do it. Hiring and promotion committees for the newly formalized procedures, for instance, consist of divisional faculty members along with writing-centre colleagues, meaning that many more people now see writing instructors' application packages, annual activity reports, and teaching portfolios—genres that give writing specialists a chance to show their achievements. Committees repeatedly express surprise and admiration for what these documents reveal about the quality of writing-centre work. Writing-centre instructors have thus been able to raise the status of their type of teaching by demonstrating its high quality through some of the key ritual displays of academic identity.

REMAINING CHALLENGES

At the University of Toronto, as in many other universities in Canada, then, writing centres have clearly expanded and established their roles within the university. We now have the critical mass to look after ourselves. But it is also clear that by responding to crises and opportunities in the situations outlined above we have accepted limitations on our roles as faculty members and perhaps even distorted our development as teaching units. Here is a summary of the challenges that writing centres at this university are still facing. I suspect that similar challenges also exist in other writing centres:

The Need to Maintain and Display Expertise in Recognizable Forms

Full-time writing-centre instructors hold faculty appointments now, but are we real faculty in the terms of a research-intensive institution? The standard teaching load of a Lecturer appointment (typically equivalent to three courses a term, usually with summer work expected in addition) does not leave much room for research, especially for large-scale funded projects with rigid reporting schedules. Lecturers are eligible for SSHRC (Social Sciences and Humanities Research Council) and other external grants if they can produce an official letter saying that their appointments allow time for research, but I can say from experience and observation that it is nearly impossible to follow through large research projects within a Lecturer's usual workload. For writing-centre directors, the multiplication of administrative duties in the 14 decentralized units also adds to the load. Writing-centre instructors occasionally brainstorm about forming an institute or other loosely linked unit, but our relative lack of research record makes that an unlikely outcome—a confining vicious circle of cause and effect. Writing-centre instructors are active in internal professional-development activities and in attending and presenting at conferences, and we have no lack of interesting teaching experiences and questions to analyse and study. However, in the absence of major crises such as the one that made us suddenly become experts on Grammatik, much of our effort now goes into learning about the disciplines in which we work rather than continuing to invent our own.

Temptations to Neglect the Unique Nature of Writing-Centre Instruction

Individual teaching is the root of all writing-centre work. But a large university with a needy student population and limited funding requires many branches of this work. All writing centres at the University of Toronto now offer group instruction of some kind as well as individual student consultations. Most full-time instructors in writing centres also teach courses of their own or team-teach disciplinary courses, as well as managing complex administrative systems of scheduling, supervision, and reporting. They also take part in committee work and meetings like any other faculty member—or perhaps more so, since their ability to speak and write clearly is much valued in these activities. Given the intensity and personal demands of one-to-one teaching, this diversification can be a welcome change of pace, but it also takes time and energy away from individual instruction. Developing new courses and, perhaps, co-teaching them with disciplinary faculty is stimulating and interesting in addition to carrying traditional types of prestige, all powerful incentives to put energy into classroom work. The cross-appointments to departments built into many new positions capitalize on this incentive, offering potential hires the challenges and rewards of classroom teaching and also some hope of continuing their discipline-based scholarly work. All full-time instructors in writing centres still offer individual instruction as part of their work. But one must now ask at what point the diversification from individual instruction will start to supplant or relegate to the margins the core work of teaching students individually.

The Strain of Adapting to Constant Change

Writing centres now take part in curriculum reform and budget planning, but they are not big enough to be the main players. They need to speak and act in terms of supporting their division's overall aims rather than concentrating on their own. Now that writing centres exist in all of the university's divisions and colleges, writing support can no longer be the first planning priority for new funding, as it was for many professional faculties in the 1995-2000 planning cycle. If the Boyer Commission made "integration" a recognized term in the 1990s, government and public pressure may do the same today for "measurable outcomes" and "accountability," terms that tend to refer to short-term change in one or a few variables delivered cheaply, not to the long-term development of students and curricula that writing centres aim at. Central planning documents raised alarm among writing centres by using such terms as "delivery of services" and "co-curricular support," and by including writing along with computer literacy and time management as one of the generic skills that students should be "given" in order to succeed. It was probably more than just good fortune that the divisional faculties rejected many of these ideas and retained the emphasis on student support and integrated instruction established and reaffirmed during the previous planning cycles. University of Toronto, Faculty of Arts and Science (2007) in particular has committed itself in both words and action to a sequence of departmental initiatives that call on writing centres as a source of teaching expertise. But worrisome terms recur in other recent planning documents, especially those driven by the Ontario government call for outcomes measures as a necessity for continued funding. Writing centres and the curricular initiatives in which they take part face the new challenge of measuring instructional impact in ways that reflect their own values, and making sure that their colleagues and supervisors understand their methods and results grounded in a research-based understanding of writing as central to knowledge production and learning in the university.

The Need to Mature and Develop New Leaders

Writing centres and individual instructors have benefitted greatly from the expansion of the last 15 years, but the figures about writing-centre staffing (Table 1, above) contain a problem for future planning. Although there are many more faculty positions now than in 1991, the proportion of full-fledged faculty members to other types of positions within writing centres is only slightly higher than in 1991 (28% of the total in 1991, 36% in 2006). More than half of writing-centre instructors are still part-time and relatively insecure. Since 2005, most instructors in this situation have been represented by a new unit of the public-service union CUPE 3902, the same organization that represents Teaching Assistants. These Sessional Lecturers continue to receive a good rate of pay and have retained some access to benefits, but their first contracts contain almost no mechanism for encouraging professional development or research of any kind. Is this key group of writing-centre instructors still faculty? Do they have the impetus and scope to develop their teaching and their ideas about teaching that the earlier generation did? In a sense their representation by a different bargaining unit makes the current writing-centre directors into management, requiring them to use elaborate hiring and evaluation procedures designed by the union with hiring preference as the reward. Besides ensuring fairness in these procedures, writing-centre directors must also find ways to ensure that their junior and less privileged colleagues can develop into the next generation of leaders.

FURTHER DISCOURSE, NEXT STEPS

This chapter has been a partial account of opportunities taken and choices made by writing centres at one university in a key time period. Under sometimes difficult conditions, multiple and diverse writing centres have developed across the university as participants in the university's teaching mission. By consolidating and capitalizing on their positions as faculty members, writing-centre instructors have been able to influence university discourse about the learning and teaching of writing. We are not yet, however, in a position to create much new professional discourse of our own, whether by investigating our own practices in more depth or by moving out into community-based research or theoretical investigation of the disciplinary practices which we now increasingly serve. One cannot wish for another crisis to impel a sudden surge of self-awareness and daring leaps into new fields of expertise, but writing-centre instructors at the University of Toronto as elsewhere cannot rest on the facts of size and contract security. Both our history and our current situation demand continuing reflection and action on the large, but sometimes conflicting, potentials of writing-centre work as vital to both the university mission and the disciplinary development of Writing Studies.

REFERENCES

Bell, J. (1996). Small-scale evaluations for writing centres in these times of trouble. *Inkshed Newsletter, 14*(7). Retrieved from http://www.stthomasu.ca/inkshed/dec96.htm#subtitle3

Bell, J. (2000). When hard questions are asked: Evaluating writing centers. *Writing Center Journal, 31,* 7-28.

Bell, S., & Hubert, H. (1996). University College of the Cariboo national writing centre survey. *Inkshed Newsletter, 14*(6). Retrieved from http://www.stthomasu.ca/inkshed/sept96.htm#subtitle4

Boyer Commission on Educating Undergraduates in the Research University. (1998). *Reinventing undergraduate education: A Blueprint for America's research universities.*

Freeman, J. (1997). *Teaching writing in a thermodynamics lab.* Paper presented at the Conference on College Composition and Communication, Phoenix, Arizona.

Gilpin, A., & Patchet-Golubev, P. (2000). *A guide to writing in the sciences.* Toronto: University of Toronto Press.

Graves, H., & Graves, R. (Eds.). (2006). *Writing centres, writing seminars, writing culture: Writing instruction in Anglo-Canadian universities.* Winnipeg: Inkshed Publications.

Graves, R. (1994). *Writing instruction in Canadian universities.* Winnipeg: Inkshed Publications.

Griffin, J., Keller, D., Pandey, I. P., Pedersen, A-M., & Skinner, C. (2006). Local practices, national consequences: Surveying and re(constructing) writing center identities. *Writing Center Journal, 46,* 3-21.

Kinkead, J. A., & Harris, J. (Eds.). (1993). *Writing centers in context: Twelve case studies.* Urbana-Champaign, IL: National Council of Teachers of English.

Hunt, R. (2006). Writing under the curriculum. Afterword/Response in H. Graves & R. Graves (Eds.), *Writing centres, writing seminars, writing culture: Writing instruction in Anglo-Canadian universities.* Winnipeg: Inkshed Publications.

Irish, R. (2006). Forging the teachable moment: Developing communication in and across an Engineering curriculum. In H. Graves & R. Graves (Eds.).

Writing centres, writing seminars, writing culture: Writing instruction in Anglo-Canadian universities. Winnipeg: Inkshed Publications.

King, D., & Cotter, E. (1970). An experiment in writing instruction. *English Quarterly, 3*(2), 48-56.

Kraglund-Gauthier, W. (2006). *Canadian undergraduate writing centres: Defining success nationally and assessing success locally.* Unpublished master's thesis, St. Francis Xavier University, Antigonish, Nova Scotia.

Murphy, C. (1996). Writing center. In P. Heilker & P. Vandenberg (Eds.), *Keywords in composition studies.* Portsmouth, NH: Boynton/Cook.

Nelson, B. (2006). *The search for faculty power: The history of the University of Toronto Faculty Association* (2nd ed.). Toronto: University of Toronto Faculty Association and Scholars' Press.

Northey, M., & Procter, M. (1998). *Writer's choice: A portable guide for Canadian writers.* Toronto: Prentice-Hall.

Priestley, F. E. L., & Kerpneck, H. I. (1976). *Report of commission on undergraduate studies in English in Canadian universities.* Montreal: Association of Canadian University Teachers of English.

Procter, M. (1994). *Software to support writing instruction.* Retrieved from http://www.utoronto.ca/writing/software.html

Procter, M. (1995). *Post-admission assessment of writing: Issues and information.* Retrieved from http://www.utoronto.ca/writing/reportw.html

Procter, M. (2006). University of Toronto: Catching up to ourselves. In H. Graves & R. Graves (Eds.), *Writing centres, writing seminars, writing culture: Writing instruction in Anglo-Canadian universities.* Winnipeg: Inkshed Publications.

University of Toronto, Faculty of Arts and Science, General Committee. (1999). Resolution on writing. Retrieved from http://www.artsandscience.utoronto.ca/docs/pdfs/plan/stepping_up.pdf

University of Toronto, Faculty of Arts and Science. (2007). The final report of the curriculum review and renewal committee, 2006-2007 (co-chairs, J. Desloges and S. Stevenson). Retrieved from http://www.artsci.utoronto.ca/main/faculty/curriculum/pdfs/crrcfinalreport15aug07.pdf

University of Toronto Governing Council. (1999/ 2003). *Policy and procedures on academic appointments.* Retrieved from http://www.utoronto.ca/govcncl/pap/policies/acadapp.pdf

University of Toronto, Provost. (2004). *Stepping UP, 2004-2010: Framework for academic planning at the University of Toronto.* Retrieved from http://www.provost.utoronto.ca/plans/framework.htm

University of Toronto at Scarborough, Task Force on Writing (chair, M. Bunce). (1998). *Final report.* Retrieved from http://www.utsc.utoronto.ca/~ctl/twc/TaskForceWriting.pdf

AUTHOR AND EDITOR INSTITUTIONAL AFFILIATIONS

Natasha Artemeva, Carleton University, Canada
Chantal Barriault, Science North, Canada
Charles Bazerman, University of California, Santa Barbara, USA
Doug Brent, University of Calgary, Canada
Janet Giltrow, University of British Columbia, Canada
Amanda Goldrick-Jones, University of British Columbia, Canada
Jeffrey Grabill, Michigan State University, USA
Heather Graves, University of Alberta, Canada
Roger Graves, University of Alberta, Canada
William Hart-Davidson, Michigan State University, USA
Miriam Horne, Champlain College, USA
Ken Hyland, City University, Hong Kong
Heekyeong Lee, Monterey Institute of International Studies, USA
Mary Maguire, McGill University, Canada
Lynn McAlpine, McGill University, Canada
Anthony Paré, McGill University, Canada
Anne Parker, University of Manitoba, Canada
Margaret Procter, University of Toronto, Canada
Martine Courant Rife, Lansing Community College, USA
Paul Rogers, George Mason University, USA
Catherine Schryer, Ryerson University, Canada
Tania Smith, University of Calgary, Canada
Philippa Spoel, Laurentian University, Canada
Doreen Starke-Meyerring, McGill University, Canada
Olivia Walling, University of California, Santa Barbara, USA
Diana Wegner, Douglas College, Canada
Larissa Yousoubova, McGill University, Canada

www.ingramcontent.com/pod-product-compliance
Lightning Source LLC
Chambersburg PA
CBHW022007300426
44117CB00005B/62